AFTER POSTSTRUCTURALISM:
WRITING THE INTELLECTUAL HISTORY OF THEORY

After Poststructuralism

Writing the Intellectual History of Theory

Edited by
TILOTTAMA RAJAN and
MICHAEL J. O'DRISCOLL

UNIVERSITY OF TORONTO PRESS
Toronto Buffalo London

© University of Toronto Press Incorporated 2002
Toronto Buffalo London
Printed in Canada

ISBN 0-8020-4791-2

Printed on acid-free paper

National Library of Canada Cataloguing in Publication Data

Main entry under title:

After poststructuralism : writing the intellectual history of theory

Includes bibliographical references and index.
ISBN 0-8020-4791-2

1. History – Philosophy.   2. Historiography – History.   3. History –
Methodology.   4. Theory (Philosophy) – History.   I. Rajan, Tilottama,
1951–   II. O'Driscoll, Michael J. (Michael James), 1964–

D13.A44 2002   901   C2001-901791-X

University of Toronto Press acknowledges the financial assistance to its
publishing program of the Canada Council for the Arts and the Ontario
Arts Council.

University of Toronto Press acknowledges the financial support for its
publishing activities of the Government of Canada through the Book
Publishing Industry Development Program (BPIDP).

Contents

Acknowledgments

We would like to begin by thanking the contributors to this volume, each and every one of whom graciously accepted our invitation to participate in this venture and, having done so, responded in a timely and helpful manner to our suggestions and queries. The essays in *After Poststructuralism: Writing the Intellectual History of Theory* represent the hard work of these scholars in expanding upon conference papers first presented at the Histories of Theory Conference, held on 16–19 April 1998 at the Centre for Theory and Criticism, University of Western Ontario.

That conference and the publication of this book were in part funded by the Social Sciences and Humanities Research Council of Canada and The Centre for Theory and Criticism, University of Western Ontario.

Our thanks to Robert Barsky for his role in organizing the conference, and also to those graduate students and research assistants who helped in either the organization of the conference or the preparation of the manuscript: Brett Buchanan, Mark Asberg, Paul Gautier, and Chris(tie) Schultz.

Finally, particular thanks to Suzanne Rancourt and Barbara Porter at the University of Toronto Press and Judy Williams for their help and encouragement in bringing this collection to fruition.

AFTER POSTSTRUCTURALISM

Introduction

TILOTTAMA RAJAN AND
MICHAEL J. O'DRISCOLL

How does one write the 'intellectual history' of theory in a time when both the conceptuality of ideas and the linearity of history have been called into question? This volume starts from the assumption that theory itself has profoundly altered the process of writing about theory. Traditional historiography has relied on notions of periodization, progress, continuity, teleology, causality, and exclusivity now questionable at a time when such positivisms have been subjected to anti-foundationalist critiques. While such notions remain useful and indeed necessary, this volume also tries to mark their limits by putting into play a new set of figures of thought – tropics of theory, as we call them here – that describe and facilitate other ways of writing about theory. Inevitably, insofar as accounts of theoretical schools, concepts, or individual careers are often underwritten by a traditional historiography, the new paradigms described here also have implications for contemporary intellectual historiography generally. The contributions gathered here thus attempt to revisit the 'history' of (theoretical) ideas – or rather their emergence, dissemination, encounter, or institutionalization – from the near side of the contemporary turn to theory in the humanities.

Deleuze's studies of a variety of earlier thinkers (including Kant, Leibniz, Spinoza, Nietzsche) are evidence that theory is not a purely presentist or futurist discourse but can also share with the so-called history of ideas an interest in the connections between bodies of thought formulated at different times, and more importantly an interest in its own relationship to the past. But is the use of the term 'intellectual history' to describe such connections itself a catachresis 'which coins a name for a still unnamed entity' (de Man 44)? This volume starts from the possibility that the 'history' in intellectual history may itself be something of a metaphor: an uneasy transplant from another field, like the 'science' in political science. Useful as the metaphor is, perhaps it also puts the mode of study at issue too much under the dominance of history, leaving it vulnerable to charges that intellectual history is an idealism that has forsaken material or 'real' history, when in fact 'history' is only a suggestive rather than determinant figure. The most important contribution made by the interdisciplinary field of theory to intellectual history may well be a questioning of the unidisciplinary model of 'history' as the sole paradigm for studying relationships between different thinkers. In so far as they draw on other areas such as psychoanalysis, literature, and cultural studies, the essays gathered here all implicitly expand the disciplinary metaphor that has hitherto limited reflection on the relationships between bodies of thought to the model of 'history.'

In articulating a new rhetoric and poetics of what, for lack of a better term, we shall continue to call intellectual history, we have tried to be descriptive rather than prescriptive. In other words, the categories we foreground – genealogies, performativities, physiologies, and technologies – name practices already at work in current writing about theory, as exemplified by the essays gathered here. These four metatheoretical figures (metatheoretical in the sense that they theorize theory) are necessarily heuristic rather than exhaustive. They can be mapped along certain axes of relationship and separation, such as time and space, the body and the machine. We could perhaps visualize them in terms of a semiotic square whose four corners constitute the limits of intellectual history as it is currently written. Yet such a structuralist diagram ignores the volatility – and indeed excessiveness – of the figures, which in practice exclude any heuristic containment, and contaminate or combine with rather than exclude one another. Indeed, as will be evident from our more detailed account of the volume, individual essays often draw on more than one figure of thought, using them to complicate and supplement one another, or discovering that one figure generates or is already inhabited by another.

In our efforts to name the tropics of theory, our first recourse was to Foucault's influential concept of *genealogy*. Genealogy offers a way of constructing sequences that is more complex, less easily totalizable and less given to closure than the term 'history.' However, in adapting Foucault's term we mean to evoke not only the discourse-oriented genealogies of his later work, but also the responsiveness to a historical unconscious that drives some of his early work. Genealogy, in short, is an 'unworking' of received histories that deploys what Foucault calls a counter-memory sensitive to the misrecognitions and aporias that trouble supposed lines of origin and influence linking various theorists. History, we could argue, moves forward and is read for the story it unfolds. Genealogy, even when it depends on the provisional construction of a 'history' that it aims to complicate, reads backwards for the resistances and missed encounters that disrupt this narrativity.

However, as our editorial task moved ahead we came to see that the impact of theory on the writing of its own intellectual history was even more varied than the problematizing of history as genealogy might allow. For genealogy still suggests a way of assembling intellectual history in terms of what has 'happened' in time. But theory has the potential to interrogate this very diachronic structure. For example, notions of the 'event' as punctual or as occurring at a point in time, and as happening actually rather than virtually, have themselves been questioned. The trope of performance, drawn from the arts, is a response to this limitation of the genealogical method: a synchronic counterpart to genealogy. *Performativities* constitute a staging of certain hypothetical intellectual encounters in which theoretical subjects share the same dramatic space and are put into dialogue, regardless of chronology and influence. Furthermore, this theoretical trope also foregrounds the thoroughly discursive nature of theory and its history, in addition to a heightened consciousness of its status as an argument that could be 'performed' differently. In this sense, the description of theoretical encounters might well be understood as 'performative' as Butler, following Derrida, uses that term: historiography as an archive of reiterative citation without origin, whose incessant repetition constitutes both the normalizing effect of received intellectual histories and their failure to be self-identical.[1]

These first two tropes assume theoretical encounters that either are or can be made fully explicit in discourse. Yet the effects (and affect) of theoretical writing, as well as the attractions and cathexes that link bodies of theory, are often more intangible. For example Derrida, even as he continues to criticize Heidegger, shows a deep attraction to him in the rhythm and grammar of his recent writings. Anxiety, abjection, incorporation, and attachment (to, again, evoke Judith Butler's term)[2] are but some of the *physiologies* or psychologies that inevitably complicate straightforward accounts of theory. To draw on the work of Julia Kristeva, these are instances of 'genotextual' rather than phenotextual exchange. Such figures convey an understanding of history as a bodily encounter that occurs within the space of the semiotic chora of pulsational drives and desires, and they suggest a libidinal economy of history that operates beyond the more restrictive schema of mere influence.

The trope of physiologies – informed as it is by psychoanalysis and/or biology – addresses the question of how one might *feel* the movement of intellectual history, how one might sense its sense. Yet, finally, to organize accounts of theory in and around the space and subjectivities of the body invites yet another counterpart that is both obvious and profound. The trope of *technologies*, then, points towards a tendency to recognize intellectual history not in relation to the machine as some form of crude technological determinism but rather in relation to technologies as they are deployed in economies of information, the construction of subjects, and the practice of craft or art in the Greek sense of *technē*. In this sense the technological foregrounds the writing of intellectual history as yet another imposition. It is an ordering of our experience of the world in reference not to the dynamic, yet curiously transcendent, organicisms of the body, but to the shifting and particularized machineries that constitute our interventions into the genealogical, performative, libidinal body that is history.

I. Genealogies

Our first contribution, Stanley Corngold's 'Some Theoretical and Historical Complications in Hegel's Aesthetics of Comedy,' starts with the way theorists are incorporated into a normalizing intellectual history. To a history that resists the difficulties in Hegel's texts so as to make him a systematic thinker, Corngold opposes a genealogy that approaches the texts through these very aporias. But rather than turning to Foucault for this counter-memory, Corngold turns to Paul de Man. De Man's readings of Hegel in *Aesthetic Ideology* are both Corngold's model and his subject. More specifically, he focuses on Hegel's *Aesthetics*, and on the tangled, self-interrupting relation between 'subjectivity' and 'substance' in the little-discussed section on comedy which precedes the more famous thesis of the 'end' of art. As is well known, this relation goes to the heart of Hegel's supposed view of history as the reconciliation of subjectivity and substance, so that the issue of how to read Hegel is tied up with the question of whether his own theory of history is formed around or in resistance to its difficulties. At the centre of these difficulties is the question of what Hegel means by subjectivity, and thus how he judges it. For subjectivity is at once a certain arbitrariness (*Willkür*) implicated in perverse forms of attachment, and an 'unbounded freedom and self-determination' – including freedom from this very arbitrariness. As Corngold argues, its irreducibly aporetic character emerges both within and between the theories of comedy and other genres such as tragedy and lyric. Moreover, the aporias in Hegel's text render two questions undecidable: a) whether he wants to dissolve, preserve, or sublate subjectivity into substance; and b) whether comedy – placed as an (anti)climax at the end of the *Aesthetics* – is the successful dissolution of a persistent problem in the end of art, or the deliberately ironic symptom of the fact that art and history have precisely *not* come to an end.

'Aporia' is of course de Man's term, and it is here that the historiographic interest of the essay lies. For inasmuch as Corngold begins but departs from de Man's readings of Hegel, his essay is also a reflection on the limits of de Man's historiography. And here it is worth recalling Corngold's own earlier – but hardly binary – distinction between mistake and error, wherein mistakes are wrong but errors, as tropes or turnings caused by getting the story crooked, can be fruitful.[3] De Man's readings trace a series of errors in Hegel and are themselves produced by error. De Man's 'error,' we could say, is that highly idiosyncratic view of language as a random positional power that Rodolphe Gasché describes as 'linguistic materialism' – a view powerfully adumbrated in 'Shelley Disfigured' and 'Phenomenality and Materiality in Kant.' As Gasché argues, de Man's chaos-theory of language makes of language a blind, singular power. His analyses are thus 'in-different' to philosophy: they do not seek to contribute to a philosophical argument, but simply expose the operations of language as 'position' and 'figuration.'[4] In this view, a text's aporias are not phenomenally retrievable; they can only materially interrupt the text's transparency. By contrast Corngold, in his own words, deploys a 'phenomenological-historical' method. Corngold's method finds its stimulus in de Man's error, which it continues through its own error or wandering away from de Man. But this very concern with phenomenology and history requires that one also call a halt to 'error' and recognize the mistakes that error produces.[5] And among these is de Man's foreclosure of the possibility that aporias, in Hegel at least, might be phenomenally knowable through the 'labour of the negative' as the process of thinking things through.

Whereas Corngold seeks to return error to the mistakes it elides, our next essay tries to revision certain mistakes as errors. Beginning from Corngold's distinction, Tilottama Rajan's 'The Double Detour: Sartre, Heidegger, and the Genealogy of Deconstruction' approaches philosophical error as the creative ground for a history that unfolds through combination and metamorphosis rather than through filiation and con-tinuity. Accordingly, Rajan tries to unravel a series of misprisions that complicate any account of the development from phenomenology to deconstruction. On one level, she reads against the grain of two mis-taken histories: one that sees Sartre's *Being and Nothingness* as a 'mon-strous' misunderstanding of Heidegger's *Being and Time*,[6] thus missing Sartre's seminal critique of the latter's idealism; and another that links deconstruction in the 1960s to Heideggerian but not Sartrean phenom-enology, thus missing *its* crucial difference from a later deconstruction that is either poststructural or post-Heideggerian. On another level, however, Rajan is also concerned with the richly knotted histories pro-duced by 'error' as a kind of performativity, albeit one that has already happened and is thus part of a genealogy.

Rajan begins with the discarding of Sartre from the canon of theory, due to his supposed misreading of Heidegger. On the contrary, she sug-gests, the difference between the two philosophers is actually the space within which French theory emerges as an attempt to use each one to think through and against the other. As is well known, the French read-ing of Heidegger was mediated by Sartre; and this 'error,' Rajan argues, was constitutive for deconstruction as the resistance, synthesis, and/or cathexis between multiple, intersecting phenomenologies. Rajan traces, with reference to different theorists, three representative ways in which error performs in the transference of phenomenology into deconstruc-tion. Briefly, these can be described – borrowing Sartre's own term – as the internal negation of one philosopher by the other (in the case of Blanchot and Levinas), as a resistance between them (in the case of de Man), and as a dialogical overlapping and supplementation of one by the other (in the case of Foucault). In this way, Rajan's essay also offers the beginnings of a grammar of error that might help in the genealogy of historical transmission.

While attention to the misprisions of history facilitates the critical practice of recovery, the genealogical also foregrounds historiography as a process of othering as well as forgetting. In 'The Premodern Condi-tion: Neo-Primitivism in Baudrillard and Lyotard,' Victor Li presents us with a genealogy in which the troubled intellectual history of Eurocen-tric ethnography returns in the moment of contemporary theorizations of radical alterity. Li begins with the way in which Baudrillard (in his challenge to the coextensive myths of productivity and semiology) and Lyotard (in his challenge to the metanarratives of Western intellectual discourse) effectively reinscribe the pre-modern condition as the very possibility of interrogating the historical and anthropological impulse towards universalization. In Baudrillard's treatment of the social relations of the gift in primitive societies, as formulated by Marcel Mauss, and in Lyotard's treatment of narrative in South American Cashinahua culture, as formulated by André-Marcel d'Ans, Li discovers a 'bizarre logic in which the primitive dies as a presence to serve as an irreducible, internalized idea.' The Cashinahua, to take one of Li's two examples, operate as a purely discursive rupture in Lyotard's challenge to the idea of a universal history, and are subject to the very 'cosmopolitical' process that, following Kant, Lyotard himself identifies. Lyotard represents primitive authenticity as, in fact, the ahistorical. In what amounts to a genealogical critique of a mystified performative encounter with the Other, Li plays upon the irony that Lyotard, by invoking the differend of Western intellectual history, 'rejoins that venerable European tradition since Montaigne at least, that has imagined and relied on a valorized Other in its internal quarrel with its own culture.' Li's analysis points up the fact that Baudrillard's 'principle of reversibility' – the inevitably fatal revenge of the object on the subject – is as true of the historical moment as it is of the cultural other.

Our closing essay in this section, Ian Balfour's 'The Sublime between History and Theory: Hegel, de Man, and Beyond,' returns the reader to both Hegel's *Aesthetics* and, more briefly, the work of de Man. Whereas Corngold recognizes genealogy as a process of unknotting, Balfour unveils the intriguing possibility that history, as the 'resistance to theory,' may in fact also *be* theory. Balfour begins with the return of contemporary criticism (in the work of Lyotard, Hertz, and most notably de Man) to late eighteenth- and early nineteenth-century thinking on the sublime. In so far as the sublime is a form of 'anti-representation,' much discussion of it is really 'theory in the guise of history.' What a genealogy of the sublime discloses is thus the complex, chiasmatic relation between the 'theory' and the 'history' of ideas. Indeed it is arguably Hegel who invented the 'history of theory,' thus setting in motion the enmeshment of theory and history. For it is Hegel who both articulated history as the theoretical – that is, transhistorical – potential of ideas rather than their mere recording, and also subjected theory to its own historicity.

Despite this seminal contribution, Hegel's treatment of the sublime in the *Aesthetics* exemplifies the conservatism of a simpler 'history,' and requires the supplement of a further reading to bring out its potential both for his own text and for the relationship of theory and history. This

conservatism of a history that resists theory is most obvious in his placement of the sublime. Unlike Kant (who considers it atemporally), Hegel
starkly circumscribes the sublime by identifying it with Hebraic poetry
and locating it in the earliest or 'Symbolic' phase of his three-part dialectic. He thus relegates it definitively to the past. In this sense Hegel
exemplifies the way a history of ideas limits their theoretical potential. And indeed it is this resistance of history to theory that de Man
criticizes, in rereading the Hegelian sublime as a moment of anti-
representation that is *permanently possible*. In effect de Man retrieves the
theoretical core of the sublime by taking Hegel's (historical) account of
the category and de-historicizing it. Yet as Balfour also argues, in a radical revision of our sense of the historical, this de-historicization makes
de Man's sublime more historical than Hegel's. Indeed one could argue
that it renders theory more historical than history: in the double sense
that the sublime can erupt at any moment, and that it is in history that
the work of theory happens.

II. Performativities

Rodolphe Gasché's 'Theatrum Theoreticum' sets the stage for our second figure, which seeks to produce rather than recover the history of
theory. Beginning with the derivation of both 'theory' and 'theatre'
from the Greek word *thea* (as spectacle or contemplation), Gasché takes
up the archaeology of the term 'theory' from Plato to modernity. He
thus asks what the relation is between theory and theatre, or between
theory as cognition, vision, 'seeing,' and theory as that which must stage
itself for a spectator. Inasmuch as theory is not just seeing, but must see
itself seeing, Gasché's concern here is the problematic of reflexivity that
he analyses elsewhere.[7] Here Gasché approaches this problem through a
series of metaphors that link theory to light, or to what Derrida calls
'the *phenomenological* metaphor' which, in its 'varieties of *phainesthai*, of
shining, lighting, clearing...opens onto the space of presence' (Derrida
132). But he also transposes this philosophical view of theory onto a
material stage through an exploration of actual dramatic lighting (interestingly, a move also made by Merleau-Ponty).[8] Theatre, then, is Gasché's
own figure for questioning a pure phenomenality of theory associated
with light as the matrix-figure for logos, logic, and illumination.
    Gasché starts with the shift in the optics of knowledge consolidated by
the invention of limelight in 1826, which made it possible to manipulate
vision through a 'focused and measured ray of "direct lighting."' In the

modern theatre, light is surrounded by darkness such that 'one only sees what is in the spotlight.' For Gasché this new deployment of light as a technology stands in contrast to an ancient *theatrum philosophicum* in which everything was 'already in the light...[and] offer[ed] itself to a gaze to be seen.' Both versions of theory claim a certitude that derives either from the contemplation of 'the ever-present originary forms' or from the legitimation of a particular truth through the light of 'method.' That theory is theatre means, by contrast, that theories have plots and characters, and perform certain acts for the purpose of theorizing. Theory becomes theatrical at the point when the apparatus of seeing is itself seen by an observer. Yet because theory cannot see itself seeing, it cannot coincide with itself in a reciprocity of the performer's and the observer's gaze. And it is this asymmetry, Gasché argues, that makes possible a 'history' – rather than a pure self-identity – of theory.

Gasché's essay deals with a mirror-stage of theory produced by the fact that theory cannot achieve identity through the reflection of the onlooker. Our other essays, however, extend the idea of theory as theatre beyond the mediation between theorist and audience, to the relations among theorists themselves. This performativity, as distinct from theatricality, is evident in our second contribution, Arkady Plotnitsky's 'Topo-philosophies: Plato's Diagonals, Hegel's Spirals, and Irigaray's Multifolds.' Though Plotnitsky deals with three historically distinct figures, his aim is not to show one as responding to the other, nor is it to uncover an existing – even if hidden – genealogy connecting them. Instead he gathers these theorists into a synchronic space where he can reperform their relationship through two key cognitive technologies that he names 'reflection' and 'explication.' The former is itself a performative metaphor condensing Hegel's philosophy of reflection with Irigaray's speculum, while 'ex-pli-cation' – meaning 'unpleating' or 'unfolding' – reworks exegesis through Deleuze's well-known figure in *The Fold: Leibniz and the Baroque* (thereby also reminding us that genealogically Hegel comes after Leibniz).

Plotnitsky focuses on three 'geometries' – or more accurately 'topologies' – of thought and subjectivity: the diagonal, the Hegelian spiral, and the orbifold (as a regendering of Deleuze's Leibnizian fold). These topologies are, of course, historically distinct: the spiral continues to harbour connotations of teleology, while both the spiral and the diagonal figure a certain rational and spiritual potential of humanity. Yet Plotnitsky's method is not to distinguish them on a historical axis but to let them interact. Hegel's spiral turns out to be a baroque rather than strictly linear figure. As such it unfolds forward into a regendering of politics which Irigaray could not elaborate without the idealist pre-text of Hegel's dialectical, teleological desire. The three topologies mirror and reflect on each other; they unravel and extend each other, even as the orbifold is used to unfold or explicate the Hegelian spiral. Interestingly, this approach is legitimized by the logic of the orbifold, which constructs the multiply in-folding space of theory so as to permit Hegelian, Platonic, and Irigarayan discourses to exist simultaneously. In this sense, Plotnitsky's essay is both a performance in its own right and a metatheory of history and performativity. As performance, it deploys Hegel and Irigaray interactively, to restage philosophy as politics. As metatheory it rethinks the trope of 'history' (as fold instead of line), and also provides us – through reflection and explication – with new technologies for such rethinking.

Peter Dews's essay 'The Eclipse of Coincidence: Lacan, Merleau-Ponty, and Žižek's Misreading of Schelling' also unfolds genealogy as performativity. Dews focuses on the central role played by Lacan in cultural studies, and more specifically on Slavoj Žižek's reading of Lacan with the Romantic philosopher Friedrich Schelling. Žižek's work is itself an exemplary case of performativity, which uses post-Kantian Idealism to restage contemporary cultural and political issues in a philosophical theatre, while performing the political consequences of philosophy. The Lacanian subject, Dews argues, is a *manque-à-etre*, split between activity and being, and present only in the moment of enunciation, before falling into language and objectivity. Worse still, Lacan gives us no way of overcoming this fundamental alienation of the subject as divided between an 'elusive ungraspable *sujet de l'énonciation*' and an 'opaque, inert, objectified ego.' Žižek gives the split subject a certain historical privilege by tracing it back to Schelling. Thus the *Urgrund*, which in Schelling's *Freedom* essay precedes and underlies the subject's existence, becomes an allegory of the Lacanian Real, from which an empty subject is forever separated.

As against this attenuation of Schelling, Dews himself poses the possibility of a different genealogy connecting Schelling to Lacan's contemporary Merleau-Ponty. In this exchange of genealogies 'Schelling' becomes the stage on which Dews performs a debate between Lacan and Merleau-Ponty. Reading Lacan back to Schelling 'historically' legitimizes the pessimistic political vision that tacitly accompanies Žižek's Lacanian view of the subject. Reading Schelling with Merleau-Ponty opens a way forward to a different future by clearing a path back to a different past. This Schelling provides a pre-text for Merleau-Ponty's own seemingly utopian reconciliation of self and world, as a response to the trauma of separation for which Lacan uses the figure of castration. Both readings, Dews reminds us, miss the point, in that 'Schelling's fundamental philosophical struggle was to hold this complex vision of plenitude and negativity, of essential conflict and potential reconciliation, together.' Or to put it differently, each reading discloses a partial truth that requires the performance of historiography through multiple, overlapping genealogies.

III. Physiologies

'Performativity' creates a dialogue between theorists that is purely hypothetical. The term 'physiologies,' however, names a form of inter- or intra-theoretical contact that is real but not easily accessible through models of historical 'influence' between fully constituted subjects or separate texts. It may also point to an economy at work in theoretical texts that is not strictly cognitive: what Julia Kristeva calls a genotext rather than a phenotext. As is well known, Neil Hertz has discussed how de Man's rigorously technical and analytic focus on rhetoric is interrupted by melodramatic figures of violence and death (Hertz 82–104). Within this volume itself Rajan's essay supplements a conceptual genealogy of deconstruction with a 'physiology' that looks at the more intangible ways in which Sartre's *Being and Nothingness* touches French thinkers after Heidegger, including Levinas and Blanchot. On this level 'Sartre' figures what Lyotard has called the 'darkening of ... the Enlightenment' for which French thought has made itself responsible. Any tracing of how Sartre *affects* French theory is thus necessarily in excess of a 'representational, reversible forgetting': a repression that can be undone by a corrective, counter-history of ideas (Lyotard 4–5).

The essays in our third section address the problem of the 'corpus theoreticus'[9] in two different, mutually implicated, ways. Anthony Wall and Mani Haghighi proceed metatheoretically by considering intellectual history itself as a body, whether it be the history of a particular theorist's work or of theory generally. Dealing with Bakhtin, Foucault, and Deleuze, they provide a general framework and rationale for approaching theory as body rather than concept. Brian Wall deals with a specific physiology: the cathexis between psychoanalysis and phenomenology in the work of Georges Bataille and its consequences for an issue also taken up by Haghighi, that of 'transgression.'

Anthony Wall's essay 'Contradictory Pieces of Time and History' ranges across Bakhtin's texts but starts with his work on the chronotope: a work that began in the 1920s under the influence of biology and vitalism, and which Bakhtin stopped and resumed repeatedly, until he began it again with his 'Concluding Remarks' in 1973. In so far as the chronotope is the lived experience of time and space, Bakhtin's work on this concept, as he performs and reperforms it over the years, itself creates a chronotope for its own reading. In other words Bakhtin's practice is itself a theory of his work as a lived body which, as such, changes, differs from itself, and takes shape as 'fragmentary,' performative writing. The fragmentary nevertheless has its own organic imperatives, which Wall ex-plicates through the figure of the 'loophole' as a telescoping of beginnings and ends. An image not unlike Plotnitsky's fold, the loophole is a spatial figure for the opening created by the overlapping of the first edge and the last edge. Yet this spatial figure finds a more organic parallel in Bakhtin's writings on the body in *Rabelais and His World* as well as in related (only recently published) texts. Reading these texts through recent work on the body, mainly by Elizabeth Grosz, Wall approaches them as Bakhtin's theory of his own volatile, historically embedded practice. Since for Bakhtin metaknowledge is always embodied in practice, it is also significant that his intellectual concerns move 'away from explicit language towards bodies, images, and languages in performance.'

Wall's way of reading the excessive, non-totalizable parts of Bakhtin's theoretical corpus verges on what Deleuze will later describe as the 'body without organs.' It can thus be expanded in directions that the other contributions to this section explore. It can be extended (as Haghighi does) to readings of the corpus of history itself as a body of resistance that is neither utopian and futuristic, nor natural and pre-discursive. Alternatively, it can be extended (as Brian Wall suggests) to the zones of contact between bodies of theory that can never quite be totalized under names such as 'phenomenology' or 'psychoanalysis' considered as bounded theoretical spaces.

Following the first path, Mani Haghighi's 'The Body of History' responds to two appositional critiques of Foucault's history of the body that, together, create a critical aporia. On the one hand there is Charles Taylor's account of Foucault's refusal to posit a space of liberation outside the passive body subject to the forces of discourse. On the other hand, there is Judith Butler's contradictory charge that the genealogical reading of cultural inscription on the body unwittingly admits to the existence of powers outside the body itself. Arguing that intellectual history 'is neither simply the story of the transformations endured by the body' nor 'the force that inscribes these transformations upon the body,' Haghighi contends, through a rereading of Foucault's seminal 'Nietzsche, Genealogy, History,' that history, as Foucault understands it, is an actual body. Foucault's body of history, rather than his history of the body, is proximate to Deleuze and Guattari's 'body without organs,' in the sense that it can be understood not as a natural, pre-historical body upon which history is then inscribed, but rather as the very coming together of the expressions and articulations of the historical. Furthermore, this body cannot be conceived in anthropomorphic or developmental terms: it is a non-human, heterarchical, contemporaneous zone actualized by a series of subjugations defined, in turn, by what escapes them. It is through this possibility of 'escape' that a space emerges for a discussion of resistance, and as importantly creation, in the political sphere. Yet by the same token Foucault's amorphous body of history escapes being placed either in terms of Taylor's hope for an evolution towards freedom or as a space of limitation, as Butler would have it.

Haghighi accomplishes two things crucial to this section of the volume. He develops a way of reading (intellectual) history as a body in which the biological is metamorphosed into concepts; he also engages in a physiological reading of Foucault's work itself, as a 'body without organs' whose effects cannot be totalized and identified under the heading of a single concept (such as 'power'). Haghighi provides a model of such a methodology in an affective reading of Foucault that refuses either stable origins (Foucault writes through and is written through by a Nietzsche who is contemporaneous with Deleuze and Guattari) or singular conclusions (the reading itself arrives at the paradoxical conclusion of a series of anti-foundationalist maxims). As Haghighi himself suggests, 'the discursive forces of history are to be understood as inscribing themselves not upon a natural, prehistorical body' – and here we might read into this Haghighi's treatment of the body of Foucault's own corpus – 'but rather upon each other.' In this sense, neither anthropomorphic bodies nor textual bodies stand somehow prior or anterior to the Nietzschean *Herkunft* and *Entstehung* of history, but are themselves the always illusive interweavings of multiple, even radically incongruous, histories.

This idea of a body of theory that resists the stratification or organization of its organs grows out of the figure of the acephalic or 'headless' body developed by Georges Bataille, who is the subject of our next contribution, 'Written in the Sand: Bataille's Phenomenology of Transgression and the Transgression of Phenomenology.' Focusing, like Haghighi, on questions of resistance (or 'transgression'), Brian Wall also approaches Bataille's heteronomous corpus as one in which 'something always escapes.' Wall avoids dealing with Bataille's more familiar essays on restricted and general 'economies.' Instead he turns to *Inner Experience* as the point at which Bataille's reflection on the social escapes (or transgresses) our attempt to organize his corpus under the heading of the social. Wall treats this notoriously difficult text as itself a body without theoretical organs. More specifically he approaches it as a missed encounter between phenomenology and psychoanalysis, which generates 'inner experience' as a limit to which social practice must be taken in order to be thought transgressively. As Foucault argues in 'A Preface to Transgression,' Bataille's 'transgression' cannot be recuperated as 'resistance,' as positivity. 'Transgression' escapes both resistance – in a political sense – and the limitation of a more negative, psychoanalytic 'resistance.' Put differently, Bataille does indeed want to integrate the for-itself of the social subject with the in-itself of inner experience. But this latter notion is deeply aporetic, conveying an interiority breached by a phenomenological thought of transcendence, which in turn is transgressed by its cathexis with the unconscious. Thus the for-itself and the in-itself enter only into a non-synthetic relation, in which the energies deployed in the social leave their own excremental – and transgressive – excess in the realm of inner experience.

On one level Wall's essay returns to the theoretical scene traced by Rajan, and contributes to a 'history' of phenomenology as a thought that exceeds itself. But this excess cannot be unravelled genealogically, nor can the performativity it generates be staged or represented. Hence Wall's emphasis on the physiology of Bataille's thought: on the way his key notions of excess, waste, and transgression are not only theorized but also em-bodied in a corpus that moves between fiction and analysis so as to exceed the borders between rigorous philosophy and more transgressive modes of writing. Nancy's word for this writing is 'exscription' – a process by which meaning 'spills out of itself' as writing opens 'within itself, *to* itself ... as the infinite *discharge* of meaning' (italics added).[10] Thus Bataille's condensed, self-displacing text can be seen to *ex-scribe* 'inner experience' in a movement of constant self-negation. In this process phenomenology, Wall argues, is at once what transgresses the synthetic social paradigm of Bataille's 'general economy,' even as it exscribes its own waste, its own remainders.

IV. Technologies

Physiology necessarily opens historiography to its 'unthought'; technology, on the other hand, opens historiography to the machineries of power. Under the influence of Heidegger's 'The Question Concerning Technology,' technology – whether understood as the Greek *technē* or in its more recent form, following Foucault, as the fashioning of subjectivities, bodies, and world – has traditionally been associated with the domination of nature by man, with the delimitation of praxis and discourse, and with a certain ill-fated positivism.[11] Taking up these multiple sensibilities of technology, the essays in our final section further complicate the term, either by discussing critical technologies as they turn and return in history, by tracking the operations of the technologies of theory, or by implicating themselves in technology's own self-questioning. The merits of foregrounding such a theoretical trope lie largely with its potential for making us rethink not only the constructed nature of critical machines but their complicity with those normalizing mechanisms which, whatever their character, are necessarily ideological. Furthermore, at the intersection of such technologies of theory and their implicit or explicit theories of technology we discover a way to bring the practice of intellectual historiography into the fold of cultural studies. Such critical positions as those afforded by the trope of technologies make evident the possibility of understanding intellectual history not simply as the reconfiguration of pure idealisms but as the mapping of materialist practices within the bounds of their own socio-historic moment.

Linda Salamon's 'Theory *avant la Lettre*: An Excavation in Early Modern England' provides a clear example of the opening created by approaching theories as technologies, both as the practical deployment of knowledge, and as an arena of ideological struggle. Working from Pierre Bourdieu's *The Logic of Practice* and Michel de Certeau's *The Practice of Everyday Life*, Salamon argues for the proliferation of Renaissance 'art-texts' as embedded in the prehistory of theory. These 'artes of' everyday life (such as Juliana Barnes's 1496 *The Treatyse on Fysshing with an Angle*) codify the technologies of everything from falconry to war within a highly polysemous writing culture that is not organized by birthright or higher education. In so doing they constitute a field of discourse in which theory as practice escapes the standard binaries of mind versus body, high versus low culture, or professions as distinct from crafts and hobbies. As regularities rather than rules, art-texts inscribe aspects of the habitus and 'subvert the dominant culture in, and on, which they work.' Salamon traces the eclipse of this form of epistemic management, as cultural capital increasingly accrues to Baconian models of 'science.' She suggests that it is this displacement of art by science that has also made 'theory' (or 'high' theory) in our time unfertile ground for the recovery of what is effectively a 'cultural studies' *avant la lettre*. At the same time, Salamon argues not so much for a genealogy linking Renaissance art-texts to contemporary cultural studies, as for a dialogic relationship – one of anticipation or intervention-between the writing culture of Elizabethan craftsfolk and the critical discourse that informs the late twentieth-century study of material culture. In the process Salamon's essay also offers a further example of the interrelatedness of the models deployed in this volume. For she describes a certain performativity between the two fields, which allows us to reflect on another eclipse now occurring, as a high theory underwritten either by philosophy or science gives way to the new technology of cultural studies.

Michael O'Driscoll's 'Derrida, Foucault, and the Archiviolithics of History' both extends and redirects Salamon's contribution. Like Salamon, O'Driscoll pays particular attention to the technologies of theory as a material practice situated within a specific socio-historic framework; however, in an examination of Diderot's and d'Alembert's *Encyclopédie*, he decouples the management of knowledge from the management of texts, which he regards as a condition of modernity that informs the writing of theoretical histories. Such a distinction allows O'Driscoll to locate the practice of intellectual historiography within the archive as a technology of theory that authorizes certain discourses, and to recognize that practice as strategically self-violating or, to borrow Derrida's term, as 'archiviolithic.' O'Driscoll contends with the paradox that poststructuralism, particularly at its most exemplary moments, situates the writing subject squarely within the archive, as a central figure of theory's own historicity, even while effacing the machinations of theory's own archival technologies. This paradox emerges in the interstices of Derrida's critique of the archaeological as origin in *Archive Fever* and Foucault's critique of the archival as law in *The Archaeology of Knowledge*. Both critiques, O'Driscoll reminds us, draw from practices of textual management mediated by the poetics of modernism, which shares its own agonistic relationship to the material archive. As enacted either through a crude techno-determinism or a radical constructivism, the effacement of the archive as a topo-nomological structure, as both a site and an operation of citation, dissimulates the power of which the archive is a material effect. In this sense, the archive, whether understood in Derrida's terms as the space of living memory in its 'insistent impression through the unstable feeling of a shifting figure' or in Foucault's terms as a network of discursive regularities that constitutes 'the general system of the formation and transformation of statements,' is as much violated by intellectual history as it violates that history. As a way to test the archontic limits of intellectual history, then, O'Driscoll turns to the recent work of German theorists Friedrich Kittler and Bernhard Siegert, who, in their bringing together of poststructuralist rigour and materialist critique, demonstrate a sensitivity to the manner in which technologies of theory are constituted by and of historiographic archives.

This mutual disruption between the technologies of intellectual history and the archive supporting them is also the concern of our final essay, Orrin Wang's 'De Man, Marx, Rousseau, and the Machine.' Focusing, appropriately enough, on the machine – which condenses the topoi of instrumentality, *technē*, and simulacra – Wang's essay brings the figure of technology and the technologized body to bear on the rivalry between Marxism and deconstruction. He begins with Fredric Jameson's reconfiguration of deconstruction, in *Postmodernism, or, the Cultural Logic of Late Capitalism*, as 'an essentially eighteenth-century philosophical strategy.' As Wang argues, Jameson's critique of Paul de Man as a 'mechanical materialist' curiously elides, except as an adjective, the figure and the reality of the 'machine.' Wang responds dialectically to Jameson: he recognizes that Jameson's defamiliarizing argument allows deconstruction to be approached from a new literal and anthropological vantage; on the other hand, this same argument reciprocally transforms Marxist critique itself into a historically situated technology. Thinking through this chiasmic relation between the two discourses, Wang argues that the presence of the machine in de Man's treatment of Rousseau, and its absence in Jameson's treatment of de Man, confound our expectations of both deconstructive and Marxist thought. Deconstruction cannot simply be reduced to readings of the misrecognition of the figurative and literal, for the machine-like figurations of language return as literal self-descriptions; neither can Marxist thought be reduced to a literalization of deconstructive figural concerns, for the figure of the machine finds its place in Marx's *Capital* as the 'robotic catachresis underwriting abstract labour and the concept of value.' In other words, Wang stages a performative engagement between the histories that Marxism and deconstruction construct for each other. As important, in so doing he recognizes both as critical technologies exceeded by their own 'technological unconscious.'

NOTES

1 See Butler's *Gender Trouble: Feminism and the Subversion of Identity* and *Bodies That Matter: On the Discursive Limits of 'Sex,'* particularly 1–16 and 27–36.
2 See Butler, *The Psychic Life of Power: Theories in Subjection* 31–62, 90–8.
3 See Corngold, 'Error in Paul de Man.' The phrase 'getting the story crooked' is from Hans Kellner's *Language and Historical Representation: Getting the Story Crooked.*
4 See Gasché, *The Wild Card of Reading: On Paul de Man* 73–113.
5 Corngold criticizes de Man for a self-justification of error as a blindness that is always the other side of insight: in de Man's theory 'there is no place for mistakes' ('Error' 93).
6 Jacques Derrida's phrase in 'The Ends of Man' 115.
7 See Gasché's *The Tain of the Mirror: Derrida and the Philosophy of Reflection* 13–108; *Inventions of Difference: On Jacques Derrida* 29–35. In the latter Gasché borrows Merleau-Ponty's term 'hyperreflection' to describe the breaking open of that 'reflexivity' by which the self, by reflecting on itself, actually confirms and grounds its identity as self-consciousness.
8 See Merleau-Ponty, *Phenomenology of Perception* 309–11.
9 Cf. Jean-Luc Nancy's figure of the 'corpus academicus' in his essay of that name in *The Birth to Presence.*
10 Nancy, 'Exscription,' in *The Birth to Presence* 319, 338–9.
11 Martin Heidegger, 'The Question Concerning Technology,' in *The Question Concerning Technology and Other Essays* 3–35. See also Gianni Vattimo, *The Transparent Society* 12–18.

WORKS CITED

Butler, Judith. *Bodies That Matter: On the Discursive Limits of 'Sex.'* New York: Routledge, 1993.
– *Gender Trouble: Feminism and the Subversion of Identity.* New York: Routledge, 1990.
– *The Psychic Life of Power: Theories in Subjection.* Stanford: Stanford UP, 1997.
Corngold, Stanley. 'Error in Paul de Man.' *The Yale Critics: Deconstruction in America.* Ed. Jonathan Arac, Wlad Godzich, and Wallace Martin. Minneapolis: U of Minnesota P, 1983. 90–108.

de Man, Paul. 'Hypogram and Inscription.' *The Resistance to Theory.* Minneapolis: U of Minnesota P, 1986. 27–53.

Derrida, Jacques. 'The Ends of Man.' *Margins of Philosophy.* Trans. Alan Bass. Chicago: U of Chicago P, 1982. 109–32.

Deleuze, Gilles. *The Fold: Leibniz and the Baroque* (1988). Trans. Tom Conley. Minneapolis: U of Minnesota P, 1993.

Gasché, Rodolphe. *Inventions of Difference: On Jacques Derrida.* Cambridge: Harvard UP, 1994.

– *The Tain of the Mirror: Derrida and the Philosophy of Reflection.* Cambridge: Harvard UP, 1986.

– *The Wild Card of Reading: On Paul de Man.* Cambridge: Harvard UP, 1998.

Heidegger, Martin. 'The Question Concerning Technology.' *The Question Concerning Technology and Other Essays.* Trans. William Lovitt. New York: Harper, 1977. 3–35.

Hertz, Neil. 'Lurid Figures.' *Reading de Man Reading.* Ed. Lindsay Waters and Wlad Godzich. Minneapolis: U of Minnesota P, 1989. 82–104.

Kellner, Hans. *Language and Historical Representation: Getting the Story Crooked.* Madison: U of Wisconsin P, 1990.

Lyotard, Jean-François. *Heidegger and 'the jews.'* Trans. Andreas Michel and Mark Roberts. Minneapolis: U of Minnesota P, 1990.

Merleau-Ponty, Maurice. *Phenomenology of Perception.* Trans. Colin Smith. London: Routledge and Kegan Paul, 1962.

Nancy, Jean-Luc. 'The Corpus Academicus.' *The Birth to Presence.* Stanford: Stanford UP, 1993. 91–207.

– 'Exscription.' *The Birth to Presence.* Stanford: Stanford UP, 1993. 319–40.

Vattimo, Gianni. *The Transparent Society* (1989). Trans. David Webb. Baltimore: Johns Hopkins UP, 1992.

GENEALOGIES

Some Theoretical and Historical Complications in Hegel's Aesthetics of Comedy

STANLEY CORNGOLD

In 'Reply to Raymond Geuss,' the last chapter of Paul de Man's posthumously published *Aesthetic Ideology*, de Man writes: 'What is suggested by a reading such as the one I propose [in the essay 'Sign and Symbol in Hegel's *Aesthetics*'] is that difficulties and discontinuities ... remain in even as masterful and tight a text as the *Aesthetics*. These difficulties have left their mark or have even shaped the history of the understanding of Hegel up to the present' (191–2).[1]

Supposing this to be true, it will be interesting to pose the following questions to Hegel's theory of comedy in the *Aesthetics*:

(1) What signs, if any, of the difficulties and discontinuities that remain in this text are visible in Hegel's treatment, in III:3:C:III:3, of 'the essence of comedy [*das Prinzip der Komödie*]' (*Aesthetics* III:520) – despite the triads![2]

(2) What history of the understanding of Hegel's theory of comedy has been shaped by these difficulties – or, as this question might have been put, more emphatically, by de Man: What history of the understanding of Hegel's theory of comedy has been shaped by readers' resistance to these difficulties?

Finally, (3), in light of de Man's readings of Hegel in *Aesthetic Ideology*, what would be a more nearly adequate reading of Hegel's theory of comedy in the *Aesthetics*?

My essay attempts to indicate the directions that answers to these questions could take. I shall be dwelling mostly on question 1 – the question of the difficulties and discontinuities in Hegel's theory of comedy in the *Aesthetics*. As such, however, I shall also be addressing question 3 – what would a more adequate reading of his theory of comedy look like, especially as it bears on Hegel's famous thesis of the End of Art, since it is precisely at the close of his discussion of comedy that this bold prognosis is elaborated? What can Hegel have discovered in his essay on comedy that leads him to his valedictory reflections?

Some of the tension in Hegel's aesthetics of comedy is certainly forecast by difficulties in the *Aesthetics* as a whole. Hence it will be useful to heed de Man's account of 'difficulties and discontinuities' throughout the system, particularly as they turn on Hegel's conception of the self or subject as it might be realized through the internal preservation of embodied ideas or, as de Man puts it, 'the recollected emotion of a bygone perception' (*AI* 100). The radical problematizing of such constitutive activities of the self or subject occurs, for de Man, under the head of an ideology critique in Hegel, which leads him to detect a subversive political thrust in the *Aesthetics*. The argument appears to follow this route: an attack on the normative view of the integral, reconciled self or subject amounts to an attack on our chief certitude (or fiction of authority) and hence amounts to an attack on the certainty in the name of which power is exercised in the modern state, especially in the post-Hegelian modern liberal state, namely the subject's right to life, liberty, and the pursuit of happiness; and, more recently, in the academic state, the subject's right to see punishment brought down on those whose language causes it discomfort. In a good deal of Hegel's writing, meanwhile, the connection between the self-constituting subject and the State as executive is even more direct – indeed, it is apodictically evident. As one expert reader of the *Aesthetics* puts it, pretending to surprise: 'What is peculiar about Hegel's theory is that it understands human institutions as subjects, most notoriously the State' (Bungay 217).

In my own question 2, I broached the question of the traditional, normalizing reception of Hegel's theory of comedy. How that matter might be developed could follow directly from the place in *Aesthetic Ideology* where de Man evokes the '"ideology of the symbol" as a defensive strategy aimed against the implications of Hegel's aesthetic theory' (*AI* 190). Since Hegel's theory is founded on an enhanced subjectivity, but for him the freedom of thought is based on the activity of signs not symbols, Hegel's views on mentation and language are bound to produce an internal critique of his aesthetic ideology. 'Memory,' too, belongs to this ideology, being 'a truth of which the aesthetic is the defensive, ideological, and censored translation' (*AI* 102).[3] This aesthetic, however, is countervailed, according to de Man, by a sign-based poetics implicit in Hegel's work although also everywhere available in it – a counter-aesthetic, more properly, which, for de Man, in turn resists the ideology of the symbol. The counter-aesthetic turns chiefly on a theory of art as a type of memorization (*Gedächtnis*) and not, as Hegel is traditionally understood, a type of remembrance or recollection, of *Erinnerung* or 'internalization.' The counter-aesthetic of memorization 'implies notation and inscription,' being 'structured like a linguistic inscription in a memorization,' and hence implies the leading activity of the sign (*AI* 191). Primacy goes, with certain reservations (*AI* 96), to the arbitrary sign over the mystifying symbol in art and, with it, conclusions as to the non-phenomenal representability or, put more radically, the unrepresentability of knowledge – so-called knowledge being, in de Man's reading of Hegel, a repetition of materially inscribed, non-transparent signs. (One could compare and contrast the actual recurrence in Hegel's writing, as in the *Phenomenology of Spirit* and in the *Science of Logic*, of the trope of self-transparency [*sich durchsichtig sein*] as the marker of the fully self-conscious subject.)[4]

I think the sign-symbol distinction in Hegel is fertile, especially for its bearing on the question of the subject, even though the account de Man gives of this distinction contains mistakes, so that here one has the right to speak of 'mistakes' that do not neutralize the disclosive power of the 'error.'[5] The effect of de Man's critique on a reading of Hegel's theory of comedy would be to bring about a radical break, since Hegel's aesthetics until now has been generally understood as a historical metapsychology of consciousness and not as a type of intermittent linguistic materialism.[6] My own reading, which follows a historical-phenomenological track, intends to respond only to certain implications of de Man's perspective, avoiding altogether his stress on the alleged mechanical character of thought. I shall return to the matter of the historicity of readings of the *Aesthetics* when discussing 'The End of Art' in Hegel.

In order, then, to describe some of the difficulties in Hegel's theory of comedy in the *Aesthetics*, it will first of all be useful to say what Hegel's theory seems to be and where its stress lies – and this is a point that must be hammered home. Comedy is an affair of subjectivity – of subjectivity displayed in two coincidental moments: a moment of triumphant self-assertion and a moment of dissolution (*Auflösung*), where what is dissolved by and for the subject are its false attachments. Stephen Bungay offers a neat summary of the matter:

> In comedy, the powers with which the individual identifies are insubstantial, and the character is not destroyed by the failure of his end, but survives to stand above the conflict. The resolution is the affirmation of

subjectivity, which is able in this way to gain insight into the triviality of the conflict, and laugh at it. (Bungay 151)

But what is the meaning of the term 'subjectivity' in this context? The term is not graspable as one single thing, as we shall see.

We can proceed by looking at dramatic poetry in general. It is first and foremost action – actions performed by individuals aiming to realize purposes, ends, and goals. Like every genuine action, action in drama mediates between, on the one hand, a certain substance (*Substanz*) – the eternal content (*Gehalt*) of 'divinity' as it is realized in the world – and, on the other hand, 'subjectivity – subjectivity as such, in its unbounded freedom and self-determination' (III:520). These two categories – or *Grundmomente* ('substance' and 'subjectivity') – define the purposive actions of individuals. The actions of every individual, real or staged, as well as the conflicts between such acting individuals, real or staged, exhibit a determinate relation between the substance of the action and the subjectivity of the actor. Hence, distinctions can be made between comedy, tragedy, and drama in the narrower sense, as theatre – according to whether, in the actions of its players, the category of substance or the category of subjectivity is mainly 'adhered to [*festgehalten*]': whether, in other words, what comes to the fore 'in individuals, acts and conflicts, [is] the aspect of substance or, contrariwise, the aspect of subjective arbitrariness [*Willkür*], foolishness, and absurdity – that is, preposterous actions and perverse deeds' (III:521). In comedy, as distinct from tragedy, 'subjectivity, as such, in willing and acting, as well as outer contingency and accident' dominate all relations and purposes.

Now, precisely at this point, a point of conceptual unclarity, it will be useful to recall de Man's citation of Hegel's term '*Meinen* [opine, mean to say]' as it is found in the *Encyclopedia*. There Hegel writes: 'When I say "I," I *mean* myself as *this* I to the exclusion of all others, but what I say, "I," is precisely anyone [Wenn ich sage: "Ich," *meine* ich mich *als* diesen alle anderen Ausschließenden: aber was ich sage, Ich, ist eben jeder']' (*AI* 98).[7] Here, and in related propositions in the *Aesthetics*, de Man finds

an ever present point of resistance in the Hegelian system: if truth is the appropriation in thought and, hence, in language, of the world by the I, then truth, which by definition is the absolutely general, also contains a constitutive element of particularization that is not compatible with its universality. (*AI* 190)

In this perspective, there is cause to worry about the way Hegel's theory of comedy has mingled the terms (1) 'subjectivity' as 'freedom' and (2) 'subjectivity' as 'arbitrariness [*Willkür*]' – the way it has mingled 'subjectivity as such' and 'contingency.' Are these apparent opposites intelligible in their imputed distinction? Can this distinction be discerned? This aporia will recur in Hegel's definition of comedy triumphant.

To highlight the difficulty, we could look for a moment at tragedy, where we see a comparable difficulty crystallizing. In tragedy, substance (e.g., family, politics, religion) comes to the fore, as these different purposes are realized in the working-out of concrete designs. To the extent that individuality can be assigned to the tragic actor, it is part of the *content* of his or her life. On this height, 'the mere contingencies of immediate individuality disappear' (III:522).

This formulation, however, will once again prove troublesome. True, we are inclined to honour the idea of an individual tragic consciousness stripped of 'the mere contingencies of immediate individuality,' and one could think of Hölderlin's eliminating from the first, the Frankfurt-plan of his *Empedokles*-tragedy, the quarrel that first drives Empedokles out of the house and up onto Aetna (Hölderlin 21). But as soon as the factor of subjectivity is described in a different register, and what is stripped from the individual tragic consciousness is 'subjectivity as such, in its *unbounded freedom and self-determination*' (emphasis added) (III:520) and subjectivity in 'its *infinite [self]-certainty*' (III:527), then we will find little to honour in this idea of the tragic consciousness. For to stress the general character of subjectivity as what in this case is *lost* is to jeopardize the high valuation of tragic impersonality, since subjectivity, so defined, has immeasurable value, and it would be this value, in tragic action, that would be cast off.[8] But what is it that allows Hegel to sacrifice within the tragic formula the term of 'subjectivity' defined *only* in its partiality, its one-sidedness, its perverseness and not in its generality? The answer belongs to the requirements of a historical system that, despite traditional expectations, places tragedy *before* and *below* comedy as a vehicle of the return of Spirit to itself, a positioning act that is itself, however, prey to a conceptual uncertainty arising from Hegel's obsessively bifurcating thought, as I shall illustrate. Meanwhile, it is clear that the definition of the tragic depends on the possibility, the intelligibility, of a subjectivity actually purified of all particular interests and at one with its substantial goal. To this end, to bridge this difficulty, Hegel writes, in 'tragedy the individuals destroy one another through the one-sidedness of their intrinsically valuable [*gediegen*] acts of will and their intrinsically valuable character,' which is to say that although one-sided – and, hence, perverse – their willing is nonetheless valuable.[9]

At this point Hegel brings us back to our more immediate concern, as he proceeds to the example provided by comedy: 'What comes to light in comedy, [however], in the laughter of individuals, who through themselves and in themselves dissolve away all obstacles, is the victory of their subjectivity, which stands forth all the same secure in its own being' (III:527). The point is progressively strengthened:

> What belongs to the comic above all is the infinite cheerfulness [*Wohlgemutheit*] and confidence of being elevated through and through above its own contradiction and not, let us say, [being] bitter and unhappy within it – the bliss and delicious comfort of subjectivity, which, sure of itself, can endure the dissolution of its purposes and realizations. (III:528)

A *literary* reading of this text, I think, will be inclined to throw up its hands – in bliss – and declare, with full certainty, that the delicious ease of subjectivity that Hegel conjures here is not a description of a state realizable in any other world except the world of this text – a fullness, a oneness, an at-homeness of a fictional being called subjectivity remote from the fate of anyone's being-a-subject *ici-bas*.[10]

Now, it is important to stress that Hegel has not failed to make use earlier in the *Aesthetics* – and all throughout his corpus – of the distinction between a sort of substantial subjectivity and one with an only invidiously particular claim on truth. The 'classical' art of the Greeks, for example, attains to its high privilege in the *Aesthetics* by individualizing as sensory appearance an essential substance become subjectively luminous, allowing it to shine through the corporeal shape that perfectly veils it. On the other hand, 'subjectivity' also appears as the deficient pseudo-absolutization of 'Romantic' inwardness that no longer has an interest in representing itself. And in a still more grievous form, subjectivity, as in the *Philosophy of Right*, turns into something altogether nugatory and threatening.

Consider a few further salient examples of this diremption. The first involves a distinction Hegel makes in the *Aesthetics* in his treatment of the lyric.

The optimal condition for the flourishing of lyric (unlike epic) is a point of ripe national development, one in which 'the prose of [everyday] reality' has been settled. For lyric is an affair of inwardness, which can only come into being vis-à-vis 'a more or less finished order of life-relationships.' 'The individual reflects himself in himself in opposition to this external reality' and secludes himself in his inwardness in order to achieve there a final autonomous totality of feeling and imagination. The interesting final term in Hegel's argument is *sich abschließen*, meaning 'to cut oneself off, to go into seclusion' but also 'to achieve for oneself a final reckoning' (III:431).

But everything will depend on just how the subject takes itself as subject, for it is 'the subject as subject that supplies the form and content.' Here is the proviso:

> This may not be understood as meaning that the individual, in order to be able to express himself lyrically, must cut himself off from everything and every connection with national interests and attitudes and in an only formal way stand entirely on his own two feet. On the contrary, in such abstract independence, the only remaining content would be the entirely contingent and particular passion, while the arbitrariness of desires and preferences, the queerheadedness of impulses, and the bizarre originality of feelings would enjoy unlimited scope. The task of genuine lyric, like all true poetry, is to express the true substance [*Gehalt*] of the human heart. As the content of lyric, however, even the most concrete and substantial entities must appear as having been subjectively felt, viewed, imagined, or thought. (III:431)

Again, on examining closely the so-called Note to the famous Paragraph 139 of the *Philosophy of Right*, where 'subjectivity' is given a philosophical *coup de grâce*, we will see that here too Hegel obsessively bifurcates the term into an essential good, namely: 'subjectivity – (Freedom – absolute thinking – form[:] Unity with myself, – differentiating consciousness)' and only thereafter lowers it into the 'evil' of particularity, namely ' – [consciousness] that gives itself a *characteristic/particular* content.' The word 'particular' and its cognates are parlous markers of degradation, as indeed, further in this paragraph, subjectivity is declared to be nothing less than 'evil': 'The individual subject *as such* has the guilt of his evil.'[11]

There is good and bad subjectivity, but how can the distinction between these two modalities be clarified aside from the *mise en abîme* of attributing to subjectivity in one or another of its higher forms – as spirit (*Geist*) or as the concept (*Begriff*) – a self-authenticating power?[12]

We shall not be spared these troubling uncertainties on examining Hegel's account of comedy as a dynamism. Comedy is an affair of subjectivity as it is marked by a disparity, a difference, a tension in its activity. Hence, it is marked by movement – a movement aiming towards resolution, indeed, towards triumphant resolution. In such comedy triumphant, there is an evident redeeming of subjectivity (as freedom) from *Willkür* (as arbitrariness) – yet in this model of an active, progressive purification, we are again confronted with a version of the same difficulty. It lies in the impossibility of articulating as a dramatic trajectory, as a historical movement, the purging of perversity (or error) and its emergence into its own truth – the liberation of a subjectivity aligned with contingencies into a subjectivity ecstatically self-assured. The question here is the temporal one of whether subjectivity is ever able to strip itself clean of particular and perverse forms of attachment, so that we might speak of a subjectivity triumphantly pure. This entanglement jeopardizes the intelligibility of comedy as a goal-oriented narrative history.

There is another way to pose this aporia. We can note that in this process, subjectivity, which has been alienated from itself by being seated in small characters or by being attached to small goals, is restored to itself in its *natural* tonality – a being natively good-natured[13] and full of well-being (*Wohlgemutheit*), if one can say this. But the intelligibility of this account depends on being able to think subjectivity as a quasi-natural entity *and* as an intentional process, alienating itself in ever different – here, spurious – goals and concerns until it is 'finally' able to take itself fully back into itself as its own goal and concern. This is a requirement laid on our understanding that flies in the face of the thesis on intentionality.[14]

Sartre's phrase for this Hegelian rule, arising from a phenomenological tradition, is: 'toute conscience est conscience de quelque chose.' The comedic return of subjectivity in Hegel occurs, after all, as an apprehension of itself, as a moment of meaning. Kristeva made the shrewd observation: 'Far from being an epistemological perversion, a certain subject is present from the moment that there is the consciousness of a meaning' (149). For the purposes of our argument, we could vary this proposition as follows: 'Far from being a metaphysical perversion, a certain meaning is present from the moment that there is the consciousness (by a subject) of a subject.' The implication should be clear: Where there is the mineness of a subject however conceived, there is meaning. What subjectivity returns to in every case, along with the impression of mineness, is a certain meaning; but this 'consciousness of a meaning' (Kristeva 149) implies an articulation of the meaning

as object, and this articulation, which is not that of subjectivity but of its
object, necessarily divides subjectivity from itself. It is not subjectivity to
which subjectivity returns but a certain apprehension of itself as object,
and it remains divided from itself by precisely this meaning, this object,
this barrier, which de Man prefers to call 'the linguistic sign.' If, then,
subjectivity at the end of the *Aesthetics* celebrates a return to itself, it can
celebrate it only as a measured triumph; and in this perspective it is not
surprising that Hegel has situated the discussion of comedy precisely at
the end, the absolute end of the *Aesthetics*, and says as much, for comedy
brings about not only the *Aesthetics* but 'the dissolution of art as such.'
After all,

> the aim, the purpose, the goal of all art is the identity brought forth by the
> Spirit, in which the eternal, the divine, and that which is true in and for
> itself are manifested in real appearance and shape for our external senses,
> for our soul, and for our imaginative ideation. But if comedy represents
> this unity only as its self-destruction, in that the Absolute, which wants to
> bring itself forth into reality, sees this realization as itself annihilated
> through interests in the sphere of reality that are freed for themselves and
> directed only towards the contingent and subjective, then the presence
> and the activity of the Absolute no longer comes forth in positive
> unification with the characters and purposes of real existence but instead
> prevails in only negative form, in the sense, that is, that everything that
> does not correspond to it is sublated, and at the same time only subjectivity
> as such, certain of itself and assured in itself, emerges in this dissolution.
> (III:572–3)

Comedy concludes art, yet not in the sense that it brings about even the
fulfilment of subjectivity; it concludes art by holding up the difficulty
that represented individuals could ever authentically represent a coming into its own of enlightened subjectivity.

In Hegel's thinking explicitly of an art (Romantic and also comedic)
that repeatedly announces a self-satisfied subjectivity, history has proved
Hegel wrong; but in so far as the thesis on intentionality can, as it
should, be attributed to him, he is implicitly right. For it is precisely
through the impossibility that a subject could return securely to itself
that art has precisely *not* come to an end. And if Hegel is understood, as
he must be, as announcing not the death of art but the further development in art of a subjectivity detached from essence, then this great
thinker is explicitly right.

What is finally at stake is whether such an art taking its course in its separation from substance is, as Hegel has it, a modern phenomenon (or one not older than Aristophanes, at the least), or something that has always been the case, whereupon the concept of an 'end' in art, whether construed as art's 'death' or art's 'goal' in beauty, emerges as ideology and delusion. I make this ricorso to de Man's initial argument, for one thing, as an acknowledgment, since his reflections on sign and symbol began these reflections on comedy. For another, the reinsertion at this point of a severely deconstructive reading of the *Aesthetics* will provoke a number of useful questions. They are set down here less in the form of answers than as spurs to reflection.

To the question of whether the End of Art has always been the case, so that historical, genetic, phenomenological models of its 'death' are merely ideological defences, de Man's reading of Hegel's system proceeds directly to such a conclusion. At the same time, the great many disparities it produces along the way throw up clouds of resistance.

One important objection is that Hegel himself explicitly conceded that beautiful art, with its dependency on sensory representation, is an inferior form of the Absolute Spirit, well worthy of dissolution. In this light, Hegel has already de-ideologized 'the aesthetic' and does not require the supplementary proof of the alleged superiority of 'sign'-based intellectual constructions on grounds of the freedom that the sign, unlike the symbol, allows to thought. A (de Manian) proof of the nullity of the aesthetic or of *beaux arts* on the grounds of the little freedom that they allow to their heroes or their maker is in another sense otiose, because, as Hegel makes plain enough in his theory of Romantic and comedic art, the subjectivity that belongs to these genres is characterized by unbounded freedom, self-determination, and play.[15] Furthermore, to de Man's claim that, for Hegel, there can never have been a classical/'symbolic' art that preserves the experience of inwardness, since 'Art, ... like memorization, ... leaves the interiorization of experience forever behind it' (*AI* 103), Hegel explicitly says the opposite. Art does in principle preserve inwardness; the *Encyclopedia* reads: 'In imagination [*Phantasie*], intelligibility [*allgemeine Vorstellung*] is constituted by the subjective, by subjectivity, that through the image gives itself objectivity and this way preserves itself [*sich bewährt*]' (III:269). Finally, in the de Manian perspective, comedy's failed engagement with substance could not be grasped in opposition to tragedy, which speaks of authentic engagement. De Man's view is sustained, it is true, by what we have noted as the elimination of subjectivity from the awareness of the tragic figure – subjectivity being also a vital affair of freedom and self-determination and hence a provocation and minimal condition of understanding. De Man would have Hegel's *Aesthetics* demonstrate the only mad illusoriness of identification (with substance) as such. This conclusion would mean that the experience of tragedy can exist only as self-interested bad faith. This conclusion cannot be Hegelian.

I want to return to my own way of reading the aporias in Hegel's conception of subjectivity to see what questions it produces. What light does it throw on the fate of subjectivity? In one sense, for Hegel, subjectivity has an absolute value: it is the being that triumphs in comedy, apprehending its freedom and self-determination as it provokes and registers the dissolution of false goals and attachments. In another sense, subjectivity in comedy is the seat of untruth, for it is an order of individuality, of particularity, and, by degrees in Hegel's argument, of wrong-headedness, of perversity. To the extent that the subject has (ineluctably) identified itself with particular and one-sided goals, it is guilty and lost.

The end crux of comedy is the dissolution of the subject's blindness in a moment of demystification, the dawning apprehension of untruth or what Hegel calls 'the negative of dissolution' (III:572). Is this moment thinkable as a restitution of subjectivity to itself in its freedom? How can subjectivity *not* have failed to return to itself as other than what it was? The matter can be ethically pointed: Can subjectivity escape from its delusory identifications with no harm done to its freedom? Can it escape the suffering and 'guilt' of its 'evil'? How can its *Sauwohlsein* (III:553), its pig's-heavenly happiness, *not* be 'evil' all over again? These paradoxes condition the possibility of an end to art's usefulness for higher purposes.[16]

It is not easy to find a model of thought suited to these tensions. Mark Roche suggests this trope: 'The complexity of forms of subjectivity is not Hegel's unsustainable thinking but an attempt to wrestle with its many sides.' The point rightly evokes factors of struggle (namely 'the labour of the Concept') and the dialectic of the 'sides,' but the work of this dialectic is not one which Hegel explicitly performs.[17]

The proposition giving additional impetus and some promise of order to these conflicts is the claim that the historical moment (ca. 1821) witnessing the triumph of modern comedy inaugurates the End of Art.

At the most explicit level, Hegel argues for the inadequacy of comedy on semantic and experiential grounds – on the insubstantiality of the hero's projects. They are without any legitimating or earnest reference to the values of life. It is not because art-language – here, the language of comedy – cannot preserve experience that art-language must come to an end; it is because an experience of substance is no longer possible in the prose of the world. Under the spell of comedy, art finds nothing substantial to preserve of the values of family, nation, religion. And if, indeed, the subjectivity caught up in such a world returns to itself in its freedom and native power, it returns, according to Hegel, without an 'acquist of true experience.'[18]

For Hegel, the *knowing* powers of subjectivity as it presents itself in contemporary art are enfeebled by its overgreat freedom as *felt* subjectivity. An art that can athletically take any velleity of the inner life or any peculiarity of outer life as interesting (whether it is an oddity Romantically intensified or comedically discarded) will cease to be discerning. The sovereignty of subjectivity is affirmed by an evacuation of substance from its concerns. The Romantic emotionalizing of the subjective and the comedic citation of any and all ties or whims of reason as its subject matter are possible only as easy functions of their insubstantiality (*Wesenslosigkeit*). The ease of art robs subjectivity of its purpose;[19] the attribution of high terms like freedom and self-determination to subjectivity in the context of comedy has an ironic character.

The ultimate impossibility of construing comedies as themselves progressive histories (because the polar values of subjectivity, the hero of comedy, are so conflicted) redounds to the question of how to figure such a thing as a past and future reception of Hegel's theory of the comedically inaugurated End of Art.

Readers of the *Aesthetics* will be obliged to decide whether Hegel's obliquities and dissonance-engendering contradictions operate a thoroughgoing, systemic disarticulation of a causal, historical, phenomenological system. One result of affirming this claim is, to say the least, that the End of Art may *not* be read as it has been, as keyed to the definitive passing away of a finite period and type of art called by Hegel, classic, and by de Man, 'symbolic': forget Graecomanic melancholy.

From this reading, we project ('with certain reservations'!) a history of reading that has come to its 'end' in its leave-taking from a reading of the *Aesthetics* as a history of finite, separate stages of artistic consciousness organized by their greater or lesser proximity to a posited goal (Substance become Spirit), the latter 'end' being proleptically present at the origin. In short, this reading takes leave of a normative reading of Hegel's text as at once history and system: it interrupts, at places difficult to survey, the intelligible causality of history and the systematicity of system by detecting the rumblings of repressed contradictions.

If Hegel's counter-aesthetic had been evident to Hegel's readers, then the End of Art could never have been understood as the Death of Art, worthy of being mourned – 'death' being a very poor translation of even Hegel's explicit word *Auflösung* for dissolution. The End would have been understood as another way of emphasizing a late stage, a having come on the scene too late, a lateness that is in principle the motor of thought, that, indulging the freedom of its diremption, must forever thrust apart from its object – and not because it is too feeble a thing vis-à-vis its object, but because it is too great. Comedy, then, as the modern art-form par excellence, would be cast in a metaphor of arrival and return, with the provision that subjectivity recover itself as a play of signs, always itself unreconciled, and return to its normal tension and self-difference. But this scene of homecoming cannot be grasped as a finite example because it is dissonant along lines of tonality: it is attuned by Hegel to two different sorts of bliss. On the one hand, in Hegel's stirring finale, it is the bliss of a not to be missed 'self-gratified, absolute subjectivity, freely moving intellectually in itself' (III:572). On the other hand, the contentment is no more (or less) than a pig's-heaven. It cannot be an exemplary station, except as a pit stop, in the career of the Spirit.

It is possible to hear in such sly difficulties and discontinuities the voice of a great ironist. Then, to the extent that Hegel does key the End of Art, with its definitive 'history,' to classical art as a thing of the past, he is writing with the irony of the esotericist. This stance puts him in a history of esoteric writing that ranges from Socrates to Nietzsche and requires a special reconfiguration of the idea of reception. The riddle of esoteric writing is not exhausted when the 'oblique, figural, and implicit' meaning (*AI* 192) is allegedly revealed.

NOTES

1 The essay 'Sign and Symbol in Hegel's *Aesthetics*' also appears in *Aesthetic Ideology* 91–104. Citations from this volume will henceforth be indicated in the body of this essay by *AI* followed by the pertinent page number.

2 G.W.F. Hegel, *Werke in zwanzig Bänden* III:520. Subsequent citations from Hegel's *Aesthetics* (*Vorlesungen über die Ästhetik*) will be indicated in the body of this essay by roman volume number (I, II, or III) and arabic page number.

Roman numerals correspond to volumes 13, 14, and 15 in the *Werke*. All translations are my own.

3 The exact location of this heavy work of 'translation' – namely in a psychoanalytically mapped unconscious or in the social ambitions of the ego or in the coercions of the art market or the comminations of an official ministry of culture – is left to de Man's reader to discover.

4 Examples: 'The truth is thus the Bacchanalian revel, in which no member is not drunk; yet because each member dissolves as soon as it dissociates itself, the revel is just as much *transparent* and simple repose' (*Phenomenology of Mind*, 'Preface,' paragraph 47. Commentary in Jean Hyppolite, *Logique et Existence: Essai sur la Logique de Hegel* 213). Again, on the idea of the good, 'There are still two worlds in opposition, one a realm of subjectivity in the pure regions of *transparent* thought, the other a realm of objectivity in the element of an externally manifold actuality that is an undisclosed realm of darkness' (*Science of Logic* VI:544). And on 'the absolute idea': 'Hence logic exhibits the self-movement of the absolute Idea only as original word, which is an outwardizing or utterance, but an utterance that in being has immediately vanished again as something outer; the Idea is, therefore, only in this self-determination of apprehending itself; it is in pure thought, in which difference is not yet otherness, but is and remains perfectly *transparent* to itself' (*Science of Logic* VI:550).

5 Raymond Geuss will also point out mistakes in his 'A Response to Paul de Man.'

6 We will leave to one side the putative bearing of Hegel's 'oblique' poetics (*AI* 192) on de Man's own critical procedure, which is to have Hegel 'say' and 'assert' this oblique poetics as the author of the *Encyclopedia*, with the guarantee of a free intelligence. The question of whether these aporias are produced intentionally by Hegel or rather by the blind, aporia-engendering positional power of language as such is left to Hegel to argue; it is enough for de Man to declare that, for Hegel, 'thought is entirely dependent on a mental faculty [namely, memorization] that is mechanical through and through' (*AI* 102).

7 See also G.W.F. Hegel, *Enzyklopädie der philosophischen Wissenschaften, Werke in zwanzig Bänden* 8:74.

8 In a letter to me, dated 11 October 1997, following his paper 'Subjectivity and Negativity in Hegel's Theory of Comedy,' presented at the German Studies Association, Washington, DC, September 1997, Mark Roche warns against readings of Hegel's views on comedy that 'elevate subjectivity as the model of certitude in a way foreign to Hegel's treatment of subjectivity in the discussion of aesthetics (here subjectivity would negate the value of objective *Sitt-*

lichkeit).' But this warning cannot hope to be heeded by readers in a case where Hegel supplies all the language necessary to come to such a conclusion.

9 In the same letter, Mark Roche insists that the one-sidedness of comedy has to be differentiated from that of tragedy, which is characterized by 'one-sidedness of a different kind.' This point is useful, to a degree: the main sense of the 'one-sidedness' of the tragic hero is his adherence to only one aspect of the eternally substantial – a blindness to the truth of what holds these aspects together. The chief argument in Hegel about the failure of the tragic hero lies in his inability to grasp the apparent opposition between his substantial value and that of his protagonist as a moment of discord within a disavowed totality that holds both values together through their difference. And yet a tension survives between this way of reading the tragic hero's one-sidedness and another: there is also the one-sidedness of a tragic consciousness from which all traces of subjectivity have been eliminated, a point made not *only* obliquely or figurally or implicitly in a less conspicuous part of the corpus. These questions are additionally studied in Roche's excellent *Tragedy and Comedy: A Systematic Study and a Critique of Hegel.*

10 In the *Phenomenology,* Hegel finds the one place where this bliss can actually be experienced – in Aristophanic comedy, identifying 'such certainty in a state of spiritual good health and of self-abandonment thereto on the part of consciousness, in a way that, outside this [Aristophanic] kind of comedy is not to be found anywhere.'

11 G.W.F. Hegel, *Grundlinien der Philosophie des Rechts, Werke in zwanzig Bänden* 7:262–3. This note, by the way, is not included in the capable translation of S.W. Dyde: G.W.F. Hegel, *Philosophy of Right.*

12 Yet this is finally how the distinction would have to be made: the Absolute Subject posits, in only ostensible contradiction, a subjectivity in its 'unbounded freedom and self-determination' that is yet privative, a false subject, for being unable to advance along the path of truth except by having to do with the accidents and contingencies it takes for substance. See Helmut Schneider, 'Hegels Theorie der Komik und die Auflösung der schönen Kunst' (an unpublished paper presented at the conference 'Hegel and Hölderlin: The Language of Philosophy and the Language of Poetry,' Yale University, October 1987) 5–6.

13 A proviso about the words 'native' and 'natural': Hegel does not use them but allows this paraphrase, I think, by describing the subjectivity at the basis of comedy in such terms as 'the *cheerful* [*heiter*] life of the mind [*Gemut*], absolutely at peace with itself' (III:552) and, more memorably, in the world of Aristophanic comedy, untranslatably, as that element in man that *wallows* in happiness, grunts with *animal* satisfaction: 'Without having read Aris-

tophanes,' Hegel writes 'one could never know what it is like to wallow in [or, perhaps, to swill down] happiness [*wie dem Menschen sauwohl sein kann*]' (III:553).

14 In proceeding with an argument that associates 'subjectivity' with the 'thinking subject,' I should stress that I am least on de Man's ground, since he takes pains, in his 'Reply to Raymond Geuss,' to distinguish his view on the subjectivity of the thinking subject from Geuss's allegedly more 'canonical' view. De Man writes: 'That this "thinking subject" (of the *Enzyklopädie*) is in no way subjective, in the ordinary sense of the term, nor even specular, in the Cartesian mode, is something that any careful reader of Hegel knows' (*AI* 189). At the same time this proviso should scarcely rule out the point that even 'subjectivity in the ordinary sense of the term' remains unintelligible except as having the structure of the linguistic sign – and hence as constraining *its* readers, including itself, into the toils of that one-sided, particular, and perverse attachment we call interpretation.

15 We deal here with the 'self-transcendence' of art in the form of art. See John Sallis, 'Mimesis and the End of Art.'

16 De Man has one (implied) response, if his voice may once more be heard, that would allow at least for a restoration of good cheer, but with a drawback. Regarding the 'pathos' of the 'state of suspended ignorance' arising from an undecidable reading (of 'the rhetorical mode of a literary text'), de Man notes: 'The resulting pathos is an anxiety (or bliss, depending on one's momentary mood or individual temperament) of ignorance' (*Allegories of Reading: Figural Language in Rousseau, Nietzsche, Rilke, and Proust*). Ergo, de Man is willing to concede Hegelian 'bliss' as the *comic* temperament's response to a moment of cognitive chastisement. But this bliss is accompanied by a sense of ignorance and is not at all a sense of 'infinite [self]-certainty' (III:527). For to learn, according to de Man, that the money in your pocket is counterfeit is not to get good money in its place, and so the elation is only of the weak Messianic kind. (This point is not inconsistent with Hegel's final position on the shortcomings of comedy: though we end with comedy, with comic laughter, our response to the awareness that with comedy we come to the end of art is not itself laughter.)

The linguistic correlative of the 'fusion' of subjectivity with its higher goal (as in tragedy), meanwhile, is silence; the fusion of subjectivity with its merely particular goal is the lie. Of the alleged restoration of subjectivity to itself in its basic tonality of cheer and security, the pig's-heavenly happiness of the subject, there is no equivalent in de Man's thought. I do not think it would exist for him except as the 'inhuman.'

17 The deconstructive reading also does not find Hegel incoherent but sug-

gests, rather, that older readings are, for failing to hear another voice in the *Aesthetics*, another 'saying,' namely 'what is being said obliquely, figurally, and implicitly [though not less compellingly] in less conspicuous parts of the corpus' (*AI* 192).

18 The phrase is Milton's, at the very close of *Samson Agonistes*; to Samson is attributed 'new acquist / Of true experience.'

19 For Adorno and Thomas Mann's Adrian Leverkühn, art worthy of its name is 'too hard.' Hegel would suggest: 'Gib's auf!'

WORKS CITED

Bungay, Stephen. *Beauty and Truth: A Study of Hegel's Aesthetics*. Oxford: Oxford UP, 1984.

de Man, Paul. *Allegories of Reading: Figural Language in Rousseau, Nietzsche, Rilke, and Proust*. New Haven: Yale UP, 1979.

– 'Sign and Symbol in Hegel's *Aesthetics*.' *Aesthetic Ideology*. Ed. Andrzej Warminski. Minneapolis: U of Minnesota P, 1996. 91–104.

– 'Reply to Raymond Geuss.' *Aesthetic Ideology*. Ed. Andrzej Warminski. Minneapolis: U of Minnesota P, 1996. 185–92.

Geuss, Raymond. 'A Response to Paul de Man.' *Critical Inquiry* 10.2 (December 1983): 375–91.

Hegel, G.W.F. *Aesthetics* (*Vorlesungen über die Ästhetik*). *Werke in zwanzig Bänden*. Ed. Eva Moldenhauer and Karl Markus Michel. Frankfurt: Suhrkamp, 1978.

– *The Phenomenology of Mind*. Trans. J.B. Baillie. London: George Allen and Unwin, 1979.

– *Philosophy of Right*. Trans. S.W. Dyde. Amherst, NY: Prometheus, 1996.

– *Science of Logic*. New York: Macmillan, 1961.

Hölderlin, Friedrich. *Sämtliche Werke, Kritische Textausgabe*. Vol. 12, *Empedokles I*, 'Frankfurter Plan.' Luchterhand: Darmstadt, 1986.

Hyppolite, Jean. *Logique et Existence: Essai sur la Logique de Hegel*. Paris: Presses Universitaires de France, 1953.

Kristeva, Julia. 'D'une identité l'autre.' *Polylogue*. Paris: Seuil, 1977.

Milton, John. *Samson Agonistes*. Ed. Stephen Orgel and Jonathan Goldberg. Oxford: Oxford UP, 1991.

Roche, Mark. Letter to the author. 11 October 1997.

– 'Subjectivity and Negativity in Hegel's Theory of Comedy.' German Studies Association Conference. Washington, DC. September 1997.

– *Tragedy and Comedy: A Systematic Study and a Critique of Hegel*. Albany: SUNY P, 1998.

Sallis, John. 'Mimesis and the End of Art.' *Intersections: Nineteenth-Century Philosophy and Contemporary Theory.* Ed. Tilottama Rajan and David L. Clark. Albany: SUNY P, 1995.

Schneider, Helmut. 'Hegels Theorie der Komik und die Auflösung der schönen Kunst.' Conference on Hegel and Hölderlin: The Language of Philosophy and the Language of Poetry. Yale University. October 1987.

The Double Detour: Sartre, Heidegger, and the Genealogy of Deconstruction

TILOTTAMA RAJAN

I. Sartre against Heidegger

This essay begins with Sartre's supposed mistranslation of *Being and Time* as *Being and Nothingness,* and traces its legacy for a deconstruction that emerges in the crossing over of 'phenomenology' from Germany to France. That the French understanding of Heidegger was initially mediated by Sartre is well known. French intellectuals such as Jean Beaufret came to Heidegger *à travers* Sartre, as Sartre himself came to Husserl via Levinas, or as Lacan came to Hegel by way of Kojève. Correcting this misprision, younger theorists such as Derrida recovered a place for Heidegger in deconstruction, so that Sartre, once a key figure in continental philosophy, was displaced as philosophically incorrect by Heidegger. As various commentators note, the eclipse of Sartre was the condition of possibility for the linguistic turn as well as for the rise of Heidegger (Dosse 1:3–10; Rockmore 95). Though the influence of the two is irreducibly intertwined, 'Heidegger' has come to figure what can be kept and purified from the phenomenological pre-text of deconstruction, while the 'naïve' parts of this legacy have been condensed in 'Sartre.'

But this history of the relation between phenomenology and deconstruction conceals two mistranslations. First, Sartre's appropriation of Heidegger is not (as often alleged) a 'mistake,' a case of a second-rate philosopher pillaging Heidegger without understanding him. The rendering of *Eigentlichkeit* as *authenticité* and of *Dasein* as *réalité humaine* by Heidegger's first French translator, Henri Corbin, may be a mistake. But Sartre's appropriation of Heidegger is more like what Stanley Corngold calls an 'error': a carrying over or troping constitutive for subsequent theory (92–7). As important, this error has itself been covered over by a second polemical misprision: Heidegger's representation of Sartre, which in its acceptance by subsequent theorists has generated a second error. For when Heidegger 'corrects' Sartre, he reduces the latter's work metonymically to *Existentialism Is a Humanism*, thus eliding the difference between Sartre's existentialism and his phenomenology, his political self-popularization and his more serious philosophical work. Indeed Heidegger, it seems, never read *Being and Nothingness*.[1] Depicting Sartre as straightforwardly 'anthropological,' Heidegger's mistake thus sets the stage for the second phase of French theory: its turn from a 'deconstruction' that develops its understanding of 'language' from a radicalization of phenomenology's focus on consciousness, to a 'poststructuralism' that sees language and consciousness as irreducibly opposed.[2]

Heidegger's claim in 'The Letter on Humanism' (1947) that he had been misrepresented by Sartre is well known, particularly as repeated by Derrida in 'The Ends of Man' (1968). Alluding to Corbin's translation of *Dasein* as *réalité humaine*, and then implicating Sartre too in this 'monstrous' mistranslation (115), Derrida speaks of the continued usefulness of phenomenology, 'but not – especially not – in the versions proposed by Sartre or by Merleau-Ponty.'[3] Briefly, Heidegger's criticisms converge on the issues of anthropology and nihilism which will continue to haunt deconstruction's anxiety about Sartre's precursory influence. Arguing that there is no essence without existence, Heidegger accuses Sartre of treating existence in Hegelian fashion as the immanent working out of essence, instead of understanding it in terms of ek-static temporality. Sartre is said to mistranslate Heidegger's terms 'ek-sistence' and 'projection,' thus recentring the latter in his own notion of the project as 'a representational positing' that is 'an achievement of subjectivity' (231).

Sartre's nihilism, Heidegger complains, is likewise a consequence of his emphasis on man rather than being. Sartre sees the structures of being and consciousness, or the *en-soi* and *pour-soi*, as fundamentally incommensurable. As the fullness of matter, the in-itself or *en-soi* is a plenitude, while the for-itself or *pour-soi* is a void (*néant*) that lacks being. Constructing a dualism that divides existence between extended and thinking matter as being and nothingness respectively, Sartre 'pitch[es] everything that does not stay close to the ... positive into the previously excavated pit of pure negation.' This negation 'negates everything, ends in nothing, and so consummates nihilism' (250). Most importantly, Sartre misrecognizes nihilation as something that unfolds 'in the existence of man' rather than in 'Being itself' (261). He therefore excludes the human as infinite absolute negativity from the world as an undialectical and non-human positivity.[4]

That Sartre enlisted Heidegger on the side of existentialism is as puzzling as his own self-vulgarization in *Existentialism Is a Humanism* – though Sartre had always seen Heidegger as a kind of humanist, and with reason.[5] But it is clear three years earlier in *Being and Nothingness*, when politics is not the issue, that Sartre – after an initial enthusiasm for Heidegger in the mid-1930s – does not misunderstand but, rather, disagrees with him. Sartre borrows from Heidegger's 'What Is Metaphysics' the terms 'nothing' and 'nihilation.' But his phenomenology of negativity translates the latter's postmetaphysical idealism only in the sense that Heidegger himself uses the word 'translation,' to denote a process by which one cultural experience is transferred into 'a different way of thinking' (149), in this case French rather than German.

Far from mistaking *Dasein* for his own *réalité humaine*,[6] Sartre foregrounds the difference between the two, as the difference between spirit and consciousness, being and existence. Heidegger, he observes, begins 'with the existential analytic without going through the *cogito*,' thus in a way sidestepping existence. The Sartrean *cogito* is not to be conceived on the model of Descartes, Kant, or Husserl. Husserl 'has shut himself up inside the *cogito* and deserves – despite his denial – to be called a phenomenalist rather than a phenomenologist' (*BN* 119). Yet in avoiding this 'sovereign transparency'[7] of the phenomenal *cogito*, Heidegger brackets the *cogito* altogether, so as to engage in his own transcendental reduction. Insofar as it 'does not and never can lead to self-consciousness,' *Dasein* thus tends towards what Foucault, echoing Sartre, will call 'inertia' (*OT* 322). Similarly Sartre writes that since *Dasein*

> has from the start been deprived of the dimension of consciousness, it can never regain this dimension. Heidegger endows human reality with a self-understanding ... But how could there be an understanding which would not in itself be the consciousness (of) being understanding? This eksta[sis] ... will lapse into a thing-like, blind in-itself. (*BN* 119–20; cf. also 134)

At issue here is the subject as vulnerability – a vulnerability also disclosed by Hyppolite when he translates the German Hegel of the *Logic* into the French Hegel of the *Phenomenology* and the unhappy consciousness. Writing on Husserl, Levinas marks the difference between logic and phenomenology: logic 'which deals with the general form of being can say nothing of its material structures' and thus 'lies outside of any psychology' (*Theory of Intuition* 78). Despite his early allegiance to Heidegger, Levinas will go on to discern a continuity between Husserlian logic and Heideggerian being as philosophies of light. That 'nihilation unfolds ... in Being' and not in the existence of man thus means, for Sartre, that nothingness does not happen *to* anyone and in a sense does not happen, materially or psychologically. Nothingness, by not being grounded upon a subject as 'negative being,' becomes a form of 'transcendence' (*BN* 53).

To put it differently, Sartre retains the *cogito* not as a positive term but as a moment of responsibility: 'In truth the *cogito* must be our point of departure ... but it leads us only on condition that we get out of it.' As Sartre explains, his ontology and ethics have as their goal precisely this exit: to 'question the *cogito* about its being,' by furnishing the 'instrument that would enable us to find in the *cogito* itself the means of escaping' it (*BN* 120). Sartre's phrase strikingly anticipates Derrida's definition of deconstruction as 'using against the edifice the instruments ... available in the house' ('Ends' 135). Indeed Sartre seeks to deconstruct the *cogito* by disclosing its aporetic structure as 'being what it is not and not being what it is' (*BN* 28). But he also insists that this deconstruction must be known and felt by a 'cogito' if it is to have any urgency.

Insofar as he short-circuits the *cogito*, Sartre sees Heidegger as recontaining nothingness – which is to say otherness and difference – in a being closer to spirit than to the unhappy consciousness.[8] This vicarious reunification of the self through the figure of 'being' is a displacement to which Levinas will also point when he notes the complicity of Heidegger's seemingly non-violent ecstasis with appropriative knowledge: whereas in the latter 'the object is absorbed by the subject,' 'in ecstasis the subject is absorbed in the object and recovers itself in its unity. All these relationships result in the disappearance of the other.'[9] Sartre makes the same point four years earlier, when he describes Heideggerian transcendence as 'a concept in bad faith.' Sartre further comments that 'undoubtedly' *Dasein* '"exists outside itself." But this existence outside is precisely Heidegger's definition of the *self*' (*BN* 336). For Sartre, then, the reduction or putting under erasure of the *cogito* in ecstasis is an idealization that restores the subject as spirit redeemed from consciousness.

This idealization, in turn, opens Heidegger to a second criticism, namely that 'the characteristic of [his] philosophy is to describe *Dasein* by using positive terms which hide the implicit negations' (*BN* 52). Sartre's aim, then, is to deconstruct Heidegger's thinking by unearthing these negations:

> *Dasein* is 'outside of itself, in the world'; it is 'a being of distances'; ... it is 'its own possibilities,' etc. All this amounts to saying that *Dasein* 'is not' in itself, that it 'is not' in immediate proximity to itself, and that it 'surpasses' the world inasmuch as it posits itself as *not being in itself* and as *not being the world* (52).

In this vein Sartre takes issue with Heidegger on a range of issues including negativity, temporality, being-with, death (697–8), ethics (128), the other (333–7), and the whole question of the 'clearing' or the phenomenon as the showing of being (8–9) as against what for Sartre is the opacity of being as solid or 'massif' (28).

Sartre notes that the essential structure of Heidegger's thought is positive, or that the 'nothing' is no more than the 'ground' upon which *Dasein* appears (251–2). In effect he finds in Heidegger – but in terms of ontology rather than language – what Derrida will analyse as a metaphysics of presence. Indeed Sartre is one of Heidegger's earliest critics in this regard, breaking with Levinas's early reading of Heidegger as an existential phenomenologist, and foreshadowing his later criticisms of the German philosopher.[10] Sartre admits that Heidegger may indeed *seem* to move to a 'concrete apprehension of nothingness' (50). *Dasein* 'rises up as an emergence of being in non-being,' even as 'the world is "suspended" in nothingness. Anguish is the discovery of this double, perpetual nihilation' (51). Still, in so far as nothingness is only that 'by which the world receives its outlines,' Sartre argues that Heidegger renders nothingness marginal: 'Here then is nothingness surrounding being on every side and at the same time expelled from being' (51). This in turn has to do with its transcendental, merely theoretical character. For 'If I emerge in nothingness *beyond* the world, how can this extra-mundane nothingness furnish a foundation for those little pools of non-being which we encounter each instant in the depths of being' (53)?

II. The Language of Nothingness

These little pools of non-being, by contrast, are the concern of Sartre, who finds them in the very microphysics of perception and language. Sartre's resistance to theory is often located in an insensitivity to language, of which Merleau-Ponty is seen as more aware. To be sure, unlike Merleau-Ponty in the 1950s, Sartre in the period 1938–43 does not mention Saussure. Yet he finds in *consciousness* the same difference and nonidentity that deconstruction later finds in language. Moreover, Sartre does not entirely bypass language, which he prophetically analyses as the discourse of the Other (*BN* 464, 485–7). He discerns the negative in language not by focusing on the diacritical nature of the sign, but by analysing ordinary language in the tradition of logical positivism. One could say that he engages with language as it was thought in his time. And as we shall see, even his analysis of perception, drawn from *Gestalt* theory, is organized by what becomes for de Man a linguistic model of 'figuration.'

For Sartre nothingness is everywhere. Considering a line segment, he argues that the 'positive attribute' of length is also 'distance' and 'intervenes here by virtue of the negation of an absolute ... proximity.' If one considers length as the bridging of distance, then 'the negation, expelled from the segment and its length, takes refuge in the two *limits*' of a line that '*does not* extend beyond this point' (54). Sartre seems compelled to find the negative in every situation, however one sees it: nothingness, he says, 'lies coiled in the heart of being – like a worm' (56). Sartre writes of negation, nothingness, non-being, and nihilation. As if these terms are inadequate he invents a further term, *négatités*, to signify the 'transcendent' or primal nature of nothingnesses that nevertheless arise only in situations of engagement 'in the world' (59). Though he sometimes relapses into a hypostasis of nothingness, Sartre is deeply aware that it is neither a substance nor a structure: 'One does not *find*, one does not *disclose* nothingness in the manner in which one can find, disclose a being' (126). Sartre's legacy to theory is thus the way he 'exscribes' a nothingness that cannot be logically contained or 'inscribed' within the text. As Nancy explains, in exscription 'meaning spills out of itself, like a simple ink stain on a word': 'the exscribed is exscribed ... not as an "inexpressible"' but 'as writing's opening, within itself ... to its own inscription as the infinite discharge of meaning.' But 'discharge' in the present context is less a bursting into presence than an opening into abjection that Nancy also signals by evoking Bataille. By trying vainly to 'inscribe' and internalize nothingness through so many synonyms, Sartre thus 'exscribe[s] the presence of what withdraws from all significations,' only to erupt in his final discussion of the viscous as the 'torment' of an 'inner experience' that is neither inside nor outside because it has breached the boundaries between them (Nancy 339–40; Bataille *Inner Experience* 8–9, 178).

We shall consider just one example of *négatité*: Sartre's famous appointment with Pierre in the café. In the first part of the scene Sartre seems to entertain the claims of the positive, as he describes the café with 'its mirrors, its light' as 'a fullness of being.' Pierre's anticipated presence is also a 'plenitude': 'We seem to have found fullness every-where.' Yet Sartre observes that

> in perception there is always the construction of a figure on a ground. ... When I enter this café to search for Pierre, there is formed a synthetic organization of all the objects in the café, on the ground of which Pierre is given as about to appear. This organization of the café as the ground is an original nihilation. Each element of the setting ... attempts to ... lift itself upon the ground constituted by the totality of the other objects, only to fall back once more into the undifferentiation of this ground. ... For the ground is that which is seen only in addition, that which is the object of a purely marginal attention. ... Thus the original nihilation of all the figures which appear and are swallowed up ... is the necessary condition for the appearance of the principal figure, which is here the person of Pierre. (*BN* 41)

In other words, thetic consciousness, as an act of focusing, eliminates that penumbra of difference sensed by the pre-reflective *cogito*. These other objects, moreover, are not simply marginalized, they are 'nihi-lated,' in a positing that Blanchot sees as a form of 'murder' and that Derrida and de Man will refer to as 'violence.'[11] When Pierre fails to appear this nihilation is redoubled. He is not absent from 'some precise spot' but 'from the *whole* café,' which is consumed by his absence (42). Nihilation, moreover, attacks not only the ground but the very possibil-ity of figuration, which is not positing but a double erasure:

> the café remains *ground* ... [but] slips into the background; it pursues its nihilation. Only it makes itself ground for a determined figure. ... This figure ... is precisely a perpetual disappearance; it is Pierre raising himself as nothingness on the ground of the nihilation of the café ... it is the nothingness of the ground, the nihilation of which summons and demands the appearance of the figure, and it is the figure – the nothingness which slips as a *nothing* to the surface of the ground. (*BN* 42)

We cannot fail to recall de Man's traumatic reading of the 'positional power of language' as a repetitive, 'arbitrary' erasure. In 'Shelley Disfigured' de Man writes that 'language posits and language means ... but language cannot posit meaning,' because it describes 'the emergence of an articulated language of cognition by the erasure, the forgetting of the events this language in fact performed.' The trace is not retention as in Derrida's Husserlian version of the concept. It is rather what Sartre calls a 'nihilating thesis' (*BN* 62): an erasure of what is already an erasure, a forgetting of the 'knowledge achieved by the forgetting that precedes it' (*RR* 116–19).[12]

Sartre, as we have seen, coins the word *négatité* to describe the unconcealing of 'original' nothingness in the commonalities of daily life. Since 'they are dispersed in being' these *négatités* cannot be 'throw[n] ... back into an extra-mundane nothingness,' as Sartre says Heidegger does (*BN* 55–6); instead they are 'constituted in immanence as transcendences.' In other words they are 'secondary,' existentially concrete 'nihilations' that disclose an 'original' 'nothingness' (84). As we have suggested, Sartre also finds these *négatités* in ordinary language. And here it is useful to approach him through one of his most astute readers, Blanchot. Blanchot's 'Literature and the Right to Death' (1947) is often taken as a rebuke to Sartre's contemporaneous and highly political *What Is Literature?* (1947). But as I argue later, it is also an extension of his texts on imagination and ontology: a radicalization of a Sartre whose earlier work was already among the most radical contributions to de(con)structive thought, or to what Blanchot calls 'the powerful negative contemporary movements responsible for this volatizing and volatile force which literature seems to have become' (*GO* 23).

Whether Blanchot read Saussure is unclear, yet he seems peripherally aware of him, in a way that may also indicate Sartre's residence in the intellectual environment that led to deconstruction. Referring to the notion that there are no positive terms in language, Blanchot comments on the diacritical nature of signs as a missed encounter with original nothingness. Thus the image, he says, does not 'designate the thing, but rather, what the thing is not; it speaks of a dog instead of a cat.' 'Common' language recontains this negation by making it the ground against which predication appears: it accepts that 'once the nonexistence of the cat has passed into the word, the cat itself comes to life again ... in the form of its idea.' By contrast, literary language returns us not 'to the absent thing, but to absence as presence' (*GO* 44–5), to the very phenomenon of nothingness rather than to its intentional correlate in the object designated as absent. Literary language turns from a merely logical to an ontological reading of the negative (*GO* 85–6, 88).

Finding absence not just in literature but at the very heart of ordinary language, Sartre similarly plays with the logical option. He allows that the mind may possess 'the *not* as a form of sorting out and separation': I find '1300 francs in my wallet' because there are 1300 and not 1500 or 1100 francs (*BN* 43); or I see a cat, which means that I do not see a dog. But as against the negative judgment that is the basis for an affirmation, Sartre would rather say 'I find only 1300 [francs]' (38). He would rather point to a disappointment, to the 'non-being that always appears within the limits of a human expectation' (38). This non-being is not a logical 'category' but an 'irreducible and original event' (43). It is, moreover, irreducibly human, since it is only through man that '*nothingness comes to things*' (57). Things cannot feel the negative which pertains to them only as a mechanism of sorting. Things are separated by an 'external' relation 'established between two beings by a witness':

> When I say, for example, 'A cup is not an inkwell,' ... the foundation of this negation is neither in the cup nor in the inkwell. Both of these objects are what they are and that is all. The negation stands as a categorical ... connection which I establish between them ... without enriching them or impoverishing them. (243)

But man, by contrast, is traversed by an 'internal negation.' By this 'we understand such a relation between two beings that the one which is denied to the other qualifies the other at the heart of its essence – by absence' (243). In this form of negation the very being of the one is put under erasure by the other, as the two terms 'constitute' each other, either through lack (135) or through the 'collapse' of a positivity onto its internal bond to 'what it denies' (243, 245).

Sartre's move from the negative as a form of sorting and identification to a 'negative synthesis' through which the non-identity of each term appears 'within and upon the being which it is not' (243, 245) prefigures what Derrida will later do with Saussurian linguistics. For Derrida too departs from structuralism's repositivizing of difference, to claim that signs are connected by internal negation, such that 'no element can function as a sign without referring to another element which itself is not simply present' (*Positions* 26). In the 1968 interview with Kristeva from which this statement is taken, Derrida uses the terms *différance*, gram and trace. That these terms build on *négatité* is, however, apparent in his earlier account of indication as 'the process of death at work in signs' (*Speech and Phenomena* 40). Derrida's phrasing recalls Sartre's account of the Other as 'the death of my possibilities in so far as I live that death as hidden in the midst of the world' (*BN* 354). By transferring 'death' from the transcendental sphere of being to the ordinary sphere of language Derrida marks its inescapability, its imperceptible penetration of our daily existence through the signs by which we live in the world.

Indeed Sartre's notion of *négatité* casts light on what many see as a Derridian aporia: namely that *différance* is at once transcendent and inescapably immanent. *Différance* is in fact a transcendence constituted in immanence.[13] As transcendence it is the disclosure, within the particular, of 'an essential relation ... to the world,' a 'rubric ... which presides over the arrangement and the redistribution of great masses of being in things' (*BN* 59). But as immanence it cannot be thrown back into the theoretism of being a category: it is rather 'hidden in the midst of the world' as the underlying condition of all our 'relations of instrumentality' (59). Sartre speaks of 'an infinite number of realities' which are thus '*inhabited* by negation' (55; emphasis mine). Like the death that Derrida discerns in signs, he locates these pools of non-being throughout mundane life: in a visit to a café or a meeting with a stranger in the park.

III. No Exit: The Double Bind of Nothingness

We could say that a world thus 'affected with non-being' (*BN* 59) is the product of a certain projection. And indeed Sartre admits this, inasmuch as it is man who brings death into the world, thus disclosing more about his relation to being than about being itself. We could then partition the field of being and nothingness and allow Heidegger to speak for this 'Being' that Sartre neglects. However, we are concerned here not with philosophical fairness, but with the unfolding of the errors constitutive for a certain phase of theory. In this context, Sartre's power as a contemporary thinker lies not only in his dissemination of the negative but precisely in his radical, even unreasonable foreclosure of any exit to Being.

Sartre's early work, 'when existentialism was not yet a humanism' (Hollier 145), is an unrelenting deconstruction of the transcendental and Being. French commentators on *Nausea* were correct to see in Roquentin's encounter with the sheer superfluity of things in the public garden a thematization of Heidegger's *Dasein*. But here it is a question not of *Dasein* as the being-there of man but of the being-there (*être-là*) of things in their fullness and redundancy. In other words, Sartre dehumanizes the relation to Being: he deliberately rereads *Dasein* as the nauseating abject of a materiality that is *de trop*, so as to close off any escape into Spirit through 'the original openness of beings' (Heidegger 103).

In *Being and Nothingness* Sartre similarly unworks but then *also* disfigures both Being and the identity with itself that Being represents for the human. First he unworks the *en-soi* as a positive term, recasting it diacritically. The *en-soi* is linked to the *pour-soi* in a relationship of internal negation, such that it discloses the radical contingency of consciousness, but without functioning as Being in any conventional sense. On the one hand the for-itself stands in a seemingly binary relation to the in-itself as a nothingness that lacks being. It is from this opposition that the self derives its nihilating structure as a 'being that is not what it is and is what it is not.' Yet the relation of the terms is structured more by supplementarity than by opposition. For the in-itself is itself a lack of negativity, which for Sartre is the internal distance and difference that generate possibility. Being is absolute identity: it 'is not a connection with itself. It is *itself*' (*BN* 27). Lacking the structure of the *pour-soi* as 'reference' and transcendence (or non-coincidence), being for Sartre is an 'immanence which can not realize itself ... an activity which can not act, because it is glued to itself' (27–8). It is 'opaque to itself precisely because it is filled with itself' in a 'synthesis of itself with itself' (28). Being

> knows no otherness; it never posits itself as *other-than-another-being*;. It can support no connection with the other. It is itself indefinitely. ... From this point of view ... it is not subject to temporality. (29)

But second, as these cloying descriptions suggest, Sartre does not stop at a supplementary relation between the *en-soi* and *pour-soi* that is still phenomenally intelligible in terms of a dialectic, albeit an aporetic one. He describes the *en-soi* in language that is at once philosophical and brutally material. As 'immanence' the in-itself does not simply put an end to transcendence or non-coincidence; it is 'glued to itself,' filled with its own 'obesity' as Baudrillard puts it (27–32). Indeed it is 'inhuman' in de Man's terms (*RT* 96),[14] or 'obscene' in the terms of Žižek, who picks up Sartre's imagery of the viscous in his own figure of the 'repelling' and 'sticky' excess that characterizes otherness in a postmodern rather than modern mode (146, 151). The *en-soi* is the corpse of being, through which Sartre defaces any possibility of being except as what Foucault describes as an 'inertia ... that does not and never can lead to self-consciousness' (*OT* 322).

On an ontological level, then, Sartre radically de-idealizes Heidegger. He renounces the possibility of a 'clearing' by transposing the phenomenality of *Dasein* into the materiality of the *en-soi*. Being thus becomes that deliverance from desire and lack that Lacan parodies as the phallus, and that Sartre himself describes as 'massif' (*BN* 27). But while he thus seals off any escape from existence to spirit, Sartre arguably falls back into a negative hypostasis of the very *pour-soi* that he also deconstructs. From this double bind there arises the self-negating and aporetic anthropology we associate with Sartrean existentialism: a supplementary recuperation of what is really (in Bataille's terms) an 'unusable negativity,' through a nihilating 'freedom' that is always already in bad faith. Nothingness as freedom is of course Sartre's 'exit,' which Levinas criticizes when he argues for a 'being without nothingness,' an 'irremissible being' which 'leaves no hole and permits no escape' (*TO* 50). The problematic nature of Sartrean freedom helps explain the turn to Heidegger after the war. Still, it is not enough to dismiss Sartre by pointing out that French theory turns away from him by returning to a radicalized Heidegger. For as late as 1962 the same Derrida who later excoriates Sartre also speaks of the latter's 'breakthrough' (*trouée*). Remembering Sartre's ontology rather than his politics, Derrida attributes to him the deconstruction that 'has so profoundly unbalanced – and then overthrown – the landscape of Husserl's phenomenology and abandoned its horizon' (*Edmund Husserl's Origin of Geometry* 125n). He admits the seminal role of the pre-war Sartre in the genealogy of deconstruction.[15]

This seminality has two aspects. One is Sartre's difference from Heidegger as 'something between mistake and error' and hence 'capable of dialectical development' (Corngold 95). To trace this difference is to incorporate Sartre into the corpus of theory. But the other aspect of Sartre's legacy is less easy to set aside or take in, as he himself never fully digested it. We can describe it in Blanchot's words as a sense of that 'unformed nothingness pushed towards us by the residue of being that cannot be eliminated' (*GO* 80): a nothingness precipitated by being and not by man, and uncontainable even in a radicalized anthropology. For Sartre's experience of the negative is profoundly split. On the one hand the emptiness of the *pour-soi*, its interior distances, and its vicious circularity as a 'reflected-reflecting' (*BN* 122) are the condition of possibility for its freedom. Negativity is productive, even if more contingently than in Hegel. On the other hand the human project is constantly menaced, not by its own hyper-reflection but by the inhuman as that which irrevocably resists reflection.[16] The very dialectic by which the *pour-soi* as emptiness makes itself different from being's repellent fullness is itself figurally constituted by the repression of a being which, as 'transphenomenal' (9), cannot actually be figured. In the last section of *Being and Nothingness* this being returns excessively, decentring Sartre's argument. It returns not as the in-itself that is 'the condition of the sharpness of [the for-itself's] outlines,' but as the viscous, which is neither solid nor liquid, and thus indifferent to any difference between *en-soi* and *pour-soi* (55, 774–6).

In the following section I suggest that this materiality or transphenomenality of being is what places Sartre's thought so much ahead of the step he is accused of not taking in *Nausea*.[17] Žižek characterizes the postmodern in terms of presence and the foreclosure of the absence that permits *différance* and the trace. Postmodernism is the 'obscene' presence of the Thing, made visible in its 'indifferent and arbitrary character,' whereas modernism lets us grasp this 'emptiness' in terms of a distance that keeps desire in being. Modernism thus proves that 'the intersubjective machine ... works as well if the Thing is lacking, if the machine revolves around an emptiness' (143–6). To be sure, *Being and Nothingness* retains the concepts of lack, difference, transcendence, and reflection, which Žižek associates with modernity. These concepts preserve the subject in the mode of alienation. But Sartre is at once a modern and a postmodern thinker, and exists in the traumatic gap between the two. In this gap lies his importance for contemporary theory.

IV. The Obscene Object of Being: Nausea, the Slimy, and Levinas's 'Horror'

Sartre comes face to face with this obscenity of the postmodern in his discussions of the body and the viscous. For the viscous is a new kind of being that is the catalyst for a different experience of nothingness. Whereas the *en-soi* is hard or solid, the viscous is the disintegration of this self-containedness which the *pour-soi* projects as its transcendent (im)possibility. As long as being was in-itself it was alien but comprehensible: as Levinas says, a world 'made up of solids' is 'stable'; it 'shows itself to us and is open to our grasp.'[18] But the viscous is this in-itself that the for-itself could be, draining away into the 'hole' of the for-itself. At the same time it is also the for-itself becoming in-itself, in a double disintegration of being-in-itself and of its supplementary replacement by a being that is at least, negatively, for-itself. Thus Sartre writes of the primal scene of the slimy:

> there is a sticky thickness in its liquidity ... a dawning triumph of the solid over the liquid – that is, a tendency of the indifferent in-itself, which is represented by the pure solid, to fix the liquidity, to absorb the for-itself which ought to dissolve it. (*BN* 774)

The viscous is the radically other, not a human but a thingly alterity. Yet as a non-self, it will not stay outside, but 'sticks to me, draws me, sucks at me' (776). It is neither one thing nor the other but a Kafkan '*metamorphosis*' (777), a horrible confusion of categories: the material 'combined with the psychic' (771). Anticipating Kristeva's abject as the disintegration of the difference between subject and object necessary to predication, Sartre says that the viscous is the disappearance of difference into the same: it 'presents a constant hysteresis in the phenomenon of being transmuted into itself,' 'everywhere fleeing and yet everywhere similar to itself' (775–6). Herein lies the nothingness with which it afflicts his text, as the impossibility of any differentiated and thus human being.

But the viscous is the catachresis of a hysteria that progressively preoccupies the text, working against the grain of its attempts to economize the negative. Thus much earlier Sartre had already spoken of the 'fresh blood [and] excrement' that 'make us vomit' (445), interrupting his argument with other lurid figures such as drain-holes and hemorrhages (343–5). These images literalize a viscosity in the text's very concepts. For example, there is the famous scene in the park that introduces the dialectic of the look. Modelled on the master-slave relation – and more specifically on Kojève's channelling of negativity into a competitive, anthropogenetic desire – this scene seems to reconfirm the founding difference of the *pour-soi* and *en-soi* as a dialectic of self and other, culminating in the unstable negation of one or other entity. But it seems this anthropogenesis is a conceptual figure used to contain a more diffuse panic, even as the other is himself a figure covering over an inexplicable 'disintegration of the universe' (344). One remembers that it was in another park that Roquentin discovered, in the trauma of things unmoored from their names, what Levinas calls the 'horror' of a '*there is* [that] resists a personal form,' 'an existing that occurs without us, without a subject' (*EE* 57; *TO* 45). In *Being and Nothingness* Sartre apprehends this existing in the 'closed "Gestalt"' of the Other, in order to have 'a full object ... to grasp.' But at 'the heart of this solid, visible form' the Other 'makes himself a particular emptying ... [and] flight' (343–4).

Let us take a second example, namely the very distinction between *pour-soi* and *en-soi*. On the surface consciousness and things, though connected by internal negation, are still protected by a Cartesian separation (*BN* 26). In other words the *pour-soi*, despite its structure as self-nihilating, aporetic reflection, at least functions in identifiable opposition to the *en-soi*. This opposition permits a dialectic, granted that it is also an impasse. In short, Sartre seems to separate *pour-soi* and *en-soi* so as to direct nothingness as human 'possibility.' The *en-soi* is in-different and thus without possibility: it is inert, 'glued to itself,' and also safely outside (27–8). The *pour-soi* in its self-cancelling nothingness is at least dynamic, a kind of negative 'spirit.'

Yet this 'absolute interiority' of consciousness (404) is disrupted by its own exteriority through the breach made by the body. For the body is constructed from the outside in. It is not known inwardly through intuition but only by analogy with the other's body: it is even given to us in language by and for the other, for example by the scientist who identifies and assembles its parts (410, 464). Alternatively it is disclosed to us by things: 'Far from the body being first *for us* and revealing things to us, it is the instrumental-things which ... indicate our body to us.' My body is therefore outside: 'on the chair, in the whole house' (428). It passes over into the body of the other: 'When a doctor takes my wounded leg and looks at it' there is no difference 'between [my] visual perception ... of the doctor's body and ... my own leg' (402). Moreover this body, though externally given, is not a totality, since one receives it in bits and pieces. Nor is it really external like a chair, since 'I exist my body' as the 'perpetual "outside" of my most intimate "inside"' (460–1). The body thus unravels the difference between *pour-soi* and *en-soi*: it is an inside that has been wrenched outside, even as it is also an outside that has appeared inside. As Sartre concedes, anticipating his description of the viscous, it 'is the in-itself which is surpassed by the nihilating for-itself and which reapprehends the for-itself in this very surpassing' (409). This indistinguishability of subject and object accounts for the nausea, the threat of nothingness, that punctuates this section (445, 450–1, 468).

It is worth pausing again over this aporia of nothingness, which goes to the heart of Sartre's relation to anthropology, as well as to the thought that instead follows a Heideggerian turn to ontology. On the one hand, Sartre is conventionally linked to Hegel via Kojève, with whom he shares an emphasis on freedom, death, and the master-slave relationship. These affinities explain why Sartrean nothingness is so often taken as the ground for a Hegelian, Kojèvian anthropology that makes man the end of history and the source of nothingness. Kojève writes, for instance, that

> Man is essentially *Negativity*, for Time is *Becoming* – that is the *annihilation* of Being or Space. Therefore Man is a Nothingness that nihilates and that preserves itself in (spatial) Being only by *negating* being, this Negation being Action. (160)[19]

In his postwar work Sartre will indeed emphasize negation as a nihilating position, thus strengthening and politicizing the negative anthropology that first emerges in *The Psychology of Imagination*. But as we have seen, in the earlier work this negativity is constantly uprooted by a different kind of nothingness, more like that described by Levinas in *Existence and Existents* (1946). Here Levinas speaks of a general reversion 'to nothingness,' which he also describes as 'being in general': 'the *there is*, inasmuch as it resists a personal form, is "being in general."' Levinas defines the *there is* only in terms of what it is not. It is not being in-itself or for-itself, but the absence of any such identity:

> We have not derived this notion from exterior things or the inner world – from any 'being' whatever. For *there is* transcends inwardness as well as exteriority; it does not even make it possible to distinguish these. (*EE* 57)

As the impossibility of distinguishing outside and inside, the *il y a* also abolishes the difference between being and nothingness. It is not being in any positive sense, even that of Heidegger, as Levinas indicates by using the words 'night' and 'absence' against the 'light' he associates with Heidegger (*EE* 47–51). And yet it is not nothingness, at least not the nothingness that 'ought' to dissolve Sartre's viscous (*BN* 774). For the *il y a* as the disappearance of all existents – things or persons – leaves behind an excessive residue of materiality:

> The disappearance of all things and of the I leaves what cannot disappear, the sheer fact of being in which *one* participates, whether one wants to or not. ... Being remains ... like a heavy atmosphere belonging to no one, universal, returning in the midst of the negation which put it aside, and in all the powers to which that negation may be multiplied. (*EE* 58)

Indeed it is through this *materiality* of being that Levinas achieves a thinking that abandons subjectivity, whereas Heidegger's immateriality of being-as-light reassimilates such thought into what Derrida calls the metonymic series reason:consciousness:spirit:subject (*Of Spirit* 18).

But this excessive materiality is precisely what Sartre also confronts in *Nausea* and in the section on the slimy. To be sure Levinas is at pains to mark his difference from Sartre, whom he cannot avoid evoking, if not by name. He thus insists on the term 'horror' rather than 'nausea':

> 'Nausea,' as a feeling for existence, is not yet a depersonalization; but horror turns the subjectivity of the subject ... inside out. It is a participation in the *there is* which returns in the heart of every negation ... [and] that has 'no exits.' (61)

But if nausea differs from horror, it is not on the ground identified here, namely its sublation into the 'negation.' There is no exit in Sartre's novel into the negation: like horror, nausea is 'immediately there' and cannot be 'grasp[ed] through a thought' (*EE* 58). Indeed as Blanchot recognized in 1938, Sartre 'takes the novel to a place where there are no longer any incidents, any plot, any particular person; to that site where the mind sustains itself' by focusing on 'existence and being' and on the nausea of 'exist[ing] without being' ('Beginnings' 33–4).

It is no accident that Blanchot uses Levinasian terminology, before Levinas himself had fully theorized an existence without existents. Coincidentally Levinas had written extensively on nausea in *De l'évasion*, three years before the publication of Sartre's novel, on which, however, Sartre was working much earlier. 'Nausea' is the term both theorists use to rethink Heidegger's enlightenment of being within the particular ethos of a pre-war Europe that Levinas, like Blanchot, figures by the word 'night.' For Levinas nausea involves the disappearance of all existents and points of orientation. Inasmuch as it is an indeterminate *malaise* irreducible to a precipitating object, nausea is not, as Levinas later says, a 'quality of an object' correlatively linked to a subject (*EE* 58). It is precisely what he later describes as horror. Nausea is the suffocating and 'revolting presence of ourselves to ourself': 'the nudity of being in its plenitude and in its irremissible presence,' which causes one to be 'riveted to oneself.' In nausea we come up against the 'pure being' that Levinas later calls the *il y à*.

As Jacques Rolland explains, this pure being radically recasts the relation of being and nothingness – a turn signalled by the replacement of the Heideggerian term 'anxiety' with 'nausea' as the mood or *Stimmung* for the 'slipping away of beings' into nothing (Heidegger 101). For Heidegger (as Sartre too observes) 'the nothing' is simply a background for being(s), and thus a night symptomatically described as 'clear':

> In the clear night of the nothing of anxiety the original openness of beings as such arises: that they are beings – and not nothing ... The essence of the originally nihilating nothing lies in this, that it brings Da-sein for the first time before beings as such. (103)

In other words, though 'human existence' can understand beings 'only on the ground ... of the nothing,' by 'being held out into the nothing' this existence 'emerges ... from the nothing' and 'relates itself to beings' (103) through 'hypostasis' (*EE* 65–72; *TO* 51–4). But as Rolland argues, for Levinas – and also Sartre – being(s) cannot be distinguished from nothing: nausea is rather the *return* of the nothingness disclosed by being, the '"coming-upon-us" of the nothing.' Levinas's images for this return are precisely 'sticking' and vomit: vomit is the attempt to expel what returns (from) inside us as a foreignness that suffocates us from within (*De l'évasion* 115–17, translation mine; Rolland, 'Introduction' 35–41).[20] Nausea is the impossibility of the hypostasis that Heidegger's ontology still allows.

By 1946 Levinas wants to distance himself from Sartre, even at the cost of giving up a term he himself had favoured. By now Sartre had moved from an anthropology riveted to its unthought, to one that felt obliged to be pragmatic. Yet the earlier Sartre enters *Existence and Existents* as an ellipsis that Levinas marks, when he attributes to the war 'the absence of any consideration of those philosophical works published, with so much impact, between 1940 and 1945' (15). It is surely these works in their unthematized historical urgency that create a space for a thought 'inspired' by Heidegger but 'governed by a profound need to leave the climate of that philosophy' (19). Sartre and Levinas both read Heidegger in the years before the Occupation, which became the pre-occupation of the thought of being with an unspecifiable nothingness. It is for this reason that Derrida echoes Levinas when he describes Sartre's relation to another German philosopher whom Levinas also associates with 'light.' For Derrida, we recall, also writes of Sartre's philosophy as a deterritorialization that overthrew 'the landscape of Husserl's phenomenology' and abandoned 'its horizon.'

Sartre's encounter with the *there is* as the defacement of his own project first unfolds in the scene in *Nausea* where Roquentin picks up a pebble that is flat and dry on one side, humid and muddy on the other. This experience begins a series of anti-epiphanies about 'changes' in the structure of objects that reciprocally unravel the *pour-soi*. As a figure for the *en-soi* the pebble discloses that the being of things is not in-itself, accessible within the order of sight and light. Things are oppressively material, unusable, excessive. And yet one cannot turn from the outside to the inside as in conventional models of alienation that Sartre is accused of following by Robbe-Grillet. For the inside of the pebble is unassimilably slimy: it is this exteriority of inner experience that evokes the feeling of 'disgust' or nausea (*Nausea* 10). Sartre, in other words, does not ascribe being to things, nor does he derive it from the inner world. And yet he is concerned with thinking being, since in the section on the viscous nothingness derives precisely from 'being in general,' or from what Sartre, anticipating Levinas, already calls the 'there is' (*BN* 770, 773).

Indeed Levinas's break with Sartre is less radical than he thinks. For one thing, in descriptions of insomnia, eating, and fatigue, he does not entirely abandon 'descriptive phenomenology' (*EE* 66). Levinas would of course argue that phenomenology 'presupposes an ego' capable of capturing the phenomenon through description (66), and indeed this is true enough of the 'regional' or descriptive phenomenologies outlined by Husserl as subdivisions of transcendental phenomenology. But Sartre's descriptions, in particular of corporeal phenomena such as eating 'oysters or raw eggs,' aim to bring out precisely their 'transphenomenality' (*BN* 770, 9). In addition Levinas's emphasis on 'physiological psychology' recalls Sartre, not Husserl or Heidegger. In emotion – Sartre's subject in *Sketch for a Theory of the Emotions* (1939) – the body overwhelms us, impeding our hypostasis as mind or spirit: emotion 'puts into question not the existence, but the subjectivity of the subject; it prevents the subject from gathering itself up, reacting, being someone' (*EE* 70).

Despite this shared territory, Levinas nevertheless differs from Sartre in what Derrida calls his 'non-violence' (*Writing and Difference* 146). He lets being be, he approaches it non-violently through 'anonymous vigilance' (*EE* 66). Levinas's withdrawal of all attributes from being is a letting-go or ascesis. By contrast Sartre evokes the absolute unacceptability of a being defined by superfluity, rather than by subtraction, detachment, and renunciation. And it is here that he is both behind and beyond Levinas.

Sartre anthropomorphizes the encounter with being by surrounding it with his own projections. But this does not mean that he preserves the subject, for nausea is the double de-facement of being and the human by each other. Let us take as an example the bizarre introduction of the viscous as an elaboration of 'existential psychoanalysis' (*BN* 764), to which Sartre has already devoted several more conventional pages. In his earlier monograph on the emotions Sartre had drawn on Husserl and Heidegger to rethink psychoanalysis as 'phenomenological psychology.' Sartre's study, including his turning of phenomenology towards 'anthropology,' sketched a theoretical basis for the more practical work of existential psychoanalysis done by Binswanger, Laing, and others. Sartre writes that for 'human reality, to exist is, according to Heidegger, to assume its own being in an existential mode of understanding.' Existential psychoanalysis studies pathological behaviour as the 'showing' of something authentically human – in other words it effects a humanization (though not normalization) of the strange.[21] Yet in the section on the viscous, Sartre disembowels his project of rethinking psychology through phenomenology, by confronting humanism with 'ek-sistence.' Evoking Bachelard, whom he had earlier credited with an internal critique of phenomenology (*BN* 428), Sartre attempts a 'psychoanalysis of things' (765) – an estrangement of the human into a thing analysed as human. Moreover, this psychoanalysis is not an anthropology: it does not 'bring to light ... the subjective choice' by which we become 'person[s]' (734). It is rather an ontology concerned with 'a certain way which being has of giving itself' (764).

Through this mutant form of existential psychoanalysis, which parodies other work by that name, Sartre con-fuses the human and thingly (771). It is as though mind is stuck in matter, or as if 'material substances have a psychic meaning which renders them repugnant, horrifying' (772). What this confusion, or abjection, threatens is a reversal in which man and thing exchange places. Indeed this last section is a *mise en abîme* of the text that disfigures its tenuous anthropology through what Merleau-Ponty calls an 'ontological' rather than existential psychoanalysis (*The Visible and the Invisible* 270).[22] But 'ontological' is also a misnomer, since Bachelard's 'psychoanalysis of things' becomes in Sartre's hands a catachresis, a trope for what cannot be named. In this context, the 'upsurge of the for-itself in being,' as the grotesque presumption to psychoanalyse things, is an 'appropriation' unveiled as 'flight' and reabsorbed by the materiality it seeks to avoid (*BN* 779). This defacement of humanism, with its disclosure of the tropological structure of 'appropriation,' seems virtually to be staged by the text as a scene of self-reading. Sartre might be speaking of his own text when he writes:

> the slimy offers a horrible image; it is horrible in itself for a consciousness to *become slimy*. ... A consciousness which became slimy would be transformed by the thick stickiness of its ideas. (778)

Through the viscous Sartre does indeed think 'being' just as much as Levinas or Heidegger, but with the difference that he cannot approach it non-violently. Because the for-itself 'exists' being (778), being cannot simply be left to itself and in itself. Being unfolds 'across human reality,' a phrase Sartre is not alone among French thinkers in retaining even after the turn from anthropology in the late 1940s.[23] And here it is worth asking what Sartre actually means by 'human reality,' a term he uses throughout *Being and Nothingness* in revisionary proximity to *Dasein*. Human reality is not a reality controlled by the human, but a pathos, a pathology. As Sartre says in his *Wartime Diaries*, human reality does not mean 'that man is anterior to the meaning of things.' Rather it suggests that being, in its transphenomenality, signifies – or perhaps utterly fails to signify – *for man*. But man is not a *cogito*; he is 'transcendence' (*BN* 767), which is to say that his being escapes him. What being signifies for man is in part his missed encounter with (his) being.

In the *Diaries* Sartre's example of human reality is precisely the viscous, which he offers as the first in an inventory of 'real categories' including elasticity and flakiness 'whence man comes slowly to himself' as to his own radical exteriority (153, 148–9). These phenomena – in the sense that they cannot be grasped noumenally but only as they appear for consciousness – are yet not 'phenomenally' knowable by the understanding in any Kantian sense; they are material and tactile, not visible and legible. They do not 'show' themselves except as a 'quality,' which is to say 'a symbol of a being which totally escapes us' (*BN* 770). Moreover, a quality such as the slimy is a trope, an anthropomorphism. In this sense what is disclosed by the being of things, or by being as a thing, is precisely *Dasein* as 'this human reality that we do not even understand is ourselves' (*Diaries* 148).

Human reality, then, includes a certain transphenomenality of the human as the Real that eludes symbolic recognition or imaginary identification. It is this insistence of the Real that gives rise to what Sartre calls nausea. And while the last section sees an uncontrollable eruption of nausea, it is also present elsewhere, notably in the cyborg descriptions of body-parts that detach themselves as hallucinatory 'figure[s] on the body-as-ground' (470, 466). This exteriority of the inside is what Bataille, writing at the same time as Sartre, describes as 'inner experience.' For Sartre I 'exist' this pre-thetic body without organs before it is named and returned to me as 'sign [and] identification' through the 'alienating, cognitive stratum' of the 'Other's concepts' (466). But this synthetic totality does not allow me to 'possess' my experience through language and concept: rather it constitutes experience as a transcendence that 'escapes me' (466). The Sartrean subject ek-sists but cannot 'gather itself up.' Indeed the *pour-soi* is itself no more than a figure. For it is founded, as Sartre says, through a repression of the in-itself which, 'engulfed and nihilated ... remains at the heart of the for-itself as its original contingency' (130).

To disclose this Real that resists symbolization, Sartre seems driven to dismember figuration and perception as the phantasmatic supports of conventional notions of experience, knowledge, and self. He begins and ends the section on the body with the scene already mentioned, where he imagines an 'arrangement of the sense organs such that a living being could see one of his eyes while the eye which was seen was directing its glance upon the world' (402). Like Bataille, who disfigures the body so as to question 'the horizontal axis of vision' that founds the *cogito* (*Visions of Excess* 83),[24] Sartre imagines bits of the self 'outside in the midst of the world' – his eye, his eyelid, hands, or arms 'without synthetic connection with the corporal totality (*BN* 402, 420, 462, 454). In the section on the body Sartre tries to absorb these descriptions into a theory of contingency that becomes the basis for 'existentialism.' Yet they obsessively exceed their place in the argument, which, instead of a philosophical system, becomes a wartime diary of phenomenology thought at its very limit. They recall the dis-figurations of surrealism that were so seminal for deconstruction, and which Foucault associates with 'the tortured body [and] the flesh' as the 'materiality' of 'unthinkable thought' (*OT* 381–2). Interviewed in 1983, de Man is evasive about his debts to phenomenology as traditionally understood, but speaks of the powerful influence on him of 'Surrealism, specifically Bataille, Blanchot, even ... Bachelard' (*RT* 118–19). But in the sections on the body and the viscous, and in the discussions of figuration as (self)nihilation that run like a *leitmotiv* through the text, Sartre comes close to this surrealization of phenomenology which will also be attempted, less cruelly, in Merleau-Ponty's *Phenomenology of Perception* (1945).

These sections are Sartre's uncanniest contribution to theory – one that returns in de Man's work and in Kristeva's notion of the abject. They approach the conjunction which Merleau-Ponty later projects between phenomenology and psychoanalysis. In 1960 Merleau-Ponty writes, 'it is by what phenomenology implies or unveils as its limits – by its *latent content* or its *unconscious* – that [it] is in consonance with psychoanalysis' ('Phenomenology and Psychoanalysis' 69–70). In its most radical moments *Being and Nothingness* unveils this inner experience of phenomenology. This is Sartre's breakthrough (*trouée*) – aptly linked by Derrida to Sartre's favourite image of the hole – by which he so unbalances the landscape of phenomenology as to prepare a space for deconstruction.

V. The Dead Runner: Three Revisionary Ratios[25]

Recognizing Sartre's role in 1962, Derrida, as we have seen, evokes the split genesis of deconstruction. Yet from the late 1960s on, he simplifies and abjects Sartre in a turn to Husserl, Heidegger, and sometimes Hegel ('Ends' 117–23).[26] In the process certain properties of Sartre are transferred to 'Heidegger,' so as to legitimate the forgetting of the one in the other. This is particularly evident in 'Différance' (1968), which displaces the Sartrean subtext of *Speech and Phenomena* (1967) with a celebration of Heidegger that strains beyond the greater cautiousness about the German philosopher in 'The Ends of Man.' What is repressed in this new version of deconstruction is a complex genealogy masked by the current idealization of Heidegger, his 'turning,' and turnings that disavow the past. What is put to rest is Sartre's remains – his tortured, aporetic *cogito*, but even more the unpalatable, viscous nothingness of nausea.

a. Chiasm: Blanchot between Heidegger and Sartre

But this is not what happens in an earlier deconstruction. For in returning to Heidegger, French theory after the war turned not to Heidegger but to an undoing of the metaphysics of identity read aslant Sartre. The early Blanchot, for instance, moves away from Sartre's anthropological emphasis to a more Heideggerian concern with a thrownness and essential solitude that unworks even Sartre's negative, deferred hypostasis of the *cogito*. Yet Blanchot is interested not in the work of art but in worklessness, not in being but in the nothingness of a Being de-posited in a Literature that is not a 'shelter' but 'a sojourn devoid of *place*' (*The Space of Literature* 41). Blanchot is Heidegger with a minus sign. As Levinas says, despite 'many points of perfect agreement,' he shifts the space of literature from 'day' to 'night,' from 'light' to 'a black light ... that undoes the world': 'In Blanchot, the work uncovers, in an uncovering that is not truth, a darkness' (*Proper Names* 132–3, 136). Lyotard has said that the critique of Heidegger is 'a "French" affair,' and that from Rimbaud to Beckett it is what the French 'call "writing" that reveal[s] ... what every representation misses.' Lyotard could be speaking of Blanchot when he writes that French literature and philosophy have 'found [themselves] in charge' of an 'irremediable' darkening of 'Enlightenment' (4–5). Blanchot's work is just such a darkening of Heidegger even as it is a 'writing' that opens Sartre to his own subtexts.

We cannot trace Blanchot's relationship to Sartre extensively, except to note with Michael Holland that at a certain stage his thought 'is so close to Blanchot's own as to pose a serious challenge to it' (22), as is evident in Blanchot's review of *La Nausée* (1938) and his essay 'The Novel Is a Work of Bad Faith' (1947).[27] In the former, as we have seen, Blanchot praises Sartre for a literature that strips away subject and plot to confront the nausea of 'exist[ence] without being.' Blanchot's critical kinship with Sartre is, however, most evident in his essay 'Literature and the Right to Death' (1947). For this essay, often taken as a repudiation of Sartre, is Blanchot's own theoretical autobiography: a return of and retreat from the Sartrean origins that inaugurate his distinctive vision of literature as the (un)working of the negative. The essay is indeed a critique of Sartre's 1947 manifesto of political conversion, *What Is Literature?* But it is also an unworking of this Sartre through a working back to an earlier Sartre whose focus on 'nothingness' had much in common both with Bataille's 'inner experience' and with what Foucault calls Blanchot's 'thought of the outside.'

Sartre's presence in the essay can be felt in its opening references to the 'nothingness' that the writer exscribes as he seeks identity through his work. As Blanchot details the process of writing from intention to finished text, he discloses little pools of non-being at every moment of this process. Literature reveals the 'emptiness inside,' and even as the author becomes one with his work, he becomes other than himself through its reading (*GO* 22, 24, 26). As a 'nothingness working in nothingness, to borrow an expression of Hegel's' (24), the writer confronts a negativity that is the very essence of language:

A word may give me its meaning, but first it suppresses it. For me to be able to say 'This woman,' I must somehow take her flesh and blood reality away from her, cause her to be absent, annihilate her [*la rende absente et l'anéantisse*]. The word gives me the being, but it gives it to me deprived of being. The word is the absence of that being, its nothingness [*néant*]. (42)

This disclosure of the word as absence is at the heart of the turn given by Derrida to Saussure's view that language has no positive terms, or as Blanchot puts it, that the image 'does not directly designate the thing' but 'what the thing is not' (45). Blanchot in turn draws this idea of the word as (an)nihilation from Sartre, who writes:

> Poets are men who refuse to *utilize* language. ... Nor do they dream of *naming* the world ... for naming implies a perpetual sacrifice of the name to the object named, or, as Hegel would say, the name is revealed as the inessential in the face of the thing which is essential. (*What Is Literature?* 6)

Sartre's theory of naming takes up his earlier analysis of perception as a positing constituted on the trace of what it nihilates. The earlier Sartre was less interested in the positing than in the 'nihilation' it disclosed. Nihilation is at the heart of positing as is 'effacement' for Blanchot and 'erasure' for de Man.[28] In *What Is Literature?* Sartre draws back from this nihilation: he takes up the task of Hegel, thus eliding nothingness to reaffirm negation as predication. But his theory of naming is a linguistic development of his early account of perception, in which predication occurred only through the nihilation of a difference that marked position as imposition. And it is to this earlier account that Blanchot returns when he speaks of the word as awakening to the absence of the being it restores.

As important in establishing a dialogue with Sartre is the description of literature as divided along two 'slopes': 'meaningful prose' and poetry (*GO* 48, 51–2). The distinction recalls *What Is Literature?*, where Sartre too partitions prose from poetry. Whereas prose for Sartre is instrumental, poetry 'considers words as things and not as signs,' thus replacing the annihilating knowledge of 'things by their name' with a 'silent contact,' a 'suggestion of the incommunicable.' Both forms of literature are linked in a 'common front' against bourgeois society, but while the prose writer is '*in a situation* in language,' the poet is 'outside of language ... meeting the word as a barrier as he comes toward men.' The poet seeks to become one with his nothingness through a 'defeat' that 'returns him to himself in his purity' (6–8, 29–30). Likewise for

Blanchot there is a productive negativity, 'turned toward the movement of negation by which things are separated from themselves and destroyed in order to be known, subjugated, communicated.' Such negation does not stop at words but reads through them: 'Hence its distrust of words, its need to apply the movement of negation to language itself and to exhaust it by realizing it as that totality on the basis of which each term would be nothing' (*GO* 48–9). Then there is another literature, also turned towards the negation of 'day' and light, but as a letting-appear, an 'endless resifting of words without content' which is a 'concern for the ... unknown, free, and silent existence' of things (49–50).

Blanchot places himself on the second slope. Literature, he says, by 'turning itself into the inability to reveal anything,' becomes 'the revelation of what revelation destroys' (47). But in moving away from Sartre, Blanchot turns not to poetry as Heidegger sees it, but to a space of literature he compares to Levinas's *il y a* (51n). The *il y a* rewrites *Dasein* in the aftermath of disaster. Blanchot turns to Levinas, but the strange thing in this turn from Sartre is the proximity of the two slopes. For the two slopes differ from other binaries deployed by Blanchot, such as his 'two versions of the imaginary,' which divide ordinary from literary perception. The first slope is *not* 'ordinary language,' which 'encloses the absence in a presence' and accepts that 'once the nonexistence of the cat has passed into the word' the cat 'comes to life again' as 'its idea' (59, 44). It is not the instrumental language chosen in *What Is Literature?*, but the activity of negation covered over by instrumentality.

In short, rather than drawing on the Sartre of 1947 – the year in which Queneau also edited Kojève's lectures – Blanchot goes back to an earlier Sartre who is interested less in positing than in the 'nihilation' or blindness that makes it possible. To be sure, Blanchot has conflated the philosopher of the war years with the postwar man of 'action,' and to do so he has gone back to Sartre's theory of the image as (an)nihilation in his even earlier *Psychology of Imagination*.[29] Blanchot's 'Sartre' claims a certain agency for language as a principle of 'deferred assassination' that 'enters the world and carries out its work' of infinite absolute negativity (*GO* 43, 34). 'Sartre' seeks to grasp the 'ideal[ity]' of the negation, and instead of accepting the 'fragmentary, successive results of this movement of negation,' seeks to grasp it in its totality (43, 49). Yet Blanchot is a more astute reader of Sartre than is Heidegger, who sees him only as a negative Cartesian. Blanchot recognizes in Sartre an endless circling back to the problem of the negative. He sees the Sartrean nihilation as the most radical encounter yet with the nothingness at the heart of language. For this reason his essay is no simple critique but rather a remembering and working through of a Sartrean moment that he finds fascinating, enabling, and problematic. Hence the curious movement of the essay, which deconstructs through retention, holding back on its rejection of Sartre until the very end when it divides negativity between the two slopes. Indeed the very figure of the slopes suggests a difference that begins from or returns to a joining. For the two slopes 'do not lead toward distinctly different works ... [and] an art which purports to follow one slope is already on the other' (51). 'Sartre' is already on a slope that leads ineluctably to 'Blanchot.'

Blanchot's difference from Sartre is that he transfers nothingness from man to writing, thus laying the basis for a Derridian *écriture* that likewise contains the trace of Sartre. In displacing nothingness away from its human origin, Blanchot aims to unwork any illusion of agency in relation to nothingness, since he does not recognize Sartre as having already problematized this agency. Yet Blanchot deconstructs the subject only as agency and not as affectivity. Blanchot's term for writing is the verb *écrire*, not the noun *écriture*, which suggests that writing happens *to* us if not *by* our agency. This residual subject is what Levinas hints at when he associates 'solitude' – perhaps Blanchot's 'essential solitude' – with 'hypostasis' (*TO* 42–4, 52–7). Replacing the in-itself of identity not with the *pour-soi* but with something closer to what Levinas calls the *sans-soi* (49), Blanchot still retains a quasi-subject. For Blanchot locates his anonymous 'vigilance' not in a 'being without nothingness' (*TO* 50) but in language as a 'situation where an existent is put in touch with its existing' (51).

b. Aporia: De Man's Repetition of Sartre

Transferring nihilation to language instead of man or Being, Blanchot translates Heidegger into a typically French form of thinking also exemplified by de Man. On the surface de Man's career proceeds from 'Sartre' to 'Heidegger.' His first major essay follows Sartre both in deconstructing consciousness through the image, and in retaining a negative hypostasis of the subject as 'intentionality' (*RR* 1–17). While for Husserl intentionality co-founds subject and object, for Sartre it is tied to lack: to be conscious of something is to be aware that I am not, or do not have, that of which I am conscious. Moreover, intentionality for Sartre is already bound up with representation. For his deconstruction of Husserl is also influenced by another translation: Levinas's distinction in his book on Husserl between intuition, which 'reaches its object,' and 'signifying acts,' which do not 'possess' but only 'think' their object. A 'signifying intention' is characterized by its 'emptiness' and 'need for the fullness ... [of] intuition.' It is 'unrealized,' 'unsatisfied': an 'expectation' threatened by 'disappointment,' as Levinas suggests in quoting Husserl, but to produce an affective reading of his texts against their exegetical grain (*Theory* 55–6, 74). First encountering Husserl through Levinas, Sartre bypasses the exegesis in chapter 3 of how intentionality founds the Husserlian ego, and is struck instead by Levinas's more radical account of *signifying* intentions, which assimilates intentionality into a potentially deconstructive problematic of signs, the image, and representation.

De Man likewise makes intentionality into the hollowing out of the subject as a lack of being discerned when the French Hegelians deconstruct spirit through consciousness. At the same time, by locating nothingness within the circuit of an unhappy consciousness both de Man and Sartre remain on the side of what Levinas calls 'hypostasis.' As consciousness, nothingness becomes a '"something that is,"' and appears in a 'situation where an existent is put in touch with its existing' (*TO* 51). On the surface, then, de Man's later work seems mobilized by the desire to purge this Sartrean residue. De Man therefore follows a general turn from Sartre to Heidegger in transferring man's radical contingency from consciousness to language, described as the 'uncontrollable power of the letter as inscription' (*RT* 37). As is well known, it was Heidegger's emphasis on language as that which speaks man that led to his popularity in the heyday of structuralism. But Heidegger, as Sartre suggests, always positivizes the negative, or as de Man says, he recuperates 'nonbeing' as 'forgotten Being' (*Blindness and Insight* 251). Indeed the continuing appeal of Heidegger's anti-humanism lies in its religiosity, what Tom Rockmore calls his 'postmetaphysical humanism' (56, 97). And de Man closes off this tropological substitution, since for him 'language' permits no transfer of residence from the human to Being. It is rather a process of dismemberment and terror caught in the 'darkening of ... Enlightenment' that Lyotard finds characteristically French.

De Man discloses this terror when he likens the 'materiality of the letter' to 'the worst phantasms of dismemberment' in Schreber's *Denkwürdigkeiten eines Nervenkranken*. Writing on Saussure's hypogram, he anthropomorphizes it as a 'proper name' cut up into 'discrete parts and groups' and dispersed as a form of chaos or 'infra-text' that disrupts any stable, phenomenal meaning (*RT* 89, 36–7). For de Man the experience of language is a loss of face, person, and property (44). As Hollier observes, this terror of existence without existents is encapsulated in Blanchot's recognition that to 'write ... is to give up saying "I."' Indeed Blanchot had already compared literature to the 'Reign of Terror' in 'Literature and the Right to Death' (*GO* 41–2) and in a review of Jean Paulhan's book on language and terrorism (1942). But as Hollier also notes, Sartre's own fascination with terrorism and the transcendence of the ego, in his wartime literary texts, is one of 'the earliest experiments' with this 'deprivatization of existence.'[30] Evoking the notion of literature as terror in the violence he associates with language, de Man comments that 'it is not at all certain that language is in any sense human' (*RT* 87, 96). The materiality of the letter, far from conveying proximity to Being, returns to the primal scene experienced by Sartre when he confronts in the *en-soi* an utter alienness to human projects. Likewise, language for de Man is 'not natural,' and 'not phenomenal, in the sense that ... no knowledge about man' can be derived from it, and it is 'not really temporal either, because the structure that animates it is not a temporal structure' (92). What Foucault, evoking Heidegger, calls the 'being of language' (*OT* 43, 300) is thus not Being in a Heideggerian sense, at least not for de Man. It is rather what Sartre calls the 'transphenomenality of being' as that which cannot be made cognitively, phenomenally present (*BN* 9).

In a 1983 interview de Man admits Sartre's enormous influence on his generation. Sartre's work was 'for many of us ... the first encounter with some kind of philosophical language which was not just academic' but engaged with literature and the political. Insisting that he 'felt closer' to Heidegger in the 'Letter on Humanism,' de Man still has more to say about Sartre (*RT* 119). Indeed he invokes Heidegger only to defer Sartre – a role he then assigns to the Surrealists and Blanchot, who are complexly intertwined with Sartre.[31] 'I felt myself ... more on the side of Blanchot,' de Man says, in 'the slight opposition which became visible' between Sartre's and Blanchot's views of literature (119). This 'slight' disagreement can be attributed to the way de Man, like Blanchot, sees Sartre's relation to the terror of language. For Sartre literature is terror(ism): an attempt to deal with the inhuman by appropriating its terror. This, at least, is how Blanchot portrays him in his account of the writer as terrorist (*GO* 37–43),[32] and in his rejection of a writing that instead of accepting the fragmentary results of 'negation ... wants to grasp the movement itself' (38–43, 48–9). Blanchot's portrait of Sartre will be confirmed by Sartre's own political development of terrorism in his *Critique of Dialectical Reason*.[33] Unlike Blanchot's Sartre, de Man cannot take charge of negation so as to claim that 'literature becomes history' (40). For him the terror of writing and criticism consists rather in a mimesis of the (non)being of language: a submission to its machine-like power, through a deprivatizing ascesis that 'substitutes a process of formal elaboration for a referential reading' (*RT* 37, 36).

Yet, as we have seen, Blanchot himself reads Sartre's work on the nothingness of imagination in two ways: teleologically as completed by his postwar Kojèvian anthropology, and archaeologically as leading back to a certain proximity to the work of Blanchot and Levinas. For Blanchot the second slope is the turn Sartre failed to take. But this view telescopes *The Psychology of Imagination* with the postwar work, thereby ignoring Sartre's intervening 'phenomenological essay on ontology.' *Being and Nothingness* hinges upon the aporia between negation and nothingness, anthropology and ontology. On one level it develops the idea of the negation as freedom; yet it also disfigures this freedom through a traumatic materialism in excess of any pragmatic anthropology.

It is this materialism in its abjected, aporetic relation to anthropology that returns in de Man's work after 1976. As he suggests, the decline of Sartre's reputation had to do with his too-direct turn to the political after the texts that engaged de Man's generation: *L'imaginaire*, *L'être et le néant* and the literary essays (*RT* 119). But if de Man is 'closer' to Heidegger in mistrusting the political, they diverge in terms of that 'other thinking that abandons subjectivity' (Heidegger 231). The 'lurid figures' that characterize de Man's descriptions of language hark back to a cathexis of literature and terror that French theory never quite works through. This cathexis, which in the *Critique* becomes Sartre's missed encounter with his own earlier ontology, returns inversely in de Man's corpus as his own missed encounter with the political. As Neil Hertz argues, despite de Man's eschewal of the term 'consciousness,' his texts are punctuated by 'drama[s] of subjectivity' played out at a primal scene of linguistic violence associated with key moments in Romantic literature. In these episodes, which focus on hanging and physical defacement, what surfaces is a quasi-subject afflicted with the 'pathos of uncertain agency':

A subject is conjured up – perhaps a killer, perhaps only the discoverer of the corpse who can serve as a locus of vacillation: did I do it? Or had it already been done?' (85–6)

This hypostasis, as in Sartre, reflects a sense that nothingness cannot simply happen. The 'nihilation' that is language happens to or through someone, who is responsible to or for it, even in his utter helplessness. Thus we can ask which slope de Man actually takes. Would he say with Blanchot that 'by turning itself into an inability to reveal anything' literature tries 'to become the revelation of what revelation destroys' (*GO* 47)? And if so, what does it mean that he discovers not the 'unknown, free, and silent existence' of things (49), but that 'the original was already dead' (*RT* 84)? Or does de Man seek the more 'murder[ous]' negativity which Blanchot finds in Sartre and Hegel: that of language as 'deferred assassination' (*GO* 42–3, 45)? De Man's own 'murder' of texts, wherein he seeks to get beyond words by 'apply[ing] the movement of negation to language itself' (42), recalls this negativity, but only as the corpse of a Sartrean anthropology that was already dead in 1943.

Yet the dead never wholly die, and de Man repeats Sartre's aporias even where he most resists him. De Man's work is actuated by a fear of 'bad faith,' from 'The Rhetoric of Temporality' where he refers to Sartre's notion (*Blindness* 208), to the chapter on 'Excuses' in *Allegories of Reading*. Indeed this element has allowed his deconstruction to be misrecognized as a form of critique,[34] although like Sartre, de Man does not believe in the possibility of good faith, only in a vigilance that sees good faith as the most insidious form of bad faith. Although de Man's work is therefore not critique in any positivist or pragmatist sense, it still feels an unfulfillable responsibility to anthropology. For vigilance requires a critical subject, even though de Man is deeply suspicious of reintroducing the subject, even to negate its mastery.

This tension leads to a counterplot in de Man's work that some see as Heideggerian: to a fascination with language not as a critical tool but as the site of a radical ecstasis figured as the inhuman. The inhuman, according to de Man, is 'linguistic structures, the play of linguistic tensions ... possibilities which are inherent in language' and which operate 'independently of any intent ... or desire' of the subject (*RT* 96). To yield to language would be to elude the fallacies of the subject, as Foucault briefly does through the figure of 'the end of man.' At the close of *The Order of Things* Foucault flirts with a temptation to permanence – albeit one that is bleaker than Heidegger's – as he reflects on man's imminent erasure, 'like a face drawn in sand' – the same image that plays a key role in de Man's 'Shelley Disfigured' (*OT* 387; *RR* 99–100). Sartre analyses this temptation with reference to Mallarmé, whom he reads through Heidegger, in the same year as Foucault: 'Through Man's very disappearance ... being [is] restored in all its purity ... If Being is dispersion, man, in losing his being, achieves an incorruptible unity' (*Mallarmé* 129, 136–7).[35] De Man, however, is closer to Sartre. He cannot cease to 'think the negation' (*Critical Writings* 39) as an ethics of reading in the essays before 1976, and thereafter, as it affects 'human reality' – itself a catachresis for the irruption of the Real in the human.

c. Hiatus: Foucault, the Human Sciences, and Literature

Much deconstruction, then, emerges as a difference or resistance between Sartre and Heidegger as well as other theorists who connect them. This genesis shapes the field in three ways: as a passage of Heidegger through Sartre in which the former returns more negatively; as an internal negation in which a later theorist reworks the aporias of the past only to be doubly bound by them; and as a tension between epistemic strands that can be brought into dialogue. This dialogue, unlike the chiasm described in the first case, does not cathect two bodies of thought at an affective level but explores their difference. We have seen how Blanchot reworks Heidegger through Sartre, touching one with the other. While de Man also works between them, he exemplifies a second revisionary ratio that is not so much a darkening of one by the other as a resistance within and between the two. The third structure of influence occurs in the work of Foucault, and can be described by a term he uses to intimate his relation to Jean Hyppolite: 'hiatus.' Foucault speaks of the openings in Hyppolite's work, which transform philosophy 'into an endless task, against the background of an infinite horizon.' In this context he refers to 'that hiatus – where I feel at once his absence and my failings' (*Archaeology* 236–7). Hiatus is a more enigmatic term than 'clearing,' suggesting a space that opens up thought but cannot be definitively (dis)closed. Hiatus as gap and opening is, moreover, the temporal gap in which the past returns to supplement the future created by what it left unfinished.

If de Man probes the aporias of Sartre and Heidegger, the early Foucault uses this hiatus to open up the vexed question of 'anthropology.' Heidegger's later hostility to anthropology can be explained by his association of it with technology as a triumph of the subjective will. This notion was already implicit in Kant's concept of 'pragmatic' anthropology in the text on which Foucault wrote his *thèse complémentaire*. Pragmatic anthropology, as man's domination of the Other in the self-service of civil society, sums up everything that French philosophy after the war rejects in 'anthropology.' But as Tom Rockmore points out, *Being and Time* leaves a space for a more radical use of the term 'anthropology' (70, 179).[36] Foucault intimates the form this might take in his first work, a monograph on the Heideggerian analyst Ludwig Binswanger. In *Dream, Imagination, Existence,* Foucault picks up on the side of anthropology Kant tries to set aside: he turns 'physiological anthropology' in a more philosophic direction,[37] promising to relocate it within 'an ontological reflection whose major theme is presence-to-being, existence, *Dasein.*' Thus he speaks of inflecting 'phenomenology toward anthropology' in a movement beyond Husserl's transcendentalism, and yet of rethinking anthropology through an articulation of 'human being ... upon an analytic of existence.' This double gesture allows him to conceive an anthropology opposed to 'any type of psychological positivism claiming to exhaust the significant content of man by the reductive concept of *homo natura*' (31).

Arguably Foucault does not create this dialogue in his first text, which remains too Heideggerian, though on the strange ground of psychology – a discipline that did not interest the German philosopher but strongly inflected French translations of phenomenology. Nor does Foucault achieve this dialogue in his other text of 1954, *Mental Illness and Personality,* whose Marxist conclusion is marred by a Sartrean pragmatism that led him to suppress it.[38] Yet an anthropology that does not forget being remains the stimulus for both *The Birth of the Clinic* (1963) and *The Order of Things* (1966). Unlike *Discipline and Punish, The Birth* is not simply a genealogy and archaeology of institutions. It constitutes a new theory type that moves between what Foucault calls the *cogito* and the unthought, by using the study of institutions to reflect on a fundamental non-being mediated and disclosed by structure. This non-being is unconcealed at the very end when Foucault refers to Nietzsche and a tradition of writers charged with darkening the Enlightenment of science. In disciplinary terms the text crosses (intellectual) history with ontology and literature. Methodologically it constructs a hinge between phenomenology and structuralism, disclosing each as the unconscious of the other. As I argue elsewhere,[39] *The Order* is an encyclopedic expansion of the *Birth* that makes explicit the philosophical hiatus in which it is implicated. The earlier text had constructed a genetic structural phenomenology: a 'noetic' analysis of the medical gaze and a 'noematic' analysis of the social world upon which it is articulated. *The Order* is a metahistory of several such 'positivities' (or 'discourses') against the margins of what is not reflected in the *cogito.* In its penultimate section

Foucault analyses man's doubled and duplicitous relation to knowledge in terms of 'four theoretical segments' (*OT* 335) with profoundly phenomenological resonances: the analytic of finitude, the empirical and the transcendental, the *cogito* and the unthought, and the return and retreat of the origin. He thus questions the present 'order' that privileges the human sciences from the perspective of the 'counter-sciences' of ethnology, psychoanalysis, and literature. In so doing he constructs an anthropology responsible to being, a theory type that prefigures such later work as that of Nancy and Agamben on community.

Foucault could be seen as following the early Heidegger, given the room left in *Being and Time* for philosophical anthropology. Still by the early 1960s, Heidegger's thought had been definitively distinguished from philosophical anthropology, so that the invocation of this crossing actually puts Foucault's work in the space created by an earlier error: the conflation of Sartre and Heidegger. Indeed the hybridizing of phenomenology and anthropology may always have been strategic as much as mistaken. Foucault's attempt to combine them may allude to a turn already made by Binswanger in 'The Case of Ellen West,' subtitled 'An Anthropological-Clinical Study' (1944). As a German speaker, Binswanger would not have been corrupted by Sartre's 'monstrous mistranslation,' and is quite clear about differing from Heidegger in his correspondence with the latter even before 'The Letter on Humanism.'[40] Binswanger writes:

> Existential analysis (*Daseinanalyse*, as we speak of it) must not be confused with Heidegger's analytic of existence (*Daseinanalytik*). The first is a hermeneutic exegesis on the ontic-anthropological level, a phenomenological analysis of actual human existence. The second is a phenomenological hermeneutic of Being understood as existence, and moves on an ontological level. The similarity of the expressions is justified by the fact that the anthropological or existential analysis relies throughout on that structure of existence as being-in-the-world which was first worked out by the analytic of existence. (269–70)

Binswanger indicates what is also a difference between Heidegger and the early Sartre: that for Sartre the ontological does not simply show itself in the ontic or mundane but is reconstituted by it. Though Binswanger is not critical of Heidegger, he allows us to see what so troubled Sartre: namely that Heideggerian 'existence' covers over a transcendentalism that withdraws actual existence into 'Being.'

Foucault's monograph allies itself with the 'analytic of existence,' and is Heideggerian in its search through dream for a 'Being understood as existence.' His goal is not any kind of therapy. Still, the fact that Binswanger provides him with his first enunciative positioning is symptomatically significant. Foucault too must think the ontological through the ontic, through an 'Archaeology' of the 'human sciences.' Thus it is appropriate that his definition of the modern *cogito* places itself between Heidegger and Sartre. For in a section often misunderstood because we assume that no contemporary theorist would use the term *cogito*, Foucault argues that man can 'neither posit himself in the immediate and sovereign transparency of a *cogito*' nor 'inhabit the objective inertia of something' that does not 'lead to self-consciousness' (*OT* 322).

This formulation echoes Sartre's criticism of *Dasein* for eliding consciousness, even as it evokes Hegel rather than Heidegger. The *modern* unlike the Cartesian *cogito* constitutes 'Man' as a 'mode of being which accommodates that dimension' that extends from 'the unthought' to 'the act of thought by which he apprehends' the unthought (*OT* 322). Foucault's reworking of the *Geisteswissenschaften* through a Nietzschean counter-phenomenology of mind differs from the work of Heidegger and Merleau-Ponty in locating this unthought not simply in perception or Being but in the 'density of the historic.' But it differs from Sartre and more especially Hegel in making 'man' answerable to his 'being' through the language in which he is articulated. In this sense Foucault, while still using the word 'man,' continues Heidegger's task of a 'thinking that abandons subjectivity,' yet without seeking any proximity to Being. For Foucault reinscribes Heidegger after Sartre, Blanchot, Bataille, and Artaud. He thus turns not to Being but to 'counter-nature, death, [and] the dark underside of disease' (*Birth of the Clinic* 195).

VI. Supplement: Literature and the Dead End of Ontology

The revisionary ratios outlined here are only suggestive. They do not exhaust the ways phenomenology returns in later theory in disparate, non-totalizable forms. As important, the relation between a given theorist and his precursors cannot be subsumed into a single structure of influence. It is overdetermined by the fact that influence is not purely a relation between individuals but involves fields, sometimes more than one field. Moreover, there can be multiple conflicting points of contact between one corpus and another even within a single text such as 'Literature and the Right to Death' where there is more than one Sartre in play. A name too is the site of a dispersion, and we are always dealing with more names than are actually named.

Indeed *The Order of Things* provides an example of this ir-resolution that disturbs any attempt to provide a simple history of influence. As suggested, by focusing synchronically on the order of knowledge Foucault constructs at the near end of his text, one discerns a dialogue between positivity and negativity in the difference between the human sciences and the 'counter-sciences' of ethnology, literature, and psychoanalysis. This dialogue brings together Heidegger and Sartre, ontology and anthropology or a radicalized epistemology, given that the concern with knowledge and the relation between the ontological and the ontic actually derives from Heidegger, while the (non)being to which science must attend has been filtered through Sartre. In other words the hiatus between Sartre and Heidegger contains further crossings between the two that make the relationship difficult to schematize. Still, we can read Foucault's text under the general figure of hiatus as opening.

Yet if we focus on the diachronic movement of Foucault's text through its near end to its end, and then place it in his corpus, the Sartre/Heidegger relation becomes one of aporia. For Foucault's epistemic history involves a darkening of his own enlightenment through a Nietzschean dialectic that moves from the Renaissance through classicism to the modern. In this process a language intermingled with 'the prose of the world' (*OT* 17) is covered over by the nominalism of classical discourse, then returning as 'literature' in the late nineteenth century. Literature is a specific form of language folded back on 'the enigma of its own origin,' so as to grow 'progressively more differentiated from the discourse of ideas' and enclosed in 'a radical intransitivity' (300). As Foucault loses faith in ethnology and psychoanalysis, he is left with literature as the only 'counter-science' (379). Thus isolated, literature is not dialogically engaged with science or knowledge but is a form of pure ontology: it 'has nothing to say but itself, nothing to do but shine in the brightness of its being' (300). As we have seen, Sartre, who first deals with this literature (or poetry) in *What Is Literature?*, later links it to Heidegger via Blanchot's work on Mallarmé. For Sartre literature as the will to failure seeks the inertia that Levinas finds in Heideggerian being when he says, 'in ekstasis the subject is absorbed in the object and recovers itself in its unity' (*EE* 41). Through literature Foucault finds himself borne towards the end of man, and returns to a being rewritten as non-being after the disaster.

And here it is useful to compare Foucault with Derrida, whose early work also takes up the hiatus described in the last section, and who is also thought to privilege literature. Whereas Foucault's 'literature' finds itself on the slope of (non)being, *écriture* works at the hinge of the two slopes that Blanchot, like Sartre, cannot bring together. For what Derrida calls arche-writing is a language not specialized as literature but present throughout discourse in the 'prose of the world.' In other words, *écriture* is not 'detached from all the values that ... keep it in general circulation' before the nineteenth century (*OT* 300). On the contrary Derrida works across the Sartrean bifurcation of prose and poetry that Foucault accepts after the classical period. Thus Derrida rarely deals with literature as separate from philosophical, anthropological, or other texts. In short he opens the aporia between prose and poetry so as to permit a dialogue between epistemology and ontology. On the one hand *écriture* is 'the process of death at work in signs,' and thus an unravelling of knowledge into its finitude. On the other hand Derrida's deconstruction is not the prelude to a negative ontology: it is always epistemic, which is to say 'affirmative.' A deconstruction, he suggests, always concerns 'systems,' with a view not to bringing them down but of opening onto other 'possibilities of arrangement' (*Speech and Phenomena* 40; *Points ... Interviews* 83, 212).

On one level, Foucault too works in this opening. Through language as 'the prose of the world,' he unravels the complicated cosmological structures fabricated by the Renaissance. Though it is covered over in the classical period, Foucault still uses language to expose the positivity of 'discourse' to its limits. Finally the 'return of language' offers the hope of a language not confined to literature but put to work within the human sciences through psychoanalysis and ethnology. In this sense Foucault does not wholly reject Kant: indeed as James Miller points out, his early work on the *Anthropology* is 'the seed' of *The Order of Things* (137–44).

But these disciplines are disappointments and fall back into various kinds of positivism. Indeed their potential as means of access to the unthought can be realized only by using them to deconstruct one another, which was not the path taken by ethnology, renamed 'anthropology' in the university of the 1960s. Thus the hiatus unravels back into an aporia between ontology and epistemology that spells the collapse of Foucault's attempt to make phenomenology the source of an affirmative deconstruction. Language, instead of being a 'process' at work in signs, becomes restricted to literature as a negative absolute. Nowhere is this more evident than in Foucault's monograph on Blanchot, also published in 1966. Blanchot, as the epitome of literature, is associated with a negative theology ('Maurice Blanchot' 16, 19). This non-being, which is so enigmatically in-itself, constitutes both the fascination and the dead end of a certain phenomenology. This may be why Foucault in his later work rarely writes on literature. And yet his turn to the poststructural social sciences after 1968 is still a return to Sartre, this time another Sartre. For Foucault's role as a disengaged public intellectual is a curious sub-version of Sartre's postwar *engagement,* which is also mobilized by the aporia between ontology and the prose of the world. Even in its exit from phenomenology, poststructuralism and its current continuations do not escape the problems left unresolved by phenomenology.

NOTES

1 This is according to Hans-Georg Gadamer, to whom Heidegger gave away his unread copy of the text (see Richard Wolin, *The Terms of Cultural Criticism: The Frankfurt School, Existentialism, Poststructuralism* 238n15).
2 For further discussion of this distinction see my articles 'Trans-positions of Difference: Kristeva and Poststructuralism' and 'Language, Music and the Body: Nietzsche and Deconstruction.'
3 See also Derrida, 'The Time of a Thesis: Punctuations' (38).
4 The phrase 'infinite absolute negativity' is Kierkegaard's and describes the infinite regress of a negativity that is projective if not exactly productive in a Hegelian sense (278).
5 Jean-Paul Sartre, *Being and Nothingness* 128. Hereafter cited as *BN.*
6 Sartre does often use the two terms side by side, but is not equating them so much as sliding from one to the other. As I shall argue, he is quite clear about the differences between his thinking and Heidegger's: he is aware that *Dasein* is a 'pure "being-outside-of-self"' (486), and slides between the two terms so as to insist on the inadequacy of *Dasein* for a concept of 'human' being.
7 The phrase is Michel Foucault's in *The Order of Things* 322. Hereafter cited as *OT.*
8 Paul Ricœur makes the distinction in the context of characterizing Hegel's work as a 'phenomenology of spirit in the element of consciousness.' Ricœur writes: 'We are not being overly schematic if we explain the difference between a philosophy of spirit and a philosophy of consciousness by saying that spirit is not directed toward another who is lacking to it, but ... is entirely

complete within itself' (228). Ricœur's understanding of consciousness draws on the foregrounding of the unhappy consciousness in Jean Hyppolite's *Genesis and Structure in Hegel's Phenomenology of Spirit* (1946) 156–63.

9 Levinas, *Time and the Other* (1947/79), 41. Hereafter cited as *TO*. Levinas further comments on the egotistical sublimity of Heideggerian being, when he writes, 'Light is that through which something is other than myself, but already as if it came from me' (*TO* 64). The term 'non-violence' is used by Derrida to describe Levinas's own thought in 'Violence and Metaphysics: An Essay on the Thought of Emmanuel Levinas' (*Writing and Difference* 147). Levinas's insistence on non-violence has much to do not only with the Jewish question but also with the French Left's fascination with 'terror,' which I discuss later.

10 In 1934 Levinas writes that Heidegger 'inaugurates' a third phase of Phenomenology, 'that of *existential phenomenology*' (*Discovering Existence with Husserl* 39). In 1940 he still reads Heidegger as an existentialist (61, 84).

11 Derrida, *Writing and Difference* (1967) 147; Paul de Man, *The Rhetoric of Romanticism*, 116, 118–19, hereafter cited as *RR*; Maurice Blanchot, 'Literature and the Right to Death' (1947), in *The Gaze of Orpheus* 42, hereafter cited as *GO*.

12 Similarly Sartre writes: 'The image must enclose in its very structure a nihilating thesis ... First it is the nihilation of the world (since the world is not offering the imagined object as an actual object of perception), secondly the nihilation of the object of the image (it is posited as not actual), and finally by the same stroke it is the nihilation of itself' (*BN* 62).

13 See for instance the essay 'Différance,' where Derrida does and does not use the words 'transcendental' and 'primordial,' even as he insists that *différance* 'is not marked by a capital letter' (*Speech and Phenomena* 130, 136, 139, 143, 153).

14 De Man's *The Resistance to Theory* will hereafter be referred to as *RT*.

15 See also Derrida's comments to Paul de Man on Sartre (*RT* 119).

16 Rodolphe Gasché borrows the term 'hyper-reflection' from Merleau-Ponty to distinguish a 'dialectics without synthesis' that is proto-deconstructive from a Hegelian 'reflexivity' that founds consciousness (28–35).

17 See for example Alain Robbe-Grillet, *For a New Novel: Essays on Fiction* 60, 68.

18 Levinas, *Existence and Existents* (1946) 42, hereafter cited as *EE*.

19 Sartre attended Kojève's lectures (given from 1933 to 1939), as did Lacan and Levinas.

20 Levinas's essay first appeared in *Recherches philosophiques* in 1935/6. Rolland points out the close proximity of Sartre's and Levinas's treatments of nausea and observes that the '*philosophical encounter*' between the two men is all the

more interesting in that Sartre, though he may subsequently have read Levinas's essay, had already written an unpublished draft of his novel in 1931. In
effect Rolland attributes to Sartre the same re-vision of Heideggerian
anguish as he does to Levinas (29, 79n).

21 See Sartre, *Sketch for a Theory of the Emotions* 24–5 and more generally 14–31.
22 Although Merleau-Ponty is not talking of Sartre here, but of Freud, this passage from the working notes is framed by two others that discuss Sartre.
23 The phrase is Jean Hyppolite's, in *Logic and Existence* (1953), 177, 179.
24 The piece from which this quotation is taken, 'The Pineal Eye,' was written
   around 1930 but not published until much later. However, many of Bataille's
   texts on body-parts including *Histoire de l'œil* (1928) had appeared prior to
   BN.
25 The term 'revisionary ratio' is used by Harold Bloom to name various structures of influence that he reads in terms of an oedipal dynamic that I am not
   evoking here. See *The Anxiety of Influence: A Theory of Poetry.*
26 Under the guise of 'rigour' Derrida rejects 'anthropology' in favour of the
   'science of the structures of the phenomenality of spirit relating to itself'
   ('Ends' 117). Hegel is praised for inventing 'a consciousness without man'
   (118). But note that this anti-humanism claims an invulnerability not offered
   by Sartre's confrontation with the inhuman.
27 The relationship is not purely one-sided. Sartre reviewed Blanchot's novel
   Aminadab in 1943. His *Mallarmé: or the Poet of Nothingness*, written in 1952,
   published posthumously in 1980, but partially published earlier, continues a
   subterranean dialogue with Blanchot, to whose work on Mallarmé he refers
   (133, 137).
28 Lycette Nelson points out in her 'Introduction' to Blanchot's *The Step Not
   Beyond* (1973) that in Blanchot's idea of the trace there 'is nothing of Derrida's idea of the trace as constitutive of the present.' The Trace is rather
   'the idea of the idea as writing as effacement, as opposed to the traditional idea that writing preserves what would otherwise disappear' (xv).
29 In *The Psychology of Imagination* Sartre struggles to attribute a kind of positivity
   to the image conceived as unreal and empty: 'an image is not ... simply the
   world-negated, it is always *the world negated from a certain point of view,* namely,
   the one that permits the positing of the absence or the non-existence of the
   object presented "as an image"' (268). But as Peter Caws says, it is difficult to
   see how 'nothingness,' as Sartre will later develop the concept, can take this
   'kind of initiative' (42). Indeed this aporia is at the heart of Sartre's attempt
   to build on his ontology a theory of praxis that must always be in bad faith.
30 See Hollier 157 and 147–57 more generally; Blanchot, 'How Is Literature
   Possible?' in *The Blanchot Reader,* 49–60.

31 Sartre claimed to have nothing in common with the Surrealists; however, his relationship to them was deeply ambivalent, as William Plank argues in *Sartre and the Surrealists* 61–72.

32 Hollier reads Blanchot's portrait of the terrorist as an account of Sartre (7–8), though there may also be a muted reference to Merleau-Ponty's *Humanism and Terror* (1947).

33 Sartre sees the political group as formed through the 'free violence' of Terror, in which individualities are negated in the common interests of the group. In so far as the 'fused group' is not a community or society but an artificial unity created by resistance to the enemy, the 'freedom' of terror is a necessary form of internalized 'counter-violence.' Sartre's terrorism, as late as *Critique*, is an example of his continuing anti-humanism: any naïve belief in the integrity of the group has to be subjected to the critical knowledge that negation always proceeds by way of a repression that makes what is posited purely figural, and that the collective ego projected by the group is 'transcendent,' and is thus an exteriority, an in-itself, something inhuman (428–44)

34 See for instance Christopher Norris, *Paul de Man: Deconstruction and the Critique of Aesthetic Ideology.*

35 Although Sartre's full text was published posthumously in 1986, a shorter version, containing the passages cited, appeared in an introduction to an edition of Mallarmé published in 1966.

36 A related point is made by Roger Frie, who notes that 'the division between ontology and anthropology in fundamental ontology is not nearly as obvious as the later Heidegger makes it out to be. For example, the distinction ... between the ontological character of existentials, such as anxiety, and their psychological dispositions is not entirely apparent' (85).

37 Arguing that 'Man ... is his own ultimate purpose,' Kant defines physiological anthropology as concerned with 'what Nature makes of man,' whereas pragmatic anthropology 'aims at what man makes, can, or should make of himself as a freely acting being' (3). Interestingly, Kant relegates to the realm of the physiological anything that is in excess of man's free cognition of himself.

38 While the book is strongly influenced by Merleau-Ponty, its second part develops the crudely Marxist argument that mental illness is caused by social alienation, and it is written in the shadow of a postwar Sartrean view that philosophical thought must be 'useful.' Foucault suppressed this section and rewrote it when he reissued the book as *Mental Illness and Psychology* in 1962. The suppressed second part reveals Foucault's links to the anti-psychiatry movement of Thomas Szasz, David Cooper, and R.D. Laing, which was

84   Tilottama Rajan

strongly influenced by Sartre. Interestingly, English translations of Foucault's early work first appeared in various series edited by Laing. A certain Sartrean activism persists in *Madness and Civilization* and perhaps returns, albeit highly qualified and complicated, in the later social studies.

39 Tilottama Rajan, 'The Phenomenological Allegory: From *Death and the Labyrinth* to *The Order of Things*.'

40 In 1942 Binswanger writes to Heidegger: 'I have repeatedly emphasized the difference between your pure ontological intentions and my anthropological endeavours. I would be satisfied if you would acknowledge that I have made use of the new "impulses" which anthropology has gained from ontological problems' (quoted by Frie, 86).

WORKS CITED

Bataille, Georges. *Inner Experience* (1954). Trans. Leslie Ann Boldt. Albany: SUNY 1988.

– *Visions of Excess: Selected Writings, 1927–1939*. Trans. Allan Stoekl. Minneapolis: U of Minnesota P, 1985.

Baudrillard, Jean. *Fatal Strategies* (1983). Trans. Philip Beitchman and W.G.J. Niesluchowski. New York: Semiotext(e), 1990.

Binswanger, Ludwig. 'The Case of Ellen West' (1944). Trans. W.M. Mendel and J. Lyons. *Existence: A New Dimension in Psychiatry and Psychology*. Ed. Rollo May et al. New York: Basic Books, 1958. 237–64.

Blanchot, Maurice . 'The Beginnings of a Novel.' *The Blanchot Reader*. Ed. Michael Holland. Oxford: Blackwell, 1995. 33–4.

– 'Literature and the Right to Death' (1947). *The Gaze of Orpheus*. Trans. Lydia Davis. Barrytown: Station Hill P, 1982. 21–62.

– *The Space of Literature* (1955). Trans. Ann Smock. Lincoln: U of Nebraska P, 1982.

Bloom, Harold. *The Anxiety of Influence: A Theory of Poetry*. New York: Oxford UP, 1973.

Caws, Peter. *Sartre*. London: Routledge and Kegan Paul, 1979.

Corngold, Stanley. 'Error in Paul de Man.' *The Yale Critics: Deconstruction in America*. Ed. Jonathan Arac, Wlad Godzich, and Wallace Martin. Minneapolis: U of Minnesota P, 1983. 92–7.

de Man, Paul. *Blindness and Insight: Essays in the Rhetoric of Contemporary Criticism* (1971). 2nd rev. ed. Minneapolis: U of Minnesota P, 1983.

– *Critical Writings 1953–1978*. Ed. Lindsay Waters and Wlad Godzich. Minneapolis: U of Minnesota P, 1989.

– *The Resistance to Theory*. Minneapolis: U of Minnesota P, 1986.

– *The Rhetoric of Romanticism.* New York: Columbia UP, 1984.

Derrida, Jacques. *Edmund Husserl's Origin of Geometry: An Introduction* (1962). Trans. John P. Leavey. Stony Brook: Nicholas Hays, 1978.

– 'The Ends of Man.' *Margins of Philosophy* (1972). Trans. Alan Bass. Chicago: U of Chicago P, 1982. 109–36.

– *Of Spirit: Heidegger and the Question* (1987). Trans. Geoffrey Bennington and Rachel Bowlby. Chicago: U of Chicago P, 1989.

– *Points ... Interviews 1974–1994.* Ed. Elisabeth Weber. Trans. Peggy Kamuf et al. Stanford: Stanford UP, 1995.

– *Positions* (1972). Trans. Alan Bass. Chicago: U of Chicago P, 1981.

– *Speech and Phenomena and Other Essays on Husserl's Theory of Signs* (1967). Trans. David B. Allison. Evanston: Northwestern UP, 1973.

– 'The Time of a Thesis: Punctuations' (1980). *Philosophy in France Today.* Ed. Alan Montefiore. Cambridge: Cambridge UP, 1983. 34–50.

– *Writing and Difference* (1967). Trans. Alan Bass. Chicago: U of Chicago P, 1978.

Dosse, François. *History of Structuralism* (1991). Trans. Deborah Glassman. 2 vols. Minneapolis: U of Minnesota P, 1997.

Foucault, Michel. *The Archaeology of Knowledge and the Discourse on Language.* Trans. A.M. Sheridan Smith. New York: Pantheon, 1969.

– *The Birth of the Clinic: An Archaeology of Medical Perception* (1963). Trans. A.M. Sheridan, 1973. Rpt. London: Routledge, 1986.

– *Dream, Imagination and Existence.* Foucault and Binswanger, *Dream and Existence.* Ed. Keith Hoeller. Special issue of *Review of Existential Psychology and Psychiatry,* 1986.

– 'Maurice Blanchot: The Thought from Outside.' Trans. Brian Massumi. *Foucault/Blanchot.* New York: Zone, 1987.

– *The Order of Things: An Archaeology of the Human Sciences* (1966). Trans. anonymous. New York: Pantheon, 1970.

Frie, *Roger. Subjectivity and Intersubjectivity in Modern Philosophy and Psychoanalysis: A Study of Sartre, Binswanger, Lacan, and Habermas.* London: Rowman and Littlefield, 1997.

Gasché, Rodolphe. *Inventions of Difference: On Jacques Derrida.* Cambridge: Harvard UP, 1994.

Heidegger, Martin. *Basic Writings.* Ed. David Farrell Krell. Rev. ed. New York: HarperCollins, 1993.

Hertz, Neil. 'Lurid Figures.' *Reading de Man Reading.* Ed. Lindsay Waters and Wlad Godzich. Minneapolis: U of Minnesota P, 1989. 82–104.

Holland, Michael. 'Introduction to Part I.' *The Blanchot Reader.* Ed. Michael Holland. Oxford: Blackwell, 1995. 1–15.

Hollier, Denis. *Absent without Leave: French Literature under the Threat of War.* Trans. Catherine Porter. Cambridge: Harvard UP, 1997.

Hyppolite, Jean. *Genesis and Structure in Hegel's Phenomenology of Spirit* (1946). Trans. Samuel Cherniak and John Heckman. Evanston: Northwestern UP, 1974.

– *Logic and Existence* (1953). Trans. Leonard Lawlor and Amit Sen. Albany: SUNY P, 1997.

Kant, Immanuel. *Anthropology from a Pragmatic Point of View* (1798). Trans. Victor Lyle Dowdell. Carbondale: Southern Illinois UP, 1978.

Kierkegaard, Søren. *The Concept of Irony.* Trans. Lee M. Capel. Bloomington: Indiana UP, 1972.

Kojève, Alexandre. *Introduction to the Reading of Hegel* (1947). Ed. Raymond Queneau. Trans. James H. Nichols. Ithaca: Cornell UP, 1980.

Levinas, Emmanuel. *De l'évasion.* Intro. Jacques Rolland. Paris: fata morgana, 1982/97.

– *Discovering Existence with Husserl.* Trans. Richard A. Cohen and Michael B. Smith. Evanston: Northwestern UP, 1998.

– *Existence and Existents* (1946). Trans. Alphonso Lingis. The Hague: Martinus Nijhoff, 1978.

– *Proper Names.* Trans. Michael B. Smith. Stanford: Stanford UP, 1996.

– *The Theory of Intuition in Husserl's Phenomenology* (1930). Trans. André Orianne. Evanston: Northwestern UP, 1973/95.

– *Time and the Other* (1947/79). Trans. Richard A. Cohen. Pittsburgh: Duquesne UP, 1987.

Lyotard, Jean-François. *Heidegger and 'the jews.'* Trans. Andreas Michel and Mark Roberts. Minneapolis: U of Minnesota P, 1990.

Merleau-Ponty, Maurice. 'Phenomenology and Psychoanalysis: Preface to Hesnard's *L'Oeuvre de Freud.*' Trans. Alden L. Fisher. *Merleau-Ponty and Psychology.* Ed. Keith Hoeller. Atlantic Highlands: Humanities P, 1990. 67–72.

– *The Visible and the Invisible* (1964). Trans. Alphonso Lingis. Evanston: Northwestern UP, 1968.

Miller, James. *The Passion of Michel Foucault.* New York: Simon and Schuster, 1993.

Nancy, Jean-Luc. 'Exscription.' *The Birth to Presence.* Trans. Brian Holmes et al. Stanford: Stanford UP, 1993. 319–40.

Nelson, Lycette. Introduction. *The Step Not Beyond.* By Maurice Blanchot (1973). Albany: SUNY P, 1992. v–xxi.

Norris, Christopher. *Paul de Man: Deconstruction and the Critique of Aesthetic Ideology.* London: Routledge, 1988.

Plank, William. *Sartre and the Surrealists.* Ann Arbor: UMI Research P, 1981.

Rajan, Tilottama. 'The Phenomenological Allegory: From *Death and the Laby-rinth* to *The Order of Things.*' *Poetics Today* 19.3 (Fall 1998): 439–66.

– 'Language, Music and the Body: Nietzsche and Deconstruction.' *Intersections: Nineteenth-Century Philosophy and Contemporary Theory.* Ed. Tilottama Rajan and David L. Clark. Albany: SUNY P, 1995. 147–69.

– 'Trans-positions of Difference: Kristeva and Poststructuralism.' *Ethics, Politics and Difference in Julia Kristeva's Writing.* Ed. Kelly Oliver. New York: Routledge, 1993. 215–37.

Ricœur, Paul. 'Hegel and Husserl on Intersubjectivity.' *From Text to Action: Essays in Hermeneutics II.* Trans. Kathleen Blamey and John B. Thompson. Evanston: Northwestern UP, 1991. 227–45.

Robbe-Grillet, Alain. *For a New Novel: Essays on Fiction.* Trans. Richard Howard. New York: Grove P, 1965.

Rockmore, Tom. *Heidegger and French Philosophy: Humanism, Antihumanism and Being.* New York: Routledge, 1995.

Sartre, Jean-Paul. *Being and Nothingness: A Phenomenological Essay on Ontology* (1943). Trans. Hazel Barnes. 1956. New York: Washington Square P, 1992.

– *Critique of Dialectical Reason* (1960). Trans. Alan Sheridan-Smith. London: Verso/NLB, 1976.

– *Mallarmé: or the Poet of Nothingness.* Trans. Ernest Sturm. University Park: Penn State UP, 1988.

– *Nausea.* Trans. Robert Baldick. Harmondsworth: Penguin, 1965.

– *The Psychology of Imagination.* Trans. Bernard Frechtman. New York: Washington Square P, 1966.

– *Sketch for a Theory of the Emotions* (1939). Trans. Philip Mairet. London: Methuen, 1962.

– *The Wartime Diaries of Jean-Paul Sartre: November 1939–March 1940.* Trans. Quintin Hoare. New York: Pantheon, 1984.

– *What Is Literature?* (1947). Trans. Bernard Frechtman. Gloucester, Mass.: Peter Smith, 1978.

Wolin, Richard. *The Terms of Cultural Criticism: The Frankfurt School, Existentialism, Poststructuralism.* New York: Columbia UP, 1992.

Žižek, Slavoj. *Looking Awry: An Introduction to Jacques Lacan through Popular Culture.* Cambridge: MIT P, 1992.

The Premodern Condition: Neo-Primitivism in Baudrillard and Lyotard

VICTOR LI

The title of my paper alludes to Jean-François Lyotard's *The Postmodern Condition* in order to make the point that the so-called postmodern critique of the modern relies heavily on the concept of the premodern or primitive.[1] Tomoko Masuzawa, in her deconstructive reading of the quest for the origin of religion, uneasily asks: '[W]e wonder ... as to the meaning of the curious appendage *post-*. Is this an extension – some kind of an afterlife, perhaps, of what it qualifies (*structuralist, modern, industrial*)? Or does it indicate a reversal of some sort, an atavistic return of what once was ... a return of the *pre-*? These are nervous questions' (13). Masuzawa is understandably nervous because her questions raise the possibility that the postmodern is not only still attached to what it seeks to supersede but that it may in fact be strangely complicit with the premodern. As I hope to show, such a preposterous convolution of the *pre-* and the *post-* exists in the work of Jean Baudrillard and Jean-François Lyotard, both of whom, though usually described as postmodern theorists, may equally be seen as neo-primitivists.

Where primitivism attempted directly to know, appropriate, or incorporate the primitive Other to serve its own (Western) ends, Baudrillard's and Lyotard's neo-primitivism sees the primitive Other as that radical alterity which, by resisting universalizing Western metanarratives, allows us to escape from what Baudrillard calls 'the hell of the Same' (*Transparency* 122). But the primitive Other's resistance also functions as a redemptive power that delivers the modern West from its own will to universality. At once resistant alterity and redemptive force, the primitive Other has little choice or say in how it is positioned and used in neo-primitivist discourses. Though critical of primitivism, neo-primitivism is, therefore, in the final analysis, similar to its predecessor in that its anti-ethnocentric relativism reintroduces a subtler theoretical recuperation of the primitive. We see an example of this critical yet redemptive logic clearly in Claude Lévi-Strauss's belief that in our encounter with primitive societies lies 'the possibility, vital for life, of *unhitching*' from our own (544). Lévi-Strauss's assertion that 'we have a duty to free ourselves' (514) from our society in order to achieve self-renewal is echoed in the following statement by Lyotard: 'The real political task today, at least in so far as it is also concerned with the cultural ... is to carry forward the resistance ... to established thought, to what has already been done, to what everyone thinks, to what is well known, to what is widely recognized' ('An Interview' 302). The break with established thought advocated in Lyotard's avant-gardist declaration finds one of its exemplifications in the challenge posed to the modern West's grand narratives of legitimation by the narrative pragmatics of a 'savage' society such as that of Lyotard's favourite Cashinahua (who pop up in *The Postmodern Condition, Just Gaming*, 'Missive on Universal History,' and *The Differend*). Similarly, Baudrillard's aphorism – 'The Other is what allows *me* not to repeat *myself* for ever' (emphasis mine) – puts as much weight on the challenge posed by radical alterity (the primitive Other) as on its role in rescuing and renewing the creativity of the modern or postmodern subject.

Baudrillard has claimed that he has 'nothing to do with postmodernism' (qtd. in Gane 47). We should not take this statement as a flat denial or as self-mockery but see in it an example of Baudrillardian reversibility in which to understand the postmodern is to readdress the premodern. Baudrillard's point, argued most clearly in *The Mirror of Production* and *Symbolic Exchange and Death*, is that the West, since at least the Enlightenment, has instituted societies based on the twin myths of production and semiology – that is, respectively, a political economy that privileges an instrumental-rational view of labour, utility, and exchange value, and a political economy of the sign based on an abstract structural-linguistic code. The myth of production governed modern industrial society while the myth of semiology has given rise to our postmodern, postindustrial culture of signs and simulacra. But these societies or cultures are made possible, according to Baudrillard, only through the denial or repression of a radical and primordial principle he calls 'symbolic exchange,' a principle he finds at work in primitive societies.

Drawing on Marcel Mauss's work on the social relations of the gift, Georges Bataille's writings on expenditure and *la part maudite*, and Marshall Sahlins's substantivist economic anthropology which challenges the orthodox economic axioms of scarcity, need, and accumulation, Baudrillard argues that the symbolic exchange of primitive societies is opposed to the productivist myth in so far as it bypasses material wealth, economic calculation, and accumulation in favour of '*symbolic* wealth which, mocking natural necessity, comes conversely from destruction, the deconstruction of value, transgression, or discharge' (*Mirror* 43). Symbolic exchange is 'based on non-production, eventual destruction, and a process of continuous *unlimited* reciprocity between *persons*' (70). In other words, in contrast to the productivist model whose economic rationality presupposes the threat of scarcity and the necessity of material accumulation, the symbolic exchange of primitive societies which privileges social reciprocity, obligation, and the ritual affirmation of community requires 'the consumption of the "surplus" and deliberate anti-production whenever accumulation (the thing not exchanged, taken and not returned, earned and not wasted, produced and not destroyed) risks breaking the reciprocity and begins to generate power' (143).

Foregrounding the reciprocal, even antagonistic, relationship between individuals in primitive symbolic exchange, Baudrillard pits its concrete, personal, and immediate qualities against that other myth of modern or postmodern society, namely, semiology or the political economy of the sign with its abstract structural code established on equivalence and substitutability. The gift, which is central to symbolic exchange, is totally opposed to the sign's decontextualized abstraction and reproductivity. As Charles Levin points out:

> The gift is, in its purest form ... something unique and irreplaceable, which cannot be substituted because it has no equivalent. It is something whose very existence symbolizes the interaction which it occasions, and which likewise could not have come into existence without the interaction. ... The gift is not a sign because it cannot be separated from its context, and transferred to any other: it simply embodies its own meaning, which is nothing other than the way the bodies of the giver and receiver have come to exist in relation to each other. (85)

The concrete reciprocity embodied in the gift takes on greater importance for Baudrillard as the semiotic order becomes increasingly simulacral in contemporary Western society with signs breaking free from their referents and becoming free-standing and self-reproducing.

The centrality of symbolic exchange to Baudrillard's thought has been noted by commentators such as Gary Genosko, for example, who sees symbolic exchange as initiating a 'revolutionary anthropology' which seeks 'to destroy the prevailing semiocracy' (xx). Similarly, Douglas Kellner states that symbolic exchange 'emerges as Baudrillard's "revolutionary" alternative to the values and practices of capitalist society' (44), and Julian Pefanis points out that it 'operates as [Baudrillard's] meta-position in the critique of political economy and its contemporary avatar, semio-linguistics' (61). The critical standpoint provided by symbolic exchange can be subjected, however, to a certain ironic reversal which might amuse Baudrillard but blunt the force of his critique of Western thought. For while the principle of symbolic exchange allows Baudrillard to critique both bourgeois and Marxist theories of social and economic organization for their universalizing tendency, their 'retrospective finality' (*Mirror* 66), which incorporates and assimilates the difference of earlier societies into their own ethnocentric and teleological paradigms, symbolic exchange, as a concept, can only function on the condition that it idealize primitive society as a positive antithesis to the West. Such a move replicates, albeit in a different register, the primitivism and ethnocentrism that Baudrillard accuses a Marxist anthropologist like Maurice Godelier of practising. Baudrillard charges Godelier with inscribing primitive society in 'the same discourse as ours: with the same code. It means looking at primitive society from the wrong end' (*Mirror* 75). But if Baudrillard's critique of Marxist anthropology is, on one level, anti-primitivist in that it seeks to correct a certain 'blindness about primitive societies' (90), on another level it is neo-primitivist in that it reinscribes an all-too-familiar binary model of a debased modern West and an idealized primitive Other.

Among the first to point out the presence of this ironic reversal in Baudrillard's theory of symbolic exchange was Jean-François Lyotard. In *Libidinal Economy*, Lyotard argues that Baudrillard falls into the trap of primitivism by appropriating the primitive Other as a lost referent or elusive alibi for his own theoretical disillusionment with Western modernity. 'How is it,' Lyotard asks, 'that he [Baudrillard] does not see that the whole problematic of the gift, of symbolic exchange, such as he receives it from Mauss ... belongs in its entirety to Western racism and imperialism – that it is still ethnology's good savage, slightly libidinalized, which he inherits with the concept?' (*Libidinal Economy* 106). Baudrillard's appropriation of the primitive Other as radical critique and alternative to Western theory becomes for Lyotard merely the reintroduction of the Western primitivist fantasy of escaping to a 'non-alienated region' (*Libidinal Economy* 107). To Lyotard, Baudrillard's critique of Western modernity ends up confirming one of its long-standing desires – the desire to escape its own limits for a forgotten truth.

Baudrillard's primitive 'non-alienated region' belongs to a utopian genre of writing that is generally careless when it comes to verifying or documenting ethnographic details. This is a criticism that the anthropologist Robert Hefner has made of Baudrillard's *The Mirror of Production*. Hefner argues that although Baudrillard is quite right to insist that non-economic social relations based on reciprocity, kinship, and ritual are embedded in primitive exchange, he is wrong in ruling that the economic values of use and need are totally unheeded in primitive society. Thus, in response to Baudrillard's claim that to the primitives 'survival is not a principle' and that for them 'eating, drinking, and living are first of all acts that are exchanged, [and] if they are not exchanged do not occur' (*Mirror* 79), Hefner points out that not only is Baudrillard indulging in a 'rather cavalier generalization' that would 'leave most anthropologists perplexed if not dumbfounded,' but also that the claim that survival is not a principle would come as a surprise to 'the starving Tikopia of Polynesia, who increasingly restricted the breadth of their social exchange outside minimal kin units in the face of an island-wide famine' (110). In short, Hefner argues, not only is Baudrillard unconcerned about 'ethnographic particulars,' but his 'romanticized' image of symbolic exchange though presenting 'a perhaps admirable notion of reciprocity ... [is] one that never operated anywhere simply for the sake of its own poetry' (113).

Though Hefner's criticisms of Baudrillard's romanticized anthropology and neglect of ethnographic particulars are cogent, they do not engage directly with the larger theoretical project of Baudrillard's work. Baudrillard is in fact not really interested in ethnographic details because for him ethnographic knowledge is part of the universalizing thrust of Western thought. As he puts it sarcastically in a critique of Lévi-Strauss's structuralist epistemology,

> This is the extreme of liberal thought and the most beautiful way of preserving the initiative and priority of Western thought within 'dialogue' and under the sign of universality of the human mind (as always for Enlightenment anthropology). ... This harmonious vision of two thought processes renders their *confrontation* perfectly inoffensive, by denying the difference of the primitives as an element of rupture with and subversion of (our) 'objectified thought and its mechanisms.' (*Mirror* 90n34)

In later works such as *The Transparency of Evil* and *The Perfect Crime*, Baudrillard's view of primitive difference as a rupture with Western thought develops into a full-fledged valorization of a radical otherness that resolutely resists ethnographic comprehension. An anti-cognitive and anti-representational stance is clearly evident in the distinction Baudrillard makes between *difference*, which is dialectical and hence intelligible and recuperable as part of a single, universal order, and *radical otherness*, which has to do with 'radical incomparability,' 'eternal incomprehensibility,' 'ultimate inscrutability,' 'unintelligibility,' and 'non-representability' (*Transparency* 128, 132, 146, 147, 152). 'Radical otherness,' Baudrillard tells us, 'is simultaneously impossible to find and irreducible. ... The worst thing here is understanding, which is sentimental and useless. True knowledge is knowledge of exactly what we can never understand in the other' (148). Advocating a form of anti-ethnography, Baudrillard recommends that one 'be ignorant of how one's subjects live' and respect 'non-representability, the otherness of that which is foreign to ... self-consciousness' (152).

The problem with Baudrillard's valorization of radical alterity is that its incomprehensibility and incommensurability open up an absolute cognitive relativism that would not permit him to know or say anything about the Other, about whom he has in fact quite a lot to say. The Other may resist ethnographic understanding but Baudrillard not only knows about its resistance, he also confidently describes its feelings towards us. Thus about other non-Western cultures he has this to say:

> Outward conversion to Western ways invariably conceals inward scoffing at Western hegemony. One is put in mind of those Dogons who made up dreams to humour their psychoanalysts and then offered these dreams to their analysts as gifts. Once we despised other cultures; now we respect them. They do not respect our culture, however; they feel nothing but an immense condescension for it. We may have won the right by conquest to exploit and subjugate these cultures, but they have offered themselves the luxury of mystifying us. (*Transparency*, 136)

But if the Other is unintelligible and inscrutable, as Baudrillard constantly reminds us, then how does he know that it scoffs at us, that it shows an 'immense condescension' towards us, that it is deliberately engaged in 'mystifying' us? Baudrillard tells us that the otherness of primitive cultures is not recuperable and that they 'live on the basis of their own singularity, their own exceptionality, on the irreducibility of their own rites and values' (*Transparency* 132). But if these primitive cultures are absolutely singular, exceptional, and irreducible, then what Baudrillard says about them cannot be true, since to be comprehended and described as such would be to have their singularity generalized, their exceptionality made into an example and their irreducibility reduced to so many adjectives. Baudrillard's paradoxical knowledge of the radical incomprehensibility of the primitive Other reaches a dangerous point when he argues that South American Indians chose to die rather than surrender the secret of their otherness to the Spanish *conquistadores*:

> When they [the Indians] found themselves obliged to become part of an otherness no longer radical, but negotiable under the aegis of the universal concept, they preferred mass self-immolation – whence the fervour with which they, for their part, allowed themselves to die: a counterpart to the Spaniard's mad urge to kill. The Indians' strange collusion in their own extermination represented their only way of keeping the secret of otherness. (*Transparency* 133)

Apart from the moral and factual dubiousness of Baudrillard's argument (it would be interesting to see what contemporary South American Indians make of Baudrillard's description of their ancestors' 'mass self-immolation'), there is the epistemological question of how Baudrillard can know the intention behind the Indians' actions when these actions were precisely designed to preserve the secret of their otherness. If the South American Indians were that radically Other, then how can Baudrillard so confidently know what they were up to?

The answer to this paradox lies in the realization that despite Baudrillard's critique of Western epistemology, he is not really concerned with epistemology at all. Though he may use historical and ethnographic accounts to illustrate his theory of radical otherness, his theory does not require the actual, living presence of the primitive Other since the Other is needed only as a *discursive* element of rupture, a *structural* antithesis to Western thought. This is why Baudrillard is not bothered by criticism, such as Hefner's, that his generalizations lack ethnographic evidence, or troubled by the aporia of describing an Other he is not supposed to know. The primitive Other functions primarily as a discursive proxy or theoretical place-holder and the secondary question of its phenomenological or material actuality may in fact interfere with or muddy its primary function. The real live 'primitive' can complicate matters with his behaviour, whereas the discursive proxy can't. We can now see why to Baudrillard the extinction or imminent disappearance of the primitive Other can be turned into a theoretical advantage. The dead or disappearing Indian becomes a pure and perfect example of the Other; through his physical death, the Indian gains theoretical immortality. We have here an instance of a 'pataphysical' logic that Baudrillard elsewhere illustrates through the example of Alfred Jarry's dead cyclist who carries on cycling: '*Rigor mortis* is replaced by *mobilitas mortis*, and the dead rider pedals on indefinitely, even accelerating, as a function of inertia. The energy released is boosted by the inertia of the dead' (*Transparency* 102; also see *America* 115). Similarly, the primitive Other's death confers on it a greater power to 'destabilize Western rule.' The dead primitive returns powerfully as a 'phantom presence,' its 'viral, spectral presence ... [infecting] the synapses of our [Western] brains' (*Transparency* 137). Baudrillard's neo-primitivism thus exemplifies a bizarre logic in which the primitive dies as a presence to serve as an irreducible, internalized idea.

To be sure, Baudrillard is aware that in our time the primitive is allowed to exist only as a simulacrum, a model constructed by the human sciences precisely to replace the vanished or vanishing original. Baudrillard argues that such a simulation of the primitive occurred in 1971 when the government of the Philippines, on the advice of anthropologists, ordered that a few dozen Tasaday, a newly 'discovered' and allegedly 'stone age' tribe, be cordoned off in their remote jungle home and protected from further media and ethnological contact and attention (*Simulations* 13).[2] The ethnologists were worried that the Tasaday would lose their primitive innocence and thus lobbied that they be sealed off from further exposure to a decomposing modernity. But this seemingly generous and self-denying gesture on the part of the scientists constitutes, for Baudrillard, a self-serving justification of their own discipline, allowing them to render the Tasaday into 'simulacra Indians who proclaim at last the universal truth of ethnology' (16). Baudrillard's argument is worth quoting at length:

> Science loses a precious capital, but the object will be safe – lost to science, but intact in its 'virginity.' It isn't a question of sacrifice (science never sacrifices itself: it is always murderous), but of the simulated sacrifice of its object in order to save its reality principle. The Tasaday frozen in their natural element, provide a perfect alibi, an eternal guarantee ... The Indian thereby driven back into the ghetto, into the glass coffin of virgin

forest, becomes the simulation model for all conceivable Indians *before
ethnology.* The latter thus allows itself the luxury of being incarnate beyond
itself, in the 'brute' reality of these Indians it has entirely reinvented –
Savages who are indebted to ethnology for still being Savages: what a turn
of events, what a triumph for this science which seemed dedicated to their
destruction! (*Simulations* 14–15.)

Simulation can thus be seen as the strategy adopted by the ethnologist, or *subject* of investigation, not only to gain control and mastery over
the primitive, or *object* of investigation, but also to dispense with the
primitive/object altogether. In the simulation model Baudrillard has
sketched out, the Tasaday or primitive/object, once cordoned off and
controlled, can be entirely dispensed with, since it is only their theoretical or simulated presence that is required to prove ethnology's importance as a science of the primitive. But while this may appear to suggest
that Baudrillard has deconstructed the concept of the primitive and
shown it to be merely a discursive construct or simulation of Western
theory, a closer examination of his work reveals that, far from abandoning the concept of the primitive, he sees it as crucial and necessary to *his*
theoretical enterprise.

In fact what Baudrillard proposes is a simple binary reversal in which
the power of the formerly privileged ethnologist or Western subject is
questioned and replaced by the formerly disadvantaged primitive or
non-Western object. What Baudrillard calls the principle of reversibility
results in the fatal revenge of the object on the subject. As he describes
it,

The Object and the world let themselves be surprised for an instant (a brief
instant in the general cosmology) by the subject and science, but today
they are violently reasserting themselves and taking revenge. ... Such is the
figure of our fatality, that of an objective turnaround, of an objective
reversal of the world. (*Ecstasy* 87)

Though the object may appear passive, indifferent and inert as opposed
to the subject's active will to power and knowledge, Baudrillard points
out that the object's very indifference and passivity make it an 'insoluble
enigma,' 'an obstacle to all understanding,' 'ever more ungraspable'
and 'contemptuous of all attempts to manipulate it' (*Transparency* 172).
The object is thus uncooperative and resistant to the subject's attempt
to control and master it. Consequently, Baudrillard tells us,

Science has lost its interlocutor [the object], which, like the 'savage,' appears not to have responded with genuine dialogue. It seems that it is not a good object, ... that it secretly evades all attempts at scientific evangelization (rational objectification), and that it is taking its revenge for having been 'understood' by surreptitiously undermining the foundations of the edifice of science. (*Transparency* 173)

Through an ironic reversal, the object, thought to be mastered by the subject, turns the tables on the latter. Baudrillard shows how such a reversal is fatal to our usual ways of thinking, which assume the centrality of the subject:

The main focus of interest has always been on the conditions in which the subject discovers the object, but those in which the object discovers the subject have not been explored at all. We flatter ourselves that we discover the object and conceive it as waiting there meekly to be discovered. But perhaps the cleverer party here is not the one we think. What if it were the object which discovered us in all this? This would give us not merely an uncertainty principle, which can be mastered by equations, but a principle of reversibility which is much more radical and more aggressive. (Similarly, didn't viruses discover us at least as much as we discovered them, with all the consequences that follow? And didn't the American Indians themselves discover us in the end?) (*Perfect Crime* 55)

According to Baudrillard's reversibility principle, the object, the virus, and the Indian have the last laugh over those who had thought to master them. Similarly, returning to Baudrillard's comments on the Tasaday, it turns out that the primitive ultimately escapes its role as ethnology's simulacrum, as the alibi and guarantee of Western science, by stubbornly refusing to come alive and thus validating its simulated role, choosing instead to remain inert and enigmatic like the dead. As Baudrillard remarks, at the very moment of its putative triumph,

ethnology gives up its final and only lesson, the secret which kills it (and which the savages understood much better): the vengeance of the dead. ... It is science which ostensibly masters the object, but it is the latter which deeply invests the former, following an unconscious reversion, giving only dead and circular replies to a dead and circular interrogation. (*Simulations* 17)

The primitive is thus both an ostensibly tamed or simulated object and a vengeful or fatal one. The simulated primitive is a product of the assumption that, in the act of simulation, ethnology possesses complete control and knowledge of its object. Baudrillard's argument, however, is that the primitive as object can never be completely knowable and, as such, can never be fully simulated. Like the object that wreaks vengeance on the subject, the primitive exceeds and subverts the simulated model produced by ethnology.

In Baudrillard's thought, then, the primitive as simulation is deconstructed only to be replaced by the primitive as pure or authentic object. The primitive is a pure object, however, only if it is unknowable. As Baudrillard describes it, 'the Object is an insoluble enigma, because it is not itself and does not know itself. It resembles ... [a] savage, whom one could not understand for the same reason that he could not understand himself' (*Transparency* 172). It is precisely because the object is unknowable that it is able to master the knowing subject. There are a couple of problems, however, with Baudrillard's account of the triumph of the uncognizable object.

First, the object's (or primitive's) victory is surely pyrrhic; because it cannot know itself, it cannot know about its overcoming of the subject. The primitive as pure object may defeat ethnology's attempts to understand and manipulate it, but it has neither conscious agency nor comprehension of either its plight or its triumph.

Second, the pure primitive or object, described as being unlike the subject in that it is unknowing and unknowable, seems nonetheless to exhibit subject-like intentions, motives, and emotions such as vengeance, cunning, sly servility, and 'the *passion* of indifference' (*Ecstasy* 93; emphasis mine). Supposed to be unknowable, the object appears amenable to all kinds of descriptions and imputations. Perhaps the object is not as purely objective as Baudrillard thinks it to be, and we may thus entertain the suspicion that the object may well be the most subtle theoretical trick yet employed by the subject, the most realistic simulation currently available and one that would offer an avant-garde edge to a theorist in the highly competitive Parisian academic scene. Douglas Kellner, for example, has described Baudrillard in such terms, calling him a double agent who, while championing the object, is really in fact speaking for the subject:

[A]lthough Baudrillard wants to present himself as the voice and advocate of the object, he is really a double agent, secretly representing the subject as he anthropomorphizes the object world in an amazing creative display that out-Disneys Disney. For it is clear that, ultimately, he is projecting the categories of subjectivity, as well as his own subjective imagination, into the domain of objects (ascribing to them as objective features his subjective projections such as revenge, indifference and so on), thus secretly continuing in a different form the very philosophy of subjectivity that he pretends to combat. (180–1)

In the end, then, despite Baudrillard's valorization of the object, it is the subject that continues to run the theoretical show. Baudrillard's theory of the fatal object turns out to be a covert theory of the subject's fetishistic approach to the object in the same way that his critique of ethnology's simulation of the primitive merely reintroduces the primitive as a pure object simulated by the theorist's own subjective imagination.

Though in the past he declared, *contra* Baudrillard, that 'there are no primitive societies' (*Libidinal Economy* 106), Jean-François Lyotard appears to have shifted his position in recent years. He now opposes the self-legitimating narrative pragmatics of a 'savage' society such as that of the Cashinahua to the grand universalizing narratives of Western modernity ('Missive' 31).[3] Criticizing Baudrillard's appropriation of the primitive Other as a critical alternative to the West, Lyotard seems to have succumbed to the same temptation. Lyotard's interrogation of the universal history of the modern West is built on the Western theorist's desire for an external, utopian space – a non-universal, particular, localized, self-enclosed, and unchanging primitive society. Put another way, what Lyotard describes as postmodern incredulity towards master narratives arises from the credulity shown towards premodern narrative pragmatics.

Whenever Lyotard needs a counter-example to challenge the Western idea of a universal history of humanity he turns to the Cashinahua, specifically to the pragmatics or mode of transmission of their cultural narratives as described by André-Marcel d'Ans in his ethnographic introduction to a collection of Cashinahua traditional tales entitled *Le Dit des vrais hommes* (published in 1978, a year before Lyotard's *The Postmodern Condition* appeared). With a population numbering between 850 and 1200 (Wearne 212), the Cashinahua are a small South American Indian tribe who live on the Peruvian-Brazilian border. But though their numbers are small, they play a large and important role in Lyotard's argument against the idea of a universal history. What especially interests him about the Cashinahua is the way in which they reproduce their cultural history through narratives which not only name the Cashinahua world but are validated by Cashinahua proper names. Citing André-Marcel d'Ans, Lyotard provides the following description of the onomastic authorization of narrative practice in Cashinahua society:

> Among the Cashinahua, every interpretation of a *miyoi* (myth, tale, legend
> or traditional narrative) opens with a fixed formula: 'Here is the story of ...
> as I have always heard it told. It is now my turn to tell it to you. Listen!' And
> the recitation invariably closes with another formula which goes: 'Here
> ends the story of ... He who told it to you is ... (Cashinahua name), known
> to the whites as ... (Spanish or Portuguese name).' ('Missive' 31–2; also see
> *The Differend* 152, *The Postmodern Condition* 20, and *Just Gaming* 32)

Cashinahua culture, in Lyotard's view, employs a ritual of 'strict denom-
inations' to fasten narratives to a world of Cashinahua names, a world in
which the narrative's referent, addressee, and addressor 'are all meticu-
lously named' ('Missive' 32). Generating a self-enclosed universe around
Cashinahua names, these narratives procure 'an identity that is solely
"Cashinahua"' (*The Differend* 155). 'By inserting the names into stories,'
Lyotard explains, 'narration shelters the rigid designations of common
identity from the events of the "now". ... In repeating [the narratives] the
community assures itself of the permanence and legitimacy of its world
of names by way of the recurrence of this world in its stories' (153).
Cashinahua narratives are thus tautological in so far as the narrator gains
the authority to tell his stories from his name, which is, in turn, authorized
by the stories. We are presented, therefore, with discursive procedures
that result in what Lyotard, using an English phrase, calls 'a very large
scale integrated culture' ('Missive' 33). Identification reigns supreme in
Cashinahua culture and all unassimilable events are pushed aside or
excommunicated. Self-legitimizing and self-enclosed, Cashinahua narratives construct 'an infrangible *we*, outside of which there is only *they*' (33).
As such, Cashinahua narratives are 'absolutely opposed to the organization of the grand narratives of legitimation that characterized modernity
in the West' (33). Cashinahua narratives are ethnocentric, unlike those of
the West, which Lyotard, following Kant, calls cosmopolitical in so far as
they 'involve precisely an "overcoming" [*dépassement*] of the particular
cultural identity in favour of a universal civic identity' (33–4).

To Lyotard the cosmopolitical West overcomes ethnocentric particulars in order, however, to establish a universal history which is the West's
own ethnocentrism writ large. In his view, the *petites histoires* or 'little
stories' of primitive others like the Cashinahua are swallowed up by the
single Western story of History:

> The little stories received and bestowed names. The great story of history
> has its end in the extinction of names (particularisms). At the end, of the

great story, there will simply be humanity. The names humanity has taken will turn out to be superfluous. (*The Differend* 155)

The importance of Cashinahua narrative organization with its insistence on local particularity thus becomes clear in Lyotard's work: Cashinahua narrative resists universal history by calling attention to 'the multiplicity of worlds of names, the insurmountable diversity of cultures' ('Missive' 30–1). As the Other of Western universality, Cashinahua culture reminds us that 'traditions are mutually opaque' and that 'the universalization of narrative instances cannot be done without conflict' (*The Differend* 157). The Cashinahua, therefore, pose an instance of the differend (*différend*) to the Western idea of universal history. Lyotard defines a differend as 'a case of conflict, between (at least) two parties, that cannot be equitably resolved for lack of a rule of judgement applicable to both arguments. ... [A]pplying a single rule of judgement to both in order to settle their differend as though it were merely litigation would wrong (at least) one of them' (xi). And yet applying a single rule is exactly what the West does by attempting to assimilate Cashinahua difference to a universal history of humanity. For to see Cashinahua narrative as part of a universal history is to see it not in its own light but from an already preestablished teleological perspective. In Lyotard's words, 'having assumed a universal history, the humanist inscribes the particular community into it as a moment in the universal becoming of human communities' ('Missive' 34). As a result, the Cashinahua are done an injustice; the differend between 'savage' particularity and Western universality is either ignored or suppressed.

To observe the differend and to do justice to the Cashinahua will demand a complete epistemological break between Cashinahua culture and that of the West, a rupture not unlike that described by Baudrillard between primitive and modern society. To be sure, Lyotard admits that historical or anthropological attempts at understanding primitive cultures occur all the time. However, such cognitive genres of discourse are ultimately incommensurable with the narrative genre of primitive cultures. As Lyotard puts it:

> The heterogeneity between the cognitive genre and its referent, the 'savage' narrative genre, is not to be doubted. ... There is an abyss between them. The savage thus suffers a wrong on account of the fact that he or she is 'cognized' in this manner, that is, judged, both he or she and his or her norms, according to criteria and in an idiom which are neither those which

he or she obeys nor their 'result.' What is at stake in savage narratives is not what is at stake in the description of those narratives. (*The Differend* 156)

Lyotard's insistence on incommensurability, on the 'abyss' between cognitive descriptions of 'savage' narratives and the narratives themselves, leads, however, to a contradiction in his work. In his book on Lyotard, Bill Readings points out that Lyotard was concerned to show that we cannot derive a prescriptive judgment which refers to an indeterminate idea of justice from a descriptive statement which refers to a determinate object of cognition (108). Political injustice occurs when this incommensurability or differend is ignored and the attempt is made 'to establish the justice of a prescriptive phrase by reference to a representable order of things (a descriptive statement)' (110). We will recall that Lyotard refers to the Cashinahua in order to establish a differend between their culture and the Western idea of a universal history. But such an incommensurable differend is made possible only through Lyotard's recourse to an ethnographic description of the Cashinahua provided in André-Marcel d'Ans's book. Lyotard is thus faced with a debilitating contradiction. To uphold the justice of his case against Western universality he has to commit the injustice of using descriptive statements about Cashinahua culture to support a prescriptive critique. But if he wishes to save the Cashinahua's differend by not subjecting them to a descriptive or cognitive genre of discourse, then he loses the use of an important counter-example in his criticism of the idea of universal history. In pursuing justice for the Cashinahua by observing their differend from the West, Lyotard commits an injustice against them by re-cognizing and describing their differend. As Allen Dunn has astutely remarked of this contradiction in Lyotard's thought, 'the terms in which the differend is described revive the very cognitive systems that the differend protests' (197).

There is a further problem with Lyotard's reference to the Cashinahua. His defence and valorization of premodern particularity and the non-assimilability of difference can lead to an ironic transformation of the particular and the different into an undifferentiated cultural totality or uniformity. Opposed to the West's cosmopolitical narrative of a universal humanity, Cashinahua narratives are described as local, ethnocentric narratives of identity that result in a 'large scale integrated culture' ('Missive' 33). But such a description is beholden to a notion of culture that is far too totalizing.[4] Cashinahua narrative practices are assumed to be evenly distributed and uniformly present throughout Cashinahua society and, consequently, Lyotard does not attend to the

differences and tensions that he elsewhere scrupulously pays attention
to in his work. A brief parenthetical mention in *The Differend* and 'Missive on Universal History' that only Cashinahua men are allowed to narrate bears out Seyla Benhabib's point that Lyotard's 'characterization of
narrative knowledge as prereflexive, as a self-sustaining whole, flattens
the internal contradictions and tensions which affect narrative no less
than [modern] discursive practices' (119). One of the tensions that is
flattened by Lyotard's view of integrated primitive cultures is that of gender difference. In a recent study, the anthropologist Janet M. Chernela
has argued that when attention is paid to the 'unofficial,' alternative
narrative practices of women among Brazilian Indian tribes, we discover
'a wealth of intrasocietal diversity' that lays to rest the misconception
that 'small-scale societies are ... homogenous rather than diversified'
(73). In defending the integrity and particularity of the Cashinahua
against Western universality, Lyotard ends up ignoring gender differences and downplaying the diversity of Cashinahua society. As John
McGowan remarks, 'Lyotard's affirmation of Cashinahua cultural identity indicates that a holistic goal of communal integration conflicts in his
thought with his more usual championing of pluralistic particularism'
(190).

Moreover, in emphasizing the tautological and self-sustaining character of Cashinahua culture, Lyotard finds himself representing the
Cashinahua as a people without history, their mode of cultural and
narrative transmission untouched by change or outside influence.[5] Such
a primitivistic characterization is problematic not only because it
equates Cashinahua authenticity with ahistoricity, thereby effectively
writing off their capacity for cultural innovation and change, but also
because it ignores the telling presence of colonial history in Cashinahua
society as evidenced by the Spanish or Portuguese names the narrators
take on in addition to their own Cashinahua names. In *Just Gaming*, Lyotard tells us that 'the proper name, the Cashinahua one, is an esoteric
one that allows the localization of the speaker in an extremely exact ...
network of kinship relations' (32). Similarly, in *The Differend*, he tells us
that through the insertion of names into their stories, the Cashinahua
shelter 'the rigid designators of common identity from the events of
the "now"' (153). What Lyotard forgets to discuss, however, is that the
Cashinahua narrators not only acknowledge the adoption of foreign
names, but also do not call themselves 'Cashinahua' in their own language; it is an exoteric appellation conferred on them from the outside
world. André-Marcel d'Ans, in the introduction to his collection of

Cashinahua tales, tells us that the Cashinahua call themselves in their own language *Honikoin*, or *les vrais hommes* (true men). How, then, did they end up with the name 'Cashinahua'? D'Ans says that it was the name by which they were called when contact was first made with the Whites. In the Panoan language family, 'Cashinahua' means *la gent chauve-souris* or 'the bat people.' D'Ans is not certain, however, how they got the name. He says they didn't get it from a neighbouring tribe, the Yaminahua, who call them *Saidawa* or 'the people who cry.' All d'Ans can be sure of is that the name 'Cashinahua' is a foreign term externally conferred on them: 'Il s'agit certes d'une appellation "de l'exterieur"' (13). The proper names which are supposed to act, according to Lyotard, as an affirmation of Cashinahua identity and shelter it from external events turn out to be more historically and culturally compromised in d'Ans's ethnographic account.

'Every man,' Clifford Geertz once wrote, 'has a right to create his own savage for his own purposes. Perhaps every man does. But to demonstrate that such a constructed savage corresponds to Australian Aborigines, African Tribesmen, or Brazilian Indians is another matter altogether' (347). Geertz's attempt to separate the people from the construction that seeks to represent them reveals his desire to rescue the ethnographic subject from theory's idealism. In the work of Baudrillard and Lyotard, however, what ultimately matters is not the actual existence of primitives but their *discursive* presence, their function as theoretical place-holders, as abstract differend in a conflict with Western universalism. Baudrillard's and Lyotard's description of the premodern condition is thus also a prescription for a primitive Otherness as necessary condition or pre-condition for interrogating the Western present. Their work reveals a postmodern primitivism in which, contrary to Geertz's project, theory comes before ethnography. As such, their primitives are, to borrow a phrase from Baudrillard, nothing but hyperreal effects or simulacra. The primitives merely represent, to use Mark Poster's felicitous phrase, an 'empty alterity' (578) and are made to fit what Michel-Rolph Trouillot has called 'the savage slot,' a pre-figured category awaiting occupation. As we have seen, to both Baudrillard and Lyotard ethnographic details remain secondary to the theoretical role played by 'the savage slot' in which, to quote Trouillot, 'the savage is only evidence within a debate the importance of which surpasses not only his understanding but his very existence' (33). Arguing for an ethics of the Other, both Baudrillard and Lyotard rush to defend the singularity and incommensurability of the 'savage' from Western theoretical

7

appropriation. But their valorization of the radical singularity of alterity ends up silencing the Other once more. For, as Rodolphe Gasché has astutely pointed out, an absolute, incommensurable singularity cannot exist for us because it would be completely unintelligible:

> [S]ingularity, by refusing all translation and interpretation, becomes opaque, silent, or immediate in a non-dialectical sense. It becomes quite simply thoroughly unintelligible. Such a singular would be a failure in its own terms. No longer identifiable, it could not be recognized, let alone repeated as singular. (14)

Baudrillard's and Lyotard's sharp criticism of Western primitivism's universalizing and colonizing aim comes to depend, as we have seen, on a reconceptualization and reinscription of the primitive as culturally and cognitively incommensurable and, hence, opposed to any assimilation or appropriation by the West. Their work can thus be regarded as a form of neo-primitivism, an anti-primitivist primitivism. As such, their project, for all its ostensible avant-gardism, rejoins that venerable European tradition, since Montaigne at least, that has imagined and relied on a valorized Other in its internal quarrel with its own culture. What Michel de Certeau has said about Montaigne's effort applies to Baudrillard and Lyotard as well: 'The finest gold tradition has to offer is used to forge a halo for the cannibals' (76). Using the finest theoretical tools Western thought has to offer, Baudrillard and Lyotard likewise forge a halo for their primitives. But, as in all efforts at hagiography, it is the hagiographer who shows the most initiative and agency. The so-called cannibal or primitive may be given a halo, but the real distinction belongs to the person who forges it. What is not asked is what the primitive thinks of the halo placed on him. But he is not asked because while his discursive or theoretical presence is needed his active response is not. He is, after all, only a hyperreal effect, only present, like Baudrillard's Tasaday, to guarantee the continued vitality of Western theory.[6]

NOTES

1 Throughout my paper, the word 'primitive' refers to a discursive concept rather than to an existing people or way of life. I will therefore dispense with the use of scare quotes around the word.
2 Baudrillard's date for the cordoning off of the Tasaday is incorrect. Ferdi-

nand Marcos, then president of the Philippines, issued a presidential decree in 1972 (not 1971) that made 'the Tasaday territory a reservation on which no one could enter without prior permission' (Dumont 263). What Baudrillard didn't know, in the late 1970s or early 1980s when he wrote about the Tasaday as an example of a primitive tribe turned into a simulated ethnological example, was that the Tasaday were not as pristinely neolithic as the ethnologists had thought. They are officially 'discovered' in 1971 by Panamin, the Philippine bureau of ethnic minority protection, but the Tasaday's genuineness as an untouched 'stone age' tribe was questioned in 1986 by a Swiss journalist, Oswald Iten. In an article published in a Zurich newspaper in April 1986, Iten claimed that the Tasaday were a hoax. Jean-Paul Dumont summarizes Iten's arguments thus: 'Someone – not to say Elizalde [Manuel Elizalde Jr, then director of Panamin and close friend of Marcos] – had forced them [the Tasaday], by resorting in a grand way to false promises, to pose, half-naked, clustered at the entrance to a cave in which they had never lived but which had been for them a holy place where they had regularly brought offerings' (Dumont 263). The controversy that followed the publication of Iten's article pitted anthropologists against each other; some continued to believe that the Tasaday were a genuine primitive tribe even though they agreed that some of the earlier claims made about them were exaggerated, while others supported the hoax theory (see the Nova/Horizon BBC documentary *The Lost Tribe* for a lively account of the controversy). Whatever the complex truth of the Tasaday – whether they were *already* simulated primitives *even before* Baudrillard criticized ethnology for simulating them or whether they are indeed real primitives – what is most instructive about their rise to *National Geographic* fame and subsequent fall into suspicion and disfavour is the fascination and meaning they hold for us in the modern or postmodern world. In the words of Jean-Paul Dumont who has examined how the Tasaday have functioned as an ethnographic sign in a contested political and historico-cultural field, 'it is the extrinsic importance of the Tasaday, that is to say the meaning that they, in spite of themselves, have acquired for us as a sign which is what holds ... [our] interest. From this standpoint, there are no Tasaday *per se*, but only a social and symbolic relationship, and it is the only analysable reality here' (263).

3 Lyotard has reservations over the term 'savage' but nonetheless uses it 'for convenience' ('Missive' 31).

4 Lyotard advocated a totalizing notion of culture early in his career. In 1962, he wrote: 'Inhabiting all the relations of a people to the world and to itself, all of its understanding and all of its work, culture is simply existence accepted as meaningful. ... This weight of meaning in activity is present in *L'île nue*, in *Come Back, Africa*, in the tattered rags of living culture dispersed around the

Mediterranean basin and elsewhere, in black music. ... We are essentially cut off from it. In our society sign and signification, activity and culture, living and understanding, are dissociated' ('Dead Letter' 34). We find in this passage a holistic definition of culture coexisting with a longing for premodern or primitive cultures in which such cultural holism is thought to be found.

5 For a compelling critique of how some recent thinkers, including Lyotard, still use the antinomy of people with and without history, see Klein.

6 If postmodern theorists like Baudrillard and Lyotard depend on the concept of the premodern or primitive to launch their critiques of the project of modernity, then a staunch defender of that project such as Jürgen Habermas, for example, can be shown to rely equally on the premodern or primitive, though, in Habermas's case, the premodern is read as a condition rightly surpassed by modernity's narrative of a progressive rationality (for an analysis of Habermas along these lines, see Li). To demonstrate the progressive nature of modern social rationalization, Habermas contrasts it to the holistic and undifferentiated mode of mythic thought and action allegedly characteristic of primitive societies (see *Theory* 43–74 and *Philosophical Discourse* 114–15). In making this distinction between the 'closed' world of primitive myth and the 'open' world of modern rationality, Habermas relies on the work of Claude Lévi-Strauss and Maurice Godelier, the very anthropologists critiqued by Baudrillard for displaying Western ethnocentrism. The so-called modern versus postmodern debate between the theorists of Frankfurt and Paris can thus be recast as a debate over the status of the premodern or primitive, a debate between opposing versions of philosophical anthropology. It is clear that to both sides the primitive Other is a philosophical or theoretical necessity.

WORKS CITED

Baudrillard, Jean. *America*. Trans. Chris Turner. London: Verso, 1988.

– *The Ecstasy of Communication*. Ed. Sylvère Lotringer. Trans. Bernard and Caroline Schutze. New York: Semiotext(e), 1988.

– *The Mirror of Production*. Trans. Mark Poster. St Louis: Telos P, 1975.

– *The Perfect Crime*. Trans. Chris Turner. London: Verso, 1996.

– *Simulations*. Trans. Paul Foss et al. New York: Semiotext(e), 1983.

– *Symbolic Exchange and Death*. Trans. Iain Hamilton Grant. London: Sage Publications, 1993.

– *The Transparency of Evil: Essays on Extreme Phenomena*. Trans. James·Benedict. London: Verso, 1993.

Benhabib, Seyla. 'Epistemologies of Postmodernism: A Rejoinder to Jean-

François Lyotard.' *Feminism/Postmodernism.* Ed. Linda J. Nicholson. New York: Routledge, 1990. 107–30.

Chernela, Janet M. 'The "Ideal Speech Moment": Women and Narrative Performance in the Brazilian Amazon.' *Feminist Studies* 23.1 (1997): 73–96.

d'Ans, André-Marcel. *Le Dit des vrais hommes: Myths, contes, legendes et traditions des indiens cashinahua.* Paris: Union Generale D'Editions, 1978.

de Certeau, Michel. *Heterologies: Discourse on the Other.* Trans. Brian Massumi. Minneapolis: U of Minnesota P, 1986.

Dumont, Jean-Paul. 'The Tasaday, Which and Whose?: Toward the Political Economy of an Ethnographic Sign.' *Cultural Anthropology* 3.3 (1988): 261–75.

Dunn, Allen. 'A Tyranny of Justice: The Ethics of Lyotard's Differend.' *boundary 2* 20.1 (1993): 192–220.

Gane, Mike. *Baudrillard: Critical and Fatal Theory.* London: Routledge, 1991.

Gasché, Rodolphe. *Inventions of Difference: On Jacques Derrida.* Cambridge: Harvard UP, 1994.

Geertz, Clifford. 'The Cerebral Savage: On the Work of Claude Lévi-Strauss.' *The Interpretation of Cultures: Selected Essays.* New York: Basic Books, 1973. 345–59.

Genosko, Gary. *Baudrillard and Signs: Signification Ablaze.* London: Routledge, 1994.

Habermas, Jürgen. *The Philosophical Discourse of Modernity.* Trans. Frederick Lawrence. Cambridge: MIT P, 1987.

– *The Theory of Communicative Action: Reason and the Rationalization of Society.* Vol. 1. Trans. Thomas McCarthy. Boston: Beacon P, 1984.

Hefner, Robert. 'Baudrillard's Noble Anthropology: The Image of Symbolic Exchange in Political Economy.' *Sub-Stance* 17 (1977): 105–13.

Kellner, Douglas. *Jean Baudrillard: From Marxism to Postmodernism and Beyond.* Cambridge: Polity P, 1989.

Klein, Kerwin Lee. 'In Search of Narrative Mastery: Postmodernism and the People without History.' *History and Theory* 34.4 (1995): 275–98.

Levin, Charles. *Jean Baudrillard: A Study in Cultural Metaphysics.* Hemel Hempstead: Prentice Hall, 1996.

Lévi-Strauss, Claude. *Tristes Tropiques.* Trans. John and Doreen Weightman. Harmondsworth: Penguin, 1976.

Li, Victor. 'Habermas and the Ethnocentric Discourse of Modernity.' *Constructive Criticism: The Human Sciences in the Age of Theory.* Ed. Martin Kreiswirth and Thomas Carmichael. Toronto: U of Toronto P, 1995.

The Lost Tribe. Narrator Dan Wescott. Writer Bettina Lerner. Nova/Horizon BBC, 1989.

Lyotard, Jean-François. 'Dead Letter.' *Political Writings*. Trans. Bill Readings and Kevin Paul. Minneapolis: U of Minnesota P, 1993. 33–40.

- *The Differend: Phrases in Dispute*. Trans. Georges Van Den Abbeele. Minneapolis: U of Minnesota P, 1988.
- 'An Interview with Jean-François Lyotard.' Conducted by Willem van Reijen and Dick Veerman. *Theory, Culture and Society* 5.2–3 (1988): 277–309.
- *Libidinal Economy*. Trans. Iain Hamilton Grant. Bloomington: Indiana UP, 1993.
- 'Missive on Universal History.' *The Postmodern Explained: Correspondence 1982– 1985*. Ed. Julian Pefanis and Morgan Thomas. Trans. Don Barry et al. Minneapolis: U of Minnesota P, 1992. 23–37.
- *The Postmodern Condition: A Report on Knowledge*. Trans. Geoff Bennington and Brian Massumi. Minneapolis: U of Minnesota P, 1984.

Lyotard, Jean-François, and Jean-Loup Thebaud. *Just Gaming*. Trans. Wlad Godzich. Minneapolis: U of Minnesota P, 1985.

Masuzawa, Tomoko. *In Search of Dreamtime: The Quest for the Origin of Religion*. Chicago: U of Chicago P, 1993.

McGowan, John. *Postmodernism and Its Critics*. Ithaca: Cornell UP 1991.

Pefanis, Julian. *Heterology and the Postmodern: Bataille, Baudrillard, and Lyotard*. Durham: Duke UP, 1991.

Poster, Mark. 'Postmodernity and the Politics of Multiculturalism: The Lyotard-Habermas Debate over Social Theory.' *Modern Fiction Studies* 38.3 (1992): 567–80.

Readings, Bill. *Introducing Lyotard: Art and Politics*. London: Routledge, 1991.

Trouillot, Michel-Rolph. 'Anthropology and the Savage Slot: The Poetics and Politics of Otherness.' *Recapturing Anthropology: Working in the Present*. Ed. Richard G. Fox. Santa Fe: School of American Research Press, 1991. 17–44.

Wearne, Phillip. *Return of the Indian: Conquest and Revival in the Americas*. London: Cassell, 1996.

The Sublime between History and Theory: Hegel, de Man, and Beyond

IAN BALFOUR

It is something of a scandal for 'theory' if it has a history in the first place. For is it not usually the claim of theory to be concerned with general, even universal matters or, a little more precisely, for its claims to be of a general or universal character? Is that not what separates theory from mere observation or judgment, even if one can always trace 'theory' back to its etymological roots in the Greek *theorein* – to see or observe? If theory is of its desired generality or universality, that would seem to imply that theory is more or less impervious to the vicissitudes of history, the constancy of change and the instability of non-identity. And so a history of theory should be something of a contradiction in terms.

Yet the claim to universality never of itself guarantees just that. And one could argue that history constantly teaches us over and over again how historical 'theory' is, how time-bound and ideologically determined are the claims of that which is, in principle, not (necessarily) time-bound. Theory seems to come, despite itself, complete with a history and histories. All of which is complicated by the fact that, as Derrida noted some years ago in an essay on 'The States of Theory,' the term 'theory' itself has in the past few decades functioned in an entirely new way, unprecedented in the history of 'theory.'[1] Which is to say that the very term 'theory' is itself historically variable, such that there is no perfect coherence or constancy to all that has even plausibly been included under that word. Few propositions of what is these days called 'theory' have the status of a putatively timeless truth, like some quasi-geometric axiom in Spinoza, much less something on the model of the Pythagorean theorem or a chemical equation. In many instances, 'theory' now understands itself to be historical, through and through.

It is easy to see how Paul de Man is a theorist who comes complete with a history. And for a number of reasons it seems even more pressing in his case than in most to figure out the relations between – perhaps the mutual imbrication of – history and theory. When the scandal emerged concerning de Man's collaborationist writings as a young man in occupied Belgium, it occurred to numerous observers that the later insistence on theory in this foremost proponent of deconstruction in literary criticism was itself the product of a need to deny 'history,' a need to deny history in general in order to repress a certain history of his own. This line of argument is not without its merit: one wonders, for example, how and why de Man can generalize about the futility of historical action based on a reading of episodes from Wordsworth's *Prelude*?[2] The conclusion seems to exceed by far the text that prompts the idea – and not fortuitously. There may have well have been powerful psycho-biographical factors at work in de Man's sometime 'resistance to history.' But the relative inattention to what usually counts as history is not at all constant in de Man's career. And indeed in the last phase of his work, broken off by his death, the historical force of theory became an explicit and intense preoccupation. Moreover, I will argue that in his work theory is rendered historical in so far as de Man sets theoretical texts in motion, which may turn out to be a more truly historical procedure and potentially even a more just one than historicism's tendency to consign history irrevocably to the past.[3]

'Aesthetic Ideology' is the rubric under which de Man's late work was organized and posthumously published. In these related essays de Man tried to mobilize the potential of rhetorical or at least language-based analysis for a critique of some of the most cherished and time-honoured notions of Western thinking about art and the aesthetic, especially those concerning the supposedly unassailable value of the aesthetic. A number of the essays in the volume crystallizing that work are devoted to the sublime, a topic of high theory if there ever was one. That the past few decades have seen a revival of interest in the sublime as a theoretical topic is itself an index of the historicity of theory, even if theory cannot be reduced simply to a merely historical phenomenon. (Nor can the emergence and disappearance of topics simply be ascribed to a 'logic' of theoretical inquiry.) But the sublime offers a particularly charged instance of what can be at stake in a history of theory – in de Man, in Hegel, and beyond.

One might think that the sublime would, in principle, be subject to the forces of time, for is it not, like the beautiful, a formal affair that could be manifest at any given moment in history? If the sublime is constituted, as Schelling, for example, says in his general definition, 'whenever we encounter the infinite being taken up in the finite' (*Philosophy of Art* 85), then it would seem impossible to limit the sublime's appearance to this or that moment in history. And yet we know that the word and the concept of the sublime are by no means constant throughout history. To judge from the aesthetic examples proffered by its theorists, the sublime does not 'occur' at just any time. It has its exits and its entrances, its moments of dormancy, its vogues, even. Ernst Robert Curtius lambasted his otherwise beloved medieval intellectuals for allowing Longinus's ancient manuscript to languish in a Paris library until the sixteenth century.[4] Only with Boileau's translation and commentary did Longinus experience a real revival, whose efficacy would last well into the nineteenth century. With respect to the thinking of the sublime, things reached a point at the turn from the eighteenth century to the nineteenth when just about everyone who was anyone had to have something to say on the subject.

But why such a pronounced return to – and perhaps of – the sublime in the work of de Man and so many of his theoretically minded contemporaries: Lyotard, Nancy, Lacoue-Labarthe, Hertz, Ferguson, and Derrida, to name only some of the most prominent figures? The general answer is, I believe, relatively simple. Given the thoroughgoing critique of representation that began, say, with Nietzsche and/or Wittgenstein, continued with J.L. Austin, and then intensified in French structuralist and especially poststructuralist thought, it is no accident that there would be a concomitant return to thinking about the sublime in its heyday of the late eighteenth and early nineteenth centuries. Beyond the general indebtedness of recent French thought to German Idealist philosophy – which is massive – there is a specific debt to the theorization of the sublime, for it was there that Western philosophy, prior to the twentieth century, most resolutely probed the limits of representation. At the time the preoccupation was with a certain kind of aesthetic experience (aesthetic in the broad sense, not limited just to art, in which Kant, for one, demonstrates not a whole lot of interest) that could not be encompassed by the traditional discourses on beauty. One question posed by the return of the sublime in recent theory is whether or not there has been an excessive generalization of the circumscribed discourse of the sublime – itself the theory of a certain excess – into a critique of representation *tout court.* Has the discourse of the unbounded come itself to be unbounded and lost the specificity of its character and its power?

In his return to the sublime, de Man focused on Kant and Hegel, the latter being in this regard an unusually non-canonical figure. Though deconstruction is often popularly represented as if it were hell-bent on destroying and discrediting the illustrious texts of the past in its path, de Man's tendency in his essays on Kant and Hegel is to read back through a thicket of established mis-readings of those philosophers to get a core of theoretical insight more or less consonant with his own positions.[5] His project is, at least in part, one of rehabilitation. Thus de Man called an early essay in this project 'Kant's Materialism,' employing an unexpected rubric under which to consider the putative father of German Idealism.[6] But it is not necessarily the case that what is recovered here is the true 'intention' of Kant or Hegel: de Man's reading aims not only at interpreting the overt statements of the texts in question but also at what is produced through the mutual implication of statement and performance, which are sometimes decidedly at odds with each other. (As it happens, both Kant and Hegel, in de Man's reading, are construed as arguing for a certain materiality of the aesthetic and of the word, a non- or anti-metaphysical remainder at the centre of what is thought to be the high metaphysics of German Idealism.) Sometimes de Man presents his project as simply asking after what the text 'says,' but this is a little misleading, since de Man's allegorical mode of reading tends to produce something other than what the text manifestly says. And in establishing what the text (allegorically) says – which is easier said than done – the text becomes, via reading, an event all over again. Reading theory, in de Man's hands, renders the text historical, even provocative, in and for the present. To say nothing of the future.

In the history of theory, Hegel is not just one figure among others. It is arguably Hegel who invented the history of theory in the first place, for his thought attempted to do justice simultaneously to the twin demands of theory and history. His philosophy, in its totalizing reach, not only claimed to include all of what counted for him as history (with some predictable blind spots: Africa, notoriously, was virtually deemed a continent without a history), he wanted at the same time to think the story of history, to make sense of it. History, for Hegel, made and makes sense – and not just in a way that could be easily subsumed under traditional Christian notions of providence.[7]

In all the topics of study – aesthetics, philosophy, history, religion – to which he devoted elaborate lecture courses, Hegel narrates the dialectical movement of his subject. In particular, the *Lectures on the History of*

Philosophy might stand as the first shining example of what now is being called the 'history of theory.'[8] More directly than in most of Hegel's narratives, there he charts the transformation of 'the idea' as it is manifest in the writings and saying of philosophers from ancient Greece to his present. As he traces the continuous and discontinuous trajectory of the idea, Hegel addresses large and small matters of translation: how does one pass, for example, from Greece to Rome in philosophical terms? What happens in the transition? Something of what is at stake here for Hegel will become all the more important for Heidegger as he tracks the history of being and the history of philosophy, with its moments of lucidity and oblivion. (Heidegger, even more than Hegel, will call attention to the immense consequences of what happens, say, in the apparently innocuous translation of a Greek term into the Latin.) Hegel's great innovation was to incorporate, so to speak, history for theory, to break down the false dichotomy between being and becoming – at once the basis for and the call to the dialectical method. Whereas the Platonic and Platonizing traditions consigned appearance to the realm of pseudo-being, Hegel would counter, in his *Aesthetics*, by proclaiming that 'appearance was essential to essence,' that 'truth would not be truth if did not appear' (I:8), a dictum fully consistent with his thinking outside the realm of aesthetics.[9] That Hegel finds appearance essential to essence means that the aesthetic in the broad sense makes its (implicit) mark everywhere in the Hegelian system. It is related to de Man's claim at the outset of 'Hegel and the Sublime' that representation is an inexorable link, as both Kant and Hegel variously demonstrate, between pure and practical reason, between knowledge and action, between theory and politics.

The famously pliant and strategically ambiguous notion of *Aufhebung* (which can mean negated, cancelled, and/or raised to a higher level) allows in Hegel's dialectic for every moment (or some aspect of the moment) of the past to be taken up into its succeeding present, even if there are marked historical differences between one moment and the next.[10] (This entails the 'momentum' of the moment, to invoke one of the senses Hegel gives to that word.) There is no doubt that in the movement of historical *Aufhebung* some aspects are emphasized more than others. Not all moments of the past are, for Hegel, equally things of the past. The most striking thing about Hegel's discussion of the sublime, in these terms, is his categorical and atypical circumscribing of that 'aesthetic' mode to a past that is radically past. There is little prospect for a return of Hegel's sublime.

In general each subject treated by Hegel is viewed historically, with a view to its origin or at least starting point, and its development, even if the narrative produced is a contradictory one. And given the features of Hegel's dialectic, the narrative does tend to be contradictory (though this is in itself neither a conceptual nor a rhetorical problem for the Hegelian system) in its labourious, spiralling path towards absolute knowledge. Yet Hegel is far from simply imposing an abstract developmental schema on every given subject matter, certainly not of the order of the infamous 'thesis-antithesis-synthesis' scheme, something which finds almost no literal foundation throughout his entire *œuvre*. Whereas it is true that Hegelian narratives tend to bear a family resemblance – there are moments when one can almost predict what Hegel is going to say – Hegel is always concerned, at least in principle, to tell things as they were. As he says laconically in his *Lectures on the Philosophy of History*: 'We must proceed empirically' – a position not all that far from Marx's recurrent appeal to the 'stubborn facts' of history. That Hegel's narratives do often take the form of some version of the Gospel narrative may well cast suspicion on the empirical accuracy of these stories, but from the point of view of the system, a certain resemblance could be construed as precisely what stands to reason. History is, after all, the unfolding of reason, however cunning its forms. One of Hegel's earliest literary-philosophical projects was a *Life of Jesus*, a synthetic narrative which formed a single story out of materials from the four Gospels, the three synoptic accounts of Matthew, Mark, and Luke, and the rather different and more philosophical Gospel of John. This most fundamental narrative for Hegel came to be a model for any number of stories he would tell, with the death of Christ being the paradigm of negation and the resurrection being that of that distinctly Hegelian category, the negation of the negation. That the term 'negation' in the first instance is for Hegel, as for Spinoza, a logical category points to the omnipresence of logic as a determinant in Hegelian narrative: history, once again, is the unfolding of a logic, the elaboration of the Logos over time.[11] This applies as much to the realm of the aesthetic as any other. One might think that the 'fine arts' would not be subject to history in quite the same way as some other topics. Many Enlightenment thinkers, moreover, had argued for a more or less linear story of progress for history in general, not unlike the evolving story of freedom Hegel would tell in his *Lectures on the Philosophy of History*. But a good many Enlightenment and Romantic thinkers had debated the question of the 'progress of the arts' and decided no such linear narrative was applicable. Was there any 'progress' in the epic from Homer onward, or in tragedy beyond the era of Sophocles? Not necessarily. The 'quarrel of the ancient and moderns' – one prominent terrain in this debate – was not exactly settled unequivocally one way or the other, certainly not unanimously in favour of the modern, as is gainsaid, for example, in Winckelmann's championing of ancient Greek culture.

Even a cursory glance at the place of the sublime in the grand scheme of his history and systematic analysis of art suggests that Hegel has relegated this aesthetic mode to a decidedly minor status. Whereas Kant had devoted a long and ungainly section of his *Critique of Judgement* to the analytic of the sublime – far in excess of the analytic of the beautiful – Hegel allots only a scant number of pages to the sublime in his elephantine lectures on aesthetics. So it may seem an inauspicious quarry compared to the rich gold mine of Kant's third Critique. But I would suggest that the short shrift given the sublime is actually an index of how much is at stake for Hegel in encountering the aesthetic mode that had come increasingly to be considered the opposite – the *Gegensatz*, as Schelling termed it – of the beautiful.

Unlike most of his immediate and near contemporaries, Hegel opted out (somewhat) of the widespread tendency to divide the field of the aesthetic in two – ancient and modern (Friedrich Schlegel et al.) or naïve and sentimental (Schiller). He decided instead on a tripartite scheme of the symbolic, the classical, and the romantic (this last being very different from the current sense of the term, since it includes all Christian and modern art, from Dante and Shakespeare to what was Hegel's present). Like the ancient/modern polarity, Hegel's too is a historical schema: not just anything is possible at any given time. But it turns out that Hegel's schema is less different from the models of his contemporaries than might appear, as soon as one learns that the symbolic is not really art in the first place. This will be disconcerting to those who think so highly of the sublime, because Hegel's discussion of the sublime is wholly contained under the rubric of what he terms pre-art (*Vorkunst*). Strictly speaking, the sublime is not art, even if he can, almost in the same breath, speak of the 'art of the sublime.' (It is good to recall that Hegel specifies that the science of the aesthetic which is the subject of his lectures could just as well be called the 'philosophy of the fine arts,' where 'fine' literally reads 'beautiful' [*schön*]. By that token, there is arguably *no* place whatsoever for the sublime in Hegel's account of aesthetics.) To find out that the realm of the symbolic is not art is all the more surprising, given that the symbol, in the structural sense of the *symbolon*, is, as we shall see in a moment, the very model of all art, regardless of time or place of provenance.

When characterizing the sublime in general, Hegel not only identifies it as one mode of the symbolic, he sees the sublime as virtually built into the symbolic. Hegel says:

> [W]hen the symbol is developed independently in its own proper form, it has in general the character of sublimity, because at first, on the whole, it is only the Idea which is still measureless, and not freely determined in it-self, that is to be given shape, and therefore it cannot find in concrete appearance any specific form corresponding completely with this ab-straction and universality. ... This flight beyond the determinatedness of appearance constitutes the general character of the sublime. (I:303)

Symbolic 'art' is not art, precisely because it is characterized by the dis-junction, the incommensurability between the symbol (really a sign) and what is symbolized. For the crucial definition of art as symbol in the other sense one turns to the opening and most theoretical section of the *Aesthetics*:

> In the case of art, we cannot consider, in the symbol, the arbitrariness between meaning and signification [which characterizes the sign], since art consists precisely in the connection, the affinity and concrete inter-penetration of meaning and form [*das konkrete Ineinander von Bedeutung und Gestalt*]. (I:304)

This determination of art as symbolic, as modelled on the *symbolon*, a Greek token connoting inseparability, is consistent with the even more systematic character of the *Encyclopedia*, where Hegel distinguishes clearly between the symbol and the sign, and where he, in similar fash-ion to the relation of *Bedeutung* and *Gestalt*, sees the definitive character of art consisting in an inseparability of form and content (*Form* and *Inhalt*). Thus, returning to the *Aesthetics* proper, we are faced with the at least superficial paradox that no symbolic art is art but all art is sym-bolic, depending on which sense of 'symbol' obtains. (This is not a lapse in logic on Hegel's part, though it can create some confusion.) When discussing the 'art of the sublime' – the art which is not art – we will be dealing with the symbol in the sense of its incommensurability, the *Unangemessenheit*, between sign and referent.

In historical terms, the notion of the symbolic is tied to a certain Orientalist version of world history and culture, whereby history follows a solar trajectory from its 'dawn' in the ancient East to its 'evening' in the modern West, having reached something like its zenith, momentarily, in ancient Greece. Thus the earliest form of sublime art – which is not art – is Eastern, Indian, and Islamic, or what Hegel calls Mohammedan. Though Hegel allows one modern, Christian example of sublimity, namely the mystical poetry of Angelus Silesius, it hardly seems to count for much, for when he comes to define the sublime in the strict sense (*im eigentlichen Sinn*), it is to be found, especially given the examples he offers, only in ancient Hebraic poetry.

De Man notes the commonplace association of sublimity and biblical poetry in the eighteenth century, a notion still proverbial for Coleridge, Wordsworth, and any number of the Romantics. So Hegel's thinking the two together should come as no surprise. But what is striking – and problematic – is that Hegel can pretend to circumscribe, to limit the art of the sublime, in its proper sense, to one mode in one period of one culture.[12] Peter Szondi can even speak of the 'historical period' proper to the sublime, and he is not simply wrong to do so (388). The problem is that it is not at all certain that one can with any justification, by such terminological fiat or historical finesse, confine the sublime in quite such a way.

Hegel's only examples of the sublime, properly so called, are drawn from the Hebrew Bible, from Genesis and the Psalms. De Man reads the collocation of Hegel's examples (the *fiat lux* and then Psalm 90 beginning 'Light is your garment') as entailing an implicit theory of language – that in a system where language is not all that often explicitly the subject matter of reflection. Moreover, in related fashion, de Man seizes on Hegel's analysis of the sublime as a crucial moment in the *Aesthetics* because it is so charged in systemic terms as one of the relatively few places in the Hegelian corpus where the 'Idea' appears (though in another sense, nothing is more ubiquitous in the entire system). The idea does indeed 'appear' or perhaps better 'occurs,' albeit in decidedly negative fashion. The passage Hegel dwells on in most detail comes from Psalm 90 where the psalmist in praising his absolute God absolutely thereby establishes the utter nullity (*Nichtigkeit*) of himself and of all the created world. Wholly unable to represent God – and this in keeping with the *Bilderverbot* or prohibition against graven images of the Decalogue – the human psalmist can only name God or signal a relation to him, neither of which constitutes a verbal version of divine presence. And the relation indicated, once again, asserts the nullity of the human.

The psalm or the psalmist says, in effect: 'I am not worthy' or, more radically, 'I am not,' period.

It is noteworthy that Hegel's examples of the sublime proper are drawn from a text that few people would call a work of art: the Bible. Not that God would be denied the capabilities of a human artist. And indeed, it was just before Hegel's time that Christian scholars were at pains to demonstrate the aesthetic greatness of the Hebrew Bible, most notably in Robert Lowth's *Lectures on the Sacred Poetry of the Hebrews*, which were well known in Germany through Michaelis's annotations and their publication in Göttingen. Even so, it is striking that Hegel goes so far in identifying the sacred and the sublime: 'If there symbolic art in general may already be called *sacred* art because it adopts the Divine as the content of its productions, the art of sublimity is *the* sacred art as such which can be called exclusively sacred because it gives honour to God alone' (I:372–3).

What 'attracts' Hegel to the sublime is its lofty subject matter – the divine or the absolute (arguably the only proper subject, ultimately, for all art, according to some of Hegel's formulations) – and the power of language which presents, among other things, the divine language of power, for which the supreme 'example' (but it is not only an example) is the *fiat lux* of Genesis 1, the performative speech act to begin all speech acts. What 'repulses' Hegel, however, in this sublime moment is the incommensurability between language and its divine subject, the inadequacy of word to idea, even if the psalmist has the grace and humility to acknowledge his own nullity.

Ancient Hebraic poetry has, moreover, made a great advance over its ancient Indian counterpart by being monotheistic, which, in philosophical terms, means naming 'the one substance' in proper fashion. Concomitant with this, ancient Hebraic poetry is, in relation to God, *bildlos*, without image or figure – the right sort of non-figuration to accord with a God who is beyond visual representation and who will later come to be called by Christians the Logos. In this, Protestant iconoclasm coincides with the spirit animating the Judaic prohibition against images, which is in the first instance an interdiction of graven images of God, but sometimes strangely generalized into a refusal of visual representation, period. Hence, for the Bible (Hebrew, and to a lesser extent, Christian), the immense emphasis on the sublimity of the Word and of words. This comes to be crucial for a good many thinkers of the sublime, rather as Edmund Burke contends in the final section of his *A Philosophical Enquiry into the Origin of Our Ideas of the Beautiful and the Sublime*. There

Burke moves precipitously from a local analysis of a sublime passage in *Paradise Lost* to the virtual sublimity of poetry as such and of words – especially words in their syntactical arrangements – as inherently sublime.

That Hegel can seize on so much that is 'positive' in sacred Hebraic poetry might lead one to believe that the sublime would be an eminently sublatable moment. After all, Christianity's relation to Judaism in general could be understood as the primary model for all *Aufhebung*, as exemplified in Jesus's vocation of fulfilling the law, of the *pleroma*.[13] The Gospel story and its teachings mandate a relentless hermeneutic of the spiritual reading that informs Hegel's notion of *Geist*. Jesus claims he has come not to destroy the law but to fulfil it, and even to respect the letter of the law ('not one jot or tittle').

Once the dialectic of letter and spirit is set in motion, spirit too must find its 'notation' in letters of its own, and so there is no end in sight to the task of 'spiritual' interpretation. And yet as de Man comments laconically of the aftermath of the sublime moment in Hegel: 'there is nothing to lift or uplift.' Unlike virtually any moment caught up in the relentless dialectical machine of Hegelian story-telling, the sublime has no afterlife. As de Man notes before quoting Hegel:

> The sublime, it turns out, is self-destroying in a manner without precedent at any other stages of the dialectic. 'The difference between the present stage (that of the comparative art forms) and the sublime ... is that the sublime relationship is completely eliminated [*vollständig fortfällt*].' ('Hegel on the Sublime' 151)[14]

What this suggests is rather odd for most conceptions of literary and aesthetic history. This means that any number of art-works commonly considered sublime – Dante's *Divine Comedy*, Milton's *Paradise Lost*, the statues of Michelangelo, the paintings of Poussin, or, in Hegel's own day, Goethe's *Faust* – cannot be considered so in Hegel's schema. Not sublime in the proper sense. With ancient Hebraic poetry the sublime, in the strict sense, comes to its definitive end. A thing of the past.

That the sublime remains in the past is all the more surprising, given that poetry emerges as the highest of the individual art-forms. In order to appreciate how Hegel arrives at that point, it will help to rehearse how he proceeds from the aesthetics of the symbol to that of the sign in the course of his lectures. When in the *Aesthetics* Hegel describes the

symbol in general, he claims that it remains 'according to its own concept essentially *ambiguous* [*zweideutig*].' He continues:

> In the first place, the look of a symbol as such raises at once the doubt
> whether a shape is to be taken as a symbol or not, even if we set aside the
> further ambiguity in respect of the *specific* meanings which a shape is
> supposed to signify amongst the *several* meanings for which it can often be
> used as a symbol through associations of a more remote kind. (I:306)

Not only is a symbol ambiguous in its very essence, a certain degree of
ambiguity persists for the reader, viewer, or listener as to whether what
appears to be a symbol should be taken as such or not. Moreover,
Hegel's determination of how the ambiguity can be dissipated is rather
restricted: 'Such dubiety disappears only when each of the two sides [of
the symbol], the meaning and its shape, are expressly named and
thereby their relation is enunciated at once' (I:306). Explicit naming of
the relation between meaning and form marks only such genres as the
parable (discussed in the section immediately following that on the sublime) and so is hardly representative of art-works in general. Though all
art for Hegel, once again, is symbolic in the sense that it is defined by
the 'concrete interpenetration of form and meaning [*das konkrete Inein-
ander von Bedeutung und Gestalt*]' (I:304), most art is also haunted by its
aspect as sign. And no art, Hegel makes clear, stands under the sign of
the sign more than poetry. Hegel claims this, remarkably, of the status of
poetry in relation to the rest of the arts:

> Architecture cannot so subordinate the sensuous material to the spiritual
> content as to be able to form that material into an adequate shape of the
> spirit: poetry, on the other hand, goes so far in its negative treatment of its
> sensuous material that it reduces the opposite of heavy spatial matter,
> namely sound, to a meaningless sign [*bedeutungloses Zeichen*] instead of
> making it, as architecture makes its material, into a meaningful symbol
> [*andeutender Symbol*]. But poetry destroys the fusion of spiritual inwardness
> with external existence to an extent that begins to be incompatible with
> the original conception of art, with the result that poetry runs the risk of
> losing itself in a transition from the region of sense into that of the spirit.
> (II:968)

One is always taught that poetry loses something in translation. Hegel's point is more radical: poetry risks losing *itself* in transition, the transition from sense to spirit. All poetry is poetry in motion, so to speak – but not necessarily in a fortuitous way. Poetry risks no longer conforming to the 'original' conception of art, that is to say, art as symbol in the sense of entailing the 'interpenetration of meaning and form.' It is certainly not art for art's sake, but art for spirit's sake, which is to say, not art in the form of art.

We have claimed that Hegel's thinking is distinctive in trying to do justice simultaneously to the demands of history and theory, specificity and system. In the part of the *Aesthetics* devoted the 'system of the individual arts' Hegel discusses in turn the characteristics of architecture, sculpture, painting, music, and poetry. This sequence is articulated with the preceding (and overlapping) historical schema of symbolic, classical, and romantic art, so here too we have a conjunction of history and system. What is perhaps surprising is that there is in addition a more or less covert narrative articulating the individual art-forms, where is it not at all clear that one is called for. Yet Hegel inscribes a hierarchical scheme of values as the arts ascend in the sequence of his discussion: architecture to sculpture to painting to music to poetry. In this spectrum extending from the most symbolic to the most semiotic, from architecture to poetry, not all the individual art-forms are created equal. Poetry is the highest and in a sense 'last' or 'ultimate' of the art-forms in that it is, on the one hand, closest to philosophy – the translation to which art tends – and on the other hand that it tends to subvert its character as art. Poetry as an art of the word consists not so much of symbols as of signs – meaningless signs, Hegel insists. And to the extent that poetic art is of the order of the semiotic not the symbolic, it departs from the realm of art. This is a double-edged gesture, since the loss of the aesthetic in poetry is precisely what makes it something like philosophy, something which has to be and indeed can be, with only a little loss in translation, rendered into philosophy, the discourse of the logos in the form most adequate to itself.[15]

Given the lofty status ascribed to poetry, it is somewhat odd that we do not witness a return of the sublime at a higher level in the late phases of the ultimate art-form. For the sublime was already demarcated as an art of the Word, and an art which could at least name the human relation to the divine – the divine being *the* subject of religion, art, and philosophy, the 'holy' trinity of discourses of the absolute as set out at the end of the *Phenomenology of Spirit*. But there is something in the boundlessness of the Hebraic sublime, something in the utter self-negating quality of its poetry, that resists its dialectical absorption into the narrative drive towards absolute knowledge.

But if Hegel's sublime is relegated absolutely to the past, it becomes unmoored from its historical specificity in de Man's reading. A certain sublime returns, a sublime of the word as positing power and inscription. De Man's sublime resists being caught up in a Hegelian or pseudo-Hegelian narrative of history but is no less historical for that. Its power is disruptive, and of more than narrative.

But if de Man is correct, it is really Hegel's sublime that is already disruptive within the (allegorical) terms of his system. Like many of his contemporaries, Hegel had, officially, a rather dim view of allegory. As de Man shows in his essay 'On Sign and Symbol in Hegel's *Aesthetics*,' Hegel relegates allegory to one of the 'subordinate' genres, like parable and fable, and groups it also with tropes and figures of speech, mere instruments in the service of higher aesthetic purposes. Allegory is linked, systematically, with the prosaic – also it would seem a devalued term. But is allegory a force that can simply be contained by the volition of an author? Is it simply a genre in which one can choose to write or not? Any system like Hegel's, which is built on a principle of spiritual interpretation, modelled on the Christian *pleroma,* and which is attentive to and even performs dialectical reversals, will itself be subject to allegory, so to speak. All the more so since Hegel says in the section subsequent to that on the sublime and when he is analysing the 'subordinate' genres named above: 'Prose begins in the slave' (*Im Sklaven fängt die Prosa an*). What Hegel means overtly is rather prosaic: Aesop, arguably the first prose artist, was, tradition tells us, a slave. Yet de Man, rightly I think, seizes on this phrase as particularly resonant beyond its reference to Aesop. Hegel is, after all, author of the famous section of the *Phenomenology* on the master-slave dialectic of consciousness (*Herrschaft-Knechtschaft*), where the slave, or even just the bondsman (if that is a preferable translation of *Knecht*), is always potentially in a position to be, in de Man's phrase, 'politically legitimate and effective as the undoer of usurped authority' ('Hegel on the Sublime' 153). In the fight to death of consciousness between the master and the slave, the master, seemingly autonomous, comes to recognize that his status as master is dependent on the slave and thus in his non-autonomy he is in some sense slave to the slave, and the slave, in his turn, master to the master. Tacitly translating this to the scene of the *Aesthetics*, de Man contends: 'The enslaved place and condition of the section on the sublime in the *Aesthetics*, and the enslaved place of the *Aesthetics* within the corpus of Hegel's complete works, are the symptoms of their strength' ('Hegel on the Sublime' 153). That is to say, among other things, the sublime has a force that exceeds Hegel's attempt to contain it, in disruptive and critical ways. It is a 'moment' with no definitive end, a moment with an unpredictable momentum. Theory, then, becomes here – but not only here – historical through the event of reading, especially of allegorical reading. No longer tied just to one moment, it could, in theory, erupt at any moment. Nothing could be more historical.

NOTES

1 See Derrida, 'Some Statements and Truisms about Neo-Logisms, Newisms, Postisms, Parasitisms, and Other Small Seismisms.'
2 See de Man, 'Wordsworth and Hölderlin.'
3 For Walter Benjamin's attack on historicism, see his 'Theses on the Philosophy of History.' I have attempted a reading of the 'Theses' in 'Reversal, Quotation (Benjamin's History),' in *MLN*. Benjamin groups historicism with other problematic intellectual-political forces or movements, such as fascism and vulgar Marxism. Closer to our historical home, I would argue that the so-called New Historicism is caught, not fortuitously, between a putative attention to historical specificity, on the one hand, and a desire, on the other, to be responsive to the political causes of its own time. But without a theory of mediation – what does a specific phenomenon in the Renaissance have to do with our present? – New Historicism cannot quite have the both ways it desires. Thus it seems to me often less satisfactory in terms of doing justice to history than a Benjaminian or even a de Manian approach (the two only partly overlap).
4 See Ernst Robert Curtius, *European Literature and the Latin Middle Ages* 398ff.
5 As Martin Donougho wisely says on the status of de Man as a putative 'deconstuctor' of Hegel: 'With enemies like these, who needs friends?' See his essay 'Hegel's Art of Memory' 230n7.
6 Though most Marxists accuse Kant of being an arch-Idealist, Lukács, for one, claims that Kant's work sways between idealism and materialism. See his essay 'Hegel's Aesthetik' 99.
7 On the complicated relations of modern Western philosophy of history to the overarching biblical narrative, see Karl Löwith, *Meaning in History.*
8 The lectures on the history of philosophy are a neglected part of Hegel's corpus and could well repay a study of how the translation – in more than one sense – of philosophy works, the passage from one historical moment of

theory to the next. One of the few contemporary parallels is Schelling's *On the History of Modern Philosophy.* (On this text, see the forthcoming work of David Clark.) Herder's historicism may well have served as something of a vague precedent for Hegel and Schelling in this regard.

9 The fuller passage reads: 'But appearance itself is essential to essence. Truth would not be truth if it did not show itself and appear, if it were not truth *for* someone and *for* itself, as well as for the spirit in general too' (I:8) (*Doch der Schein selbst ist dem Wesen wesntlich, die Wahrheit wäre nicht, wenn sie nicht schiene und erschiene, wenn sie nicht für Eines wäre, für sich selbst sowohl als auch für den Geist überhaupt*). Subsequent citations from Hegel's *Vorlesungen über die Ästhetik* will be indicated in the body of this essay by roman volume number (I, II, or III) and arabic page number. Roman numerals correspond to volumes 13, 14, and 15 in the *Werke.* For the German text, I am using the 'Theorie-Werkausgabe' of G.W.F. Hegel's *Werke in zwanzig Bänden.*

10 For an excellent account of Hegelian *Aufhebung,* see Jean-Luc Nancy, *La remarque speculative: sur un bon mot de Hegel.*

11 For a good account of negation in Hegel and Spinoza, see Pierre Macherey, *Hegel ou Spinoza,* especially chapter 4, 'Omis determinatio est negatio.'

12 One might balk also at the arguably more problematic determination of Judaism as the 'religion of sublimity,' which is how Hegel characterizes it in his *Lectures on the Philosophy of Religion* delivered more or less concurrently with the lectures on aesthetics.

13 For a magisterial analysis of this notion in Hegel (and not just Hegel), see Werner Hamacher's introduction to his edition of Hegel's *Der Geist des Christentums.* This text is now available in English translation under the title *Pleroma* (Stanford: Stanford University Press, 1998).

14 The essay is also reprinted in Paul de Man, *Aesthetic Ideology* (Minneapolis: University of Minnesota Press, 1996).

15 On the 'inadequacy' of poetry and the aesthetic in Hegel's system, see Giorgio Agamben, 'A Self-Annihilating Nothing.'

WORKS CITED

Agamben, Giorgio. 'A Self-Annihilating Nothing.' *The Man without Content.* Trans. Georgia Albert. Stanford: Stanford UP, 1990. 52–8.

Balfour, Ian. 'Reversal, Quotation (Benjamin's History).' *MLN* 106.3 (April 1991): 622–45.

Benjamin, Walter. 'Theses on the Philosophy of History.' *Illuminations: Essays and Reflections.* Ed. Hannah Arendt. Trans. Harry Zohn. New York: Shocken, 1968.

Curtius, Ernst Robert. *European Literature and the Latin Middle Ages.* Trans. Willard R. Trask. Princeton: Princeton UP, 1973.

de Man, Paul. 'Hegel on the Sublime.' *Displacements: Derrida and After.* Bloomington: Indiana UP, 1983. 139–53.

– 'Wordsworth and Hölderlin.' *The Rhetoric of Romanticism.* New York: Columbia UP, 1984. 55–9

Derrida, Jacques. 'Some Statements and Truisms about Neo-Logisms, Newisms, Postisms, Parasitisms, and Other Small Seismisms.' *The States Of 'Theory.'* Ed. David Carroll. Standford: Standford UP, 1994. 63–94.

Donougho, Martin. 'Hegel's Art of Memory.' *Endings.* Ed. Rebecca Comay and John McCumber. Evanston: Northwestern UP, 1999. 139–59.

Hamacher, Werner. *Pleroma.* Introduction to *Der Geist des Christentums.* By G.W.F. Hegel. Frankfurt am Main: Ullstein, 1978.

Hegel, G.W.F. *Aesthetics.* Vol. 1. Trans. T.M. Knox. Oxford: Clarendon P, 1974–5.

– *Lectures on the Philosophy of Religion.* Ed. Peter C. Hodgson. Trans. R.F. Brown et al. Berkeley: U of California P, 1984–7.

– *Vorlesungen über die Ästhetik. Werke in zwanzig Bänden.* (Theorie Werkausgabe). Vols. 13, 14, and 15. Frankfurt am Main: Suhrkamp, 1970.

Löwith, Karl. *Meaning in History.* Chicago: U of Chicago P, 1964.

Lukács, George. 'Hegel's Aesthetik.' *Beiträge zur Geschichte der Aesthetik.* Berlin: Aufbau, 1954. 97–134.

Macherey, Pierre. *Hegel ou Spinoza.* Paris: Maspero, 1979.

Nancy, Jean-Luc. *La Remarque speculative: sur un bon mot de Hegel.* Paris: Galilée, 1973.

Schelling, F.W.J. *On the History of Modern Philosophy.* Trans. Andrew Bowie. New York: Cambridge UP, 1994.

– *Philosophy of Art.* Trans. Douglas Scott. Minneapolis: U of Minnesota P, 1989.

Szondi, Peter. 'Hegel's Lehre von der Dichtung.' *Poetik und Geschichtsphilosphie I.* Suhrkamp: Frankfurt am Main, 1976. 267–511.

PERFORMATIVITIES

Theatrum Theoreticum

RODOLPHE GASCHÉ

In 1826, Thomas Drummond's invention of limelight made it possible for theatres 'to generate, in combination with concave mirrors, lighting "effects"' which by sheer quantity of directed light surpassed the rather timid previous attempts at staged lighting found, for instance, in six-teenth- and seventeenth-century painting. With this he set the stage for opening up, in Hans Blumenberg's words, 'new possibilities for an accentuating approach to vision, one that always takes as its point of departure the dark as *the "natural" state*.' 'This manipulation is the result of a long process,' he adds. The discovery that light could be manipu-lated and directed preceded the sometimes violent development of technical devices that put this knowledge into practice. Indeed, as Blu-menberg has shown, this discovery coincides with the origins of moder-nity, that is, of the conception that truth can only be methodologically secured. According to Blumenberg, the idea of method as it emerges with Bacon and Descartes rests on the presumption that phenomena lie in the dark and that only 'a focused and measured ray of "direct light-ing"' aimed at them at a certain angle and from a certain perspective is capable of wresting their truth from them. The new concept of 'seeing' manifested throughout modernity and at the heart of modern 'theory' assumes, as its very foundation, that light is at the disposal of human beings, or that the modern subject is that light itself. Only the mastery of light can force the fetters of ignorance and pierce the darkness sur-rounding all things ('Light as Metaphor' 53–4).

Is it a coincidence if this conception of seeing and theory finds in the realm of the theatre the most powerful corollaries to their own central notions of 'illumination' and magnification of sensory perception? Do theory, and the seeing that it implies, have a natural affinity, as it were, with the theatrical stage? To argue such a point might appear to be an arduous task. Given that theory is notorious for its concern with the immobile and the invariant, how could it entertain any relations worth our attention with a medium and an institution as fleeting and inessential as the theatre? The Platonic reservations concerning the theatre in the *Republic*, and elsewhere, have shaped philosophy's judgment of the theatre up to Austin's description of stage recitation as a parasitic or non-serious use of language. Accordingly, the theatre appears to be one of philosophical theory's others. Theory must seek to distinguish itself radically from, and must have no traffic with, the theatre. Undoubtedly, it has been precisely the theatre's otherness, its fleeting and transient nature, which appealed to those thinkers in the 1960s and early 1970s in France who, seeking to overthrow metaphysics through an inversion of Platonism, discovered 'the theatre of thinking.' I think of Gilles Deleuze, in particular, but also Michel Foucault. As Foucault writes in 'Theatrum Philosophicum,' a review article of two of Deleuze's books, philosophy must no longer be understood as thought, 'but as theatre: as a mime theater with multiple scenes that are fleeting and instantaneous, and where gestures, without being seen, make signs to one another' (908). But the mere exchange of the defining characteristics of theatre and theory leaves the question concerning a possible intrinsic relation between them as improbable as before.[1] Nevertheless, if it should prove possible, if not necessary, to link theory and theatre, the questions of representation and artificial redoubling, of spatial and temporal situatedness, and of narrativity would seem to bear on theory and to have a much less superficial or extraneous relation to it than is commonly assumed. Indeed, if the theatre is an other of theory, from which it needs rigorously to demarcate itself in order to secure a specificity of its own, the trace of the theatre must inhabit theory's innermost core. To evoke, then, the theatre in regard to theory suggests that theory occurs on some stage, that it has a plot, that it takes on a worldly appearance in which it shows itself to spectators, and so forth. But although theory, no doubt, has to do with seeing, it is still far from clear at this point why it requires a theatrical apparatus, or to be seen in the first place.

The near-homophony of theory and theatre is certainly not accidental. As is well established, the two terms derive from the same root: the Greek notion of *thea*, spectacle, contemplation. Still, however suggestive such etymologies are, they cannot serve – lest one indulge in a substantialist metaphysics of etymology, or a naïve *Begriffsplatonismus* – to affirm some intrinsic relation between theory and theatre. Rather, if we are to establish any intimate rapport between them, their difference, about which theory has been quite eloquent, should not be effaced by simply assigning them a common ground. Further, and just as important, the recourse to a common root does not itself provide one with a sense of the specific material ways in which theory and theatre may be entangled. Besides the allure of the etymological short-cut, all attempts to clarify the relation between theory and theatre face a set of what I wish to call strictly necessary temptations. These are the temptations of theory itself, possibilities to whose enticement theory must respond if it is to be what it is. By extension, these temptations belong to any effort to theoretically establish the relation between theatre and theory. We can and must ask: In the event that, independently of their origin in a common root, theory and theatre are drawn together, is it because theory must take on visible, tangible shape? Is the theatre theory's inevitable aesthetic complement? Does theoretical vision require that vision take place within a theatrical space, that is, within a space in which that which is seen stages its own appearance? And in which seeing is thus necessarily a kind of spectatorship of that which exposes itself to its gaze? Finally, could it be that the theatre as a locus of visualization and offering to view is precisely that space in which the theoretical gaze seeks to see what it looks like, what its looks look like – in short, to see itself? Is the theatre mainly the setting and the event in which theory can find an answer to itself? However necessary these questions may be, they also tend to submit the space of theatre to the theoretical, and hence to blur their difference again. Still, only if these questions are asked can the theatre be seen to make, perhaps, a difference with respect to theory.

In the following I intend to discuss these issues with reference to Blumenberg's *Das Lachen der Thrakerin: Eine Urgeschichte der Theorie*.[2] Blumenberg construes the story of Thales as recounted in the *Theaetetus* as the archetypal illustration of the antique ideal of *theoria*. In this archaeology of theory, Blumenberg investigates the transformations, deformations, and extensions of this single anecdote throughout the history of the West. Before I take up this anecdote itself, and especially its status as an archetype of theory, some very brief remarks concerning the 'theoretical' (or philosophical) underpinnings of Blumenberg's own investigation are certainly in order. For his study of the various transformations that the anecdote has undergone, Blumenberg borrows the notion of a history of reception from Hans Robert Jauss, although he uses it in a sense more suited to his own purposes and at one further remove from what Gadamer has termed 'effective history.' Through the analysis of the history of reception of the anecdote, Blumenberg seeks to establish what theory is about. In the entry 'Theory' from *Begriffe in Geschichten*, we are told that 'one can learn more through intuition and free variation, which brings the hard core of the meaning of a concept into view. One can assume that the history of "theory" has already accomplished a good deal of free variation-work. All that remains to be done is to look at the model' (193). This is precisely the task Blumenberg has set for himself in *Das Lachen der Thrakerin*. In contrast to effective history, which 'unfolds the potential of an originary invention unattainable in itself, and which is actualized in always new expressions [or turns]' (*Das Lachen* 89), a history of reception is primarily concerned with the structural 'frame for positions [*Stellenrahmen*]' within the originary configuration of the anecdote, and which can be infinitely reshuffled, or recast (108). From the perspective of a history of reception, 'the anecdote [of Thales] becomes endowed with the function of standing for something that could never ever be exhausted either by itself [that is to say, the anecdote], or by its reception' (108). Consequently, it is not so much the anecdote *itself* that is of interest in a history of reception, however originary it may be, but, more essentially, the anecdote's 'imaginative (*imaginatives*) potential, one that anticipates deformations, and even the recasting of its stock figures' (109). Compared to effective history, in which continuity (tradition) is a function of the repeated innovative actualization of an identical semantic nucleus (of what Gadamer calls *die Sache*), a history of reception, as understood by Blumenberg, is discontinuous, a function of an identical model, pattern, or scheme (*Muster*, or *Typus*) whose nodal points, or positions, can be infinitely recast. For a theory of reception, the anecdote in question is important in that it, in Blumenberg's own words, literally 'prefigures,' in exemplary fashion, 'a model that one cannot shake off in a history of theory' (45). This attentiveness to the structural elements in the model which the Thales anecdote illustrates (though it is only one possible, however exemplary, version of it) allows the history of reception to focus on the discontinuity in the variations of the model, rather than on the continuity of the tradition that all effective history presupposes, even (or especially) when the latter laments the alienation from the tradition. In a reception theory the aim is not to 'diagnose in the disturbed gaze [*in dem befremdeten Blick*] upon theory something like a preliminary stage of the alienated gaze of theory itself' (44–5), Blumenberg explains. This history of the reception of the Thales anecdote is not simply discontinuous; however, a meticulous analysis of all the deformations (*Verformungen*), distortions (*Entstellungen*), dissemblances (*Verstellungen*), perversions (*Verkehrungen*), and reversals (*Umkehrungen*) of the anecdote would be required to make out the internal logic according to which the history of its reception unfolds.

Since I do not propose to carry out this analysis but merely to maintain that a logic does support Blumenberg's exposition of the anecdote's historical variations, I will limit myself to calling up his discussion, towards the end of his study, of Heidegger's interpretation of Thales' story. Occurring against the backdrop of a destruction of the history of metaphysics, Heidegger's treatment of the anecdote is, according to Blumenberg, a reversal (*Umkehrung*). Rather than interpreting the philosopher's fall as an essential consequence of the philosopher's neglect of the life-world, Heidegger, Blumenberg argues, interprets it as the very criterion of philosophical thinking (and in this continues a way of looking at the anecdote that began with Nietzsche). The fall into the well is not a sign of the philosopher's shortcomings or of his inevitable downfall but a testimony to the superiority of philosophical thought. The servant maid's laughter not only reveals total incomprehension but intrinsically lacks any critical bearing whatsoever. Heidegger can thus interpret the anecdote as an all-out vindication of philosophy rather than as a critical voice from the life-world. Without further lingering on specifics, let me only mention that with this reversal, Heidegger, for Blumenberg, has not only cut all ties to modernity and the Enlightenment and severed philosophical thought from the horizon of the life-world, but he has, especially, freed philosophical thought, or theory, from the need to seek 'agreement and consensus' (*Das Lachen* 158). Although Blumenberg does not conceptualize this reversal as an alienation from the history of the reception of the anecdote, Heidegger's treatment of the anecdote seems to suggest a point of development in which the imaginative potential of the anecdote, and along with it the potential of a structural grid of intelligibility in the history of ideas and concepts, have come to an end.[3] Implicitly, this reversal in the interpretation of the anecdote also amounts to an end of theory, the end, thus, of what Blumenberg, in the wake of Husserl, continues to understand as the unifying *telos* of European culture.

Although the anecdote in question can be traced back to one of Aesop's fables, it is only, as Blumenberg persuasively argues, in the Platonic reconfiguration of that story that the anonymous Aesopean protagonists of the fable are identified in such a way that the original *epimythion*, or moral, of the anecdote fits the philosopher and theoretician, making it into the successful archetype of theory. The anecdote as told by Socrates in the *Theaethetus* only takes two sentences. It is 'the story of the Thracian maidservant who exercised her wit at the expense of Thales, when he was looking up to study the stars and tumbled down a well. She scoffed at him for being so eager to know what was happening in the sky that he could not see what lay at his feet' (879 [174a–b]). The context in which the anecdote is evoked, and which I will take up in moment, leaves no doubt that in fact not Thales, but Socrates, is the real referent of the story. Yet even so, it is not by happenstance that Plato has recourse to Aesop's fable about the astronomer and the well. As Plato holds in *Timaeus*, philosophy derives from the contemplation of the heavens and is the greatest good that 'ever was or will be given by the gods to mortal man.' Indeed, for the Greeks, star-gazing amounts to contemplating 'the courses of intelligence in the heaven.' The cyclical revolutions of the planets in the nightly skies reveal to the astronomer the unperturbed, lasting, and steady presence of the gods. And philosophy, or *theoria*, which is first and foremost the sight of that which remains unchanged – the divine – contemplates those courses of intelligence in the heavens, according to Plato, in order to attend to 'the courses of our own intelligence which are akin to them ... and that we, learning them and partaking of the natural truth of reason, might imitate the absolutely unerring courses of God and regulate our own vagaries' (1174–5 [47a–d]). Thales of Miletus's prediction of the total solar eclipse in 585 BC, which provided the Greeks with a spectacular demonstration of the effectiveness of theory, makes him, therefore, the proto-theoretician, or proto-philosopher. What befalls him also befalls Socrates, the philosopher, and by extension philosophy and theory in general. Concern with theory in the shape of Thales' astronomy only exposes the theoretician to mockery of his oblivion to the lower realities under his nose, his helplessness, clumsiness, and constant embarrassment by situations in the real world. His lack of realism, in short, draws the laughter of the uncomprehending yet very pragmatic and down-to-earth maid. But the projection of the anecdote upon the Platonic Socrates brings out something else: the true source of the onlooker's laughter in the mistrust, contempt, and eventually the hatred of theory on the part of the onlooking community. As Blumenberg remarks, 'in the two centuries since Thales, it became clearer what was actually so ridiculous about theory. Precisely because Socrates abandoned the interest in nature which had dominated his youth and turned to questions concerning human action and life, it became clear that the spatial

distance and unattainability of the objects of the starry heaven, compared to the proximity of the pitfalls of practical existence, did not constitute the strangeness of the theoretician, but was only a representation
of it' (*Das Lachen* 16). Indeed, the way the philosopher applies himself
to issues of practical life shows him to be even more alienated from life
and the point of view of his contemporaries than when he deals with the
philosophy of nature. Socrates says in the *Theaetetus* that 'whoever gives
his life to philosophy ... is unaware what his next-door neighbour is
doing, hardly knows, indeed, whether the creature is a man at all; he
spends all his pains on the question, what is man, and what powers and
properties distinguish such a nature from another' (879 [174b–c]). Blumenberg remarks, as if responding to this statement: 'The philosopher
of the Socratic type, in busying himself, and because he busies himself,
with the essence of the human being, does not recognize the human
being in the neighbor' (*Das Lachen* 17). Like the astronomer, Socrates'
aim is also to achieve wisdom and excellence. By determining the question of virtue in terms of knowledge, however, the philosopher sets a
trap for himself. The very generality of the problem of how the knowledge is possible on which virtue is to rest drives him, in Blumenberg's
words, 'away again from the proximity of human things that he had
sought by turning away from the phenomena of nature' (23). As a
result, the object of theory, and its gaze – the true reality – rather than
being sought in the sublunar realm of the human world, is located
beyond everything that can be sensibly experienced – indeed, beyond
the stars that punctuate the night sky (29). Riveted on the ideas in an
intelligible *topos ouranios*, the philosopher not only looks stranger than
ever; he now also shows himself to be an asocial being, disdainful of the
human being's daily, practical concerns, and inattentive towards the
polis and its citizens' political activities and obligations.[4] At this point,
theory no longer provokes the laughter of a simplistic though realistic
maid, but, as Socrates' tragic end demonstrates, the distrust and even
hatred of the community. The confrontation between theory and (in
Blumenberg's Husserlian terminology) the life-world in general has
taken a form that transcends the implications of the anecdote. In fact,
the story of Socrates is the first variation on the encounter between the
proto-philosopher and the Thracian maid who witnesses his fall into a
well; that is to say, the first variation on 'the most lasting prefiguration of
all the tensions and misunderstandings between the life-world and theory' (11). This variation (even more than its Aesopean predecessor or
original) has determined theory's inexorable history, a history whose

different phases are made up by the innumerable variations, transformations, deformations, and reversals of the anecdote.

But what has this history of the archetype of theory to do with the theatre or theatricality? If one were to assume that the title of the dialogue in which the anecdote is narrated would permit a clue, one would certainly be mistaken. The name 'Theaetetus,' according to Liddell and Scott, means 'obtained from God,' and thus derives from another root than 'theatre.' Yet, if the title of the dialogue offers no clue, could the dialogue itself contain hints at an intrinsic relation of theory to the theatre? Barbara Herrnstein Smith has pointed out that as a text about philosophical instruction – one in which the young Theaetetus, by witnessing the self-refutation of the doctrines to which he adheres, is delivered to a better understanding of the nature of knowledge – the *Theaetetus* stands out by its theatricality. She writes: 'The archetypal, exemplary self-refutation, is, of course, dramatically scripted, and theatricality remains central to its re-productions. The dramatis personae are certainly among the most compelling in cultural history: the callow, showy, scoffing, hubristic truth-denier; the seasoned, gently ironic, ultimately martyred truth-deliverer; plus, as crucial parties to the scene, the mixed chorus of disciples and occasional interlocutors and, not insignificantly, the audience itself, motley representatives of the community at large' (Smith 80). Unquestionably, a certain theatricality promotes the search for truth, especially when the search has a pedagogical aim. But does this already indicate any deeper connection of the theoretical to the theatre? After all, theatricality could here be understood as merely instrumental to the learning of theory, as something that helps to carry it out, but ultimately remains exterior to it. By contrast, I would like to inquire whether there is an essential link between theory *itself* and the theatre. Does theory always, and necessarily, require to be staged? Must it always perform in front of spectators?

In order to elaborate further on this last question, I return to Blumenberg's *Das Lachen der Thrakerin*. What is this archaeology of theory, if not the history of the different ways in which theory shows itself on the basis of the permutations that one visual archetype, the anecdote of Thales and the Thracian maid, makes possible? Theory, Blumenberg notes, is 'something that one does not see. Although the theoretical attitude consists in actions that submit to intentional rules and lead to complexes of propositions in rule-governed connections, these actions are only visible on their exterior, and under the form of their "performances, or proceedings [*Verrichtungen*]." To someone who has not been

initiated into their intentionality, and who perhaps does not even sus-
pect that these acts are a specimen of "theory," they must remain enigmatic, and may look offensive, or even ridiculous' (*Das Lachen* 9). The
seeing peformed by theoreticians is not itself visible, but the acts that
they must perform for the purpose of theorizing can be seen. To the
spectator, theory offers the sight of its doings. It comes into an appearance by way of the acts of seeing, and these acts offer the sight of an
exotic ritual. According to Blumenberg, the anecdote about the Milesian astronomer/philosopher and the Thracian maid is the first figuration (*Verbildlichung*) of theory – in other words, the archetypal image in
which it shows itself to a spectator. The archetype of theory proposes as
'the configuration of theory' a 'scene,' in a theatrical sense, that is
'archaic' in the sense that it is both originary and ancient (116). In its
originary figuration, theory shows itself on stage for a spectator.
Blumenberg describes the anecdote as 'the Milesian primal scene of
theory' (120). The story of Thales is thus the première of theory, its
opening night, as it were. Moreover, the spectacle that it offers on this
occasion is a comedy. Thales, the type of the ancient theoretician, 'the
ancestor of the modern manufacturer of the product "theory"' (1), is a
comical figure. But as Diogenes Laertius reports, Thales' last fall was
fatal. Blumenberg therefore concludes that 'with theory the possibility
of tragedy is also posited' (39). If this is not an accidental possibility, it is
precisely because theory shows itself theatrically. Already in the first variation of the archetypal scene – that is, in its Platonic reconfiguration –
the comedy at the edge of the well is replaced by the tragedy before the
people's court, where the collision of worlds and concepts of reality, and
their mutual incomprehensibility, become deadly (14). In *Das Lachen der
Thrakerin*, Blumenberg takes the position of a historian contemplating
the 'view(s) offered by theory of its own distance – in terms of worlds
and times – from the *imago* of its beginning' (11). As on a stage, in fact,
these different scenes in which theory makes a show of itself parade
before him, before Blumenberg, the spectator, while he, equipped with
the theoretician's gaze, looks at what remains constant, in spite of all the
transformations of all these sights, until in the end he makes the curtain
fall when he is faced with a variation of the sight of theory that seems to
have done away with theatricality and hence with theory altogether.
Still, one needs to keep in mind that the transformative potential of the
anecdote is in principle infinite. Heidegger's reversal of it, therefore,
may merely signify a provisional end of theory. Indeed, the question to
be asked is whether the staged reversal which eliminates the theatricality

of theory presupposes not only (*ordine inverso*) the theatre of theory but is itself inherently theatrical as well. In any event, Blumenberg's archaeology of theory, as a history of scenes in which theory offers itself to view, suggests a much deeper internal connection of theory and theatre than is commonly assumed. One is even led to surmise that this whole archaeology rests on the presupposition of a theatre of theory – in other words, on the assumption that the theatre has a constitutive role in the theoretical.

Because he distinguishes between the intentionality of theory and its subsequent scenic manifestations, Blumenberg could be seen to relegate the theatrical elements of theory to a merely superficial sphere, to make them seem mere theatrics. But although theory's intentionality cannot become visible itself, and for all to see, theory cannot avoid showing something of itself. Indeed, it must come into an appearance, offer a view of itself, give itself to be seen. In order to theorize, the theoreticians must perform certain acts, the chores of theory, as it were. If theory's intentionality cannot avoid appearing, one must infer some internal necessity for its giving itself to see. Asking why theory must, precisely, show itself theatrically, or why it must make a spectacle of itself, perhaps makes it possible to clarify the necessity in question. Blumenberg distinguishes between the intentionality of theory and theory's doings. With this he hints already at an explanation as to why theory, as long as it remains theory, inescapably offers not only a view of itself, but one that is made up of gestures. Theory has the character of an act. To achieve what it intends, it must perform. Further, by appearing, and taking on an appearance, it necessarily appears to a spectator. In sum, if theory must take on a worldly appearance, one can assume that becoming seen, rather than remaining invisible, is essential to it. As Blumenberg demonstrates when he assesses Heidegger's reversal of the Thales anecdote, theory, by cutting all ties to the life-world, not only renders itself invisible again but thereby also sacrifices (or escapes) its ability to foster agreement and consensus (or dissent). As I hope to show hereafter, theoretical vision must become visible in order to accomplish what it strives for.

Theory achieves visibility in a theatre of sorts, but it is not clear at all why the theoretician's doings and the spectator's observation of them are elements of a theatre to begin with. What is it about theory that causes it to manifest itself scenically, on stage? The sight of the protophilosopher is the sight of one who stares at the heavens, rather than at what is at his feet. According to Blumenberg, 'for the Thracian maid who observes the Milesian walking at night in this inappropriate manner, it is possible to surmise that she has caught him in worshiping his gods. In that case he did well to fall, since his gods were the wrong gods' (*Das Lachen* 12). But whether or not his gods are the right ones, does the proto-philosopher's bearing not derive precisely from his setting his eyes on the divine? Blumenberg reminds us of something the Greeks knew very well, that the divine produces incomprehensible behaviour (12). Could it possibly be that, because theory sets itself the goal of viewing the divine, it cannot but offer a sight of itself that is fundamentally theatrical?

In the prospect of a possible answer to this question, I turn to an examination of the context of the story of Thales and the Thracian maid and of its precise role in the *Theaetetus*. In this dialogue Socrates engineers the self-refutation of three different determinations of knowledge directly after Theodorus has effusively praised Theaetetus, describing him not only as remarkably talented, but also as having a quaint physical resemblance (*homoios*) to Socrates himself. Socrates carries out the refutation in a dialogue before an audience, then, under the pretext of studying his own appearance as it is supposedly manifested in Theaetetus's performance. Theodorus is not a painter but, aside from being an expert in geometry, calculation, music, and the liberal arts, he is, significantly enough, an astronomer. Socrates holds that Theodorus, in speaking of their resemblance, could only have noticed a similarity of the mind, rather than a physical likeness between the two. Therefore, and in order to gain certitude about such a similarity, Socrates invites Theaetetus to perform for him, and to give him a display of what he is capable of (*soi men epideiknunai*), while he will watch, contemplate, examine him (*emoi de skopeisthai*) (850 [145b–c]). Although the verb *skopeo*, to behold or contemplate, is generally used only with respect to particulars, rather than to universals, for whose contemplation *theoreo* is the verb more commonly used (Liddell and Scott 1613), it is nonetheless clear that with this the whole ensuing debate in the *Theaetetus* is set in a space of visibility of performers and onlookers. Since Socrates is not concerned with physical likeness, this space, with its performers and onlookers, is certainly not a theatrical space in the ordinary sense, and yet resembles such a space. In spite of Socrates' obvious irony concerning Theaetetus's alleged similarity to him, Socrates' desire to test the young man's intellectual abilities does not stem from an intention of reeducating him by refuting sophistry. Rather, it concerns the philosopher himself, Socrates as a personification of theory. The philosopher wants to see himself, what he is like, how he presents himself, and to what extent the figure he cuts corresponds to himself; theory wants to see itself, what it is like, how it appears, and to what extent the appearance corresponds to its true nature. Here we can begin to surmise a reason for theory's inextricable relation to the theatrical, which goes beyond, though it is related to, theory's preoccupation with the divine. To be what it is and to secure this resemblance to itself, theory must seek out the stage. Indeed, one may wish to ask why Socrates, who rarely attended the theatre, felt compelled to witness the mockery that Aristophanes made of him in *The Clouds*.

It is a standard practice in hasty discussions of theory to recall that the term derives from the Greek *thea*, seeing, looking at. But, particularly when seeing is taken to be a mode of comportment in which one seizes an object in the sense of taking power over it, such an explanation does not do much to clarify the Greek sense of theory. To cite Hans-Georg Gadamer,

> *theoria*, in its Greek sense, refers to observation, for example, of celestial constellations, to being a spectator at, for example, a play, or a participant in a delegation to a sacred festival. It does not refer to a mere 'seeing' which establishes what is present-at-hand or stores information. *Contemplatio* does not linger with a determinable being, but in a region. *Theoria* is not so much the individual, momentary act as it is a comportment, a state and condition in which one holds oneself. (Gadamer 96; translation modified)

Even more significantly, the kind of vision specific to *theoria* in its Platonic sense – that is, *theoria* understood as knowledge (*epistemē*) – carries the assumption that such seeing, or contemplation, is the highest and most perfect mode of cognition. Indeed, contemplation is the highest and most complete mode of knowledge because it maintains a relation to Being itself, to that which is originary, the ever-present originary forms – in other words, the divine order of the world.[5] As a way of seeing, *theoria* derives its specificity from contemplative contact with the divine, from *theos*, even though the etymological root of *theoria* may be *thea*. Because of theory's prime concern with the divine, antiquity speculated already about *theoria*'s possible, though etymologically questionable, derivation from *theos*. Summing up the extensive philological research on the origin of the term, Hannelore Rausch distinguishes two main uses of the Greek word *theoria*. On the one hand, *theoria* refers to looking at, or watching in general, a meaning that permits *theoria* to refer to the phenomenon of the feast or festival. In this context *theoria* means spectacle, game, or theatre, the viewing or watching of games, or spectacles, or, further, the sending of state-ambassadors to these festive events. On the other hand, *theoria* evokes the gaze of the mind, and, accordingly, signifies observation, speculation, intuition, contemplation, and so forth. The two meanings, Rausch notes, cannot easily be accounted for on the basis of one single etymon. According to most philologists, the Greek root *theoros* holds the greatest promise for unifying the two different series of meaning of *theoria*. Since the research into the notion of *theoros* has shown the impossibility of unequivocally deciding whether *theoros* derives from *thea*, sight, or looking, or from *theos*, god, this root *theos* must also be given due consideration in attempting to understand *theoria* (Rausch 12–14). In short, in attempting to come to grips with the meaning of *theoria*, and by extension, with the archetypal scene in which it shows itself in the *Theaetetus*, one cannot ignore this essential connection of the theoretical gaze to the divine. But how are *thea*, seeing, and *theos*, god, interrelated? To answer this question, a brief detour through the pre-philosophical and, as we will see, sacral meaning of *theoria* is necessary.

Basing herself on Karl Kerényi's interpretation of Greek religion as a religion of *Schau* (show, seeing), Rausch argues that a pre-philosophical interconnection between seeing and the divine is manifest in the Greek conception of the religious or sacred feast. The feast, she holds, is the spiritual occasion and place 'in which the inner filiation of the two basic meanings of *theoros* that are under investigation, that of seeing and that of the divine, becomes clearly visible' (Rausch 37). Following Kerényi, Rausch defines the religious festival as the moment at which the ever-present gods show themselves (in human form) and in which humans associate with the divine. The *theoroi*, the official envoys from the Greek city states, constituted the theoric delegations, the *theoriai*, that travelled to the great pan-hellenic festivals. These envoys either performed an act of worship at the festive sites in their own name or participated in the feasts organized by their hosts as observers.[6] The *theoroi*, then, relate to the gods present at the festival. They partake of the divinity that takes on visible and determinate shape, figure, or form on the occasion of these sacred feasts in the capacity of spectators – in essence, by way of looking. Rausch, therefore, concludes: 'For the Greeks, festivity and the point of view of the spectator are inextricably connected, and we now understand that in the Greek feast this situation of *thea*, of seeing, is always repeated as one in which the gods and the human beings come together' (34). Now for everything that concerns us here, it is important to emphasize that the chief place where this viewing takes place is the theatre, whose name Plutarch conjectured – in a derivation that is doubtless extremely questionable, but nonetheless revealing – was, like *theorein*, taken from the *theoi* (Rausch 17). But the entire festive world also makes up a *theatron* in which the gods are both viewed and viewers themselves (Rausch 34). As Kerényi has remarked, the gods, too, 'come festally, come as *theoroi*,' to the festive shows, to be spectators of the holy games, dances, and other events (*Religion* 153). Kerényi describes the fundamental situation of Greek religion as a 'a reciprocal, active and passive, vision, a spectacle in which men are both viewers and viewed' (144).[7] In the festive world, Greek religion found its accomplishment. When the gods take on visible shapes during the sacred festivals, they do so on stage, certainly, but they also participate in the festivities as divine onlookers. In the theatre the seers are also seen, men and gods included. In the theatre those who come to see the gods are the objects themselves of a divine gaze. Finally, considering that, in *The Peace*, Aristophanes brings the feast itself, personified as *theoria*, onto the stage, one can presume that in this theatre of *theorein*, the theatre is not only a space of seeing and being seen but also the locus and the time in which theatrical space and time offer themselves to view.

This pre-philosophical interconnection between seeing and the divine glance in the phenomenon of the sacred feast still pervades the philosophical understanding of *theoria*. I mentioned the Platonic conception of *theoria* as a contemplation of the eternal, and divine, order of the world. One could as well evoke Aristotle, who derives the possibility of the highest science, the science concerned with the first causes and principles, from divine *theoria*, from god's own gazing at the world and at himself in joyful bliss. Yet, if *theoria* in the philosophical sense of contemplation implies a contact with the gods, it also reveals the sense of festivity characteristic of the pre-philosophical and sacral meaning of the term. It further follows from this prime concern of *theoria* with the divine that the world itself is like the festive world; in Rausch's words, 'a *theatron*, a place of seeing for gods and men, and in which the philosopher accomplishes, in the face of god, that of which the human being is capable' (180). Yet, it is also a fact that for the Greek philosophers the human capacity in relation to the divine is limited, and that, furthermore, the divine is no longer present for them in the way it had been in pre-philosophical Greece. We must therefore assume that theoretical vision's approximation of divine vision has intrinsic limits. These limits will certainly affect theory's theatricality, but they will not abolish it. On the contrary, they will, as we shall see, endow theory with a new sense of the theatrical, a theatricality so pervasive that it will affect the nature of its glance.

For the time being, however, let me linger a while longer on the close link between theory and theatre. I will do this by taking up the attempt made by Jacques Taminiaux to critically unseat the philosophical privilege that Plato has accorded to the *bios theoretikos*. So far we have seen theatricality to have been the intrinsic medium in which theoretical contemplation of the divine order takes place. In order to resist theory's contemplative thrust and cement the practical nature of theory, Taminiaux, too, must, significantly enough, stress the intimate connection of *theoria* to the phenomenon of the theatre. Thus in *The Thracian Maid and the Professional Thinker: Arendt and Heidegger*, while opposing along with Hannah Arendt the Aristotelian conception of the *bios politikos* to the *bios theoretikos*, Taminiaux recalls that the *bios politikos* originates in the pre-philosophical meaning of *theoria* as being related to the theatre. He writes: 'Before the Platonic invention of the *bios theoretikos*, the only *theoria* that corresponded to the isonomic city consisted in the glance that the spectators of the theatre could cast at the human affairs, not in order to become detached from their appearing and thus to reach the solitary contemplation of a higher region, but in order to discover in them the measure for a judgment [in the sense of *phronesis*] in community with others, and at the heart of plurality' (134). Practical life, a life in which thinking is secondary, and the pursuit of immortality in the public domain are governed by a *theoria* 'entirely different from that of the philosopher given to contemplating *physis*' (123), Taminiaux remarks.[8] Since this *theoria*, according to Taminiaux, is 'the tragic *theoria* whose echo is to be found in Aristotle's *Poetics*' (125) and ultimately reaches back to 'the prepolitical experience of the actions whose legends are recounted by Homer, and which afterwards inspired the tragic theatre' (118), it owes no less to the theatre than theoretical contemplation does. But the *theoria* of the philosopher, Taminiaux concludes, is only a metamorphosis of the originary glance that the spectators cast at the theatre over the much more fragile reality of human life. Whether recourse is made to the pre-philosophical meaning of *theoria* to allow one to argue that theory's intrinsic relation to the theatre determines it as the contemplation of a transcendent, and solidly unchanging, order, or whether it allows one to argue that the connection to the theatre proves theory's deep affinity to the unstable realm of human affairs, *theoria* clearly cannot be thought without the theatre. Both interpretations of the role of the theatre for theory contain the assumption that theory is impossible without a lighted space in which showing and seeing can occur.

In modernity theory directs a focused beam of light upon objects under investigation in order to dissipate the darkness that surrounds it, and the lighting effects in the theatre made possible by the invention of calcium light highlight this conception of theory. By contrast, Blumenberg reminds us, *theoria* rests on the Greek assumption that brightness fills the cosmos like a medium, that everything is already in the light and hence offers itself to a gaze to be seen ('Light as Metaphor' 34). The world is a theatre because light is everywhere. Everything shows itself (by itself), and the natural attitude of the protagonists – gods and human beings both – consists in the contemplation, in theoretical bliss, of the appearing that accrues to them. The birth of modern theory, by contrast, is contemporaneous with the transition (as analysed by Richard Alewyn) of the worldly parade, the *trionfo*, which during the Middle Ages and the early Renaissance took place under the open sky, in the unlimited public space of the streets, followed by fireworks of a magnitude which turned the night into the day, into the closed space of the theatre hall, a transition that takes place at the end of the Renaissance (21–2).[9] The modern theatre is surrounded by darkness, and one only sees what is in the spotlight, in the coerced optics owing to a directed beam of illuminating light.

At all times, both in the ancient and the modern conception of theory, an intimate connection between theory and theatre obtains. From everything we have established so far, the theatricality of theory is tied to the seeing that characterizes it. But is this theatricality of a theory of the divine exhausted by the festivity that comes with the contact of gazes, in which those who see are seen? This question is all the more important because for Plato, and the Greek philosophers as a whole, the divine no longer enjoys the immediate presence that it had previously. With theophany no longer a self-evident given, the theatricality of philosophical *theoria* can no more presuppose the immediacy of seeing and being seen that is achieved in the festival. In what sense then must we conceive of the relation between theatre and theory in philosophical *theoria*? To understand the theatricality of philosophical theory, let us first inquire into how the gazes that constitute theory are structured such that they may be said to have a theatrical dimension. More precisely, what is it that puts theatre into this theatre of gazes? With these questions, I return to the *Theaetetus*.

The inquiry into whether wisdom is related to the good or the useful is interrupted with a digression upon the kind of speech that distinguishes philosophical investigations. After having remarked that 'one theory after another is coming upon us ... and [that] the last is [always] more important than the one before,' Socrates returns to the question of resemblance raised at the beginning of the dialogue by inquiring into what those men who spend their time in philosophical studies look like. Testimony to the strict inner logic of the dialogue (and perhaps also to a much tighter connection with the ongoing argument than some scholars have tended to believe), this question conjures up the sight that the philosopher offers to an assembly of men of law. It is natural, Socrates holds, that philosophers 'should look ridiculous when they appear as speakers in a court of law' (878 [172 c–d]). What distinguishes the philosopher from the orators in court is, first, his freedom from his own discourses. As Theodoros remarks, 'we are not the servants of the argument, which stand and wait for the moment when we choose to pursue this or that topic to a conclusion. We are not in a court under the judge's eye, nor in the theatre with an audience to criticize our philosophical evolutions' (879 [173c]). In contrast to those 'men who have knocked about from their youth up in law courts and such places' (878 [172c–d]) and who are slaves to their speeches, the philosopher is free, for example, to interrupt his argument and digress. Unlike the orators or the poets, the philosopher, it would seem, does not perform for an audience. The philosophers' doings are not addressed to spectators (and their expectations). Not only that, 'from their youth up they have never known the way to market place or law court or Council Chamber or any other place of public assembly' (879 [173d]). The philosopher does not perform for a court, or theatrical audience in the strict sense, but only for a select assembly of thinkers and disciples, where, in the *Theaetetus*, a young and promising disciple can display his intellectual abilities before Socrates. In such a display, however, the philosopher cannot avoid making a show of himself, a show, in fact, that has all the characteristics of a theatre play. As the anecdote about Thales and his maid makes plain, the philosopher makes a fool of himself during this performance. But he does so even more 'on a public occasion or in private company, in a law court or anywhere else, ... [when] he is forced to talk about what lies at his feet or is before his eyes. [Then] the whole rabble will join the maidservants in laughing at him, as from inexperience he walks blindly and stumbles into every pitfall' (879 [174c]). Resembling none of his fellow men, the theoretician, consequently, offers the spectacle of one who is quite different, who is, indeed, other. His oddness derives from the fact that in addition to performing for those who like him seek the truth, he is a player on still another scene, this time with other, non-human, spectators. As Socrates explains, only the philosopher's body 'sojourns in his city, while his thought, disdaining all such things as worthless, takes wing, as Pindar says, "beyond the sky, beneath the earth," searching the heavens and measuring the plains, everywhere seeking the true nature of everything as a whole, never sinking to what lies close at hand' (879 [173e]). Keeping his 'eyes fixed on the whole,' or thinking 'of the earth as a whole' (880 [174e]), the philosopher, according to Socrates, 'take[s] flight from this world to the other, and that means becoming like [*homoiosis*] the divine so far as we can' (881 [176b]). The theoretician not only seeks to contemplate the divine. His act consists in emulating the way of looking that pertains to the gods, hence, of playing their role for them to view on the stage of this world. With them in sight, and performing under their glance, the theoretician or philosopher perfects righteousness through knowledge – a knowledge based in seeing – and nothing is 'more like the divine.' The theatre of theory, though played on several scenes, is suspended from this glance of the divine onlookers. Its very theatricality, in a sense still to be specified, lies in the encounter, or rather non-encounter, as we will see, of seeing and being seen.

Seeing, whether by the theoretician, the gods, or the public, requires the medium of visibility, but that alone does not yet make seeing necessarily theatrical. A certain theatricality, however, already comes into play where the brightness of light allows things to present themselves to a gaze; in other words, to stage themselves for an observer. Yet, as soon as this observer, in turn, becomes seen, and even steps forth into the light to be beheld, seeing becomes theatrical. Seeing's theatricality is clearly a function of seeing being seen, of a play between the gazes that suggests no limit. Seeing, here, is seen abysmally, without end in sight. But with the agent of the theoretical glance offering a view not only to spectators such as the Thracian maids, or even other philosophers and disciples, but to the gods whom he has made the object of his contemplation, theoretical vision aims at bringing the infinite exchange of the gazes to a stop, and, thus, at neutralizing the theatrical space of theory. The divine look at the theoretician should, indeed, bring the infinity of perspectives to a halt. But even this dream of theory does not do without some theatre.

Through the anecdote about Thales and the servant maid, theory, or philosophy, first stages its own worldly insignificance. It makes itself look silly. Against the backdrop of this first play, theory stages itself for the disciples of theory, and, ultimately, in order to become the object of the 'redeeming' glance of the gods. The theoretician's glance seeks out the sight of the gods, whose divine *theoria* he emulates. He needs divine onlookers not merely so that someone may witness his emulation of the gods but, ultimately, so that he may see himself in their gaze, so that he may witness his own emulation of the god's vision. As seen, *theoria* is *homoiosis theo*. The philosopher, because he is trying to resemble the gods who see him seeing, also emulates their vision of himself. As a result, theoretical vision hopes to see itself by itself. Under the eyes of the gods, it thereby hopes to see itself independently of the divine audience whose embracing gaze at itself it makes its own. Here it becomes evident why theory must show itself, and why it cannot but stage itself in such a manner as to be seen. But also the meaning of theory's theatricality becomes tangible here. The theatricality of theory derives from its impossibility to speculatively complete the closure of seeing's being seen by itself. Theatricality names theory's impossibility of achieving a reciprocity between seeing and being seen, one that would secure the possibility that it would see itself. To the maid, of whose look the theoretician pretends to be unaware, the theoretician only offers a silly sight. Being seen by her serves as the necessary backdrop for a seeing in which he aspires to recognize himself. But in the theatre of theory the gods' look cannot be confounded with that of the man of theory. Of him Plato admits that he vies with their gaze only so far as he can. The asymmetry between their gaze and that of the theoretician directed at them remains irreducible. For Plato the theoretical gaze can no longer be certain that it is seen, and therefore that it is divine vision itself. Theory is no longer the direct and immediate vision of the divine itself. It is, to use a Platonic formula, only the next best way of beholding the divine. The theatre has turned from being the provider of a space of immediate commerce between the human gaze and that of the gods to being the internal limit of the human gaze. But this limitation does not therefore invalidate the gaze in question. It is still the next best way, the only way for the human.

The maid's appraisal of the philosopher's gaze fails to see what the philosopher sees. But neither is his own gaze at the immortals rendered, or restored, to him in order for him to see himself. This asymmetry in the staging of the theoretical gaze designates a theatricality in theory that not only opens, but also immediately closes, the possibility that seeing could ever see itself. This asymmetry is owed to the impossibility that, in spite of all attempts at emulating divine vision, the gaze pertaining to the gods could ever be converted into the gaze directed at them. Since it is the gods' privilege to (actively) see seeing in the act of seeing, the theatrical dimension of theory indicates a prevalence of the moment of passively being seen (seeing) in the human theoretical gaze. The asymmetry between the gazes that constitutes the theatricality of theory also concerns a disparity in nature of the two moments. Theatricality names the inescapable necessity by which theory, of which Blumenberg held that it itself could not be seen cannot but turn itself into a spectacle in which it can be seen – without, however, ever being able to assimilate the audience's gaze directed at itself. The acts (*Verrichtungen*) in which it must engage, and which make it visible, are a function of the asymmetrical assembling of the spectators who witness a seeing that strives to become seen seeing. But to say that, therefore, there is an intrinsic theatricality of theory is also to suggest that theory redoubles, multiplies, and transforms itself without end in sight. Indeed, thanks to the failure of theory to witness its own seeing, there is a history of theory, a world theatre of theory, in which even the possibility of the 'optics of prefabrication' and the subsequent 'coerced vision' that arise with the technology of the manipulation of light is not an accident that befalls theory from the outside (*Light as Metaphor* 54). Rather, it is a possibility with which theory goes pregnant from the very beginning. Thanks to theory's theatricality, this is a history that includes the possibility of a loss, or end, of theory, of its entire theatricality, that is, of its performance for a public. Blumenberg deplores this loss at the end of his book on the Thracian maid, since it is nothing less than the loss of theory itself. But such loss can be tragic or comic. With the asymmetry of the gazes, theory is also exposed to the constant threat of becoming empty and futile. The threat of being turned into a comedy of itself, and even the temptation of turning itself into a comedy by itself, are real possibilities of theory, ones that are not accidental either. They too derive from theory's constitutive relation to the theatre and are testimony to the fact that even the end of theory is still played out in the theatre. It is a theoretical end – a theatrical end.

NOTES

1 In this context, see Derrida's critique of the idea that metaphysics can be unseated through a reversal of Platonism in *Spurs: Nietzsche's Styles.* For his own

account of how theatre combines with philosophical thought, I refer to 'Plato's Pharmacy.' See also my analysis of that relation in the chapter devoted to Derrida's concept of reading in *The Wild Card of Reading: On Paul de Man* (149–80).

2 A first version of this text appeared under the title 'Der Sturz des Protophilo- sophen – Zur Komik der reinen Theorie, anhand einer Rezeptionsgeschichte der Thales-Anekdote,' in *Das Komische. Poetik und Hermeneutik VII* (11–64). The present context does not permit a comparison of the two versions.

3 As the latest version of the Thales anecdote in Jacques Taminiaux's *The Thra- cian Maid and the Professional Thinker: Arendt and Heidegger* indicates, even with Heidegger the potential of the anecdote has not been exhausted. In Taminiaux's study of Heidegger's discussion of the Aristotelian notions of *phronesis* and *praxis* – in which he argues, pitting Aristotle against Plato, that Heidegger, in total disregard of these notions' embeddedness in a practical philosophy, reinterprets them to fit Plato's conception of the *bios theoretikos* – Hannah Arendt is shown to oppose these Heideggerian moves in the name of a thinking that originates in Aristotle's notion of the *bios politikos*, and whose understanding of theory is not alienated from the human beings' practical concerns. Arendt, Taminiaux asserts, laughs with the laughter of the Thracian maid at the philosopher's theoretical and political fallacies. He writes: 'The professional philosopher of whom she laughs with the Thracian woman who made fun of Thales, is he who for having devoted himself entirely to the activ- ity of thinking, promotes to an absolute rank what is only one human activity among others' (168).

4 As thus becomes clear, with the anecdote about Thales and the Thracian maid, Plato not only inscribes the position of anti-theory into theory itself, but also posits anti-theory as a strictly philosophical position, intelligible only in view of what theory aims at, and hence a moment within theory itself. It is appropriate, therefore, that several of the variations of the anecdote, in partic- ular the latest one by Taminiaux, can make of the Thracian maid the true phi- losopher.

5 That *theoria* is contemplation of the divine is even more obvious with Aristotle. See Hannelore Rausch, *Theoria: Von ihrer sakralen zur philosophischen Bedeutung* 11–12, 143ff.

6 Wlad Godzich evokes the Greek institution of the *theoroi* to argue that from the start, theory, for the Greeks, is a public and not a private act carried out by a lone cogitating philosopher in *The Culture of Literacy* 165.

7 For what follows, it is not insignificant to note that Kerényi understands the being-seen that is intimately tied up with seeing as a being-known. He writes: 'In the Greek sense Existence is seeing and being-seen, or more exactly, know-

ing and being-known, or most exactly at all, being and being-known' (*Religion* 150).

8 However suggestive, the gesture by which Aristotle becomes squarely opposed to Plato is highly problematic. Plato's philosophy is not exclusively a celebration of the *bios theoretikos*. After having exited from the cave, and contemplated the light, the philosopher returns intent on freeing the inhabitants of cave from the fetters of darkness. It is certainly the case that Aristotle was the first to have recognized the domain of the practical in its own right, but this does not mean at all that *theoria* has become secondary. *Sophia* is inextricably connected to *phronesis*. 'One is certainly wrong,' as Gadamer has remarked, 'when one denigrates the priority that ... [Aristotle] did grant the theoretical life by describing it as his platonic inheritance. Quite the contrary, Aristotle was the first to establish the independence of the practical-political question of the good from its older form which was theoretically oriented to cosmology. He opened his investigation into human praxis, the *Ethics*, with the compact sentence: "All striving in knowledge and deeds and choices aims at the good." But it is just as obvious to him that theoretical interest does not need a legitimation either, and that it animates every human being' ('In Praise of Theory' 88; see also 98). If *phronesis* is suspended from *sophia* and *theoria* in Aristotle, knowledge of the good remains the final standard of practical life. From what we have seen about the Greek notion of *theoria* and the inseparable connection of knowing and seeing that this notion implies, it follows that what is seen, and thus known, is always seen as form, figure, or shape. For this reason, the known is, to quote Kerényi, 'as actual and consequently as certain, indeed, as efficacious, as anything which is immediately and clearly seen' (145). Yet, for the Greeks, as Kerényi has recalled, moral or practical ideas such as justice or honour are no exception in this regard. Rather than being experienced affectively, they are understood as steady forms, or figures of being, hence as objective realities, as it were, that, as such, inevitably invite the look of *theoria*, of a seeing that beholds them, precisely, in this actuality that is theirs. In other words, conceived as forms – forms to which they owe their actuality – moral ideas require theoretical knowledge (147). (The German original is considerably more precise than the English translation. See Karl Kerényi, *Die Antike Religion: Ein Entwurf von Grundlinien* 108–9).

9 Except for the backdrop, the theatre stage in the Middle Ages was surrounded on all sides by the public. Alewyn writes: 'Only the theatre stage of the Renaissance withdraws from the public and now faces the auditorium breadthwise and with little depth, like a line. The more the baroque period unfolds, the more the depth of the stage increases, with the effect that the relations become reversed. The convex stage of the Middle Ages is replaced by the con-

cave stage of the baroque, a funnel widely open that sucks the spectators into its depth' (59).

WORKS CITED

Alewyn, Richard, and Karl Sälzle. *Das grosse Welttheater. Die Epoche der höfischen Feste.* Hamburg: Rowohlt, 1959.

Blumenberg, Hans. *Begriffe in Geschichten.* Frankfurt am Main: Suhrkamp, 1998.

– *Das Lachen der Thrakerin: Eine Urgeschichte der Theorie.* Frankfurt am Main: Suhrkamp, 1987.

– 'Light as Metaphor for Truth: At a Preliminary Stage of Philosophical Concept Formation.' *Modernity and the Hegemony of Vision.* Ed. D.M. Levin. Berkeley: U of California P, 1993. 30–62.

Foucault, Michel. 'Theatrum Philosophicum.' *Critique* 282 (November 1970): 885–908.

Gadamer, Hans-Georg. 'In Praise of Theory.' Trans. D.J. Schmidt and J. Steinwand. *Ellipsis* 1.1 (Spring 1990): 85–99.

Gasché, Rodolphe. *The Wild Card of Reading: On Paul de Man.* Cambridge: Harvard UP, 1998. 149–80.

Godzich, Wlad. *The Culture of Literacy.* Cambridge: Harvard UP, 1994.

Kerényi, Karl. *Die Antike Religion: Ein Entwurf von Grundlinien.* Düsseldorf: Eugen Diederichs Verlag, 1952.

– *The Religion of the Greeks and Romans.* Trans. C. Holme. New York: Dutton, 1962.

Liddell, Henry George, and Robert Scott. *A Greek-English Dictionary.* Oxford: Oxford UP, 1978.

Plato. *The Collected Dialogues.* Ed. E. Hamilton and H. Cairns. Princeton: Princeton UP, 1980.

Preisendanz, Wolfgang, and Rainer Warning, eds. *Das Komische: Poetik und Hermeneutik VII.* Munich: Fink Verlag, 1976.

Rausch, Hannelore. *Theoria: Von ihrer sakralen zur philosophischen Bedeutung.* Munich: Fink Verlag, 1982.

Smith, Barbara Herrnstein. *Belief and Resistance: Dynamics of Contemporary Intellectual Controversy.* Cambridge: Harvard UP, 1997.

Taminiaux, Jaques. *The Thracian Maid and the Professional Thinker: Arendt and Heidegger.* Trans. M. Gendre. Albany: SUNY P, 1998.

Topo-philosophies:
Plato's Diagonals, Hegel's Spirals, and Irigaray's Multifolds

ARKADY PLOTNITSKY

[Shall we do it] by a method very appropriate for application by Theaetetus and yourself, seeing that both of you are geometers? What is it? I would say, 'by the diagonal and secondly by the diagonal of the diagonal.' What do you mean? How is this human race of ours endowed? So far as its ... potential is concerned, is it not very like a diagonal?   Plato

The aim of this essay is to sketch certain Hegelian trajectories of Luce Irigaray's work and, reciprocally, certain Irigarayan trajectories of Hegel's, the trajectories that I shall trace via Plato, at one, and Gilles Deleuze and Jacques Derrida, at another end of the history of Western philosophy. Irigaray engages Hegel directly in her writing, as in such major works as *Speculum of the Other Woman* and *This Sex Which Is Not One*, or in her essay on Hegel, 'The Universal as Mediation.' My main concern here, however, is a certain general configuration arising at the intersection of Hegel's and Irigaray's thought, most especially in her earlier work. This configuration, I argue, enables a deeper understanding of a radical transformation of classical philosophical conceptuality entailed by Irigaray's feminist project and related developments, both in feminist or gender theory and elsewhere, such as in Deleuze's and Derrida's work. I shall also suggest several connections between these thinkers and certain mathematical ideas – some elementary and some more complex and esoteric, without making any substantive technical or disciplinary mathematical claims. I would like, especially in the context of recent debates concerning the usage of such ideas in the humanities, to stress this point from the outset.[1] The philosophical content of this essay can be recast so as to avoid any reference to mathematics altogether. To do so, however, would be, first, to impoverish the portrayal of the thought of the thinkers in question and, thus, of philosophy itself. Indeed a certain mathematical stratum appears to be irreducible in philosophy. Or, at least, philosophy appears to contain an irreducible quasi-mathematical stratum, that is, a stratum that is mathematical-like and philosophically intersecting with mathematics but not mathematical in its technical, disciplinary sense. Secondly, to do so would be, conversely, to deprive mathematics of its conceptual richness, which reciprocally makes it philosophical or quasi-philosophical. For, beyond having a significant philosophical and cultural import, mathematical concepts can be and have been converted into philosophy, just as certain philosophical ideas can be and have been into mathematics. It is, however, more difficult to speak of philosophical disciplinarity in the same way as of that of mathematics. Here, I shall adopt Deleuze and Guattari's understanding of philosophy, in *What Is Philosophy?*, as the creation of new concepts, indeed concepts that are forever new, thus also defining it as, in Nietzsche's phrase, always the philosophy of the future. While I would argue this understanding to be Hegelian, and Deleuze and Guattari indeed especially credit Hegel (*What Is Philosophy?* 11–12), I would also argue that Irigaray's project in particular (albeit not uniquely) gives a new dimension to the task that philosophy, thus, sets to itself. The term 'concept' itself must be used in the specific sense given to it by Deleuze and Guattari rather than in any common sense of it, in particular that of an entity established by a generalization from particulars or 'any general or abstract idea' (11–12, 24). According to their view, a philosophical concept has a complex multi-layered structure, or architecture. It is a multi-component conglomerate of concepts (in their conventional sense), figures, metaphors, particular elements, and so forth. So understood, concepts inevitably entail an engagement of diverse disciplines and human endeavours – say, mathematics and science, on the one hand, and literature and art, on the other.

Hegel's spiral is, arguably, the most famous geometrical image used in philosophy. It is worth observing, however, that, while a certain spiralness may indeed be associated with his philosophical vision, Hegel himself does not appear ever to have used or even had in mind the spiral as such, when the image is attributed to him, most famously in closing the first *Logic*. Plato's diagonal, while indeed used by Plato at key points, requires more explaining, although it would be familiar to connoisseurs of Irigaray, since *Speculum*, her ground-breaking philosophical work, closes with a discussion of it. *Speculum*, however, also enters a more complex tropological and conceptual 'geometry' or 'topology.' These two tropes are distinguished by their mathematical provenance: geometry has to do with, or at least fundamentally involves, measurement, while topology (disregarding measurement and scale) deals only with the structure of space qua space (topos) and with the essential shapes of figures. In so far as one deforms a given figure continuously (i.e., in so far as one does not separate points previously connected and, conversely, does not connect points previously separated) the resulting figure is considered topologically the same. Thus, all spheres, of any size and however deformed, are topologically equivalent. They are, however, topologically distinct from tori. Spheres and tori cannot be converted into each other without disjoining their connected points or joining the disconnected ones. (The holes in tori make this impossible.)[2] Obviously, in speaking of the organization or configurations (figures) of concepts, topology (or geometry) can only be used as a broad metaphor. This metaphor, however, appears to be exceptionally useful in suggesting a certain connectedness and fluidity of concepts or the complexity of their organization. I shall approach this philosophical topology via several concepts, borrowed from more arcane areas of modern mathematics, specifically topology and its mathematical extensions, and philosophically extended here. The term 'multifold' itself is my own and refers to a class of *philosophical* conceptual conglomerates that results.

I. Multifolds

I begin with geometrical images that are neither especially esoteric nor difficult to visualize, namely a helix, a kind of spiral, and a helicoid – a kind of spiral surface, extending the ideas of diagonal and spiral. For a spiral, too, can be conceived of as a diagonal. If one rolls, *folds*, into a cylinder a square with a diagonal drawn upon it, the diagonal becomes a spiral. A 'spiral,' however conceived, can be used to represent or to stand for a more or less complex and more or less vertiginous movement. It may be a movement up, say, towards God or Geist, as in Plato, Leibniz, and Hegel, or towards bottomless abysses, as in famed deconstructive vertigoes. It is difficult to say whether these result from moving or from looking up or down. Hölderlin's 'abysses above' may do best here. In any event, one can contemplate a helicoid or, to complicate the picture, clusters or (infinite) families of helicoids, topologically (continuously) deformed into each other within each family. Ultimately, one needs to combine each such family into a single object, so as to see each two-dimensional helicoid as a 'point' of a new space, and yet also to conceive of this space in terms of its more standard topology, whose points are regular dimensionless points. This will complicate the picture, since such objects are not visualizable, except by means of tentative and ultimately inadequate two-dimensional (at best three-dimensional) models.[3] Rather than moving up, or only up, towards God or even deconstruction, the 'surfaces' I have in mind extend or un*fold* in multiple directions, like the fold in Leibniz or Deleuze, explored by Deleuze in *The Fold: Leibniz and the Baroque*. I here use 'fold' in its most general sense (closer to the French *pli*) as suggested by the helicoidal imagery just introduced. Alternatively, one can think of it in terms of all possibilities in which a fabric can flow: to fold and to unfold, to pleat and to unpleat, to wrinkle and to smooth itself out, and so forth, or all of these at various points and on various scales. One can also think of a mountain landscape in all of its geometrical and topological aspects at all scales. Or one can think of a variational musical fabric, from Bach to Pierre Boulez. The latter indeed wrote a composition, inspired by Mallarmé, called 'Folds upon Folds.' The signifier 'fold' is often inserted into the terms designating the concepts, mathematical and philosophical, invoked in this essay – such as mani*folds*, multi*folds*, and so forth.

One can imagine the curved surfaces of such helicoids as mirrored and reflecting in – and, as it were, upon – each other, and further changing their forms in the process, like fun-house mirrors reflecting in each other. One can also include Derridian 'chandeliers' (*lustres*) reflecting in all these mirrored surfaces. This will shift the register of the image into that of philosophical concepts (in Deleuze and Guattari's sense) or allegory (in de Man's sense). For unlike real chandeliers, Derrida's represent or allegorize the circumstances that disallow one to unequivocally distinguish sources of light from their reflections or that which mirrors from that which is mirrored, or claim the possibility of an absolutely original source of light or even an original plurality of such sources. In the philosophical circumstances here in question, the play of reflections cannot be reduced to an unequivocal discrimination between sources and images. (This is not to say that nothing materially exists under these conditions or nothing materially produces them.) What Derrida calls dissemination, or différance/dissemination ('chandelier' [*lustre*] is part of this multi-conceptual, and itself disseminating, matrix of many, by now famous, names), *reflects* this irreducible play and plurality.[4] It does not, however, reflect or map the ultimate efficacity of such effects. This efficacity can be 'reflected upon' philosophically and rigorously related to but cannot be illuminated, or indeed otherwise accessed. I here use the term 'efficacity' in its dictionary sense of power and agency producing effects, but, in this case, without the possibility of ascribing this agency causality, or ultimately anything as exemplified by Derrida's 'différance' or Foucault's 'power.'

With the features just described combined, one might have a reasonable image of what is at stake in Irigaray's mirrors and reflections (in either sense) in *Speculum* and beyond. Epistemologically, like other works just mentioned, her works guide us to a vision of an irreducible entanglement of mirrored and mutually reflecting, multi-folded – and multi-unfolded – surfaces and sources of light without an absolute origin or centre, or an absolute reality, or, it follows, an absolute mirror. Feminist philosophy and politics demand, and are defined by, this epistemology. Mirror – speculum – is a central figure and concept, or allegory, for Irigaray. It could even be said to be *the* central figure, were her mirrors to allow for an absolutely central figure or an absolute centre.

The figure of the mirror links, on the one hand, a long history of philosophy and its curved mirrors – those of Plato, Hegel, Nietzsche, Lacan, Deleuze, and Derrida – and on the other, the history of feminist philosophy (and sometimes of literature), from Sappho to Christine de Pisan, to Mary Wollstonecraft, to Virginia Woolf, to Simone Weil, to Simone de Beauvoir, to Irigaray and contemporary feminism and gender theory. (Indeed the above 'segregation' is not right, and one should intermix these names in a more complex way.) The conjunction of the figures of the mirror and the fold is fitting, since these 'figures' *reflect* and *explicate* two great philosophemes of Western philosophy. The first is *reflection*, which concept is especially significant both in the history of classical philosophy, where it culminates in Hegel's concepts of speculative and, finally, absolute reflection, and, as it may be called, non-classical philosophy, such as that of Irigaray, or Deleuze, Serres, and Derrida. The second is ex-*pli*-cation, which, as Serres observes, literally means un-*pleat*-ing or unfolding (65). Reflection so conceived extends into an immense interplay of mirroring folds – 'the pleats of matter' and 'the folds of the soul'; the folds of history and philosophy; the folds of gender, the feminine (or, of course, the masculine) and sexuality; or the interfoldings of all these folds. At the same time, both philosophemes are transgressed in so far as the fold represents philosophy as the creation of concepts, contrasted to reflection or explication by Deleuze and Guattari. Hegel's absolute reflection, however, comes close to the creation of concepts, and indeed (this may be a problem, even *the* problem) absolute concepts, the Absolute Concept (*das absolut Begriff*).

Families of helicoids is not an unreasonable visualization (to the degree that one can visualize them) or allegorization of more complex mathematical concepts and of quasi-mathematical concepts that are derived from them and that are here assembled under the rubric of multifolds. These concepts, such as fibre bundles, sheaves, deformations of structures, topoi, moduli spaces, and so forth, were developed in the wake of Bernhard Riemann's and then Henri Poincaré's work in the nineteenth and early twentieth centuries. They were instrumental in several areas defining twentieth-century mathematics and played major roles in modern physics. Although technical details are often prohibitive for non-specialists, the conceptual essence of such objects is not inaccessible, and I shall explain it presently. In so far as these mathematical concepts are used in, or in order to approach, the philosophical topologies here considered, they give the helicoid allegory of these topologies offered above a more complex quasi-mathematical structure.[5] I shall here use three quasi-mathematical concepts of multifoldness. These concepts correspond, respectively, (a) to a particular mathematical conceptualization of geometrical figures, such as helicoids; (b) to a further mathematical enrichment of such objects through new spaces associated to them; and (c) to multiplicities of such objects, as each such multiplicity is itself given the structure of a 'space' in which each such object is a 'point.'

The concept of the manifold is due to Riemann, who, sometimes, considered such objects more geometrically than topologically. (The invention of topology as a mathematical discipline is due primarily to Poincaré.)[6] Riemann considered the so-called differential or smooth manifolds, which roughly means that one can define differential calculus on such objects. A manifold is a kind of patchwork of (local) spaces, each of which can be mapped by a (flat) Euclidean, or Cartesian, coordinate map, without allowing for a global Euclidean structure or a single coordinate system for the whole, except in the limited case of a Euclidean homogeneous space itself. That is, every point has a small neighbourhood that is (or can be treated as) Euclidean, but the overall manifold is not. Smooth, curved surfaces, such as helicoids, are manifolds in this sense. They are also smooth, differential manifolds and as such are subject to differential topology. In short, we here deal with objects that are locally flat or straight, but globally curved. The concept of manifold can be linked to the idea of non-Euclidean geometry, and the non-Euclidean geometry of positive curvature was discovered by Riemann as well. (Earlier, his teacher, another great German mathematician, Karl Friedrich Gauss was a co-discoverer of the geometry of negative curvature and a precursor of topology.) Riemannian (curved) spaces are differential manifolds and one of Riemann's many great inventions was the concept of measurement in a curved space. The concept was crucial to Einstein's general theory of relativity, his non-Newtonian theory of gravitation, according to which placing matter in space curves it, making light propagate curvilinearly. These ideas may be illustrated by considering Paul Klee's great painting *The New Harmony*, the title probably alluding to Leibniz. Klee's painting gives the Cartesian coordinate grid both curvature and a complex colour and light scheme, representing or allegorizing a curved, Riemannian or perhaps Lobachevskian (negatively curved), rather than Euclidean or Cartesian, space, while also indicating that the latter still play a role, mathematically or conceptually. Claude Monet's *Nympheas* (*The Water Lilies*) (1918), painted on the curved walls in the Musée d'Orangerie in Paris, would give another spectacular example, and both paintings may be seen (and perhaps were conceived) as allegories of both Riemannian spaces and Einsteinian general relativity.

If in the case just described at stake are spaces that are locally flat or straight but globally curved, the second form of multifoldness I consider is formed by spaces that are locally straight but globally 'twisted.' By this, however, I mean a more complex and more multifolded structure of such 'spaces,' corresponding to the so-called fibre bundles and sheaves in mathematics. The Moebius strip is the most famous example. The model of the Moebius strip is a strip of paper with its ends glued together by turning one of them upside down. Locally, in the vicinity of any given point, the Moebius strip is indistinguishable from a regular (cylinder) strip, which one obtains by gluing the ends of a strip of paper, while keeping both edges on the same side. Each point is an intersection of a vertical interval (think of each such an interval as a stalk to be added to a sheaf) and a horizontal interval common to all, drawn in the middle of the strip (think of it as a single long stalk to tie the sheaf). We can now glue the ends of the strip either regularly or twist one of them in a Moebius strip, or tie our stalk accordingly (hence the sheaf terminology). No single vertical stalk, or its intersection with a long stalk, is affected in itself, and the (tied) horizontal stalk is a circle in both cases. Two global objects are, however, different topologically. If you begin to paint on one side of the Moebius strip, say, in blue, you will end painting 'both' sides in the same colour – that is, it only has one side. Its boundary is topologically a single circle, while the boundary or, rather, boundaries of a regular (glued) strip are two separated circles. (One can paint its two sides in two different colours, say, red and blue.) A regular strip is also a sheaf, but a trivial, untwisted, one. In general, a circle and a line interval are replaced by other, usually more complex, mathematical objects. A horizontal circle or its equivalent is called the base of a sheaf, and vertical intervals or their equivalents are called 'fibres.' The space as a whole is a bundle of 'fibres' (hence the fibre bundle terminology). Technically, the terms 'sheaves' and 'fibre bundles' serve to designate somewhat different mathematical objects, but these differences are not essential for the present purposes. The essence is that one can glue a multiplicity of objects into a single object so that a global 'twist' may result, or conversely one can decompose an object such as the Moebius strip into this type of configuration in order to distinguish it from the untwisted ones. Such objects are, in general, richer in structure than manifolds, although they can be manifolds, or be built around manifolds in the way the Moebius strip is built around a circle, which is a one-dimensional manifold (obviously meaning by 'circle' the *curve* surrounding the area). Differential manifolds inherently have sheaves associated with them; for example, the so-called tangent sheaf, formed by spaces tangent to each point of a manifold – say, all planes tangent to a sphere, joined into a single object. Thus, sheaves, too, may viewed as 'spaces,' in which each point is already a 'space,' which concept takes a more radical form in the next concept I want to introduce.

This concept, while also due to Riemann, is primarily indebted to much more recent developments, in particular in the mathematics of the so-called moduli spaces, which are examples of applying the general principle of combining a multiplicity of objects of a given type into a single higher level of objects. One may describe the philosophical content of what is at stake as follows. In analysing certain objects, such as geometrical curves or surfaces, one considers jointly all – or a large enough number of – variations or deformations of structures that define such an object or are associated with it, and combines the objects defined by each such variation into a new, higher-level structure. Why do so? First of all, the structure of such objects provides new information, perhaps otherwise unobtainable, about the original object. Secondly, the process leads to a construction of new 'spaces,' which can be considered in order to approach the initial configuration, or on their own. In addition (although I can only mention this here), such objects allow one to enrich the analysis of a given original object by engaging and trafficking between different registers of analysis. Since, however, it is not effective and in practice impossible to consider all such variations, one must determine which variations are sufficiently equivalent to be subsumed within a single variation, which should be discarded, and how some among such variations can be organized. In short, one must understand how these variations unfold and how some of them can be folded or fold together. One thus deals with variations of already varied spaces, folds upon folds, and folds of folds. According to Deleuze, 'the ideal fold is the *Zweifalt*, a fold that differentiates and is differentiated. When Heidegger calls upon the *Zweifalt* to be the differentiator of difference, he means above all that differentiation does not refer to a pregiven undifferentiated, but to a Difference that endlessly unfolds and folds over each of its two sides, and that unfolds the one only while refolding the other, in a coextensive unveiling and veiling of Being, of presence and of withdrawal of presence' (*The Fold* 30). I would add, however, that the 'point' of this 'surface' of Difference must already be seen as a differentiation and folding of differentiated folds, which stretches the limits of our imagination (although this is a standard operation in modern mathematics). There is a general philosophical principle here, which I shall consider at several levels. (It is operative in the case of sheaves as well.) It may be called the principle of 'enrichment.' New, or sometimes any, meaningful information concerning a given object requires considering related objects of a much greater structural complexity. Naturally, the initial object need not be 'poor' in structure, and it as much depends on what it is being compared with. It can be quite complex, a Riemannian manifold or a sheaf, for example. Klee's space in *The New Harmony* (and we might also think of variations of light and colour here) may be seen as an *element* – a point – of a higher-level space, other points of which are variations of this manifold space. In a certain sense, as we look at the painting we 'see' such a multiplicity, albeit not all possible variations of this space. Yet another model or allegory is André Kertész's *Distortions*, which I shall consider later. Bach's *Goldberg Variations* may give us the best model here. One can see each of the variations as an unfolding or varying musical space, which spaces are then combined into the whole thirty-two-piece work, while a potential infinite expansion of this space of variations of variations is suggested. While the actual work is closed by Bach, it may be seen as the image of a multifold. A potential number of variations that can be inserted between the first and the last (which are the same, so that the whole work can be seen as a kind of Moebius strip, too) may be imagined as, in principle, uncontainable.

Now, both Hegel's and Irigaray's visions, and those that connect them – such as Nietzsche's, Mallarmé's, Blanchot's, Lacan's, Deleuze's, and Derrida's – have significant affinities with and sometimes deploy the quasi-mathematics of multifolds just described. This claim is qualified by the question whether (or to what degree) the quasi-mathematical concepts in question are part of – rather than a particular, and specifically 'topological,' allegorization (here undertaken) of – the conceptual 'topologies' of these authors. With this qualification in mind, I see the introduction of, in this sense, a multifold economy of history as one of the greatest achievements and legacies of Hegel's philosophy. It is a commonplace that Hegel was first to bring history and philosophy together in a philosophically rigorous way. According to Hegel, however, not only is any given concept, however it is overtly introduced or indeed conceived, a concept in Deleuze and Guattari's sense, but it also has the conceptual and historical 'topology' of a multifold, as just described.

Irigaray's 'topology' of the feminine, first, introduces a conceptual field analogous to, although differently multifolded from, that of Hegel. Secondly, it entails, even if it does not altogether or fully effectively enact, a radical transformation – a refolding and, as it were, re-unfolding – of all classical historico-political and conceptual economies by regendering them, philosophically and politically, to the degree that such classical economies can be retained. As Irigaray points out, some of them may need to be retained, at least for while, for complex philosophical and political reasons, in part because, from and before Plato to Hegel and beyond, these economies have always been gendered, even if in spite of themselves. Irigaray's work is, I think, best understood as interacting with and refiguring the philosophical tradition or enclosure rather than reducing or bypassing it. Indeed, as she argues, it may not be possible to do otherwise.[7] It also entails a radical refiguring of the masculine and its interaction with the feminine. In short, it refigures the whole centred – logo-centred, phallogo-centred, Oedipo-centred, and so forth – politico-philosophical economy, from Plato on. As Irigaray reminds us in *Speculum*, in Plato this economy is shaped by the idea of the diagonal, to which I shall now turn.

II. Theogonals

The diagonal of the square was both a great glory and a great problem, almost a scandal, in Greek mathematics and philosophy. The reason for this was that the diagonal and the side of a square were mathematically proved to be mathematically incommensurable: their 'ratio' is irrational; that is, it cannot be represented as a ratio of two whole numbers, and hence is not a rational number.[8] This was the first example of such a number – what we now call the square root of, for example, 2 – a number that was proved to be unrepresentable as a ratio of two positive integers. I would not be able to say – nobody would – what its exact numerical value is. It does not have an *exact* numerical value in the way rational numbers do: that is, it cannot be exactly represented (only approximated) by a finite, or an infinite periodical, decimal fraction, and, hence, by a regular fraction – by a ratio of two whole numbers. (The Greeks conceived of the situation in geometrical terms of incommensurability of the lengths of two line intervals.) The term 'irrational' – both *alogon* (outside logos) and *arreton* (incomprehensible) were used – was, at the time of the discovery of the first irrational numbers, also used in its direct sense. The discovery undermined the Pythagorean belief that, like everything rational, the harmony of the cosmos was expressible in terms of (whole) numbers and their commensurable ratios (proportions). It was also in part responsible for a crucial shift from arithmetical to geometrical thinking in mathematics and philosophy, before 'algebra,' a marvellous invention of Arab medieval mathematics (albeit indebted to some Greek mathematics, especially to the work of Diophantus of the third century), eventually entered the scene and defined mathematical modernity. For, while the diagonal of the square was self-evidently within the limits of geometrical representation, it was outside those of arithmetical representation, as the Greeks conceived of it. It was an extraordinary and, at the time, shocking – scandalous – discovery, sometimes attributed to Plato's friend and student Theaetetus (others are mentioned as well), and crucial to Plato's work, including the dialogue under the same title.[9] To cite Maurice Blanchot: 'The Greek experience, *as we reconstitute it*, accords special value to the "limit" and reemphasizes the long-recognized scandalousness of the irrational: the indecency of that which, in measurement, is immeasurable. (He who first discovered the incommensurability of the diagonal of the square perished; he drowned in a shipwreck, for he had met with a strange and utterly foreign death, the nonplace bounded by absent frontiers)' (103; emphasis added).[10]

On (for the Greeks) the positive side, in Irigaray's words in *Speculum*: 'Since no estimate in whole numbers is possible, the diagonal will supply the excessiveness as a certain non-integrality ... playing with the passage by/to the immeasurability of the greatness of the One,' or God (358). The divine itself becomes a diagonal, and the diagonal a kind of the theogonal. The mind of God, the creator of all perfect figures, such as the square, may be supremely rational and as such is the prototype of all human rationality. However – this is the scandal – at least some of the objects that God's or perhaps even human mind creates, even mathematical ones (the most rational of objects), are never accessible to human rationality, even though this inaccessibility can itself be discovered rationally. Indeed it can be discovered by means of a mathematical proof, a paradigmatic form of human (and, some argue, divine) rationality. This configuration defines the project of philosophy throughout its history, from Anaximander to Heidegger and Derrida, both of whom explore its extraordinary deconstructive potential, or Irigaray, who was among the first to reflect on the gender economy this project entails.[11]

God, too, can be thought of or allegorized as a diagonal in this sense, to subject the history of the diagonal as a signifier, first, to a quasi-Lacanian and then Irigarayan analysis here. God can perhaps be contemplated as a geometrical image, but cannot be fully accessed – only obliquely approached – by means of a ratio, mathematical or philosophic. This obliqueness becomes radical only when the divine itself is seen as incompatible with the theological determination of the inaccessible in question in it. The circle (whose measurement involves an even more complicated number, π) is a more famous image, but the diagonal offers more direct (in either sense) diagrammatical potential. The spiral may be seen as combining the circle and the diagonal, and hence offers an even richer diagonal/theogonal allegory.

The diagonal, thus, measures the difference between the human and the divine – the difference irreducible and itself ir-rational (that is, inaccessible to human rationality), but not altogether unbridgeable. The human mind may, as it were, be diagonalized, even if only to a degree, so as to approach the divine mind. The diagonal becomes a diagram and a theogram (also in the post-Derridian sense of an inscription of the divine). The 'spirituality' of the spirit can be allegorized as follows, and, I would argue, has been conceived of since Plato and before (or at

least this thought can be allegorized accordingly). The diagram is a
square with man and God in respectively the lower left and right corners, and with the rationality and Spirit of God representing the upper
right corner. One should actually think here in terms of an infinite
square or an infinite sequence of squares, with God at infinity, the picture itself unrealizable but only allegorizable by means of a diagram.
Hegel will conceive of this infinite theo-diagonalization in historical
terms. One can also 'play' various allegorical games here – for example,
stretching this square into a strip and making a Moebius strip out of it,
which would transform, twist, the position of the human and the divine.
Hegel plays this type of game at the end of the first *Logic*, where the
famous 'spiral' (Hegel himself speaks of circles and circles of circles)
multiply twists and returns upon itself, as it 'progresses' diagonally forward and upward. The task of humanity and, in particular, philosophy
becomes that of developing human rationality and spirituality that
approximate those of God. This spiritually enriched humanity can be
represented by the upper left corner of the extending square-diagram,
as it extends to, but, unlike God, never reaches, infinity.

The process may be called 'diagonal enrichment,' yet another
'enrichment' principle that has considerable significance in modern
mathematics. The question is how to give to or associate with a structurally impoverished object a kind of structural richness comparable to
that associated with an analogously defined object that is structurally
rich in the same sense, or how, as it were, to transfer such structural
richness. To return to the theological diagonalization just outlined,
God's spiritual endowment is rich, indeed infinitely rich, while that of
humanity is extremely poor, and no spiritual, upward movement for
humanity is possible without diagonally traversing through (the available portion of) divine spirituality. The task of philosophy and human
practice – the task of Plato's *Republic*, for example – is to maximally
enrich the spiritual endowment of humanity on the model of and
approximating the divine one. At one point in *Statesman*, Plato says:

> [Shall we do it] by a method very appropriate for application by
> Theaetetus and yourself, seeing that both of you are geometers? What is it?
> I would say, 'by the diagonal and secondly by the diagonal of the diagonal.'
> What do you mean? How is this human race of ours endowed? So far as
> its ... potential is concerned, is it not very like a diagonal? (266ab)[12]

That the divine endowment is itself already constructed upon or, in

Derrida's terms, supplemented by human models (mathematical or other) is often forgotten by theology or even philosophy. Both Plato and Hegel did, however, realize that in order philosophically to engage this scheme one needs to refigure both the human and the divine. Similarly, but with some momentous reversals, in Irigaray's matrix, which utilizes an analogous diagram and economy of enrichment, one must refigure both the feminine and the masculine, and indeed, yet again, the human and the divine.

The task of diagonalization is not easy. The diagonal is only a diagram and has to be justified as rigorously as possible through complex analytical or analytico-political work, which has continued throughout the history of philosophy. Here I must omit a long analysis, in particular of Leibniz, and proceed directly to Hegel, who is arguably the most crucial example of this history of dialectial diagonalization, in part because he introduces history itself into philosophy. As conceived by Hegel, this history is also the history of philosophy and, as such, the history of the diagonal diagram at issue here and of its transformations. In this transformation, Plato's diagonal becomes a grand historical fold and multifold in the above sense, with some spiral movement to it. This immense multifold, however, is and can only be an allegorical diagram relating to that which is irreducibly inaccessible by any means, allegorical or not. Nor can these (manifold) allegories, especially in their theogonal aspects, be contained by mathematical or even quasi-mathematical allegories, any more than the (mathematical) diagonal can contain the theogonal that it diagrammatizes or theogrammatizes. This uncontainable, however, is the uncontainable, the inaccessible, of the radical epistemology, as here considered. It is not the inaccessible – the divine inaccessible or the inaccessible divine – of theology (including negative theology), as the creators of such theograms, from Plato to Hegel and beyond, would 'envision' (in either sense).

Beyond its historical character, the Hegelian diagonalization has several other features crucial in the present context. The first is the irreducibly materialist character of Hegel's so-called idealist philosophy. This needs to be understood both in the sense of the materiality of nature (i.e., of the irreducible interconnections between Spirit and Nature, or matter, in Hegel) and in the sense of the materiality of history (i.e., of the irreducible interconnections between Spirit and humanity). The second feature has to do with the movement from the economy of philosophical reflection to that of the philosophy and pedagogy of concepts, which defines the very enterprise of philosophy, in

Deleuze and Guattari's sense in *What Is Philosophy?*, where they specifically refer to Hegel's idea of concept (*Begriff*) as arguably the single most important insight of that type, even if its potential was not fully realized by Hegel himself (12). Given my limit here, however, I must bypass this subject, except for indicating that it is a consequence of Hegel's multifold philosophical topology. The third key feature is, then, the richness both of its unfolding and of its folding and refolding, which makes it into what I here call a multifold. Hegel's spiral designates the gradient – towards Absolute Knowledge – of this grandiose unfolding, with many (usually ignored) complex loops and returns, often Moebius-strip-like, and so forth, rather than a reduction of its richness to a linear progression.

Hegel says in the *Phenomenology*: 'The movement of carrying forward the form of [Spirit's] self-knowledge is the labor which Spirit accomplishes as actual [and therefore material] History [*wirkliche Geschichte*]' (488). However, he also realized and pursued the enormous complexity of the process involved, which in part results from the interfold, of spirit and matter within it. To return to Deleuze's idiom in *The Fold*, 'the pleats of matter' and 'the folds of the soul' continuously interact with, interfold, and pass into each other, and mix their curvatures. Indeed, this interaction already defines Leibniz's and, more generally, the baroque vision and allegorization of the world as well. Hegel gives both of these an irreducibly temporal, and historical, character. The process can, in various degrees, be configured and understood by spirit (through its interaction with nature and history, or politics) – whether 'spirit' refers to human spirituality (and in particular philosophy) or to the divine spirituality of the Hegelian Spirit or Geist. It is, in Hegel, only to the latter that the nature of the process in question can be accessible in full measure. The complete comprehension of this nature by *Geist* or, later, the Idea is what Hegel calls Absolute Knowledge. At the end of the *Phenomenology* Hegel *unfolds* this economy via his concept of sacrifice, further refigured by Bataille, whose work is a key connecting link between Hegel and Irigaray. So is, of course, the concept of sacrifice itself, in particular in the context of Sophocles' *Antigone*, a crucial text for both Irigaray and Hegel, especially in the *Phenomenology*. An extraordinary vision, one of the greatest philosophical visions ever, is suggested in the monumental paragraphs closing – or unclosing – Hegel's *Phenomenology of Spirit*. These paragraphs would require a separate analysis, and they resist and are indeed inaccessible to a summary or gloss.[13] This vision is made possible by, in Shelley's phrase, that 'wondrous alchemy' that both mixes and separates exteriority and interiority, spirituality and materiality, philosophy and history, tragedy and knowledge, contingency and necessity, and so forth – perhaps all conceivable conceptual oppositions and multiple clusters that one might form.

The multiplicity of this network is irreducible and is played out throughout Hegel's work. Hegel conceived history as an immense conglomerate of, interactively, concepts of history and historico-political practices, with multiple economies, continuous and discontinuous, organizing both theory and practice and the interactions between them. Hegel considers *ensembles* or *families*, indeed manifolds, of conceptual and historico-political formations – locally flat, but globally curved, locally straight but globally twisted – and manifolds of the interconnections and interactions between them, rather than merely such formations themselves. His philosophy is that of conglomerates or, again, multifolds of material and spiritual structures, theoretical conceptualities and historico-political practices, continuities and discontinuities, multiple economies of necessity and chance, and so forth, and of the interactions within and between such oppositions and junctures. The question of the structure and economy of the grand whole, and of the very possibility of assigning any wholeness to this interplay, defines the Hegelian problem of history.

This manifold or multifold process is what Hegel's spiral represents or allegorizes. As I said, 'diagonalization' from the human to the divine can only be accomplished through a radical rethinking, first, of both the human and the divine, and the interaction between them, and, second, of the interaction between spirituality, human and divine, and materiality (as nature and as history, or politics). Hegel, obviously, transforms the Christian diagonalization, again through a rethinking of the concept of sacrifice. Many a Greek diagonal is refigured as well, however. The entire 'Judeo–Greek' diagonalization is *converted* into an immense historical fold.

Now, one can think (and some have thought) of this fold as a helicoidal mirror and its lamps, to return to M.H. Abrams's old metaphor, or the families of such mirrors and Derridian disseminating chandeliers, as discussed earlier. One can, however, use even this second, far more complex and radical image only as preliminary allegory or a diagram for Hegel's historical-conceptual topology as the topology of the multifold, even if still grafting the diagonal of Plato's *theos* on its unfolding. That is, as what Hegel sees in the *Phenomenology* as 'the slow moving progression of Spirits' (i.e., stages through which the Hegelian Spirit passes on its way to Absolute Knowledge) entails all variations of the conceptual and historical structures (spiritual, material, or interactively both) that it considers, such as perception, consciousness and self-consciousness, spirit; or ethics, religion, art, philosophy, history, and so forth. Each of these structures are, to begin with, conceived as varied or manifold (i.e., entailing the multitudes of maps), fibred and fibre-bundled, Moebius-strip-like, and so forth, conceptually and historically. Secondly, and most crucially, this 'progression' combines these structures into a new, higher-level structure or, again, a manifold of structures and of the interactions between them. Indeed, in Hegel such multiplicities can often be best described in terms of one another. Each may serve as a descriptive 'mathematics' ('calculus,' 'algebra,' 'geometry,' 'topology,' 'analysis,' and so forth) or translation of the other, even though all of them are, jointly, placed in the service of the inaccessible. History is a calculus or allegory (one among many) of philosophy, philosophy is (again, one among many) that of history; matter of mind, mind of matter; consciousness of the unconscious, the unconscious of consciousness; and so forth.

Hegel's spiral, if there is any, does indicate an upward movement of Spirit and humanity, but only as a diagram. At the very least, one must also envision this spiral as circling along an immense folded manifold, a kind of baroque garment, like those in El Greco's paintings, whose geometry or topology may in turn be seen as allegorizing a similar theogonal economy. Each cross-section along this spiral is in turn an immense manifold of structures and connections, which cannot be reduced to an unequivocal, unitary, or punctual simplicity. One may also imagine the process through both the terraced Mountain of Purgatorio in Dante and, especially, Peter Breughel's painting of the Tower of Babel, both of which have helicoidal geometry, if with some crucial differences as far as the outcome of the journey is concerned. Hegel was undoubtedly aware of the possibilities offered – and problems posed – by both of these images.[14]

Since, as I said, it is ineffective and in practice impossible to consider all such variations, it is important to understand how some of them are organized, or along what orbits these variations unfold and how some of them can be folded together or fold upon themselves. Hegel offers a variety of historical sequences and stages (and other classifications) throughout his works. These, however, are only various and varying modes of organization or folding of multiple historical orbits. These mappings reflect manifolds and manifolds of manifolds of configurations found at any point of history (to the extent that one may still speak of *points* of history in this topology) and still more complex formations resulting from linking them in longer historical intervals.

The process also entails discontinuities and ruptures, such as death and sacrifice, and one might also see the Hegelian dialectic as an allegory of discontinuity, as de Man does.[15] Tragic ruptures, which are among these effects, become manifestations of Hegel's negativity, or perhaps of a still more radical negativity, which emerges in Hölderlin's work on tragedy and which Hegel sometimes tries to circumvent, or the power of which he tries to contain. He, however, continuously reinscribes these ruptures in his text, as he climbs or builds simultaneously both the Mountain of Purgatorio and the Tower of Babel, and translates them into each other, as any diagonal enrichment is ultimately bound to do. As a result, while it may be the former that is desired or hoped for, it is the latter that becomes the ultimate model. And it may well be a better, more multifold model (assuming that Dante's terraces can be anything else), given its richness, complexity, and philosophical or political potential, especially in so far as it is a model of translation which also prohibits any ultimate translation.[16]

III. The Women of the House of Thebes

The grand question posed by Irigaray's work and modern feminist and gender studies in general is how this history or this Hegelian manifold or multifold of many histories is gendered – that is, how it has always been gendered (even if and because in spite of itself) and how one needs to regender it. One can actually see along these lines much of the preceding history of feminism, beginning with Mary Wollstonecraft's meditation on political justice (in part in response to William Godwin's great work under this title, which was important for Hegel as well). I cannot here discuss many significant links and trajectories, extending from Hegel to Irigaray. One trajectory or orbit cannot be bypassed, however, and must be at least indicated – the one extending to Freud and Lacan, in which the diagonal diagram is refigured in Oedipal terms, is Oedipalized.

Put schematically or diagrammatically, what was considered here as diagonalization is Oedipalization, and, according to Freud and Lacan, or (with a different evaluation) to Deleuze and Guattari's *Anti-Oedipus*, has always been, from Plato and before to Hegel and after. This Oedipalization refigures both the human and the divine. First, in Freud's Oedipal economy, God, the Father, becomes Father, the God. Then, in Lacan, this (always political) economy is refigured, via, among others, Hegel (in part in Kojève's and Bataille's readings), as the economy of the symbolic, controlled by the Oedipal triangle as a signifier, which triangle can be conceived of as one-half of Oedipalized Plato's square divided by its diagonal. Ultimately, once the Lacanian register of the Real becomes engaged, this economy acquires the epistemology here considered. This economy is also irreducibly multifold.[17]

That which makes the human human and produces the divine is the Oedipal diagonalization from sons to fathers, which one might call 'the house of Thebes' diagram, taken more or less from Lévi-Strauss. Society and its ideological state apparatuses – its family fathers, king-fathers, priest-fathers, teacher-fathers, God-fathers (in either sense), and so forth – and history alike become a reproduction (also in either sense) of the Oedipal diagonal or theogonal. In Lacan's and Althusser's terms, they reproduce the conditions of Oedipal production, which production in turn extends from Oedipal politics as family politics to ideological state apparatuses considered by Althusser, via Marx and, thus, Hegel. Historically, the diagram extends and multiplies itself in both directions, to the earliest history of civilization and its discontents, and into the future.

What Irigaray's work shows is that this diagram irreducibly contains another diagram, which is, arguably, her greatest philosophical and political contribution, whether or not she manages ultimately to work out the resulting configuration and its implications most effectively, theoretically and politically. I make no strong claim in this respect. This is the secondary point here, as against the fact that her work makes it imperative to do so, however difficult such a task may be, theoretically and politically. This second diagram was in fact grafted by Freud and Lacan onto their Oedipal diagram, and indeed had already been grafted by Plato or Sophocles onto theirs. This diagram was, however, never considered by any of them and was repressed by all of them, especially in its potential for rediagonalization of all diagonals, and theogonals hitherto conceived. All these diagrams contain (in either sense) mothers, daughters, sisters – say, archetypally, Iocasta, Antigone, and Ismene, alongside Laius, Oedipus, and Polynices in the house of Thebes. Whether they considered the question of woman (as did Hegel, Freud, and Lacan, including in the context of Greek tragedy, especially *Antigone*) or not, the thinkers of these diagrams, diagonals, and theogonals have never considered the radical implications of the supplementary diagrams that their diagrams entail. Or, more radically, they never managed to fully consider the uncontainable supplement of the diagram or the theogram in Derrida's sense of supplementarity, which entails irreducible epistemological complications concerning the classical ideals of causality and reality, or, conversely, representation.[18] It also entails, however, equally irreducible complications as concerns the gender economies, philosophical and political, involved. This supplement can never be contained in the way the Oedipal diagrams aim or claim to do. One must, accordingly, rethink the irrationality (in either sense) of the diagonal and, in Irigaray's language, the excessiveness of the One which, as she says, the diagonal helps to temper.

Put diagrammatically, Irigaray's philosophy suggests that one must draw the second diagonal in the square of the (extending) Oedipal theogram, the diagonal from right to left, rather than from left to right. It proceeds from the masculine (say, in the lower right corner) to that, as yet unknown (but then nothing is as yet known), excessivity that defines the feminine as feminine and through which one must rethink and transform the whole diagram. It may not be possible to quite abandon it, at least for now. Even so this refiguration is radical. The diagrammatic diagonal description, just given, is of course too schematic to convey its radical nature, which is one of the reasons that one needs at least Hegel's multifold, analogously transformed. Furthermore, in accordance with the radical epistemology of this type of philosophical program, as outlined at the outset, at stake here is something that is ultimately inconceivable by any means that are or possibly will ever be available to us, but through which certain conceptual and performative, including political, effects, such those of the feminine and gender, become possible. That said, the refigured diagram would represent something that has always been in place, from (and before) the very beginning, in spite of and in part because of all the efforts to contain it by means of diagrams or otherwise. In Derridian terms, along with the supplementary economy of the human and the divine, imperceptibly inhibiting the theogonal program considered earlier, there is an, equally irreducible, supplementary economy of the feminine or gender, inhibiting the Oedipal diagonalization. Indeed these two supplements are, in turn, irreducibly interlinked. In a way, Irigaray's argument is that the theogonal would remain fundamentally intact, unless that second supplement, the supplement defined by gender, is introduced into the picture. All Oedipal diagrams have always concealed what Irigaray analyses, via the diagonal, as Plato's *hystera*. This *hystera* is also Hegel's, or

Freud's or Lacan's, in short, that of the long history of philosophy and/ as psychoanalysis – from Plato to Lacan and from Lacan to Plato, from top to bottom and from bottom to top, from left to right and from right to left.

This is not to say that the (re)gendering at stake in Irigaray amounts only or even primarily to an excavation or recovery of the feminine or gender unconscious in the classical text – literary, philosophical, psycho-analytical, or other, conceivably, even mathematical – whether this excavation proceeds (more or less) along psychoanalytic lines, Freudian or Lacanian, or along archaeological lines, as in (early) Foucault, or along deconstructive lines, as in (early) Derrida. Quite the contrary; at stake is a much more radical restructuring and a very different economy of diagonal enrichment. They are concerned more with the future than with the past, and in this sense would be closer to Deleuze and Guattari's anti-Oedipal program, or its earlier precursors in Nietzsche and Bataille, and in a certain sense in Hegel, this, in Nietzsche's phrase, great philosopher of the future. This restructuring entails both the usage of such proce-dures at certain points and within certain limits, and an investigation of the conditions of their possibility and necessity. To return to Irigaray's passage on or along Plato's diagonal and Plato's *hystera*:

> *A Diagonal Helps to Temper the Excessiveness of the One* [up to a point]. The method, the path, the shaft, the neck, the split even, will certainly have proved useful in ensuring the Father's [God's or Oedipus's] authority. But how are they to be found, these holes in an imperious unity? In the squaring of the circle of its glory? A potency whose squareness would have swallowed up the potency of the *hystera*. Playing with the *passage* by/to the *immeasurability* of his greatness. Since no estimate in whole numbers is possible, the *diagonal* will supply the excessiveness of a *diaphragm* non-integrality. A paraphragm on the slant, dividing and thus duplicating and determining the primitive dyad of big and small. A matrix that remains material and whose diagonal, or diameter, will halt, or cut, the infinite progression or regression, and oppose it with the definition of a second side. Symmetry that will artificially have organized, by a *reversing projection*, the first as such: half of one same whole square. The geometric construction will have eliminated the reliance on a [square?] *root* to which no value can be assigned – in its extraction or its power – because it lacks a common measure with the finite. The operation of duplication will use the, possibly, fictive tracing of a line through the middle to achieve the possible reduction to a *relationship of equality*. But, as soon as the figure has

been traced, the *inverted* shadow produced by that fraction will appear, or at least *its mirror image*. Plato's *hystera*. And, *by mimicking them on the inside*: space of magicians, space of prisoners, the di-lemmas of Plato's *hystera* will, hey presto, have concealed the fact that there is no common measure with the unrepresentable *hystera protera*, the path that might lead back to it and the diaphragm that controls the cavity opening. The plan(e)s that establish the similarity of numbers must therefore be raised up in the thinking and not allowed to be too much controlled by designs upon the earth. The mother. (*Speculum* 357–8; emphasis added in some cases)

I cannot here consider this remarkable passage in detail. Beyond offering significant suggestions for writing a 'gender genealogy' of the origin(s) of geometry or of the discipline (in either sense) of mathematics and/as philosophy in general, the anti-Oedipal restructuring, announced here, entails momentous changes in the diagonal and theogonal economy that has governed all history hitherto. That includes the history of our interactions with the earth or what Michel Serres calls our 'natural contract,' along with all social contracts. 'Geometry' is here given a new direct geopolitical sense, a new measure of the Earth. In truth, the philosophico-political economy in question in this passage entails a radical renterpretation – and a radical re-enrichment – of everything. Perhaps it will even lead to the death of the *dia*gonal, in part since, after Nietzsche, the *theo*gonal is already dead. The feminine and gender (both masculine and feminine, and their interactions) must – this is my argument – be refigured along the lines of the Hegelian multifold as here considered, but also by gendering and regendering the latter in turn.

First, contrary to many misconceptions (which still persist), what Irigaray sees as the feminine is both a material (this is more acknowledged, although often misconceived) and (this is most often forgotten) a socio-political economy, just as, and contrary to many misconceptions, Hegel's idealist economy is. Indeed, while I would not go so far as to suggest that this Irigarayan economy is a translation of Hegel's Spirit, *Geist*, it may well offer us a crucial allegory of Hegel's allegory. The latter, conversely or reciprocally, may well be (if imperceptibly for Hegel himself) an allegory of an Irigarayan allegory. What it is ultimately an allegory of becomes ever less determined, exposing the ever greater abysses of the unknowable, and yet making this allegory or all allegories here involved more, and differently, productive. In other words, the efficacious potential of the process is explored more richly and in a more complex, and different, way with respect to the knowable and the unknowable alike. The Irigarayan economy is perhaps best conceived on the joint model of Derrida's economy of writing and Deleuze and Guattari's anti-Oedipal economy of the body without organs and desiring machines, which refigures, via Nietzsche and Marx, Freud's and Lacan's Oedipal theograms. Conversely, one can conceive of both Deleuzian and Derridian economies on the model of Irigaray's and related feminist economies, to which both are indebted.

Secondly, therefore, manifold as even such a single economy may be, one must, once again, see it not as a single conglomerate, say, a single body without organs with desiring machines emerging on its surface, but as a fold of such conglomerates as here considered earlier. At this point, one can supplement (in either sense) a number of models and allegories (their multiplicity is, again, itself irreducible) with yet another one, André Kertész's *Distortions* – a series of photographs of distorted images of the naked female body taken from their images in a fun-house mirror. (It must be considered with a suitable gender deconstruction in mind.) While the topology of many images *reflects* continuous, smooth transformations of the 'original' form, in some cases the interplay of the surface of the mirror and light produces fantastic twisting and dislocations, complementarily continuous and discontinuous, both the Hegelian (continuous) positive and the Hegelian (discontinuous) tragic negative. The body can in principle spread, twist, and fracture across the surface of the mirror, forming multiple pictures. There is no original form distorted in a mirror, but only effects of a more 'twisted' play. At the same time, this play entails a radical enrichment and a radical regendering of the emerging multifold, which can and must be given a political structure as well. One must consider irreducible, if structured, this multiplicity of images, or of deformations and 'distortions,' some of which (in different situations, different) are sometimes seen or function as relatively undistorted or, as we naïvely call them, normal figures.

We must understand from a critical (rather than uncritical or utopian) perspective how gender affects these multiplicities and their organization. We must, for example, understand how it intersects with the economy, including political economy, of sexuality, or of so-called homosexuality or heterosexuality (to the degree such terms can still be applied), whether, say, it doubles or multiplies, or entails a complex interplay of duality and multiplicity. Some of these possibilities or indeed necessities are in part responsible for the possibility of regendering and rediagonalizing such families and families of families, from Oedipus to Antigone and from Antigone to Oedipus. These are of course key figures (in either sense) for Irigaray, for whom, as for Hegel, Sophocles' *Antigone* is arguably the single most important classical text.

The new 'topologies' thus emerging are not the end but a new starting point of a philosophical and historical analysis, and of political practice. An immense theoretical-political work remains ahead, even as one acknowledges, by now, decades of crucial research and action, to both of which Irigaray made so significant a contribution. This analysis and practice may, as I said, entail a radical reinterpretation of everything – of the body and the soul of everything – for example, the nature and history, and in some measure perhaps practice, of science and mathematics. Once again, I mean here rethinking, rather than abandoning much of what they have to offer. One will certainly need to rethink the history of the idea of the diagonal of the square, as the diagram and as the theogram, if not as mathematics. One might, then, also arrive at a different understanding of Plato's appeal to the diagonal in *Statesman*: 'How is this human race of ours endowed? So far as its potential is concerned, is it not very like diagonal? Yes, Socrates, and I now know what you mean. A woman-philosopher I know explained it all to me by using Sophocles' *Antigone*. She also explained why you say that the art which is the closest to that of the art of governing is the art of weaving. Unless it is the art of folding. Have you heard, Socrates, that two artists, a wife and a husband, plan to wrap the whole Acropolis in fabric, and they say that the whole point of the project is how the folds of the fabric flow – diagonally, from Gods to humans, and from humans to Gods, from women to men, and from men to women?'

NOTES

1 These debates are sometimes referred to as the 'Science Wars.' I have addressed the subject in detail in *The Knowable and the Unknowable: Modern Science, Nonclassical Thought, and the 'Two Cultures' via Bohr, Heisenberg, Lacan and Derrida.*

2 Michel Serres stresses the difference between geometry and topology, and sees the latter as a preferable model for philosophical thought. See Michel Serres with Bruno Latour, *Conversation on Science, Culture, and Time* 60–1. There are, however, deep connections between geometrical and topological structures in mathematics itself, and one cannot unequivocally juxtapose

them in the way Serres appears to do. These connections have been a source of rich and productive mathematical work throughout the history of modern mathematics.

3 This may also mean that even in mathematics one may not be able to speak of multidimensional (that is, four and higher) geometry, as geometry or even of higher-dimensional spatiality (topology), except metaphorically or allegorically. I have commented on this issue in an article 'The Aesthetics of Mathematics.'

4 See, in particular, Derrida's reading of Mallarmé in 'The Double Session' in *Dissemination.*

5 This structure itself may not be visualizable or even conceivable otherwise than metaphorically or (with de Man's work in mind) allegorically. I have discussed allegory in this context in 'Algebra and Allegory: Nonclassical Epistemology, Quantum Theory, and the Work of Paul de Man.'

6 This would be a good example of the mutually defining and mutually enriching relationship between geometry and topology, which I mentioned earlier (note 2), and between both and analysis and function theory.

7 See, in particular, 'Questions,' in *This Sex Which Is Not One* 119–69.

8 There is a 'slippage' here from the Greek terminology and conception of incommensurability and the related terms concerning the irrational (mentioned below) to the Latin 'ratio' and 'rationality.' This 'slippage' does not affect the present argument as such. One might, however, argue, with Heidegger, that this terminological (and conceptual) shift is significant in shaping the history of these questions.

9 One might say that it was the 'Gödel's theorem' of Greek mathematics. It is worth noting here that the method used in the proof – an argument based on the excluded middle (still the most common form of mathematical proof, used by Gödel as well) – was originally used by Parmedines and Zeno. It formed one of the foundations of dialectic and linked diagonal and dialectic forever. Cf. John Kadrany, 'Dialectic and Diagonalization.'

10 Blanchot probably has in mind Hipassus, who is sometimes mentioned as a discoverer of the irrationals.

11 One might argue that the proper mathematical definition of irrational numbers (a momentous achievement in its own right) 'removes' the incomprehensible and restores the mathematical situation to its proper order. This is true to some extent, although the situation is far more complex epistemologically. On this point, I permit myself to refer to the discussion of Lacan in *The Knowable and the Unknowable.* I here speak of the 'paradigmatic,' model-like, significance of this configuration, which can be realized otherwise.

12 The actual context of this statement is not without relevance for the present essay, especially in relation to the Oedipal economy, discussed below. In question are 'peripatetic potential' and 'a potency of two feet.' I shall not, however, develop this context here.

13 I have considered them in detail in *In the Shadow of Hegel* 198–205.

14 To some degree, the present analysis repositions Hegel's philosophy away from its more pronounced and much more discussed relationship to Kant and German Idealism or, earlier, Descartes, and towards Leibniz and Spinoza. One might argue that Hegel's 'topological' philosophy, as here considered, is unique in German Idealism.

15 On this point I permit myself, again, to refer to *In the Shadow of Hegel* 270–74.

16 This argument has significant connections, and is indebted to, the recent work on 'translation,' developing the ideas of Walter Benjamin, on the one hand, and Derrida, on the other. The subject, however, would require a separate discussion.

17 I consider some of these questions in *The Knowable and the Unknowable,* referred to above (note 11).

18 See also Derrida's analysis of the supplement of the code in 'Signature Event Context,' in *Writing and Difference.*

WORKS CITED

Blanchot, Maurice. *The Writing of the Disaster.* Trans. Ann Smock. Lincoln: U of Nebraska P, 1981.

Deleuze, Gilles. *The Fold: Leibniz and the Baroque.* Trans. Tom Conley. Minneapolis: U of Minnesota P, 1993.

Deleuze, Gilles, and Félix Guattari. *What Is Philosophy?* Trans. Hugh Tomlinson and Graham Burchell. New York: Columbia UP, 1994.

Derrida, Jacques. *Dissemination.* Trans. Barbara Johnson. Chicago: U of Chicago P, 1981.

– *Writing and Différance.* Trans. Alan Bass. Chicago: U of Chicago P, 1978.

Hegel, G.W.F. *Phenomenology of Spirit.* Trans. A.V. Miller. Oxford: Oxford UP, 1977.

Irigaray, Luce. *Speculum of the Other Woman.* Trans. Gillian G. Gill. Ithaca: Cornell UP, 1985.

– *This Sex Which Is Not One.* Trans. Catherine Porter. Ithaca: Cornell UP, 1985.

Kadvany, John. 'Dialectic and Diagonalization.' *Inquiry* 34 (1991): 3–25.

Monet, Claude. *Nympheas (The Water Lilies).* 1918. Musée d'Orangerie, Paris.

Plotnitsky, Arkady. 'The Aesthetics of Mathematics.' *Encyclopedia of Aesthetics*. Ed. Michael Kelly. Oxford: Oxford UP, 1998.

– 'Algebra and Allegory: Nonclassical Epistemology, Quantum Theory, and the Work of Paul de Man.' *Material Events*. Ed. Thomas Cohen, J. Hillis Miller, and Andrzej Warminski. Minneapolis: U of Minnesota P, 2000.

– *In the Shadow of Hegel.* Gainesville: U Presses of Florida, 1993.

– *The Knowable and the Unknowable: Modern Science, Nonclassical Thought, and the 'Two Cultures' via Bohr, Heisenberg, Lacan and Derrida.* Ann Arbor: U of Michigan P, 2001.

Serres, Michel, and Bruno Latour. *Conversation on Science, Culture, and Time.* Trans. Roxanne Lapidus. Ann Arbor: U of Michigan P, 1995.

The Eclipse of Coincidence: Lacan, Merleau-Ponty, and Žižek's Misreading of Schelling

PETER DEWS

I

Why has the thought of Jacques Lacan played such a central role in the formation of the field of research and debate which is generally known as 'cultural studies'? One answer would be that cultural studies evidently needed an account of the subjective dimension of the production and consumption of meanings. Lacan provided a theory of the subject which seemed able to survive deconstruction, to absorb and move beyond the influential demotion – even dissolutions – of the subject which have emerged from recent French thought. In Lacan's work the concept of the subject is indispensable, but the subject is no longer sovereign, no longer given to itself prior to any system of representation. The Lacanian subject appears unable to master its own position, being torn between the 'field of the Other' (the domain of signifiers) within which it emerges, on the one hand, and its ineffable pre-linguistic 'being' on the other (Lacan, *Psychoanalysis* 211). Such an account has seemed highly congenial to theorists who have wished to stress the historically and culturally situated – and the gendered and desiring – character of the subject, by contrast with the epistemologically detached and formally universal subject of experience regarded as central to the philosophical tradition.

But is Lacan's account of the subject as innovative as it seems, or is he himself reworking well-established philosophical themes? One obvious fact which seems to speak against the unprecedented status of the Lacanian subject is that, in his *Seminar XI* (and elsewhere), Lacan underlines the parallels between Freud and Descartes. Indeed, he goes so far as to suggest that 'Freud's method is Cartesian – in the sense that he sets out from the basis of the subject of certainty' (35). What Lacan means by this is that 'it is by taking its place at the level of the enunciation that the cogito acquires its certainty' (*Psychoanalysis* 140). In other words, as Jaakko Hintikka was one of the first to emphasize in the recent philosophical literature, the 'cogito, ergo sum' is only *certain* at the very moment of its enunciation. For it is the *fact* of its enunciation, and not any reality to which it unerringly refers, which establishes its momentary indubitability.[1]

On this view, the distinction between Cartesianism and the psychoanalytic tradition (which were traditionally taken to be antithetical) cannot be established with reference to the performative character of the self. Rather the distinction consists in the fact that Descartes substantializes the existence which is disclosed in the performance of the *cogito*, transforming it into a *res cogitans*. According to Lacan, Freud's innovation was to accept the existence of a subject which thinks, for example behind the surface of the dream signifiers, without attempting to capture or define this existence. Thus, in *Seminar XI* he states: 'it is here that the dissymmetry between Descartes and Freud is revealed. It is not the initial method of certainty grounded on the subject. It stems from the fact that the subject is "at home" in this field of the unconscious that the progress by which he changed the world for us was made' (*Psychoanalysis* 36). This is because 'the subject of the unconscious manifests itself, it thinks before it attains certainty' (37).

In Lacan, then, the subject is not to be substantialized; its mode of existence is radically distinct from that of entities in the world. As we know, Lacan himself describes this mode of existence as a *manque-à-etre* (a lack in relation to being, or a 'want-to-be'). But what does it mean for the subject – as lack – to *be*? For the majority of theorists who have taken up and applied Lacan's work in recent decades, this question does not seem to have caused much disquiet. Yet, in fact, it is one of the most difficult issues raised by Lacan's work. Of course, there is no particular difficulty in describing a relative lack, a lack which emerges in relation to some system of symbolic coordinates, like the book absent from its place on the library shelf. This is because the missing book is not sheerly lacking, but rather present elsewhere. Yet in the case of the Lacanian subject we are confronted with the notion of an *absolute* lack – a lack which cannot be filled by any symbolic or hermeneutical shift of perspective. And it is this notion of absolute lack which poses the philosophical problem. How are we to make sense of it?

We can note, first of all, that Lacan's use of the notion of being, in the phrase *manque-à-etre*, seems to presuppose that being belongs primarily to the inertly given – as given to which modes of activity or performativity can be opposed. Nowhere is this clearer than in 'The Agency of the Letter in the Unconscious,' where Lacan writes: 'if ... I refuse to seek any meaning beyond tautology, if in the name of "war is war" and "a penny's a penny" I decide to be only what I am, how even here can I elude the obvious fact that I am in that very act' (165). The use of the word 'act' is significant here: for it is the subject which is implied by the act, and more specifically by the utterance (the *sujet de l'énonciation*, in Lacan's terms), which is incapable of any objectifying determination in the statement. It is 'left behind,' as it were, by the transition of the utterance from act to past event, leaving only its objectified residue 'alienated in the signifier,' to take up the terms which Lacan will employ a little later in his career. If such a subject can said to 'be' only in the very act of its self-alienation, then this is a perplexing and paradoxical form of being.

Of course, this conception of a subject split between activity and being is not strictly speaking Cartesian, but it certainly has many precedents within the philosophical tradition. These begin with Kant, who argues in the *Critique of Pure Reason* that the synthetic activity of the subject cannot be known in the same way as an empirical phenomenon. 'Synthesis as an act,' Kant suggests, 'is conscious to itself even without sensibility'; 'awareness of the act is ... not indeed in but with intuitions' (B153, B161). This conception of the subject's unique status in the field of knowledge is continued in an even clearer form by later idealists such as Fichte, who develops an explicit opposition between act and being, describing the primordial self-positing of the subject as a 'seeing' which is logically prior to, and opposed to, all being (126). These precedents and parallels (arguably, Sartre is an even more recent one) raise a genuinely perplexing issue concerning Lacan's thought. For it seems that his defence of the radicality of Freud's discovery of the unconscious in fact depends on the adoption of a model of the subject which has well-established precedents within the philosophical tradition. The opposition between the elusive, ungraspable *sujet de l'énonciation* and the opaque, inert, objectified ego is – it could be argued – simply Lacan's version of the opposition between the transcendental and the empirical self.

At the political and cultural level, the problem with this conception of the subject as lack is that it seems to leave no space for the possibility of an overcoming – or even attenuation – of the fundamental 'alienation' of the subject which Lacan describes. The incommensurability between the subject and the signifier, the absence of any common ground between them, means that no signifier can capture the non-essence of the subject better than any other. Lacan's famous pessimism, it seems, has a metaphysical foundation.

II

At this point I would like to refer to the thought of Lacan's friend and contemporary Merleau-Ponty. For, if Lacan's conception of the subject is indeed dependent on some version of the distinction between the transcendental and the empirical, if the subject's lack is specifically a lack of inert, opaque, or objectified being, then the very dualism which this conception seems to presuppose might be open to Merleau-Pontyan objections. At the beginning of chapter 3 of *Le Visible et l'invisible*, Merleau-Ponty writes:

> The destruction of beliefs, the symbolic murder of others and of the world, the cutting off of vision and the visible, of thought and being, do not establish us – as they claim – in the negative; when one gets rid of all that, one finds oneself amidst what remains, sensations, opinions; and what remains is not nothing, nor something of a different kind from what has been cut off: they are mutilated fragments of the vague *omnitudo realitatis* against which doubt was exercised. ... It is in the name of and for the benefit of these floating realities that solid reality is put in doubt. (148)

Essentially, Merleau-Ponty claims, 'methodical doubt, which is carried out in the voluntary zone of ourselves, refers to Being, since it resists the factical evidence, represses an involuntary truth which it admits is already there' (144).

For Merleau-Ponty, therefore, there is no radical gap or gulf between our openness to the world and the world itself. As he says in one of the working notes for *Le Visible et l'invisible*, 'the nothingness [*néant*] (or rather non-being) is a hollow and not a hole. The opening in the sense of a hole is Sartre, is Bergson, it is negativism or ultra-positivism (Bergson), which are indiscernible. There is no *nichtiges Nichts*' (249). The significance of the metaphor of the hollow, of course, is that a hollow is not discontinuous with the surface in which it appears, and does not allow a passage right through the surface to the other side. Accordingly, in place of the Lacanian notion of *manque* we find, in Merleau-Ponty's late thought, the notion of an *écart* – of a gap or disjunction. By definition, the *écart* cannot be absolute, for it is always a disjunction between two surfaces, one of which functions as the foil or contrast for the other, but which can in turn be relativized. Thus for Merleau-Ponty we must understand the subject 'not as a nothingness, not as something, but as a unity of transgression or correlative overlapping of "thing" and "world," or as the *écart* or space between figure and its background' (*Le Visible et l'invisible* 254, 245).

One obvious criticism of this approach would be that Merleau-Ponty's thought is essentially nostalgic. Merleau-Ponty wants to remind the subject of its history, of the fact of its emergence from the world. He asserts that 'we will not accept a preconstituted world, a logic, unless we have seen them emerge from our experience of brute being, which is like the umbilical cord of our knowledge, and the source of meaning for us' (*Le Visible* 209). The problem here, of course, is that the 'umbilical link' has to be cut in the first minutes of life in order for the child to initiate an independent existence. Merleau-Ponty's constant effort to discover an implicit, incipient meaning of things by descending phenomenologically below the level of reflection could be regarded as a refusal to acknowledge that meaning only arises through our inevitable reflective separation from the world. At times Merleau-Ponty comes close to acknowledging this dynamic. In the working notes to *Le Visible et l'invisible*, for example, he considers the fact that perspectival forms of representation cannot simply be seen as arbitrarily *imposed* upon a world of perception whose spontaneous evidence is irrefutable. He writes:

> My position is to be defined in the problem of the 'return to the immediate,' the perceptual in the sense of the non-projective, vertical world. And yet someone like Piaget has no knowledge of this, has totally covered his perception with cultural-euclidean perception. So what right do I have to call immediate an original which can be forgotten to this extent? ... With life, with natural perception (with the savage mind) we are given the means to relativize the universe of immanence – and yet, this universe tends inherently to make itself autonomous, inherently to bring about a repression of transcendence. The key is in this idea that perception is in itself ignorance of itself as wild perception, an imperception which tends inherently to see itself as an act and to forget itself as latent intentionality, as being at [*être à*]. (267)

This paradoxical definition of perception as 'ignorance of perception' suggests that the haunting sense of a dimension of experience which objectifying awareness 'represses' – to use Merleau-Ponty's own word – seems to be insufficient to halt the objectifying dynamic. What is worse, this paradoxical awareness seems to be precisely what Lacan understands by castration: the phallus, as the promise of ultimate pleni-tude, cannot be given up, even while – at a different level – the subject must acknowledge the reality of castration, of reflective separation. From such a standpoint the 'repression of an involuntary truth' (i.e., the truth of the continuing immersion in Being), which is a condition of the *cogito* on Merleau-Ponty's account, cannot function as an argu-ment against the possibility of the detached, empty subject of the *cogito*. For this supposed evidence of Being, which Merleau-Ponty himself describes as a matter of 'perceptual faith,' cannot trump reflection. Rather, it remains in a relation of tension with it, which – we could say – *defines* the position of the subject.

III

At this point we seem to have reached an impasse. I suggested that the thought of Merleau-Ponty might be able to help us avoid the problems raised by Lacan's notion of lack. Yet, as we have found, Merleau-Ponty appears finally unable to escape the same dynamic of 'alienation' – of the inevitable occlusion of the primordial subject (whose primordiality is thereby put in question) – which we found in Lacan. But, to test whether this really is an impasse, I would like to introduce another voice into the discussion, that of one of the major thinkers of the post-Kantian idealist generation: Friedrich Schelling.

Recently, the connection between the thought of Schelling and con-temporary debates in philosophy and cultural theory, particularly with respect to the question of the subject, have been brought to attention by the work of Slavoj Žižek. In his book *The Indivisible Remainder* and in his introduction to a translation of the second draft of *The Ages of the World*, Žižek has proposed a Lacanian reading of Schelling which rightly stresses the central role which the problem of inadequation, of lack of fit between the originally boundless freedom of the subject and the inev-itably finite, bounded realizations of this freedom, plays in Schelling's thought. Schelling's fundamental insight, on Žižek's account, is that 'the Word, the contraction of the Self outside the Self, involves an irre-trievable externalization-alienation' ('The Abyss' 42).

In general Žižek deserves credit for having proved to the cultural studies audience that the decentring of subjectivity is not an invention of twentieth-century philosophy, but runs right back into the heart of German Idealism. The affinities appear graphically in the opening paragraph of Schelling's 1809 treatise on freedom, where Schelling describes the difficulty of getting a philosophical hold on the experience of freedom. He begins by remarking that there are two ways of approaching the essence of human freedom philosophically. On the one hand, he suggests, the immediate 'feeling of freedom' (*das Gefühl der Freiheit*) is ingrained in everyone, yet at such a deeply implicit level that it would require 'an unusual purity and depth of sense' (*eine mehr als gewöhnliche Reinheit und Tiefe des Sinns*) merely in order to express it in words. On the other hand, no concept can be fully determined in isolation from others, and it is only the demonstration of its interrelation with the whole of a scientific world view which gives the concept its completion. This must be especially the case with the concept of freedom, Schelling states, because – if it has reality at all – it cannot be a mere 'subordinate or subsidiary concept, but must be one of the dominating middle-points of the system' (*Über das Wesen* 33). Schelling is fully aware that this two-pronged approach seems to generate a fundamental inconsistency – for how can what he knows through immediate feeling or awareness be determined through its insertion into a differential circle of concepts? Such an insertion would rob freedom of the very immediacy which makes it a 'dominating middle-point of the system,' as he puts it. It is not difficult to perceive, therefore, that Schelling is describing a structure which for Lacan is the very definition of the subject: freedom – which is the essence of subjectivity – is both inside and outside, at the centre and yet at the periphery, determinable and indeterminable. Indeed the title of the treatise (*Philosophische Untersuchungen über das Wesen der Menschlichen Freiheit*) refers explicitly to this paradoxical conjunction of the finite, the 'human,' and the unbounded, of conditionality and unconditionality.

However, Žižek's reading plays down the fact that this contradictory structure poses a crucial philosophical problem for Schelling, even though – at the same time – Schelling regards it as being so all-pervasive that, in the form of a fundamental torsion or lack of self-coincidence, this structure marks even God himself. To put this in historical terms, Žižek ignores the fact that one crucial challenge to which Schelling is responding in the treatise on freedom is that of Friedrich Jacobi. Jacobi provoked his contemporaries by suggesting that the philosophical drive for comprehensive explanation, which – in its own terms – is entirely justified and legitimate, necessarily excludes the free human subject and undermines our confidence in the reality of the perceived world.

The implication he draws is that we have to shift into another dimension – risk what he calls a *salto mortale*, a leap into faith – in order to avoid the destructive mechanism of theoretical reason.[2] It is this irrationalist implication, however, which Schelling wants to avoid. His aim, as he states at the beginning of the treatise on freedom, is precisely to contest the assertion that 'the concept of freedom is entirely unreconcilable with the system, and [that] every philosophy which makes a claim to unity and totality must result in a denial of freedom' (Schelling, *Über das Wesen* 33). Žižek, however, must ignore this in his one-sided assertion of 'Schelling's insistence on the gap that separates forever the Real of drives from its symbolization' ('The Abyss' 28).

Indeed, what I now want to suggest is that, with respect to his philosophical intentions at least, Schelling can be read just as plausibly from a Merleau-Pontyan as from a Lacanian perspective. In fact it may turn out that Schelling's thought can be viewed as an attempt to *reconcile* the conflicting intuitions which we find in Merleau-Ponty and Lacan. In other words, Schelling is not content to remain with the thought that Spirit is merely what Žižek calls the 'substanceless void of non-Nature, the distance of Nature toward itself' ('The Abyss' 44). Like Merleau-Ponty, he wants to show that there must be *some* ontological – or perhaps better: *pre-ontological* – affinity between spirit and nature, subject and signifier, while at the same time emphasizing the bitter reality of their non-coincidence.

Non-coincidence is acknowledged by Schelling as an irreducible feature of the world. He gives a new twist to the traditional conception of God as containing the ground of his own existence, suggesting that philosophy has spoken of this ground as 'a mere concept, without making is something real and effective' (*Über das Wesen* 52). By contrast, for Schelling, 'This ground of his existence, which God has within himself, is not God regarded absolutely, in other words in so far as he exists; for it is of course only the ground of his existence. It is nature – in God; a being which is indeed inseparable from him, but yet distinct from him' (53).

The major part of the *Freiheitschrift* follows the way in which the dialectic of ground and existence plays itself out. For Schelling, existence (a term for which a twentieth-century analogue might be Sartrean 'transcendence') only becomes fully transparent to itself in the life of human beings – where it struggles to escape entirely from the constraints of the ground (or 'facticity'). Yet this facticity is in fact the necessarily particularized core of our selfhood, which – in an almost impossibly demanding balancing act – must be acknowledged as the anchoring centre of our existence, without being allowed to dominate it. ('Evil,' for Schelling, consists in precisely such an inversion, one which is almost inevitable, since its possibility arises from the diremption of God himself.) However, Schelling anticipates a moment at which this dualistic struggle, and the perversions to which it gives rise, will be overcome. He has to do so, since otherwise his initial aim of reconciling freedom and system would be exposed as unacheivable. Yet at this point a fundamental difficulty arises. For, on the one hand, if there is no 'common middle point' between ground and existence – as Schelling calls it – we will be left with an irreducible dualism. And dualism, Schelling states at an earlier point in the book, is 'a system of the self-dismemberment and despair of reason' (*Über das Wesen* 49). But, on the other hand, if an ultimate identity of the opposites is proclaimed, then a collapse of oppositions will occur – subject and object, light and dark, good and evil – which is equally incompatible both with the conditions of coherent thought and our fundamental moral intuitions.

In an attempt to confront this dilemma, Schelling, towards the close of his treatise, introduces the notion of a primal ground (*Urgrund*) of both ground and existence, which he then describes as an 'Un-ground' (*Ungrund*), since it must be conceived as 'prior' to the very distinction between ground and existence. Just as the Un-ground is not a ground in the normal sense, neither can it be said to exist: it precedes the distinction between existence and the ground of existence whose coincidence alone constitutes actual entities. But if the Un-ground cannot be said to exist, what is the purpose of invoking it?

Essentially, Schelling's insight is that there must be a common *space* of comparison, and thus of difference, as the condition of possibility of any duality. If ground and existence are to enter into a dialectical tension with each other, then there must be a dimension within which their incompatibility can become apparent, can be felt. The Un-ground is thus not the 'identity' of ground and existence, for this would still not provide a space of distinction – indeed, their incompatibility would tear it apart. Rather, as Schelling writes,

> The essence of the ground, as of that which exists, can only be that which precedes every ground, in other words the absolute viewed without qualification, the unground. It can only be this however ... by splitting apart into two equally eternal beginnings, not that it is both simultaneously, but that it is in both in the same way, in other words is in each the whole, or an independent essence. (*Über das Wesen* 99)

Schelling's basic notion in the *Freiheitschrift* is that, at the logical beginning, prior to the distinction of ground and existence, the Un-ground is
'as' nothing. But after ground and existence have separated, and particularly when – in the redoubling movement which typifies human history
– the *priority* of ground over existence (evil) begins to struggle with the
priority of existence over ground (good), then the unground makes
itself felt as the ungraspable, because all-pervasive, reconciling power of
love.

As I have suggested, Žižek is completely insensitive to this aspect of
Schelling's thinking. He presents the opposition around which the
Freiheitschrift revolves as one between an 'impenetrable-inert' ground
(*Indivisible Remainder* 20), which he equates with the Lacanian Real, and
the void of the subject who essentially separated from it. At the very
least, this interpretation misses the duality inherent to both ground and
existence in Schelling's account – and it does so because it transforms
what in Schelling are proto-ontological 'wills' (in other words, strivings
towards being, towards the melding of ground and existence) into
entirely discrete ontological registers. In Schelling's treatise the 'will of
the ground' is torn into two directions: far from being merely the force
of particularistic involution, the ground is described by Schelling as 'a
will to revelation' (68). The ground wants to reveal itself, to be, but it
can only do so by overcoming its own resistance, it must 'call forth own-
ness and opposition' (68), as Schelling puts it. Similarly, if the 'will of
love,' the contrary will, 'wished to shatter the ground, it would struggle
against itself, find itself at odds with itself, and would no longer be love'
(*Über das Wesen* 68). As Schelling's phrasing makes clear ('at odds with
itself' [*mit sich selbst uneins*]), there cannot be an *absolute* distinction
between ground and existence: from a speculative standpoint, each is in
fact its other, as the account of their common 'origin' in the unground
later makes clear – yet they find themselves locked in a chiasmic, overlapping relation of cooperative opposition, of supportive antagonism.

IV

The affinities between Schelling's thought and that of Merleau-Ponty
should already be clear by this point. In one of the most striking phrases
in *Le Visible et l'invisible*, Merleau-Ponty announces that 'the originary
explodes' (*l'originaire éclate*), and that 'philosophy must accompany this
explosion, this non-coincidence, this differentiation' (165). The parallel
with Schelling's account of the irruption of ground and existence from

the unground is striking here. For it is clear that Merleau-Ponty's point cannot be that we must conceive of a unitary ontological point of departure (the 'originary') which subsequently bursts asunder. The 'essence' of the originary is to explode, to fragment – in which case, we can ask in what sense it merits the term 'originary.' As Merleau-Ponty himself puts it: 'The difficulties of coincidence are not merely factual difficulties which would leave the principle intact' (165). And he concludes by remarking: 'What there is is not a coincidence in principle or a presumed coincidence, and a factual non-coincidence, a bad or failed truth, but a privative non-coincidence, a coincidence at a distance, a gap, and something like a "good error"' (166).

The most readily appreciable example of this structure in *Le Visible et l'invisible* is the touching of a part of the body which is itself touching: 'My left hand is always on the point of touching my right hand as it is touching things,' Merleau-Ponty writes, 'but I never reach coincidence' (194). However, this is not the end of the story. For Merleau-Ponty does not accept absolute non-coincidence. Rather, he goes on to say of that coincidence that it 'is eclipsed in the very moment it occurs' (*elle s'éclipse au moment de se produire*), and of the incommensurable experiences of activity and passivity that they 'escape at the moment when they come together' (*elles échappent au moment de se rejoindre*) (194). Thus coincidence is always 'imminent,' we can say, employing Merleau-Ponty's own term, but never explicitly realized. Correlatively, non-coincidence should not be hypostatized into an ontological void. A little later in the same section he writes:

> I can experience, as often as I want, the translation and metamorphosis of one of these experiences into the other, and it is merely as if the hinge between them, solid and unshakable, remained permanently hidden from me. But this hiatus between my right hand touched and my right hand touching, between my voice heard and my voice articulated, between one moment of my tactile life and the following, is not an ontological void, a non-being. (*Le Visible* 194–5)

This description could be seen as a vivid phenomenological specification of Schelling's apparently abstruse speculative structure of unground, ground, and existence.

But what of the objection raised earlier, that Merleau-Ponty's philosophy vainly invokes a coincidence which is incompatible with the inevitable drive towards theoretical distance – which is merely a nostalgic residue? Is Žižek not right to suggest that, since the transition from the featurelessness of the unground to the duality of ground and existence (or in Merleau-Ponty's case, the explosion of the originary) cannot – by definition – be explained, it has the status simply of a retroactive phantasy? Indeed, since Merleau-Ponty himself asserts that 'metaphysics is coincidence,' would not the imminent coincidence which he evokes represent a lapse into metaphysics? Is Merleau-Ponty simply unable to confront the trauma of a separation, a self-division which can never be healed, and for which Lacan employs the figure of castration?

Against this objection one might point to the fact that Merleau-Ponty explicitly appeals to Schelling's notion of 'first nature' (*erste Natur*, i.e., the ground in its objective manifestation) as a 'barbaric principle.' In his lecture course on the concept of nature, dating from 1956–7, he affirms that 'There is nothing solid in a natural history, where this force, which is undoubtedly wild and destructive, and yet necessary, is ignored' (*La Nature* 62). Yet the echoes of Schelling in *Le Visible et l'invisible*, where Merleau-Ponty speaks of *l'être brut* or *l'être sauvage*, stress the untamed, raw, pristine character of nature prior to reflection, but not its disruptive and unquenchable internal contradictions. There is undoubtedly a founding moment of violence or rupture in Schelling's thinking which Merleau-Ponty does not fully acknowledge. But this is counterbalanced by other passages in Schelling which sound thoroughly 'Merleau-Pontyan,' and which Žižek, in his turn, ignores. Thus, Schelling writes in the second draft of *The Ages of the World*: 'In even the most corporeal of things there lies a point of transfiguration that is often almost sensibly perceptible ... something else in and around them first grants them the full sparkle and shine of life. There is always an overflow, as it were, playing and streaming around them' (151). Yet, at the same time, for Schelling, 'the entire fullness and future splendor of nature is only built upon the ground of an eternal self-negating will that returns into itself, and without which nothing could be revealed anywhere' (140). Schelling's fundamental philosophical struggle was to hold this complex vision of plenitude and negativity, of essential conflict and potential reconciliation, together.

Žižek's insistence on interpreting the ground as an inert, opaque version of the Lacanian Real makes him incapable of grasping this fact. Thus he writes that Schelling's notion of the subject emerging through a primordial act of decision/differentiation (*Entschiedung*) 'aims at the gesture which opens up the gap between the inertia of the pre-historic Real and the domain of historicity, of multiple and shifting narrativizations; this act is thus a quasi-transcendental, unhistorical condition of possibility and, simultaneously, a condition of the impossibility of historicization' ('The Abyss' 37). But Schelling does not set up a stark contrast between object and subject, between a radically inert, ahistorical real and ultimately delusive historicizations. On the contrary, his aim is to make possible a history of the subject, in the sense of a recovery by the subject of the narrative of its own genesis, of the emergence of freedom from the facticity of nature, from the ground. 'Science [i.e., philosophical science (*Wissenschaft*)],' Schelling claims in the introduction to *The Ages of the World*, 'according to the very meaning of the word, is history' (113). It involves a continuous weaving back and forth in a *space* which encompasses the past and the present, the tacit and the explicit, facticity and transcendence:

> This separation, this doubling of ourselves, this secret intercourse between two essences, one questioning and one answering, one ignorant though seeking to know, and one knowledgeable without knowing its knowledge; this silent dialogue, this inner art of conversation, is the authentic secret of the philosopher. (115)

This 'doubling of ourselves' would be impossible outside the space of (always eclipsed) coincidence. For otherwise the doubling would become a splitting, in which the subject would be churned around in an endless cycle between opaque particularity (lack/the ground) and vacant universalization (the signifier/existence). In fact, this splitting explains the underlying pessimism of Žižek's political vision. He writes, in a typical passage:

> The key fact of today's world is the unheard-of expansion of capitalism, which is less and less bound by the form of the Nation-State, capitalism's hitherto fundamental unity of contraction, and asserts itself more and more in direct 'transnational' form; the reaction to this boundless expansion which threatens to sweep away every particular self-identity are 'postmodern' fundamentalisms as the violent 'contraction' of social life into its religious-ethical roots. (*Invisible Remainder* 27)

Despite his ostensible left-wing stance, Žižek gives us no philosophical reason to assume that the dismal cycle of abstract, universalistic expansion and particularistic contraction should ever be progressively attenuated or overcome. And in this respect his vision is ultimately indistinguishable from the familiar forms of conservative *Kulturkritik*. It is arguable whether this is the inevitable political consequence of Lacan's thought.[3] But undoubtedly, such a conclusion can only be the result of a myopic reading of Schelling.[4]

NOTES

1 See Jaakko Hintikka, 'Cogito, Ergo Sum: Inference or Performance' 3–32. See also Karl-Otto Apel, 'The Problem of Philosophical Foundations in Light of a Transcendental Pragmatics of Language' 277–80.

2 See Friedrich Jacobi, *Über die Lehre des Spinoza, in Briefen an Herrn Moses Mendelssohn.*

3 See Peter Dews, 'The Tremor of Reflection: Slavoj Žižek's Lacanian Dialectics' 253–5.

4 This essay first appeared, in a slightly different form, in *Angelaki* 4:3 (1999): 15–24.

WORKS CITED

Apel, Karl-Otto. 'The Problem of Philosophical Foundations in Light of a Transcendental Pragmatics of Language.' *After Philosophy: End or Transformation.* Ed. K. Baynes, J. Bohman, and T. McCarthy. Cambridge: MIT P, 1987. 250–90.

Dews, Peter. 'The Tremor of Reflection: Slavoj Žižek's Lacanian Dialectics.' *The Limits of Disenchantment: Essays on Contemporary European Philosophy.* London: Verso, 1995. 253–5

Fichte, J.G. 'Letter to Schelling.' 31 May–7 August 1801. *Fichte–Schelling: Briefwechsel.* Ed. Walter Schulz. Frankfurt am Main: Suhrkamp, 1968. 124–32.

Hintikka, Jaakko. 'Cogito, Ergo Sum: Inference or Performance.' *Philosophical Review* 71 (1962): 3–32.

Jacobi, Friedrich. 'Über die Lehre des Spinoza, in Briefen an Herrn Moses Mendelssohn.' *Werke.* Vol. 4/1 and 2. Darmstadt: WGB, 1980. Reprographic reprint.

Lacan, Jacques. 'The Agency of the Letter in the Unconscious or Reason since Freud.' *Écrits: A Selection.* London: Tavistock, 1977. 146–78.

– *The Four Fundamental Concepts of Psychoanalysis.* Harmondsworth: Penguin, 1979.

Merleau-Ponty, Maurice. *La Nature.* Paris: Seuil, 1996.

– *Le Visible et l'invisible.* Paris: Gallimard, 1964.

Schelling, F.W.J. *The Ages of the World.* Slavoj Žižek/F.W.J. von Schelling, *The Abyss of Freedom/Ages of the World*. Trans. Judith Norman. Ann Arbor: U of Michigan P, 1997. 107–82.

– *Über das Wesen der Menschlichen Freiheit*. Frankfurt am Main: Suhrkamp, 1975.

Žižek, Slavoj. *The Abyss of Freedom*. Slavoj Žižek/F.W.J. von Schelling, *The Abyss of Freedom/Ages of the World*. Trans. Judith Norman. Ann Arbor: U of Michigan P, 1997. 3–104.

– *The Invisible Remainder: An Essay on Schelling and Related Matters*. London: Verso, 1996.

PHYSIOLOGIES

Contradictory Pieces of
Time and History

ANTHONY WALL

Mikhail Bakhtin's writing contains no theory of history per se, but his writings on the chronotope, scattered throughout his work, provide indispensable clues for understanding how he performatively 'felt' about history. In the case of Bakhtin, we are dealing with a thinker whose thoughts on time and history can only be revealed if we are willing to let them play themselves out in what he writes rather than seeking all the keys to his thoughts by poring over everything he explicitly said. In other words, Bakhtinian times and histories must be performed by someone other than Bakhtin himself, not only because he is no longer there to do any performing, but also because performance is a two-way street. It is in the performance of his various pieces, achieved through reading as 'doing,' that a zone of contact, spatial-temporal in nature, can be established between Bakhtin the writer and the readers who perform him. Indeed, we modern-day readers execute these thoughts much the same way in which Roland Barthes talks about the amateur pianist who must not only read the musical scores he has in front of his eyes, but also play those scores out with his body, and in particular with his fingers, as he works his way through that written text that he is trying to 'play' by sight. As Barthes goes on to show, there is indeed a profound difference between 'listening' to a Schumann recording and playing Schumann oneself on the piano (260).

One of the joys, but also one of the major problems, of Bakhtin the herald of chronotopes is that he himself never seems to be able to do two or more performances of his own thinking on time and history that are exactly the same. That is to say that when we deal with Bakhtin the theoretician trying to sort out the interconnections between time and space, we soon come to realize that there is, as Jay Ladin has aptly

pointed out, a certain 'trouble with chronotopes' (213) that needs serious reckoning. Reflection on Bakhtin's variously construed, and variously enacted, stances towards history – history understood as physical
time lived out by concrete human beings – becomes possible only when
we examine his writing on the chronotope as specifically fragmentary
writing, writing whose bits and pieces, strewn throughout his manuscripts and published works, often lead to contradictory statements or
aporetic conclusions. Not only are there contradictions between the
young neo-Kantian Bakhtin who writes about the times and spaces of
aesthetic consummation and the later cultural philosopher Bakhtin who
writes about the ambivalent time-spaces of carnivalesque celebrations –
and these contradictions play themselves out continually in what he says
about time-space relationships in art and in life – but there are also
important contradictions that display themselves 'synchronically,' if you
will, as they repeatedly, and variously, rehearse a highly significant scene
for understanding how Bakhtin, sometimes in a single piece, lets contradictions in his own theoretical selves and positions come into the open.

The most interesting aspect of performing Bakhtin's contradictions
about time and space, while attempting to contextualize these contradictions in his own time and in space, consists in the fact that such read-
erly performances inevitably entail the involvement of one's own body. I
am proposing here to include recent work being done on the body,
mainly by Elizabeth Grosz, who herself talks about time and space in the
context of her bodily analyses.[1] This I shall do in an attempt to show
how the fragmentary and contradictory nature of the chronotope, as it
appears in Bakhtin's writing, can be plausibly linked with the contradictory and fragmentary pieces that he posits as being part of both the
human and the cosmic body (as discussed in his work on the carnival,
both in the Rabelais book and in other related – some only recently
published – texts).

I. History as Lived Time

I wish to argue here that the volatile nature of Bakhtin's conceptual
thinking in general is inextricably linked to the volatile nature of his
thinking on the body in particular. Not only does this volatility extend
to what he says about language and cultural expression, but it is also
steeped in the flux of what he says and does in relation to time. Body,
fragment, space, and time form various configurations in his thinking
and they expose themselves on a theoretical stage where repetition as

variation and improvisation is more the norm than it is the exception. Even though it would seem, as historians are wont to emphasize, that 'the more an event becomes distant, the more opportunities for fruitful research into a historical object are expanded and enhanced' (Kögler 29), we will not be using this piece of common-sense knowledge in an effort to reestablish wholes, to reconstruct lost historical pieces, or to erase the fragmentary and contradictory nature of the objects that are placed before us. Quite to the contrary, 'opportunities are expanded and enhanced' in Bakhtin's thinking on time and history precisely because objects moving further and further from us in time and space are increasingly subjected to the vagaries of the competing discourses that attempt to monopolize them. Human history is indeed a form of cultural memory, but history as lived human time only arrives on stage when there are repetitions, just as it can only be seen as productive when we are prepared to accept these same *repetitions* in the sense of a theatrical *répétition générale*. In other words, repetition and return in Bakhtin's work are inevitably imperfect, and they thus become the very engines of the interesting dynamics of history that shows itself in his theoretical thinking. In my own attempts to talk about what Bakhtin himself says about time, space, and the body, and as I observe various places and chronotopes of his manuscripts and works, I shall sometimes use the word 'choppy' to describe what I see. This I shall do in an effort to show that the inconsistent, irregular, and changing conceptions of time and history that we can uncover in Bakhtin's thinking must be thought of as pieces and parts that will never fit together just right.

Let me begin by proposing what is (for me) a neat analogy that helps to illustrate what I am attempting to say: history is to time and space, I want to say, as dialogism is to language; that is, history is lived times and spaces, not just abstract, or purely physical time and space, just as dialogism is a form of a lived heteroglot language, not merely abstractly conceived language, or the type of pre-packaged language that is found in the dictionary. In this preliminary way of understanding the distinction between physical time-spaces and lived human history, our conception of the chronotope would necessarily need to move into the territory of what is lived time – in other words, the chronotope becomes part of history (and not the other way around).[2] Given the indelible links they signify by definition, or indeed given that they *are* the very bridge that links time and space in the way we inhabit the world, Bakhtin's chronotopes are thus constituted as lived times and spaces, from the fact that life itself, as a series of social events, arises in the ways in which social beings inhabit space in time, and time in space. 'Thus, the traditional and Kantian conceptions of time and space become undermined, each taking on the properties of the other, as they lose their identities in a kind of ontological cross-dressing' (Mihailovic 47). The Bakhtin of the 'middle' period is often said to be primarily a philosopher of language, and what at first glance appears to be 'merely' a theory about language – Bakhtin is after all thinking about chronotopes in the 1930s, that is, after his 'linguistic turn' has occurred – is in fact (and this is the point of departure for this essay) a profound reflection on how we live language through contradictions as we move through time and space, or rather as we move through our lives with others *by means of* times and spaces.

Owing to the fact that history is lived or performed, not *discovered*,[3] it is subject to the same sorts of vagaries and variables that govern cultural utterances in general. The utterance, as we know, can only gain currency when it circulates from 'one mouth to another, from one context to another context, from one social collective to another, from one generation to another generation' (Bakhtin, *Problems* 202).[4] Such circulation continuously occurs – and reoccurs – through variously constituted utterance acts, i.e., performances of cultural languages. As Michel de Certeau would claim, we not only live in language but we especially 'do' language.[5] History, then, must be seen as a type of cultural utterance in that it is 'lived' time, time that has been 'done,' as it were, or time that has been articulated into the spaces and cracks of cultural memory. Its utterance-like nature can be further observed in so far as it must continually be acted out. History can thus be seen as the loosely assembled series of lived cultural utterance acts that take place in any number of human contexts, sometimes appropriate, and sometimes not so appropriate. It thereby becomes definable as the humanized dimension of physically lived time and consequently falls under the influence of inconsistency and change.

One of Western modernity's greatest, if not its most controversial figures, Charles Baudelaire, once remarked in his reflections on culture and literature that one of the most important, but probably the most neglected of human rights – besides, of course, the fundamental right to leave someone else's company – had to be the right to contradict oneself.[6] Although recognized by no existing political constitution, neither in the Universal Declaration of Rights of 1789 nor in any other constitution, including that of Mikhail Bakhtin's former Soviet Union, Baudelaire's declaration of the fundamental need of humanity to have the semantic space available to it for contradiction, or for the human individual to change his or her own mind, found a truly strong, although implicit, endorsement in Bakhtin's cultural philosophy. As a thinker in history and a thinker reflecting on time and space, Bakhtin is much more a practitioner of contradiction than a full-fledged theorist thereof. Baudelaire's cries for the universal respect of the fundamental right to contradict oneself therefore did not fall on totally deaf ears, in Bakhtin's case at least,[7] for the latter readily avails himself of this same right for self-contradiction, a right he exercised in changing his theoretical mind on a number of occasions, and in several fundamental ways, especially when talking about time and space and about the ways in which the human body fits, or does not fit, therein.

One readily notes in many recent studies of Bakhtin's work, and in this respect Alexandar Mihailovic's *Corporeal Words* is no exception, a general yearning for consistency that is shared by Western and Russian interpreters alike. The fact that Bakhtin, throughout his writing, but in particular in his later texts, very often returned to ideas that he had already discussed in his very first texts should be read – it has been suggested – as a clear sign that there is a clear and fundamentally unified core of thought in everything that he said and did. This may not be a methodological unity – one can after all find a sociological Bakhtin, a neo-Kantian Bakhtin, an aesthetic Bakhtin, a literary Bakhtin, a psychologist Bakhtin, a biologist Bakhtin, and so forth – but, as such readings suggest, these continual returns to the old themes provide the most convincing proof possible of a remarkable consistency in his thinking, even if this consistency often remains hidden from many readers. The fact of his eternal returns does not, however, constitute incontrovertible evidence that he is as consistent and as non-contradictory as some of his readers would like him to be. It should be pointed out that Bakhtin himself seems rather surprised, near the end of his life, to discover that his editors had drawn a sense of coherence out of the various essays, stemming from a variety of periods and phases of his intellectual trajectory, which they had assembled under the title *Questions of Literature and Aesthetics*.[8] In his notes from the early 1970s, Bakhtin expresses a certain wonderment when he remarks, 'This collection of essays is unified by one theme in various stages of its development' ('From Notes Made in 1970–71' 155), failing, however, to give the slightest indication about what that unifying theme is supposed to be. My point here would be to claim that there is no plausible semantic theme that unites all of Bakhtin's thinking but rather that there are certain 'imagic patterns' and 'arts de faire' that run through his writing (just as a style of brushstrokes runs through a painter's works).[9] This is, of course, more than just a 'question of style,' for it goes right to the heart of Bakhtin's writing, loosely strung together texts that should be seen not as abstract semantic material but as concrete somatic events.[10]

In the following, I propose to follow a tack for discussing Bakhtin's works and their putative harmonies and disharmonies that is slightly different from those readings strategies that seek consistency. This proposal to read his writing as one would read moving images is profoundly connected with several underlying practices, all frequently exercised by Bakhtin in his writing, of living through time and space (that is, of conceiving history). Rather than viewing Bakhtin's forever reoccurring remakes of his former theoretical selves, and instead of explaining his eternal returns to his previously written work as indisputable signs of his underlying (even if only implicit) unified and unchanging philosophical attitudes, I submit that the problematic moments of repetition that occur throughout his life-work should be read as variants in a continually refitted and readapted *mise en scène*, the eventful restaging of a choppy view of time and space that is not afraid to contradict itself in its words and deeds. In displaying varying degrees of inconsistency and contradiction in these numerous remakes, Bakhtin is enacting an apparent belief in the non-permanence of what he had once said or thought, a belief that underscores a generally temporalized series of changing positions with regard to virtually all his previously held views. I propose here to regard Bakhtin's repeated, but variously consummated, reconstructions of his former selves as always varying enactments of the fundamentally Baudelairean right to contradict oneself. Such fleeting moments of inconsistency, or (we might say) such fleeting moments of a most profound humanity, are all part and parcel of a further-reaching set of theoretical practices and tactics in which times, spaces, and bodies, both great and small, are always playing the lead roles.

II. The Indispensable Nature of Contradiction

By this insistence on the right to change one's mind, I do not wish to suggest that there are absolutely no pockets of 'consistency' in Bakhtin's thinking. Nor do I wish to deny that the earlier work absolutely lacks any 'kernels' of the theoretical thinking which, although barely noticeable in the early unpublished work, will miraculously develop into something important in Bakhtin's later work. What I do mean to suggest, however, is that we need a broad enough *frame of reference* for thinking about

Bakhtin that allows us to see both the changes in (in-)consistency as well as the (in-)consistency in the changes. This way of avoiding the dead-end problematic of understanding Bakhtin as *either* consistent *or* inconsistent has the further advantage of directing us towards the *edges* of the various facets of his thought as they come into contact with one another.[11] It also allows us to look at Bakhtin's thinking over time and across theoretical spaces as it opens a way of looking at Bakhtin that stresses multiple edges, that is, multiple beginnings and multiple endings. In this respect, Bakhtin's thinking can be said to be consonant with Gilles Deleuze and Félix Guattari's unorthodox view of modern philosophy, a view according to which it is entirely unclear whether philosophy can be described as even having a single beginning: 'Even the first concept, the one with which a philosophy *begins*, has several components, because it is not obvious that philosophy must have a beginning, and if it does determine one, it must combine it with a point of view or a ground' (Deleuze and Guattari 15).

The notion of the chronotope necessarily deals with the times and places that thinking itself fills up within the unfolding of Bakhtin's own work. The chronotopes of Bakhtin's own productivity constitute starkly 'poetic' examples – 'poetic' in the sense of the poetic function discussed by Roman Jakobson[12] – of a conceptual configuration that draws attention to itself through the fact that it literally *does*, on the level of performance, what it would *like to say* on the level of its semantics. Conceptually developed in the 1920s in connection with biology and vitalism,[13] then written down in legible form only in the 1930s in a loosely strung together series of more or less connected notes (that were never openly intended to be part of a finished whole), and finally revisited in 1973 by the aging Bakhtin, who agreed to write his 'Concluding Remarks' for an essay on the chronotope that he had never really written[14] – the chronotope can be seen as that which forges the artistic unity of his own work in its 'relationship to an actual reality' ('Forms of Time' 243). Most remarkably, and no less significantly, it can be observed that these 'Concluding Remarks' actually provide a number of inconsistencies in relation to the series of smaller chapters, or case 'studies,' for which they are supposed to provide a few 'final words.' This is a vintage Bakhtinian performance of Bakhtin the theorist who revisits his former theoretical selves. He first purports to 'sum up' what was previously said, that is, to cast the expressed ideas in a tightly construed and encapsulated form, but then, as it very often occurs with most instances of Bakhtin the theorist who attempts to be tightly construed and encapsulated, the elder Bakhtin fails with flying colours to achieve his purported aim (i.e., to write a clear and concise summary). The 'conclusion' itself is no less 'choppy' than the series of studies that it follows and, in particular, it introduces a totally new conception of the chronotope in comparison with the definitions and demonstrations that were provided in the first nine sections. This 'new' chronotope could at best be said to exist *in nuce* in the various texts on the chronotope that he had written much, much earlier, some of which had indeed been included in the essay he is purporting to conclude, while others remained inexplicably absent.

Moreover, the newness of these 'Concluding Remarks' can be seen, first and foremost, in that, in constant contrast with the earlier nine studies, this last section recognizes its *own chronotopicity*. All the 'contra-dictions' and 'inconsistencies' it displays in relation to the studies it dis-cusses derive from this metatheoretical point of view that is egregiously absent in the earlier parts of the essay. In fact, if indeed it is at all per-missible to speak of 'facts' in Bakhtin's work, the conclusion will not *con-clude* anything at all, at least not in any traditional sense of the word, as it, quite explicitly, sets out to introduce new material on the chrono-tope: 'As we draw our essay to a close, we will simply list, and merely touch upon, certain other chronotopic values having different degree and scope' ('Forms of Time' 243). Bakhtin will ostensibly proceed by synthetic generalizations here, and he develops certain notions such as the road that he sees running more or less consistently through a vast array of literary texts written in England, France, Germany, and Russia. But the chronotopic notions he now proposes at the very end are them-selves *so general and overtly metaphoric* that they do not permit us to move towards any concrete analysis of any of the texts he mentioned earlier, unless of course these attempts at analysis are to be accompanied by yet another arsenal of much more precise analytical tools. In other words, when Bakhtin concludes his essay on the chronotope, he (unwittingly?) reveals the major inadequacies of everything that has been discussed in so far as his reader cannot help but notice that the chronotopes that he talks about can be used to discuss virtually anything, that is to say, noth-ing at all in particular.[15] The concluding remarks are supposed to leave Bakhtin's readers with the final word on the chronotope, but they actu-ally create more questions about what the chronotope might be – and might not be – than they provide concrete answers.

It does not take too long to notice that the version of the chronotope discussed in Bakhtin's 'Concluding Remarks' is much less a device for distinguishing between several different generic types, as it was in the preceding case studies, than it has become a tool for capturing a fundamental aspect of semantic *dynamism* at work within the texture of a given body of thought. Time and space 'shift gears,' as it were, and move from the realm of taxonomy, the typical procedure of immature inquiry, to that of explaining, the surest sign for what Bakhtin praises as mature thinking ('Contemporary Vitalism' 78). The most important element of the comprehension of this dynamism is the chronotope of the author-creator, a new conception of the chronotope that is introduced only in the second half of these concluding remarks. This 'new and improved' chronotope cannot therefore conclude anything at all about what has preceded it, for it itself *introduces* new things, at the very end of the essay. In fact, this new chronotope is designed to accomplish a number of tasks that are totally different from those accomplished by the chronotopes in the earlier parts of the essay.

Given this last and *new* aspect of the chronotope, we can say, without the slightest exaggeration, that the ending of the chronotope essay is, quite literally, the beginning of a brand new chronotope. As is so often the case with Bakhtin, it is in those moments where he begins to sum up what he has previously said, i.e., those very moments where he ostensibly is trying to give us an appropriate ending, that he inadvertently (or perhaps even purposely) begins to embark upon something entirely new. It is as if he forgets what he wanted to do when he set out to summarize what he had already done, as if the past can no longer determine indefinitely that which the future will perhaps one day reveal. This aspect of the conclusion leads us to believe that Bakhtin's work is characterized by a remarkably fertile *confusion* between endings and beginnings. Linked with the Roman god of entrances and passageways whom Bakhtin mentions on numerous occasions, the confused beginnings and endings that we can discern in this non-conclusion are made of the same mythological *Stoff* that fuels Bakhtin's predilection for images of Janus. In his view, and especially in his study of speech on the open square, this god and his symbolism penetrate into the very heart of language: 'The billingsgate idiom is a two-faced Janus' (*Rabelais* 165). In the concluding remarks of the chronotope essay, as he moves from the level of represented chronotopes to that of the representation of chronotopes, Bakhtin is slowly slipping into a state of total confusion. Arriving in the final paragraphs of this conclusion that concludes virtually nothing, his remarks are worth quoting *in extenso*:

> But even in the segmentation of a modern literary work we sense the
> chronotope of the represented world as well as the chronotope of the

readers and creators of the work. That is, we get a mutual interaction between the world represented in the work and the world outside the work. This interaction is pinpointed very precisely in certain elementary features of composition. Every work has a *beginning* and an *end*, the event represented in it likewise has a beginning and an end but these beginnings and ends lie in different worlds, in different chronotopes that can never fuse with each other or be identical to each other but that are, at the same time, interrelated and indissolubly tied up with each other. ('Forms of Time' 254–5)

My contention is that this curious passage that insistently creates a confusion between beginnings and endings is just one example of what I would call a Janus-like compulsion on Bakhtin's part to link every beginning with an ending and every ending with a beginning. In Bakhtin's thinking, I'd like to argue, beginnings *are* endings, just as endings *are* beginnings. The poetic (Jakobsonian) quality of this fundamentally Bakhtinian confusion – one hesitates in calling it an insight – can be seen once again in the concluding remarks of the chronotope essay inasmuch as the conclusion enacts this same confusion: it is both a beginning and an end.

III. A Necessary Confused State

This confusion necessarily occurs in Bakhtin's thinking at the metatheoretical level. In terms of the implicit theory of history it exemplifies, another name we can give to this confusion is the 'loophole.' In terms of time, loopholes give us, then, what the Janus-like confusion between the first edge and the last edge gives us in terms of space. This confusion of first and last, beginning and ending, or even inside and outside, can be described, using the theoretical framework provided in Françoise Susini-Anastopoulos's reflection on fragmentary writing in general, as a classical characteristic of a fragmentarist attitude in relation to the world. In a remark where she refers to Paul Valéry, but which can be used to understand the phenomenon of fragmentary writing in general, Susini-Anastopoulos makes an important observation. Even though she is not thinking of Bakhtin here, I find it appropriate to apply it to Bakhtin's way of writing in fragments. She writes that 'what the fragmentarist author seeks by way of this dream of conflating the beginnings and the endings of the utterance is a *coincidentia oppositorum*, a situation that assures that a perfectly fitting meeting will occur between writing per se and the object of this writing, that is theory or experience' (108; my translation). If we adopt Susini-Anastopoulos's terms, Bakhtin is basically a fragmentarist. The use of such a label is justified by the constant confusion that we can point to in the 'Concluding Remarks,' a state of bewilderment that occurs at precisely that moment where he half-heartedly insists on the separation that must be maintained between representing chronotopes and represented chronotopes. Of course, it is a natural consequence of the notion of an 'ending' that it should be accompanied by its conceptual opposite, that is, by a beginning. It is also natural, at least in terms of the history of Western philosophy of time, especially since Aristotle, that fragments should play such an important role in understanding what time is, or rather what it is not.[16] In a thorough theoretical examination of what it means to say that one has arrived at the end of something, Karlheinz Stierle clearly shows that it is impossible to think of an ending without realizing that, for every ending, there has to be a beginning – somewhere or sometime.[17] Endings actually create opportunities for new beginnings, and this they do by their inherently paradoxical nature, which lies at the confusing conceptual crossroads between 'no more' and 'not yet' (Stierle 578). As Stierle goes on to show, the very fact of believing that one has begun something new implies a second belief that that same start is destined to find its own ending in the future.

However paradoxical the notions of beginnings and endings are, it would seem that fragmentary writers, and Bakhtin is no exception, push their paradoxical semantics to the limit. In the quotation taken from the final pages of the 'Chronotope' essay, cited above, it is clear that no attempt is made on Bakhtin's part to reconcile the differences between the conflicting semantics of concluding and that of starting anew. This confusion between endings and beginnings is not, however, confined to the chronotope essay alone, inasmuch as the thinking that Bakhtin put into the carnival also partakes of this same fertile conceptual mixture: 'all these acts are performed on the confines of the body and the outer world, or on the confines of the old and the new body. In all these events, the beginning and the end of life are closely linked and interwoven' (*Rabelais* 317). We see then that Bakhtin often *assumes* these beginning-and-ending contradictions, as they have become an essential component of his idiosyncratic way of thinking in verbalized images.[18] We rather sense, in fact, that he is willingly displaying a confused state that lies at the very heart of what he is trying to *do* as he writes a conclusion for a set of fragments that he had written some forty years earlier.

This type of *showing* through *doing* is not unlike the illuminations through fragmentary thinking that are so characteristic of an innovative thinker such as Walter Benjamin, for example. Not only was Benjamin interested in the effects that actual physical lighting exerted on inhabitants of the modern city, a point admirably shown by Susan Buck-Morss (308–12), but he was also keenly fascinated by the ways in which human thought is able to appear 'in a flash,' as it were, as an illuminating moment that gives us a fleeting, but powerful, glimpse of a much larger, and thereby unfathomable, body of thought. Any such glimpse, a momentary fixing of an evolving and moving target – what for Benjamin is normally unconscious and invisible to the naked eye – is hopelessly caught in a situation where it can only be sensed, but never grasped, as a 'momentary flickering-up' (Weigel 115). In other words, as Benjamin himself writes, the 'dialectical image is one that flashes through the mind' (591; my translation). Indeed, conscious and unconscious thinking are not very far at all from processes of vision, owing to the fact that both have a 'flow,' and, because of this, neither lends itself to operations bent on 'grasping' them as a single, static or immobile entity. 'Consciousness is like vision. The similarities are probably not accidental since the eye is anatomically an extension of the brain, and since for most of us vision is so fundamental a part of conscious experience' (Chafe 53).

Just as time, the impenetrable past, texts, and images can only be 'downloaded' by our minds in bits and pieces (the most important philosophical question consists in asking *how many* pieces the mind can process at a time),[19] so too the body as a whole is a far too complex piece of informative living matter for us to be able to take it in 'in a single go.' It is no coincidence, then, that both time and the body are 'lived' by humans in a fragmentary fashion. As the philosopher Philip Turetzky remarks, while speaking of Henri Bergson's philosophy of time, 'Through their habits, needs, actions, and techniques, people fabricate the stabilities necessary for practical life. Because of these practical needs, consciousness artificially breaks up the whole of *durée* into mutually external things' (202).

Indeed, Bergson's notion of *durée* has taken up a significant place in many contemporary critiques of Western notions of time and space. Among the critics, feminist theoreticians have recognized the importance of *durée* as a notion that permits us to understand how human beings *live* time. Gail Weiss is one of them when she harnesses the conceptual power of Bergson's *durée* as she strives to offer a cogent opposition to currents of thinking that tend to 'reduce bodies to organisms, organisms to organs, and in the end, evacuate human (and especially female) agency by doing away with the very notion and experience of *durée* or becoming in time' (106). Elizabeth Grosz could be said to be another, although she does not mention Bergson explicitly, referring rather to Bergson's innovative reader Gilles Deleuze. This Bergsonian tinge that colours Grosz's vantage point can be observed when she discusses the need to understand the body in terms of the types of agency that it can potentially fulfil. She contests all the philosophical and otherwise theoretical conceptions of the past that 'never questioned the body's status as an *object* (of reflection, intervention, training, or remarking), never considered the possibility that the body could be understood as subject, agent, or activity' (*Space, Time, and Perversion* 2). Indeed, Grosz contrasts the concept of a 'pliable' or 'docile' body with that of an active body, one that must be 'understood as more than an impediment to our humanity' (2). This opposition is something that she readily recognizes not only as a part of her long-term interest in 'research on how to reconceive the body as socio-cultural artifact' (103) but also as a component of her desire to engage in a project of 'spatiality studies' which can take on the aim of questioning theories that 'seek validation in terms of their moral force rather [than] their intellectual, political, or ethical weight' (5).

These types of issues lead us to reexamine the relationship between human beings and the humanized times and spaces in which they live. These same issues also allow us to study the body as an unfolding language whose very corporeality must be seen as a form of human subjectivity in and of itself. Seeing the body as language implies seeing language as a body. This seeing compels us to look at phenomena such as quotation and indirect speech, two favourite topics discussed by both Bakhtin and Voloshinov,[20] as telling examples of how language takes on interactive dimensions. The use of quotation, for example, can be understood as the type of borrowing of another's words, an apprehension by which the very act of quoting 'embodies language' and gives it a new space and time (Weigel 38).[21] The important issue here has to do with the fundamental links between time, space, and the body, relationships that become perceptible when we examine the ways in which we create semantic and somatic fragments. Quotation is after all an encapsulated piece of someone else's flowing discourse. From such practices of fragmentation, we can attempt to understand just what fragment fits where, and just whose fragments we are allowed to take, and when. Fragmentary practices have to do, in the final analysis, with how, in the social spaces that we are assigned, we live through pieces of the bodies and pieces of meaning. They show us how we live through pieces of time.

I think that it is here that the importance of Elizabeth Grosz's work can be most clearly seen, an importance that extends in particular to readers of Bakhtin, even though Grosz does not herself give much, if any, explicit recognition of Bakhtin's ideas in her own work.[22] We need to deal with what Grosz calls '*discursive positioning*,' something she defines as the 'complex relation between the corporeality of the author, that is, the author's textual residues or traces, the text's materiality, and its effects in marking the bodies of the author and readers, and the corporeality and productivity of readers' (*Space, Time, and Perversion* 18). 'Positioning' is indeed a useful notion for thinking about spaces and bodies that *move*. Language too is on the move and this movement can be readily seen in the to-and-fro oscillation between speaker and hearer, a movement that characterizes linguistic 'turn taking.' Modern philosophy of language has learned to move from a conception of language as statement to a view of language as act. An essential part of acting in language, and of the productive utilization of time in this *acting out* of language's movement, is precisely the practice of asking questions. 'In relation to life in general and man in particular, *why* and *for what purpose* become the problems of central importance, not *because* or *for this reason*' (Bakhtin, 'Contemporary Vitalism' 80). As Bill Readings pointed out in his recent critique of the contemporary Western university, at the present time we are unfortunately relinquishing, with much too much willing compliance, our readiness to spend the precious time that is needed to ask each other questions. We no longer seem to understand what Readings calls the 'temporality of questioning' (19) that is a necessary part of any living body of language in use. In other words, thinking processes (deeply rooted in curiosity and wondering), like bodily processes, are subject to time and space constraints and this combination of thinking and embodiment is in turn part and parcel of processes of fragmentation.

Time and space can never be considered in relation to the human body without serious consideration being given to the social matrices within which, and from which, bodies are able (or not able) to say what they have to say. That this is so can be seen *ab contrario* when, in fiction or in our private imagination, we attempt to release the body from its physico-social environment. Writings on utopia consistently try to imagine, most often unsuccessfully, a setting where 'the use of time and the use of space are different' (Roudaut 114; my translation). Significantly, however, the very possibility of inserting corporeality into our imaginary worlds provides us with opportunities for reconceptualizing how we imagine bodies in real life. 'If bodies are to be reconceived, not only must their *matter and form* be rethought, but so too must their environment and *spatio-temporal location*' (Grosz, *Space, Time, and Perversion* 84). There are several ways to deal with such fundamental considerations: one can refer for example to the idea of time and bodies as expressed by the gaps between generations, as Richard Fenn does (196). Or one can alternately refer, as Jean-Marie Tréguier does, to discussions of flesh and time that take part in our traditional thinking derived from Saint Augustine (183–90). It is thereby important to note that the idea according to which fragmentation is an essential component of our human existence is not an invention of postmodernism. Saint Augustine pointedly saw fragmentation as the necessary scourge of human understanding, something that provided the most unbridgeable gulf between our own fragmented human capacity to have limited opinions and God's continuous capacity to know.[23]

This issue of necessary human fragmentation is of course also related to how our memories function. For indeed human memory depends on the fragments, which are stored away mechanically, or in an in almost automatic fashion, as Bergson would have it (83–96).[24] These bits and pieces must be subsequently sewn together in a type of artistic montage. It is precisely this reconstructive performance that human memory constantly enacts, a performance that can be understood as a type of semiotic/somatic utterance. This fundamental characteristic of memory has important consequences for historiography, as pointed out by many philosophers of history.[25] Memory can only reconstruct its bits and pieces as best it can in a semantic and somatic process that fascinated Bergson and, after him, Gilles Deleuze. When, in his studies of time and movement in film, Deleuze turns his attention to the ways in which films (re-)assemble thousands of isolated photographic frames into a continuous flow of imagic movement, he is inevitably led to a rereading of Bergson's work on memory as montage. Deleuze talks in particular about *nappes du passé*, horizontally organized spaces or spans of time that can be mounted together and reorganized into various configurations. We thereby see that memory seen is a sort of temporal 'machine' that must play itself out through continued and repeated performances (*L'Image-Temps* 129–64).

Grosz too is attracted, via Deleuze, to the potential of Bergson's phi-

losophy of memory. She links all such semiotics of bodily movement to
the ultimately bodily foundation of most of what *moves* in discourse. Discourse is forever putting us in our place(s), as we might say in reference
to Michel Foucault's early work on the insane asylum.[26] Grosz, for her
part, stresses the point that, if we buy into the idea of the body's potential position as a subject of social discourses, we must nevertheless not
smudge over the fact that there is always a fundamental 'mismatch'
between the types of representation that the body can make on its own
accord and those that are embarked upon through language (*Space,
Time, and Perversion* 21).[27] Body languages are not pure languages of the
exterior, however, owing to the fact that the body provides the essential
bridge between our interior selves and the external world. 'By the very
ways in which it inspects its environment and ... turns itself into an
object among other objects, the body provides an opening onto what is'
(Thierry 92; my translation). Despite this bridging function fulfilled by
our bodily nature, it is still often difficult for us, especially from within
our minds, which are caught in the languages of interiority, to understand the degree to which bodies speak not merely to express a secret
interior that the mind's prodding eye would like to 'hear,' but rather to
express their own and specific ways of being and their own interiors –
on their own terms. It is all a question of methodology, as Bakhtin would
say, a matter of learning to listen from within a methodology that is
open to questions. 'Methodology in science is nothing other than the
main direction in which questions are formulated' ('Contemporary
Vitalism' 78). A fixed and hard-set methodology will of course determine the answers it wants to hear by the very types of questions it asks:
'The proof is determined in [the] descriptive terminology which moves
from a hidden to a manifest state' (91). Grosz's interest in letting bodies
do their own talking converges with Bakhtin's project of learning how to
listen to languages other than one's own. In both instances, a problem
arises as to the best way of understanding the transfer of knowledge
about the outside to knowledge possessed on the inside. As we have just
seen, this is where the body, as the link between the individual and the
outside social world, plays a crucial role. A basic characteristic of the
human body and its dealings with its environment is, just as the carnivalesque Bakhtin has remarked, that the body is busy ingesting all that is
placed outside of its own limits. Grosz sees the body in a strikingly similar way:

Food, dieting, exercise, and movement provide meanings, values, norms, and ideals that the subject actively ingests, incorporating social categories into the physiological interior. Bodies speak, without necessarily talking, because they become coded with and as signs. They speak social codes. They become intextuated, narrativized; simultaneously, social codes, laws, norms, and ideals become incarnated. (*Space, Time, and Perversion* 35)

It is precisely in this sense, i.e., in the reading according to which the body *literally* incorporates (and thereby comes to embody) everything and anything with which it comes into contact, that it will always be able to say, in its temporal-spatial movement, very much more than anyone could ever predict in advance. This is why it is impossible, as we stressed above, to pry the body languages that the body is speaking away from the social chronotopes in which and from which this speaking is being done.

IV. Loopholes as Meta-Knowledge

In Bakhtin's thinking, the important moment where fragmentation and knowledge come cogently together occur in those passages where we sense the presence of his famous loopholes. Loopholes, like the fragmentarist confusion between ending and beginning that we earlier discussed, occur in the epistemological environment created by meta-knowledge. It is no accident that, in those texts where Bakhtin sees and discusses the chronotope of the threshold in terms of the loophole, that is in *Problems of Dostoevsky's Poetics*,[28] such discussion occurs in the context of 'anti-heroes' who suffer from acute cases of hyperbolic self-consciousness, or an over-abundance of meta-knowledge. Once again, what at first glance simply appeared to be merely a part of Bakhtin's theory of language, one that is elaborated in terms of dialogic interaction and novelistic polyphony, turns out, upon closer inspection, and in this fundamental connection between endings and beginnings, to be an integral element in a theory of lived time or history. Meta-knowledge is less a state than it is a highly significant and mobile sign that human time unfolds in a non-linear fashion.[29]

While the chronotope is that which gives lived time a discernible form, time becomes 'lived' in order to become a story, and seemingly inert space is temporalized in order to let it be 'lived.' This transformation of physically inactive time-spaces into energetic chronotopes is intelligently studied by Wolfgang Kemp in his fascinating Bakhtinian study of European art. In his analyses of Giotto and van der Weyden, as well as of several other artists, Kemp demonstrates that a participation of spectators is encouraged whereby a special type of seeing sensitive to the interaction between time and space is taught to the eye, a seeing that is thereby able to pry the life and movement out of the canvas through the ways that divergent chronotopes are juxtaposed and put into action (27). For Kemp, it is the juxtaposition that occurs on a single canvas space of inside and outside, before and after, or in front and behind that injects time, i.e., narrativity, into the spaces that are painted.

Such explanations depend on the fact that continuous times and spaces are broken up into smaller pieces and placed side by side. It may therefore not be necessary to enter into an anachronistic, and perhaps peripheral, discussion of chaos theory and fractals in order to sense the importance of how pieces of time and space become lived, but it does seem important to grasp the constitutive roles and the potential uses that can be assigned to the fragments of Bakhtin's way of thinking, especially in the context of the ways in which time is choppily lived through, and enacted, by Bakhtin the writer. What we have here is neither a 'causal theory of time'[30] (let us no longer say that Bakhtin wrote about y in text b *because* he wrote about x in text a) nor a time that is totally subjected to the insuperable 'direction of time.' The multi-directionality and undirectedness of Bakhtin's times not only have to do with his thinking, which is irretrievably steeped in metalanguages of all sorts, but also have intimate connections with the enormous importance placed by Bakhtin on the multiple processes he studies of cultural memory. In Bakhtin's thinking, something that is unequivocal in *Rabelais and His World* for example, there is actually a tendency towards *historical inversion,*[31] a secret nostalgia that is felt for the beauties of lost cultural worlds whose absence Bakhtin starkly regrets as he writes from his standpoint in the present. Bakhtin does not specifically talk about historical inversion in the Rabelais book (this he does, as just noted, in the chronotope essay); rather, he *shows* historical inversion in the very ways that he idealizes the lost carnival semiotics that he admires in Rabelais's time in comparison with the atrophied capability for laughter under which modern society suffers. 'Historical inversion' is really just one other symptom of the Bakhtinian tendency we have observed that consists in confusing beginnings and endings. This is a pattern he inevitably imputes to *someone else,* for example when in 'Contemporary Vitalism' he points out the propensity of Hans Driesch to look at life processes 'from the point of view of the already realized, wished for end,' a perspective that forces him into 'looking back from the end to the beginning' (95). In the

Rabelais book, however, Bakhtin literally 'does' a certain temporal inversion of his own, particularly in the way that he studies the carnival. In that 'inverted' performance that is part of an imagic pattern, the time of laughter from Rabelais's environment slowly becomes 'history' for Bakhtin, a story that he himself must play out in the body of his text. My point here is encapsulated by what Samuel Kinser has written about 'Bakhtin's discovery' in a passage where Kinser says that 'the systematization of images, not the representation of Rabelais' populist orthodoxy, is Bakhtin's secret theme' (257). Time and time again, Bakhtin not only speaks about time in his writing, but he especially plays time out in the ways that he actively organizes his fragmentary 'images' through a confusion of beginnings and endings.

This organizational quality stems not from systematized structures but from imagic patterns, i.e., 'body-signs,' forever making their presence felt rather than being explicitly or clearly visible. These body-signs characterize the invisible metalanguages at play not only in Bakhtin's Rabelais book, but also in much of his writing. The remarkable thing about Bakhtin's metalinguistic dimension ('metalinguistic' in the Jakobsonian sense) is that, contrary to what most semioticians of Saussurean persuasion seemed to believe,[32] his meta-knowledge expresses itself not from within the confines of codified linguistic semantics, but instead uses the resources of the non-verbal side of language. In other words, metalanguages are not necessarily about fixed codes, and they are not necessarily that which reinforces those expressive elements and cultural forms that most resemble verbal language. They lead rather to those dimensions of verbal language that, in the final analysis, are the least 'verbal' of all. This Bakhtinian movement away from explicit language towards bodies, images, and languages in performance is prominent in his study of the cultural life-forms that transform time into history. Since living in time means transforming time into history, the fact of being able to situate oneself on an historico-cultural map always involves the ability to *listen for* and to *listen to* where one has (already) been. One needs to look back to the beginnings to be able to point oneself in the direction of some desirable ends. The utmost importance of the reoccurrence of what has already been said should be sensed less as a proof of permanence than as a means to discovering how and where any socially determined individual, a creator of history, can be concretely situated. The histories and stories we tell about ourselves are no less significant than those histories and stories that we hear about others. They are in fact 'moving pictures' that we show about ourselves.

As the narrated version of how an individual came to be where he or she now is, and as an imagic story about what the individual might possibly become, history must be just as fragmentary as the partial visions that go into its elaboration. As such, history and fragments are both the product and the producers of loopholes. Bakhtin's chronotopes are produced and occur in a generalized broken thinking that places heavy stress on the roles that fragmentary forms play in cultural transmission. They all point in the directions of a history that, as the dynamic depository of all the cultural storiés one is constantly (re)telling oneself in order to *be*, must continually turn back upon itself. This very motion of turning back gives 'flesh' to the very stories which compose it. As time is lived, its propensity to generate meta-knowledge in the agents that live it (and thereby produce it and are themselves produced therein) becomes increasingly strong and irresistible. In other words, as Bakhtin would have it, there is no history without meta-knowledge, no history without memory, no time that does not turn back on itself. As meta-knowledge is at once that which enables history to unfold and that which, as a loophole, disables any strict linear unfolding of that same history, Bakhtin's thinking is less a reflection in the direction of a full-fledged theory of time than it is a form of thought that flees the very closure that time, as the ultimate form of meta-knowledge, might one day produce. Bakhtin's fragmentary theory of history can thus be seen to unfold in the fragmentary nature of his own writing, in the conflictive spaces and times that open up owing to the contradictory metaphorical domains that are used as his numerous explanatory bases and in the multifariously configured bodies that he uses as actors in an open-ended story that mutates in its successive regenerations.

It is only logical, then, if there is any 'logic' in this fragmentary thought, that the absence of clear endings in this way of thinking would have as its necessary corollary a corresponding lack of clear beginnings. Stories are not that which give us a story of our birth; they are rather that which much be continually re-counted. From the fact that there are no Adamic or first words for Bakhtin, this lack of clear beginning is only 'natural' in a cultural world constituted in fragments, one in which endings and beginnings are productively 'confused' and where the absence or proliferation of the one will necessarily entail the absence or proliferation of the other. For Bakhtin, utterances are always already-used and previously owned. The history we can *live through* by means of Bakhtin's own theory of culture is therefore not one of origins but rather one of continual metamorphoses, of partial reoccurrences, of variable adaptations, and especially of second-handedness. Time is the name we can give to the movements that propel us from one cultural imperative to another, the set of forces that allows us to cross borders from one domain to another. If today we are busy worrying about theories of history, I do not think it is necessary to lament and to decry such activity as being necessarily derivative or culturally parasitic. Let us not confuse, as Thomas Pavel once did, cultural meta-production with cultural decadence (125–45). When enacted in a conscious effort to leap with greater efficiency, and when constituted as a reflective attempt to understand where we are going by looking at where we have been, the manifestation of meta-knowledge, the production of contradictory bodily fragments, the uneven juxtaposition of times and places, and the appearance of loopholes are about as culturally 'natural' as you can possibly get.

NOTES

1 In the course of this study, I shall be always referring implicitly, when mentioning Elizabeth Grosz's work, to her *Volatile Bodies: Toward a Corporeal Feminism* and to the collection of essays she coedited with Elspeth Probyn in *Sexy Bodies: The Strange Carnalities of Feminism*. I shall be referring explicitly, on several occasions, to her interesting *Space, Time, and Perversion*.

2 This is not so much to say that history can never be part of a given chronotope but rather that history is made up of all the culturally constituted timespaces that we as human beings both *live in* and *act out*.

3 This fact has to do with what Peter Kivy calls 'authenticity as practice' in his *Authenticities: Philosophical Reflections on Musical Performance* 80–107.

4 The contention that repetition is 'doing,' and not vacuous reproduction, is a basic point in feminist criticisms of traditional conceptions of womanhood that see women as destined for reproduction in a world bereft of history and change. On this point see Moira Gatens, *Imaginary Bodies* 95.

5 The crucial book for understanding de Certeau's concept of cultural utterances remains his *L'Invention du quotidien*. A variant of this point of view can be seen in Jean Chesneaux's work as he talks about turning time into something that human beings can 'do.' See Jean Chesneaux, *Habiter le temps*.

6 See Charles Baudelaire, 'Edgar Poe, sa vie et ses œuvres,' 306: 'Parmi l'énumération nombreuse des *droits de l'homme* que la Sagesse du XIX siècle recommence si souvent et si complaisamment, deux assez importants ont été oubliés qui sont le droit de se contredire et le droit de s'en aller.'

7 We know that Bakhtin knew Baudelaire very well, as he can be heard citing

Baudelaire's poetry by heart in the interviews with Viktor Duvakin that were taped in the latter years of his life. The transcript of these extensive interviews was recently published *in toto* under the title *Besedy V.D. Duvakina s M.M. Bakhtinym.* The English translation, underway with Brian Poole, is forthcoming: *M.M. Bakhtin in Dialogue with V.D. Duvakin.*

8 See M.M. Bakhtin, *Voprosi literaturi i estetiki.* The essays from this collection, all seen and reread by Bakhtin before his death – he died during the year of this publication – have been published virtually all over the Bakhtinian map as far as English-language translations are concerned. Four of the essays are found in *The Dialogic Imagination;* another in *Art and Answerability: Early Philosophical Essays by M.M. Bakhtin* 257–325; yet another as an appendix to *Problems of Dostoevsky's Poetics* 283–302; and finally another (not yet in any official Bakhtin translation) in 'Rabelais and Gogol' 284–96.

9 By the term 'art de faire,' I am referring once again to Michel de Certeau's *L'Invention du quotidien* and, in particular, to his way of understanding culture in terms of how we humans have clever ways of 'doing' things to our environment in order to adapt it to our needs, both immediate and long-term. This we do by continually performing cultural utterance acts that incorporate that same environment into the very texture of our lives. When using the term 'imagic patterns,' on the other hand, I am thinking about the description of carnival, offered by Caryl Emerson, which implies that Rabelais's humour 'lay in a Renaissance worldview that could still grasp directly a spontaneous, contradictory carnal image as a unified whole, without logical or linear explanations' (*The First Hundred Years of Mikhail Bakhtin* 97). My particular take on Bakhtin's 'thinking-in-images' (or *Bilddenken,* to use a Benjaminian term) is to lay less stress on the idea of the internal unity that these images can possess than on the internal temporality that they put into motion. To this extent I am trying to digest all the theoretical and practical consequences for reading what Mieke Bal suggests when she shows in her recent work that an image should be understood as figuration 'by projecting onto it an entirely literary poetics that is nonetheless articulated according to principles derived from fundamental characteristics of painting' (16).

10 The importance, for an adequate understanding of Bakhtin's cultural thinking, of not separating semantics from 'somatics,' or 'sema' from 'soma,' is emphasized in Renate Lachmann, *Memory and Literature: Intertextuality in Russian Modernism,* 150–7. Lachmann develops her argument not only with reference to Bakhtin's work on the carnival but also – and this is a most useful aspect of the argument – in relation to the underutilized notion of 'body-sign' that was first introduced by Bakhtin/Medvedev in *The Formal Method in Literary Scholarship,* 12. What is at stake here is the temptation to consider

human meaning-making practices independently of the corporeal site from which they are enacted, that is their bodily 'eventness.' In an entirely different framework, Mary Russo also insists on the necessity of 'treating signifying systems and "events" together' (*The Female Grotesque* 60).

11 On this point, see my 'A Broken Thinker.' In this article I try to show that it is pointless to attempt to demonstrate, on the basis of Bakhtin's earliest fragmentary texts, where he thought he was going to go in all his future thinking. This problematic stance has to do with Bakhtin's fascination with the relationship between parts and wholes, something that is very evident in his early article 'Contemporary Vitalism,' an article to which we shall be referring several times here. To a large extent, observations on the fragmentary nature of Søren Kierkegaard's philosophy are appropriate for characterizing Bakhtin's propensity for fragmentary thinking: 'The whole stands in pieces, but these pieces do not even add up to a whole work; they are incidents of reading, each of which is, as an incident, unruly and unauthorized' (Peter Fenves 211).

12 The famous text in which Jakobson develops his conception of the poetic function of language is found in his 'Linguistics and Poetics.'

13 Bakhtin's 1920s fascination with biology is closely connected with his intensive study of the French philosopher Henri Bergson. A remarkable Bakhtinian text that Bakhtinians rarely discuss, except of course to dispute whether or not it was 'really' written by Bakhtin (see Katerina Clark and Michael Holquist, *Mikhail Bakhtin* 146; and Gary Saul Morson and Caryl Emerson, *Mikhail Bakhtin: Creation of a Prosaics* 115), is the article on 'Contemporary Vitalism' that was originally published under the name of I. Kanaev. Bakhtin includes Bergson among the six 'most published representatives of vitalism in Western Europe' ('Contemporary Vitalism' 81). The reason for stressing here Bergson's often invisible influence concerns the need for establishing a plausible link between, on the one hand, bodily processes that unfold in time and space in the physical world and, on the other, bodily processes that occur in humanized time and humanized space, and in particular memory processes.

14 The chronotope essay was assembled by Bakhtin's editors, and it is far from constituting a unified 'whole.' It is also not 'complete.' Let us not forget that it does not include all the remarks and notes Bakhtin had either jotted down, or had at times carefully written out, about the notion of the chronotope. One notable omission from the 'chronotope essay' would be all the work Bakhtin did on Goethe's ability to see time in space. Bakhtin wrote a large study of Goethe but the sole complete manuscript of that study was destroyed during the Second World War. Most of what survives of that study

was published after Bakhtin's death. The relevant pages on 'Time and Space in Goethe's Work' can be found in his 'The *Bildungsroman* and Its Significance in the History of Realism.'

15 'It is obviously impossible to suggest any neutral methodology. It is impossible to say: search both for causal determinants and systematicity, both physical-chemical, and vital; whatever you find will be fine; that is the same thing as saying: look for nothing' ('Contemporary Vitalism' 78).

16 See Robin Le Poidevin and Murray Macbeath, eds., *The Philosophy of Time* 16.

17 See Karlheinz Stierle, 'Die Widerkehr des Endes. Zur Anthropologie der Anschauungsformen.' The logic that Stierle uncovers is essentially the same one that Mihailovic reads into Bakhtin's notion of the act: 'Bakhtin's understanding of *postupok* is twofold, denoting behavior in general, while connoting conduct, which is the movement or direction of a particular actor that is implicit in the locution "postupat" *kuda* (to proceed *where)*' (Mihailovic 54).

18 Bakhtin's way of assuming the consequences of what he does when he mixes endings and beginnings contrasts starkly with philosophers of the analytic tradition for whom such a confusion creates the 'danger of entering a morass of non-sense.' See on this point W.H. Newton-Smith, 'The Beginning of Time' 169. This *assuming* is characteristic of an imagic pattern in his thinking whereby, as André Belleau has written, 'opposites are maintained and placed side by side without being undone' (145). This logic of *both x and not-x* can be observed in many places in Bakhtin's writing, one significant moment being in 'Contemporary Vitalism' (82–3) where Bakhtin discusses the independent-interdependent regeneration of spliced hydras that both grow together and maintain their separate biological 'identities' at the same time. Such a logic underwrites his notions of 'outsidedness' and how he conceives a chronotope such as the road, a time-space where various forms of heterogeneity find a time and place to meet, but not to blend. On this last point see Paulo Venturelli, 'Deus e o diablo no corpo dos meninos' 315.

19 Bakhtin-inspired semiotics would claim that, whatever the final answer is to the question of whether or not we are able to *process* in our minds more than one piece of information at a time, we are indeed able, because of the polyphonic and hybrid make-up of cultural languages, to *say* more than one thing at a time. The cultural spaces we live in are always, for Bakhtin, much more than the physical space that they occupy just as language is always much more than the phonological sound units and the dictionary meanings that constitute it. Indeed, it has often been noted that space, too, has this inherent characteristic of preventing more than one object or person from occupying it at one and the same time (for some philosophers of time this prevention is precisely the role of time in the physical world). In this context,

the Bakhtinian chronotope can be seen as a tool to overcome this restrictive conception of space. That such limitations ought to be overcome is aptly demonstrated by Gail Weiss, who shows that more than one human body can indeed occupy a single space at one and the same time, and this she does while discussing the difficulties that traditional philosophies of the body have in conceptualizing pregnancy. See Gail Weiss, *Body Images: Embodiment as Intercorporeality* 54.

20 The most sustained linguistic discussion of indirect speech occurring in Bakhtin's autograph work is found in *Problems of Dostoevsky's Poetics* 189–203. The important discussion in Voloshinov's/Bakhtin's sociological understanding of indirect discourse is found in *Marxism and the Philosophy of Language* 115–59.

21 Working from a Bakhtinian perspective, Marilia Amorim believes that the possibility of quotation is specific to humanity. See her *Dialogisme et altérité dans les sciences humaines* 75–6.

22 One of the most convincing points of convergence can be found in what can be called 'languages of excess,' something that not only characterizes Bakhtin's later reflections on the carnival in *Rabelais and His World* but also some of his earliest work, when he stresses, for example, the idea of an 'excess of seeing' ('Author and Hero in Aesthetic Activity' 22–3 and passim). For Bakhtin, excess is whatever is inherently able to move beyond borders and reach into realms other than those that have been strictly assigned by fixed social codes. These languages of excess come into play when Elizabeth Grosz and Elspeth Probyn acknowledge 'the disquieting effect of sexuality as it spills the boundaries of its proper containment, the unease of bodies breaking and flowing over their limits.' ('Introduction,' *Sexy Bodies* xi). In much women's writing of the contemporary period this 'spilling over of boundaries' has been seen as an essential poetic feature (see for example Lucie Joubert, 'Les gâcheuses de *party* ou les femmes et le carnival'). Such overflowing creates feelings of unease in the face of Berlin Walls that seem to be falling down everywhere. These feelings are no doubt related to the fact that Western knowledges are generally unable to conceptualize 'their own materiality and the conditions of their (material) production' (Grosz, *Space, Time, and Perversion* 26).

A second important point of convergence can be seen in both thinkers' conception of the body as inherently incomplete. Bakhtin stresses this idea in his carnival studies when he points to the orifices of the body which open it up to the outside world: 'All these convexities and orifices have a common characteristic; it is within them that the confines between bodies and between the body and the world are overcome: there is an interchange and an interorientation' (*Rabelais* 317). Grosz too is interested in cracks and openings, but for different reasons from those of Bakhtin. She is mostly interested in seeing how the 'incomplete' nature of the body's materiality constantly draws the human actors of society to draw on the body's inexhaustible, and hence unpredictable, capacity to generate meanings. 'The body is, so to speak, organically, biologically, *incomplete*; it is indeterminate, amorphous, a series of uncoordinated potentialities that require social triggering, ordering, and long-term *administration*' (*Space, Time, and Perversion* 104). When combined with Bakhtin's stress on how the body constantly seeks to move outside of itself, Grosz's discussion, here following Irigaray, of the importance of contiguous relations in female-to-female sexual love-making that are 'always surface effects, between one thing and another – between a hand and a breast, a tongue and a cunt, a mouth and food, a nose and a rose' (182) takes on interesting dimensions. One of these dimensions is that, for the philosophy of time, incompleteness and the fragmentary nature of time are themselves signs of a continuous becoming (Turetzky 113). I stress here the importance of both incompleteness and openings because I think these two notions are conceptually related to the Bakhtinian notion of 'loophole' to which I shall soon be turning. As we shall see, these openings are vitally productive in yet another fundamental way, that of being able to produce meta-knowledge.

23 The famous sentence from Saint Augustine's *City of God* (7.17) – *hominis est enim haec opinari, Dei scire* ('It is for man to think these things, for God to know them') – neatly encapsulates this postulate. For our purposes here, the Augustinian opposition between, on the one hand, the inevitable fragmentary ways in which we are compelled to function semiotically as human beings caught in our bodily world of mere seeing and, on the other, the wholeness of divine vision is provocatively hinted at by Anselm Haverkamp in 'Auswendigkeit: Das Gedächtnis der Rhetorik,' and especially in 'Lichtbild – Das Bildgedächtnis der Photographie: Roland Barthes und Augustinus.' To play with Haverkamp's use of light metaphors and imagery, we could say that, for Saint Augustine, we humans are forever trapped in 'glimpses' or 'flashes' but we will unfortunately never have the overall 'moving picture' that will always and forever escape us.

24 This semi-automatic memory which stores virtually anything and everything is accompanied by a second type of memory that has an inventive side to it.

25 For example, see Hans Michael Baumgartner, *Kontinuität und Geschichte*, 12.

26 See Michel Foucault, *Madness and Civilization: A History of Insanity in the Age of Reason*. For Mary Russo it is important to study those cultural instances which 'refuse to keep every body in its place' (16).

27 As François Chirpaz has written: 'when borne by flesh, meaning is never completely sure of being able to appear in the way it wanted' (97).

28 'A loophole is the retention for oneself of the possibility for altering the ultimate, final meaning of one's own words. If a word retains such a loophole this must inevitably be reflected in its structure. This potential other meaning, that is, the loophole left open, accompanies the word like a shadow. Judged by its meaning alone, the word with a loophole should be an ultimate word and does present itself as such, but in fact it is only the penultimate word and places after itself only a conditional, not a final, period' (Bakhtin, *Problems* 233). Bakhtin first mentions this notion of the loophole in his 'Author and Hero in Aesthetic Activity.' Here Bakhtin writes: 'I always have an outlet along the line of my experience of myself in the act [indecipherable] of the world – I always have a loophole' (40).

29 The productive environment that is created when languages are confused with metalanguages, something that often occurs in images, and particularly in body-images, is analysed with clarity by Eduardo Peñuela Cañizal, 'O corpo e os veús da metalinguagem.'

30 For an explanation of what philosophers mean by a 'causal theory of time,' see Bas C. van Fraasen, *An Introduction to the Philosophy of Time and Space*, 170–98.

31 Bakhtin discusses the notion of *historical inversion* in 'Forms of Time and of the Chronotope' 147.

32 An egregious example of this belief can be seen in the opening page of Josette Rey-Debove's monumental study of metalanguages, where the author states quite clearly that 'only verbal language is able to describe non-verbal semiotic systems' and only language 'finds itself in the position of speaking about itself' (1; my translation).

WORKS CITED

Amorim, Marilia. *Dialogisme et altérité dans les sciences humaines.* Paris: L'Harmattan, 1996.

Bakhtin, Mikhail. *Art and Answerability: Early Philosophical Essays by M.M. Bakhtin.* Trans. Vadim Liapunov and Kenneth Brostrom. Austin: U of Texas P, 1990.

– 'Author and Hero in Aesthetic Activity.' *Art and Answerability: Early Philosophical Essays by M.M. Bakhtin.* Trans. Vadim Liapunov and Kenneth Brostrom. Austin: U of Texas P, 1990.

– 'The *Bildungsroman* and Its Significance in the History of Realism.' *Speech Genres and Other Late Essays.* Trans. Vern W. McGee. Austin: U of Texas P, 1986. 25–54.

- 'Contemporary Vitalism.' *The Crisis in Modernism: Bergson and the Vitalist Controversy.* Trans. Charles Byrd. Ed. Frederick Burwick and Paul Douglass. Cambridge: Cambridge UP, 1992. 76–97.
- *The Dialogic Imagination.* Trans. Caryl Emerson and Michael Holquist. Austin: U of Texas P, 1981.
- 'Forms of Time and of the Chronotope in the Novel.' *The Dialogic Imagination.* Trans. Caryl Emerson and Michael Holquist. Austin: U of Texas P, 1981. 84–258.
- 'From Notes Made in 1970–71.' *Speech Genres and Other Late Essays.* Trans. Vern W. McGee. Austin: U of Texas P, 1986.
- *Problems of Dostoevsky's Poetics.* Trans. Caryl Emerson. Minneapolis: U of Minnesota P, 1984.
- *Rabelais and His World.* Trans. Hélène Iswolsky. Cambridge: MIT P, 1968.
- 'Rabelais and Gogol.' *Semiotics and Structuralism.* Ed. Henryk Baran. White Plains, NY: International Arts and Science P, 1976. 284–96.
- *Voprosi literaturi i estetiki.* Moscow: Khudozhestvennaya Literatura, 1975.
Bakhtin, Mikhail, and Viktor Duvakin. *Besedy V.D. Duvakina s M.M. Bakhtinym.* Moscow: Progess, 1996.
- *M.M. Bakhtin in Dialogue with V.D. Duvakin.* Trans. Brian Poole. Austin: U of Texas P, forthcoming.
Bakhtin, Mikhail, and P.N. Medvedev. *The Formal Method in Literary Scholarship.* Trans. Albert J. Wehrle. Cambridge: Harvard UP, 1985.
Bakhtin, Mikhail, and V.N. Voloshinov. *Marxism and the Philosophy of Language.* Trans. Ladislav Matejka and I.R. Titunik. Cambridge: Harvard UP, 1986.
Bal, Mieke. *The Mottled Screen: Reading Proust Visually.* Trans. Anna-Louise Milne. Stanford: Stanford UP, 1997.
Barthes, Roland. 'Aimer Schumann.' *L'Obvie et l'obtus.* Paris: Seuil, 1982.
Baudelaire, Charles. 'Edgar Poe, sa vie et ses œuvres.' *Oeuvres complètes.* Ed. Claude Pichois. Vol. 2. Paris: Gallimard, 1975. 249–88.
Baumgartner, Hans Michael. *Kontinuität und Geschichte.* Frankfurt am Main: Suhrkamp, 1997.
Belleau, André. *Notre Rabelais.* Montreal: Boréal, 1990.
Benjamin, Walter. *Gesammelte Schriften.* Vol. 5.1. Frankfurt am Main: Suhrkamp, 1982.
Bergson, Henri. *Matière et mémoire.* Paris: Presses Universitaires de France, 1939.
Buck-Morss, Susan. *The Dialectics of Seeing.* Cambridge: MIT P, 1991.
Cañizal, Eduardo Peñuela. 'O corpo e os veús da metalinguagem.' Ed. Ignacio Assis Silva. *Corpo e sentido: A escuta do sensível.* São Paulo: Editora da UNESP, 1996. 211–27.
Chafe, Wallace. *Discourse, Consciousness, and Time.* Chicago: U of Chicago P, 1994.
Chesneaux, Jean. *Habiter le temps.* Paris: Bayard Éditions, 1996.

Chirpaz, François. *Le Corps.* Paris: Klincksieck, 1996.

Clark, Katerina, and Michael Holquist. *Mikhail Bakhtin.* Cambridge: Harvard UP, 1984.

de Certeau, Michel. *L'Invention du quotidien.* Paris: Gallimard, 1990.

Deleuze, Gilles. *L'Image-Temps.* Paris: Minuit, 1985.

Deleuze, Gilles, and Félix Guattari. *What Is Philosophy?* Trans. Hugh Tomlinson and Graham Burchell. New York: Columbia UP, 1994.

Emerson, Caryl. *The First Hundred Years of Mikhail Bakhtin.* Princeton: Princeton UP, 1997.

Fenn, Richard. *The End of Time.* Cleveland: Pilgrim P, 1997.

Fenves, Peter. *'Chatter': Language and History in Kierkegaard.* Standford: Standford UP, 1993.

Foucault, Michel. *Madness and Civilization: A History of Insanity in the Age of Reason.* Trans. Richard Howard. London: Tavistock, 1965.

Gatens, Moira. *Imaginary Bodies.* New York: Routledge, 1996.

Grosz, Elizabeth. *Space, Time, and Perversion.* New York: Routledge, 1995.

– *Volatile Bodies: Toward a Corporeal Feminism.* Bloomington: Indiana UP, 1994.

Grosz, Elizabeth, and Elspeth Probyn, eds. *Sexy Bodies: The Strange Carnalities of Feminism.* New York: Routledge, 1995.

Haverkamp, Anselm. 'Auswendigkeit: Das Gedächtnis der Rhetorik.' *Gedächtnis-kunst: Raum – Bild – Schrift.* Ed. Anselm Haverkamp and Renate Lachmann. Frankfurt am Main: Suhrkamp, 1991. 37–46

– 'Lichtbild – Das Bildgedächtnis der Photographie: Roland Barthes und Augustinus.' *Memoria.* Ed. Anselm Haverkamp and Renate Lachmann. Munich: Wilhelm Fink, Hermeneutik und Poetik 15, 1993. 47–66.

Jakobson, Roman. 'Linguistics and Poetics.' *Style in Language.* Ed. Thomas E. Sebeok. Cambridge: MIT P, 1968. 350–77.

Joubert, Lucie. 'Les gâcheuses de *party* ou les femmes et le carnival.' *Les Littéra-tures d'expression française d'Amérique du Nord et le carnavalesque.* Ed. Denis Bourque and Anne Brown. Moncton: Editions d'Acadie, 1998. 297–316.

Kemp, Wolfgang. *Die Räume der Maler: Zur Bilderzählung seit Giotto.* Munich: Verlag C.H. Beck, 1996.

Kinser, Samuel. *Rabelais's Carnival: Text, Context, Metatext.* Berkeley: U of California P, 1990.

Kivy, Peter. *Authenticities: Philosophical Reflections on Musical Performance.* Ithaca: Cornell UP, 1995.

Kögler, Hans Herbert. *The Power of Dialogue.* Trans. Paul Hendrickson. Cambridge: MIT P, 1996.

Lachmann, Renate. *Memory and Literature: Intertextuality in Russian Modernism.* Trans. Roy Sellars and Anthony Wall. Minneapolis: U of Minnesota P, 1997.

Ladin, Jay. 'Fleshing Out the Chronotope.' *Critical Essays on Mikhail Bakhtin.* Ed. Caryl Emerson. New York: G.H. Hall, 1999.

Le Poidevin, Robin, and Murray Macbeath, eds. *The Philosophy of Time.* Oxford: Oxford UP, 1993.

Mihailovic, Alexander. *Corporeal Words: Mikhail Bakhtin's Theology of Discourse.* Evanston: Northwestern UP, 1997.

Morson, Gary Saul, and Caryl Emerson. *Mikhail Bakhtin: Creation of a Prosaics.* Stanford: Stanford UP, 1990.

Newton-Smith, W. H. 'The Beginning of Time.' *The Philosophy of Time.* Ed. Robin Le Poidevin, and Murray Macbeath. Oxford: Oxford UP, 1993. 168–82.

Pavel, Thomas. *The Feud of Language: A History of Structuralist Thought.* Trans. Linda Jordan and Thomas Pavel. London: Basil Blackwell, 1989.

Readings, Bill. *The University in Ruins.* Cambridge: Harvard UP, 1996.

Rey-Debove, Josette. *Le Métalangage.* Paris: Dictionnaires Le Robert, 1978.

Roudaut, Jean. *Les Villes imaginaires dans la litterature française.* Paris: Hatier, 1990.

Russo, Mary. *The Female Grotesque.* New York: Routledge, 1995.

Stierle, Karlheinz. 'Die Widerkehr des Endes. Zur Anthropologie der An-schauungsformen,' *Das Ende: Figuren einer Denkform.* Ed. Karlheinz Stierle and Rainer Warning. Munich: Wilhelm Fink, Poetik und Hermeneutik 16, 1996. 578–99.

Susini-Anastopoulos, Françoise. *L'Écriture fragmentaire: définitions et enjeux.* Paris: Presses Universitaires de France, 1997.

Thierry, Yves. *Du corps parlant: le language chez Merleau-Ponty.* Bruxelles: Ousia, 1987.

Tréguier, Jean-Marie. *Le Corps selon la chair: phénoménologie et ontologie chez Merleau-Ponty.* Paris: Éditions Kimé, 1996.

Turetzky, Philip. *Time.* New York: Routledge, 1998.

van Fraasen, Bas C. *An Introduction to the Philosophy of Time and Space.* New York: Columbia UP, 1970.

Venturelli, Paulo. 'Deus e o diablo no corpo dos meninos.' *Diálogos com Bakhtin.* Ed. Carlos Alberto Franco, Cristovão Tezza, and Gilberto de Castro. Paraná: Editora da Universidade Federal do Paraná, 1996.

Wall, Anthony. 'A Broken Thinker.' *South Atlantic Quarterly* 97.3–4 (1998): 669–98.

Weigel, Sigrid. *Body- and Image-Space.* Trans. Georgina Paul, Rachel McNicholl, and Jeremy Gaines. New York: Routledge, 1996.

Weiss, Gail. *Body Images: Embodiment as Intercorporeality.* New York: Routledge, 1999.

The Body of History

MANI HAGHIGHI

The works of Michel Foucault are often read as histories of the body, and the controversies that surround his corpus often amount to a disagreement over the status of the body in these writings. Some critics, Charles Taylor among them, have charged that by presenting the body as thoroughly imbued by the discursive practices that are said to shape it, Foucault has left nothing for the forces of resistance to liberate ('Foucault on Freedom and Truth'). Others, notably Judith Butler, have argued that even though the body is supposed not to exist outside the terms of these discursive practices, Foucault's examples and tropes imply that the forces of discourse are necessarily external to the body itself ('Foucault and the Paradox of Bodily Inscriptions'). This, they argue, betrays Foucault's unacknowledged belief in the body as a 'passive' and even 'natural' substratum upon which history makes its marks.

Both Taylor and Butler claim to have discovered a 'paradox' in Foucault's work. For Taylor, the paradox takes several forms, all of which are reducible to one version or another of the 'relativist's conundrum,' the uninspired and inconsequent claim that all relativist postulates are self-undermining. Looking for the place of truth and freedom in Foucault's work, Taylor explains that

> the 'truth' manufactured by power also turns out to be its 'masks' or disguises and hence untruth. The idea of a manufactured or imposed 'truth' inescapably slips the word into inverted commas, and opens the space of a truth-outside-quotes, the kind of truth, for instance, which the sentences unmasking power manifest, or which the sentences expounding the general theory of regime-relativity themselves manifest (a paradox). (94)

Disregarding the problematic equation of disguise with untruth, Taylor argues that this paradox implies another, similar paradox. If truth is always manufactured by a system of power and if, therefore, no truth can ever be espoused against a system of power, the negation of an 'evil' power structure would amount not to the promotion of a 'good,' but rather to a lateral slippage into another evil power structure. Hence, the body can never be free, because it is thoroughly imbued with the historical discourses that determine the truths it can claim for itself. Taylor finds this 'rather paradoxical' because it seems to undermine the utility of Foucault's argument: 'what is the point of analyzing the "evils" of power,' asks Taylor, 'if such an analysis merely reproduces, and is in fact nothing but the effect of, a new series of power effects?' (69–70).

Judith Butler's exposition of Foucault's paradox resembles Taylor's argument viewed from the opposite angle. Taylor worries about Foucault's refusal to posit a free, utopian 'outside' towards which the forces of an enlightened resistance would carry the body. Butler, on the other hand, argues that Foucault's reliance on a model of genealogy as cultural 'inscription' unwittingly reintroduces such an outside into his work:

> Although Foucault appears to argue that the body does not exist outside the terms of its cultural inscription, it seems that the very mechanism of 'inscription' implies a power that is necessarily external to the body itself. The critical question that emerges from these considerations is whether the understanding of the process of cultural construction on the model of 'inscription' – a logocentric move if ever there was one – entails that the 'constructed' or 'inscribed' body have an ontological status apart from that inscription, precisely the claim that Foucault wants to refute. (603)

Butler sees the process of 'inscription' not as an expression, but rather an etching, a 'disfiguration and distortion of the body, where the body is figured as a ready surface or blank page available for inscription, awaiting the "imprint" of history itself' (603).

Butler and Taylor are therefore concerned about the same aspect of Foucault's discourse. Taylor deplores the absence of an outside, free of the oppressive inscriptions of power, wherein the body can be liberated at last. Butler, on the other hand, laments the presence of just such an outside, arguing that the very notion of 'inscription' implies an outside surface that exists prior to the inscribing mechanism and is distorted by it. Both critics point to a paradoxical dissonance between Foucault's implicit claims about what he is doing and the logical effects of what he actually does. For Taylor, a description of an evil should amount to the suggestion that overcoming that evil is good. But by describing power as omnipotent, Foucault resists this suggestion and thus traps himself in a paradox. For Butler, the omnipotence of power makes it impossible to think of a body in a free or natural state, untouched by the inscriptions of power. But the logic of inscription, again paradoxically, suggests the logical possibility of just such an untouched state.

Both these accounts point to an uneasy tension in Foucault's work between the body and the power that is said to construct it. In short, they describe a strictly dialectical encounter between the body and its history. What they fail to acknowledge is that, for Foucault, history is itself a body – in the most literal and concrete sense of the word. History is neither simply the story of the transformations endured by the body, nor is it, just as simply, the force that inscribes these transformations upon the body. History *is* a body, and its being a body must matter more than it has to Foucault's readers and critics.

The effort to ground this claim leads us to Foucault's famous early essay, 'Nietzsche, Genealogy, History,' and to the distinction made there between two kinds of history: 'traditional history,' which concerns itself with the Platonic modalities of reality, identity, and truth, set against what Nietzsche has called 'actual history,' or genealogy. However, as we shall see, the logical conclusions that follow from this distinction ultimately fail to give us a satisfying account of the sort of body the Body of History can be. To resolve this, we will turn to the works of Gilles Deleuze and Félix Guattari as a lens through which to reread Foucault's essay in more fruitful ways.

In 'Nietzsche, Genealogy, History,' Foucault argues that genealogy concerns itself with the body and with the masks that cover or shape it. Abandoning the transcendental position of traditional history, which seeks out truths by reducing the everyday to the epochal, genealogy clings to the body, expressing its microscopic becomings. It 'shortens its vision to those things nearest to it – the body, the nervous system, nutrition, digestion and energies' (89).

The modalities of traditional history call for a disembodied gaze which seeks an essential identity behind the random transformations of the body. This identity often takes the form of exaggerated masks: Roman prototypes for the French Revolution, for example, or the Knight's armour for Romanticism (Foucault, 'Nietzsche, Genealogy, History' 93). Genealogy, in contrast, seeks to 'unrealize' identity. Rather than tearing away these masks in an effort to discover a foundational truth behind them, it shamelessly intensifies the possibilities of the masks by basking in the fun of overdoing the masquerade. Genealogy thus replaces the Historian's quest for stable emblems of identity with an affirmation of the provisional and temporary status of the body.

But what is it about the body that gives genealogy its power to transform the traditional notion of history so radically? Foucault's bold answer is that history *is* already a body. 'History,' he writes, 'is the concrete body of a development, with its moments of intensity, its lapses, its extended periods of feverish agitation, its fainting spells' ('Nietzsche, Genealogy, History' 80).[1] His justification of this odd claim involves a slide from the general and overcodified uses of the concept of 'History' to a number of molecular concepts that, hovering on the margins of History, both define and transgress it. The most important of these microconcepts – appropriated by Foucault from Nietzsche's analysis of genealogy – are *Herkunft* (descent) and *Entstehung* (emergence).

Herkunft denotes a multiplicity of points of departure which converge to form what is then interpreted, falsely, as a singular historical bedrock. The myth of a historical *archē*, a single, solid ground of identity, is thus unravelled through an analysis of its unbound and aleatory beginnings. *Entstehung* effects a similar unravelling, this time of the myth of a historical *telos*, or a single point of arrival. Rather than a grand culmination of a teleological progression, the emergence of a historical concept is to be interpreted as a transient moment in a 'series of subjugations' ('Nietzsche, Genealogy, History' 83). There is no fate, this implies, no historical destiny; there is only the passing of time. And if this temporal flow is ever curdled into a definite shape, the task of the genealogist is to reveal and unravel the system of subjugation that is responsible for its emergence and, in doing so, deprive this shape of its claim to a single historical meaning.

Herkunft (descent) and *Entstehung* (emergence) are in fact refined and distilled versions of Nietzsche's more cumbersome concept of *Ursprung*, or Origin. But, as Foucault has shown, at a certain moment in the development of Nietzsche's thought *Herkunft* and *Entstehung* actually turn against their own conceptual origin, *Ursprung*, and define themselves in opposition to it. This differentiation occurs most explicitly in Nietzsche's preface to his *Genealogy of Morals*, where he is tracing the source of his preoccupations with genealogy to his reading of Paul Rée's book, *The Origin of Moral Sensations*. (*Der Ursprung der moralischen Empfindungen* was the German translation of the title.) Here, in reviewing the works he wrote in response to that book, Nietzsche speaks of his *Herkunfts-Hypothesen*, (his 'hypotheses of descent' or, in Kaufmann and Hollingdale's translation, his 'genealogical hypotheses' [*Genealogy* 18]), and as Foucault quite shrewdly points out,

> This use of the word *Herkunft* cannot be arbitrary, since it serves to designate a number of texts, beginning with *Human All Too Human*, which deal with the origin of morality, asceticism, justice and punishment. And yet the word used in all these works had been *Ursprung*. It would seem that at this point in the *Genealogy* Nietzsche wished to validate an opposition between *Herkunft* and *Ursprung* that did not exist ten years earlier. ('Nietzsche, Genealogy, History' 78)

The emergence of *Herkunft* as a new genealogical concept opposes the traditional modalities of history in a number of ways. Now, wherever the historical discourse of *Ursprung* looks for essences and identities, the genealogical discourse of *Herkunft*, in response, discovers disparity and disguise; wherever history attributes innocence and solemnity to a birth, genealogy unearths its lowly lineages and mocks them; wherever history invokes a unity, genealogy multiplies and proliferates it. The genealogical operations of *Herkunft*, says Foucault, replace reality with parody, identity with dissociation, and truth with sacrifice ('Nietzsche, Genealogy, History' 93).

How is it that this relentless attack on the metaphysical foundations of traditional history manages also to transform history into a 'concrete' body? The genealogical method establishes the body as an arbitrator, not only of hunger, excretion, and penetration, but also of truth and error, as well as good and evil. The body is a machine that transforms its biological drives into moral imperatives. The hunger of the slaves transforms into their virtue in the face of the well-fed master. And if the body is the place where the biological is metamorphosed into a system of values, then *Herkunft* is the historical *expression* of this metamorphosis.

The body thus becomes 'an inscribed surface of events' ('Nietzsche, Genealogy, History' 83) and *Herkunft*, becomes the articulation of this inscription. As we have seen, Foucault's employment of the language of 'inscription' raises the question of whether these events are external or posterior to the body upon which they are inscribed. However, to separate the forces that act upon the body from the body as such and, further, to separate the body from its expression as *Herkunft* would amount to the first of Nietzsche's Four Great Errors, the error of mistaking cause for consequence.[2] The body is nothing but a weave of the forces that are said to be 'inscribed' upon it and it has no choice but to express these forces.

Thus, the discursive forces of history are to be understood as inscribing themselves not upon a natural, pre-historical body, but rather upon *each other*. What is called the natural body is the synthesis, and not the substratum, of these mutual inscriptions. It is for this reason that *Herkunft*, in so far as it expresses the body, is nothing but the body.

The absence of a substratum behind the conflicts of the body implies that the *topos* of these conflicts is a 'non-place.' *Entstehung* is here accorded the function of a non-extensive *spatium* by Foucault: 'emergence [*Entstehung*] designates a place of confrontation, but not as a closed field offering a spectacle of a struggle among equals, [but rather as] a "non-place," a pure distance, which indicates that the adversaries do not belong to a common space' ('Nietzsche, Genealogy, History' 85). Here again, it would be a mistake to think of the place of *Entstehung* as a space *within* which the forces of inscription come face to face. The place of the encounter does not precede the encounter; rather, it is produced by the encounter. This means that *Entstehung* expresses a non-conjugated and non-subjective verbal notion: to confront. 'No one is responsible for an emergence, no one can glory in it, since it always occurs in the interstice' (85).

The most significant feature of *Entstehung* is the radical incongruity of the forces that shape it. Speaking of the perverted cartographies of Borges' fiction in the *Order of Things*, Foucault describes this incongruity as a

> disorder in which a large number of possible orders glitter separately, in the lawless and uncharted dimension of the *heteroclite*; and that word should be taken in its most literal etymological sense; in such a state, things are 'laid,' 'placed,' 'arranged' in sites so very different from one another that it is impossible to find a common place beneath them all. (xvii)

A similar account of this non-belonging appears in Foucault's monograph on Magritte, *This Is Not a Pipe*, where the encounter between the image of Magritte's pipe and the words that refuse to accept it as a pipe is described in terms of a disjunctive cohabitation:

> The slender, colorless, neutral strip, which in Magritte's drawing separates the text and the figure, must be seen as a crevasse – an uncertain, foggy

region. ... Still it is too much to claim that there is a blank or a lacuna: instead, it is an absence of space, an effacement of the 'common place' between the signs of writing and the lines of the image. ... No longer can anything pass between them save the decree of divorce. ... (28–9)

The bizarre incongruities of Borges' and Magritte's surrealism, however, transform into a generative battle once Nietzsche is introduced to the scene. Now the problem of the mutual exclusion of the forces from their respective fields is aggravated by their perpetual struggle to overcome one another ('Nietzsche, Genealogy, History' 85).

The Nietzschean combat among forces is generative in two senses. On one hand, it unspools various scenes of violence into life and designs rituals which regulate and augment these scenes: civil law, for instance, perpetually instigates new dominations; the function of its institutions is to stage rituals of violence in the name of justice. On the other hand, the perverted or stabilized *image* of this violent combat is equally capable of generating values and concepts: justice itself, for example, is simply a static misrepresentation of the law's inherent violence.[3] In short, 'all events in the organic world are a subduing, a *becoming master*, and all subduing and becoming master involves a fresh interpretation, and adaptation through which any previous "meaning" and "purpose" are necessarily obscured or even obliterated' (Nietzsche, *Genealogy* 77).

The most important generative function of *Entstehung* is the generation of the body itself: just as *Herkunft* is the body because it expresses the body, so *Entstehung* is the body because it is the weaving-together of the conflicts that articulate the body. It is in this sense that history, as a disjunctive synthesis of *Herkunft* and *Entstehung*, is literally a 'concrete body.'

To rearrange the formula in this way, so that, instead of speaking of the History of the Body, one has to speak of the Body of History, leads to a number of puzzles. If history is a body, it becomes important to know what we actually mean by the term 'body.' Given Foucault's references and images in 'Nietzsche, Genealogy, History,' it is not surprising that his readers have been all too willing to think of his concept of the body in anthropomorphic terms. But the image of the human body as an archetype for the Body of History seems ontologically inappropriate. *Herkunft* and *Entstehung*, as the elementary functions of genealogy, already efface the image of the human body. When a body takes a human form, to follow Nietzsche's postulates, it presents an image of a coagulated flow in equilibrium: a human body-image is a stratified surface with an internal compass.[4] But the body proper to the genealogical project resembles, to revive a Lacanian joke, not an *homme*, but an *hommelette*: a yolky fetal shape unburdened by the traumas of self-recognition.[5]

This particular body-image is the ignored and unspoken, yet soundly derived conclusion of Foucault's genealogical syllogism. The genealogist, rather than pouting about the inauthenticity of the traditional Historian's exaggerated masks, affirms and revels in them: he is preoccupied not so much with disguises *per se* as with the velocity with which they are replaced. What Foucault has called a 'mask' is therefore not so much a veil to hide behind as a limit to strive towards. Thus, a single or fixed mask, in Foucault's lexicon, is 'simply a disguise,' while the mask of an 'excessive persona' that unhinges the meagre trials of historical identification, or a mask whose sole function is to be whisked off a face in order to be replaced with a new one, is perverted and good:

> The new historian, the genealogist, will know what to make of this masquerade. He will not be too serious to enjoy it; on the contrary, he will push the masquerade to its limit and prepare the great carnival of time where masks are constantly reappearing. No longer the identification of our faint individuality with the solid identities of the past, but our unrealization through the excessive choice of identities – Frederick of Hohenstaufen, Caesar, Jesus, Dionysus, and possibly Zarathustra. Taking up these masks, revitalizing the buffoonery of history, we adopt an identity whose unreality surpasses that of God, who started the charade. ('Nietzsche, Genealogy, History' 93–4)

What Foucault pays less attention to, however, is that a *real* push to the limits of the carnival, where underneath each torn mask one is to find another disguise, cannot simply culminate yet again in the emergence of an organized human figure, with a face and a proper name, no matter how 'excessive' this figure is. The only *Entstehung* that this carnival can tolerate is the emergence of difference itself, and the only body that can emerge out of the pure difference that imbues this non-place is a destratified or 'chaotic' body made up of what Foucault has called 'subindividual marks.'[6] In order to understand what these 'subindividual marks' may be, and to grasp their relation to the 'historical sense' that is the hallmark of genealogy, we must briefly turn to Nietzsche's writings on race.

The 'historical sense' that distinguishes the genealogist from the traditional historian is the outcome, writes Nietzsche, of 'the mad and fascinating *semi-barbarism* into which Europe has been plunged through the democratic mingling of classes and races' (*Beyond* 152). This mingling has turned the nineteenth-century European into 'a kind of chaos':

> Through our semi-barbarism in body and desires we have secret access everywhere such as a noble age never had, above all the access to the labyrinth of unfinished cultures and to every semi-barbarism which has ever existed on earth; and, in so far as the most considerable part of human culture hitherto has been semi-barbarism, 'historical sense' means virtually the sense and instinct for everything, the taste and tongue for everything. ... (*Beyond* 153)

Genealogy, which Nietzsche equates with this 'historical sense,' thus implies a free drifting across all cultures and epochs, an unreflexive ability to slide back and forth into and out of the distant past and faraway places at infinite speed. Quite appropriately, the most significant attribute of this sense is its velocity: Nietzsche describes it as a quick, almost instinctual capacity to 'divine' the hierarchy of values according to which a people, a society, or a person has lived.

Germans, it turns out, are particularly good at this, because they are, in the proper sense of the term, 'monstrous': their soul is 'above all manifold [*vielfach*], of diverse origins, put together and superimposed rather than actually constructed' (Nietzsche, *Beyond* 174). Nietzsche's writing presents the German soul as if it were one of Kafka's serpentine buildings: '[It] has corridors and interconnecting corridors in it, there are caves, hiding places, dungeons in it; its disorder possesses much of the fascination of the mysterious; the German is acquainted with the hidden paths to chaos' (*Beyond* 175).[7] But what does Nietzsche mean, when he speaks of 'Germans'? He is not simply speaking about a people or a race, but rather about an interraciality, a proto-race that is 'in-between.' For him, the apparent incomprehensibility or enigma of Germans has to do with the fact that they are, in his words, 'the people of the middle' (*Volk der Mitte*) (*Beyond* 174). This condition of middleness, moreover, is not limited to Germans – they simply exemplify it; in itself, it is the cultural condition of late nineteenth-century Europe as a whole.

For Nietzsche, 'Germany' is the non-place of *Entstehung*, it is a network of confrontations among European races; or, more precisely, it is a diagram that unfolds between racial strata: the racial forces that are in relation across this diagram are inseparable from the variations in their relations – variations that are expressed by the diagram.[8] In light of Nietzsche's genealogical postulates, therefore, it would be a mistake to reduce 'Germany' to the status of a 'nation' or a 'race' in equilibrium; rather, it is to be understood as a field of differential relations, which is not to say that it designates a mere multiculturalism, if by that we mean the lugubrious cohabitation of various self-same cultural entities in the name of tolerance. It denotes the intermingling and confrontation of heterogeneous and non-subjective singularities or particles, 'sub-individual marks,' that are defined according to their differences with each other: it is a place of mutation, or a matrix of transformation.[9]

Now the question arises: doesn't this apparent move away from the 'concrete' forms and functions of the body towards a diagrammatic theory of 'sub-individual' particles or marks imply a homogenization of the body? In this account, isn't there only a single difference, a 'pure' difference or a difference 'in itself,' compared to the rich multiplicity of several bodies? In critiquing the substantialist or essentialist understanding of the body, in other words, are we not offering instead a bland univocal abstraction of the social field in which a contingent convergence of individuals or races is no longer possible? The reason why these worries are misplaced is that Nietzsche's attractive Spinozism, as extracted from his works by Foucault as well as by Gilles Deleuze and Félix Guattari, demonstrates that these 'sub-individual marks' which, in themselves, are incorporeal and infinitive, nevertheless *belong* to an individual. In Deleuze's account, these abstract marks, which have neither form nor function, are perfectly real in spite of their abstraction:

They are distinguished solely by movement and rest, slowness and speed. They are not atoms, in other words, finite elements still endowed with form. Nor are they indefinitely divisible. They are infinitely small, ultimate parts of an actual infinity, laid out on the same plane of consistency or composition. They are not defined by their number since they always come in infinities. However, depending on their degree of speed, or the relation of movement and rest into which they enter, they belong to a given Individual, which may itself be part of another Individual governed by another, more complex, relation, and so on to infinity. There are thus smaller and larger infinities, not by virtue of their number, but by virtue of the composition of the relation into which their parts enter. (*A Thousand Plateaus* 254)

The semi-barbaric and sub-individual co-mingling of different particles over the body of 'Germany' does not reduce these particles to a
homogeneity of pure difference. These particles are crucially sub-
individual, but they belong to individuals. Individuality and agency thus
retain certain strands of their autonomy in the face of difference. What
they happily discard, instead, is their claim to originality and founda-
tionality: the organic or stratified body (or body-politic) and the agency
that animates it are simply the effects of the speeding infinitesimal particles that traverse them. The trajectories of these particles' speeds and
rests, in effect, add up to another body that is coextensive with the
organic or 'lived' body of the individual. From the weaving-together and
expression of these singular particles arises the body of 'Germany,' an
unconjugated or 'virtual' body without a name and without a race – a
Body, in other words, without Organs.

Studying the similarities between Foucault's accounts of the body in
'Nietzsche, Genealogy, History' and Deleuze and Guattari's descriptions
of the Body without Organs is as useful as it is perilous. Interpreting
Foucault's historical corporeality in terms of the Body without Organs
could lead to a vast number of misunderstandings unless four important
points are made clear.

Above all, the Body without Organs is not a body that has no organs;
rather, it is a body that has resisted or escaped the stratification and
organization of its organs. 'The Body without Organs is not defined by
the absence of organs, nor is it defined solely by the existence of an
indeterminate organ, it is finally defined by the temporary and provisional presence of determinate organs' (Deleuze, *Francis Bacon*).[10] This
temporary presence structures temporality and history in terms of the
rhythms of the Body without Organs. The 'time' of the Body without
Organs is determined neither by the calculations of a conventionally
standardized time (the vibrations of electrically charged quartz), nor by
the operations of a phenomenological *Stimmung* (bored time, excited
time), but rather by what we can call a '*Gestalt* rhythm.' The anthropologist José Gil has invoked the example of a *Gestalt* 'in which the gaze cannot hold steady either on the figure or the background.' What is the
form of this particular figure/background assemblage?

We are no longer in the presence of figures, but a kind of scansion between
two forms that have the tendency to appear and disappear. Considered
globally, these forms make up a whole, they therefore have a form, that is

no longer a representation, but is something we could tentatively call a 'rhythm,' the rhythm of the appearance and disappearance of each of the figures. We now have time in addition to space. (Gil 132–3)

The appearance of determinate organs against the background of the Body without Organs and their spontaneous dissolution into this background is the 'rhythm' that introduces time into the emerging *spatium* of the body. It is precisely the peculiar *Gestalt* quality of this new time, its chaotic indeterminacy, that guarantees the elliptical and discontinuous quality of Nietzschean history.

Secondly, the emancipation of the Body without Organs from the stratifications of the organized body does not reduce it to the status of a natural body. In fact, the Body without Organs vigorously rejects the distinction between nature and artifice, since it defines itself not according to functions or essences, but only in terms of affects. The Body without Organs is defined in two simultaneous ways. Kinetically, it is defined in terms of the relations of speed and slowness among the particles that compose it:

> Global form, specific form, and organic functions depend on relations of speed and slowness. Even the development of a form, the course of development of a form, depends on these relations, and not the reverse. The important thing is to understand life, each living individuality, not as a form, or a development of form, but as a complex relation between differential velocities, between deceleration and acceleration of particles. (Deleuze, *Spinoza* 123)

Dynamically, the Body without Organs is defined according to its capacity to affect and be affected by other bodies. Each body is defined according to its optimal and pessimal thresholds for being affected. By defining the body in terms of speeds and affects, Deleuze and Guattari multiply the possibilities of its becomings: you cannot know what a body is capable of doing, nor will you discover the lineages from which it has issued, unless you open it up to the potentials offered by all kinds of new affects. The implications of this methodology for the study of history are vast: genealogy and historiography can no longer limit themselves to the investigation of chronologies, resemblances, and deviations among historical entities, since the very taxonomy of these entities is now fundamentally rearranged. Deleuze's example is quite revealing in its simplicity: 'There are greater differences between a plow horse or draft horse and a racehorse than between an ox and a plow horse. This is because the racehorse and the plow horse do not have the same affects nor the same capacity for being affected; the plow horse has affects in common rather with the ox' (*Spinoza* 124).[11] The same principle informs Deleuze's own peculiar approach to the writing of intellectual history: Lucretius the atomist, Hume the empiricist, Spinoza and Leibniz the rationalists, Nietzsche the genealogist, Bergson the vitalist, Foucault the archivist, Proust and Kafka the novelists, Artaud and Beckett the playwrights, Bacon the painter, Boulez and Messiaen the musicians – all of them are great philosophers and all of them belong to the same lineage or stock, according to Deleuze. What list could have seemed more eclectic and haphazard? And yet there is a secret link, an affective genealogy, that weaves these figures together: 'their critique of negativity, their cultivation of joy, the hatred for interiority, the externality of forces and relations, the denunciation of power' (*Negotiations* 6).

The definition of time in terms of a '*Gestalt* rhythm' conjoined with the kinetic and dynamic postulates of Deleuze's affective philosophy implies, thirdly, that the Body without Organs is not a romantic or pre-discursive *chora*, nor does it invoke the maternal and pre-Oedipal body of psychoanalysis. It is, rather, a zone of contemporaneity:

> The BwO is a childhood block, a becoming, the opposite of a childhood memory. It is not the child 'before' the adult, or the mother 'before' the child: it is the strict contemporaneousness of the adult, of the adult and the child, their map of comparative densities and intensities, and all the variations on that map. The BwO is precisely this intense germen where there are not and cannot be either parents or children. (*A Thousand Plateaus* 164)

The fact that the Body without Organs is a zone of contemporaneity already precludes the language of regression and projection. This contemporaneous quality beckons us to construct and reconstruct the Body without Organs, even though it is always already there, beside us:

> there is a very special relation of synthesis and analysis between a given type of BwO and what happens on it: an *a priori* synthesis by which something will necessarily be produced in a given mode (but what it will be is not known) and an infinite analysis by which what is produced on the BwO is

already part of that Body's production, is already included in the body, is already on it (but at the price of an infinity of passages, divisions, and secondary productions). (*A Thousand Plateaus* 152)

History, therefore, is at once synthetic and analytic: it generates new events, but this generation is already a repetition. This is the reason why both Foucault and Deleuze have described the emergence of newness in time in terms of a theatrical event: 'historical actors or agents can create only on condition that they identify themselves with figures from the past' (Deleuze, *Difference* 91).[12] This identification, however, is neither 'intracyclic' (in which one historical age regenerates a former age analogically) nor 'cyclic' (where the 'intracyclic' analogy is itself repeated). The constructivism of history, its introduction of newness into time, is, in fact, an eternal return: a return in which differences are the only repeated elements.[13] Deleuze's famous description of his own histories of philosophy illustrates this insight beautifully:

The history of philosophy plays a patently repressive role on philosophy, it's philosophy's own version of the Oedipus complex: 'You can't seriously consider saying what you yourself think until you've read this and that, and that on this and this on that.' ... I suppose the main way I coped with it at the time was to see the history of philosophy as a sort of buggery or (it comes to the same thing) immaculate conception. I saw myself as taking an author from behind and giving him a child that would be his own offspring, yet monstrous. It was really important for it to be his own child, because the author had to actually say all I had him saying. But the child was bound to be monstrous too, because it resulted from all sorts of shifting, slipping, dislocations and hidden emissions that I really enjoyed. (*Negotiations* 5–6)

Deleuze's histories of philosophy (not to mention his books on cinema) are, in this sense, monstrous masquerades or (it comes to the same thing) original repetitions.

Finally, Deleuze and Guattari insist that the capture of the Body without Organs by an organism will always remain necessarily incomplete. Something always escapes. This possibility of escape is what opens up a space for a discussion not only of resistance but also, and more importantly, of creation in the political sphere.[14] Liberation, for Deleuze and Guattari, is always a liberation from the organized body and its identity: it is not, contra Taylor, an evolution towards a utopian structure beyond the contemporary limits of the social, nor is it, contra Butler, a parodic or ironic repetition of those very limits. Rather, it is an involution towards the immanent Body without Organs that is always coextensive with the body of the social:

> The final word on power is that *resistance comes first*, to the extent that power relations operate completely within the diagram, while resistances necessarily operate in a direct relation with the outside from which the diagrams emerge. This means that a social field offers more resistance than strategies, and that the thought of the outside is a thought of resistance. (Deleuze, *Foucault* 89–90)

The 'outside' reappears: Taylor had bemoaned its conspicuous absence; Butler had derided its insidious presence. It is neither utopian or futuristic, nor natural or pre-discursive. It is, above all, creative.

In conclusion, we can draw six axioms from our Deleuzian reading of Foucault's essay:

(1) As a disjunctive synthesis of descent (which expresses the body), and emergence (which weaves the body together), history is already a body.

(2) The Body of History is a Body without Organs and is, therefore, primarily inhuman. The human form is not the only form in which it can actualize itself.

(3) The Body of History must never be distinguished from the process of construction it undergoes. It is nothing but a weaving of forces converging over a 'non-place.'

(4) The Body of History, as a Body without Organs, is defined by the contemporaneous presence of all of its organs. The time of the Body of History, therefore, is not the successive time of causality, habit, or memory, but rather the simultaneous time of intensity, affectivity, and repetition.

(5) The fact that the Body of History is only a weave of its expressions, together with the fact that it is also a zone of contemporaneity, means that the emergence of an event upon the Body of History always takes the form of an inscription upon an inscription, or more accurately, the expression of an expression.

(6) The series of subjugations that stratify and organize the Body of History on the social field are defined by what escapes them. This means that escape and liberation are the primary and necessary condition for the genesis of the social field.

NOTES

1 The English translation seems quite free here. The French original reads: 'L'histoire, avec ses intensités, ses défaillances, ses fureurs secrètes, ses grandes agitations fiévreuses comme ses syncopes, c'est le corps même du devenir' (150–1).
2 Compare Friedrich Nietzsche, *Twilight of the Idols* 47.
3 Compare *On the Genealogy of Morals* 77; and Friedrich Nietzsche, *Gay Science* 172–3.
4 Nietzsche goes as far as to describe the belief in the existence of the body as 'an erroneous article of faith.' See *The Gay Science* 169.
5 Compare Jacques Lacan, *The Four Fundamental Concepts of Psycho-Analysis* 197.
6 'The analysis of *Herkunft* often involves a consideration of race or social type. But the traits it attempts to identify are not the exclusive generic characteristics of an individual, a sentiment, or an idea, which permits us to qualify them as "Greek" or "English"; rather it seeks the subtle, singular and subindividual marks that might possibly intersect in them to form a network that is difficult to unravel' ('Nietzsche, Genealogy, History' 81).
7 Compare Nietzsche's remarks with Deleuze and Guattari's meditations on Kafka's corridors in *Kafka: Toward a Minor Literature* 72–80.
8 On the concept of the diagram, see Gilles Deleuze, *Foucault* 85.
9 Compare Michel Foucault, *The History of Sexuality: An Introduction* 99.
10 From 'Chapter Seven: Hysteria.' It becomes apparent that the 'Body without Organs' is, technically, a misnomer. The term is derived by Deleuze and Guattari from Antonin Artaud's text, 'The Body Is the Body.' Artaud identifies the 'organs' of the body with the body as an 'organism': 'The body is the body / alone it stands / and in need of no organs / organism it never is / organisms are enemies of the body.' Unlike Artaud, Deleuze and Guattari distinguish between 'organs' as such and the organization of organs as an 'organism.' The 'Body without Organs' therefore describes a set of unorganized organs which escape the organism.
11 For a provocative criticism of this point, see Keith Ansell-Pearson, *Germinal Life: The Difference and Repetition of Deleuze* 185–9.
12 For a clearer account of the notion of simultaneity, see Deleuze's remarks on the third synthesis of time (*Difference* 87–94). On the relation between 'simultaneous history' and the return of difference in 'eternal return,' see Deleuze, *Nietzsche and Philosophy* 39–72.
13 See Deleuze's remarks on the three repetitions (intracyclic repetition, cyclic repetition, and the eternal return) in *Difference and Repetition* 93.

14 Deleuze and Guattari break away from Foucault's discourse of resistance, which they describe as reactionary by definition. They write that in every assemblage, the lines of flight are primary and that they are 'not phenomena of resistance or counterattack of the assemblage, but cutting edges of creation and deterritorialization.' See their two points of disagreement with Foucault in *A Thousand Plateaus* 531n39.

WORKS CITED

Ansell-Pearson, Keith. *Germinal Life: The Difference and Repetition of Deleuze.* New York: Routledge, 1999.
Artaud, Antonin. 'The Body Is the Body.' Trans. Roger McKeon. *Semiotext(e), Anti-Oedipus* 2.3 (1977): 59.
Butler, Judith. 'Foucault and the Paradox of Bodily Inscriptions.' *Journal of Philosophy* 86.11 (1989): 601–7.
Deleuze, Gilles. *Difference and Repetition.* Trans. Paul Patton. New York: Columbia UP, 1994.
– *Foucault.* Trans. Seán Hand. Minneapolis: U of Minnesota P, 1988.
– *Francis Bacon: The Logic of Sensation.* Trans. Dan Smith. Forthcoming.
– *Negotiations.* Trans. Martin Joughin. New York: Columbia UP, 1995.
– *Nietzsche and Philosophy.* Trans. Hugh Tomlinson. New York: Columbia UP, 1983.
– *Spinoza: Practical Philosophy.* Trans. Robert Hurley. San Francisco: City Lights, 1988.
Deleuze, Gilles, and Félix Guattari. *Kafka: Toward a Minor Literature.* Trans. Dana Polan. Minneapolis: U of Minnesota P, 1986.
– *A Thousand Plateaus.* Trans. Brian Massumi. Minneapolis: U of Minnesota P, 1987.
Foucault, Michel. *The History of Sexuality: An Introduction.* Trans. Robert Hurley. New York: Vintage, 1990.
– 'Nietzsche, Genealogy, History.' *The Foucault Reader.* Ed. Paul Rabinow. Trans. D.F. Bouchard and S. Simon. New York: Pantheon, 1984. 76–100.
– 'Nietzsche, la généalogie, l'histoire.' *Hommage à Jean Hyppolite.* Paris: Presses Universitaires de France, 1971. 145–72.
– *The Order of Things.* Trans. Alan Sheridan. London: Tavistock, 1970.
– *This Is Not a Pipe.* Trans. James Harkness. Berkeley: U of California P, 1983.
Gil, José. *Metamorphoses of the Body.* Trans. Stephen Muecke. Minneapolis: U of Minnesota P, 1998.
Lacan, Jacques. *The Four Fundamental Concepts of Psycho-Analysis.* Trans. Alan Sheridan. New York: Norton, 1977.

Nietzsche, Friedrich. *Beyond Good and Evil.* Trans. R.J. Hollingdale. New York: Penguin, 1990.
– *Gay Science.* Trans. Walter Kaufman. New York: Vintage, 1974.
– *On the Genealogy of Morals.* Trans. Walter Kaufmann and R.J. Hollingdale. New York: Vintage, 1989.
– *Twilight of the Idols.* Trans. R.J. Hollingdale. New York: Penguin, 1985.
Taylor, Charles. 'Foucault on Freedom and Truth.' *Foucault: A Critical Reader.* Ed. David Hoy. New York: Basil Blackwell, 1986. 69–102.

Written in the Sand: Bataille's Phenomenology of Transgression and the Transgression of Phenomenology

BRIAN WALL

> I thought of keeping the Book of Sand in the space left on the shelf by the Wiclif, but in the end I decided to hide it behind the volumes of a broken set of *The Thousand and One Nights.*   Jorge Luis Borges, 'The Book of Sand'

Bataille is not – or not *only* – a thinker of the social. When his name arises it is most often associated with notions of value, or negatively, non-productivity: *la part maudite*, sovereignty, sacrifice – all of these concepts are cut adrift from their debt to Hegel in particular and phenomenology in general. An important exception, of course, is 'From Restricted to General Economy: A Hegelianism without Reserve,' where Derrida enlists Bataille to critique Hegel – but this is less than half the story: Bataille's thought traces a trajectory that evokes a way beyond sheer negativity, past the phenomenological valorization of experience and post-structuralism's critique of experience and beyond the oscillation of value and non-value, subject and object. Habermas is typical here in seeing Bataille through Foucault, who

> is fascinated by Bataille as someone who stems the tide against the denaturing flood of enlightened discourse about sexuality and who wants to give back both sexual and religious ecstasy their proper, specifically erotic meaning. But, above all, Foucault admires Bataille as someone who ranges texts in fiction and analysis, novels and reflection, alongside one another; someone who enriches the language with gestures of waste and excess and transgression of limits, in order to break out of the language of triumphant subjectivity. (238)

Habermas stresses Bataille's and Foucault's critique of subjectivity at the expense of a more profound relationship between the two thinkers. If, for Habermas, the relationship between Derrida and Heidegger is a genealogical one, the relationship between Foucault and Bataille then is physiological – a relationship of bodies of thought and thought of bodies.[1] Habermas also emphasizes the range of Bataille's thought, and while the lack of a systematized, coherent corpus betrays Bataille's fundamental irrationalism and anti-enlightenment program, Habermas also emphasizes the extent to which Bataille's thought is 'headless' – a philosophical body without organs.[2] Disciplinary boundaries form for Bataille part of a restricted economy that must be transgressed, not just in theory but in the practice of writing. Thus Bataille's texts – whether on sociology, anthropology, economics, literature, or erotics – constantly transgress themselves, each other, and the disciplinary borders that seek to keep them apart, leaving an essential excess.

In emphasizing the heterogeneous nature of Bataille's corpus – but especially its ecstatic and erotic dimensions – Habermas's portrayal obscures the profoundly philosophical dimension of Bataille's writings, specifically Bataille's relation to phenomenology, and how that relationship informs the complex interdisciplinary weaving of anthropology, economics, sociology, psychoanalysis, and aesthetics in his work. But such an impulse towards transgression entails that Bataille's *œuvre* cannot, will not coalesce into a seamless whole, and thus his texts can often appear contradictory, fragmentary, and rebarbative. 'The Psychological Structure of Fascism,' an early text, bears within it a bricolage of methods and binary economy of value:

> This [the absence of an elaboration of methodology] is obviously the principal shortcoming of an essay that will not fail to astonish those who are unfamiliar with French sociology, modern German philosophy (phenomenology), and psychoanalysis. As a point of information, it can nevertheless be insisted upon that the following descriptions refer to *actual experiences* and that the psychological method used excludes any recourse to abstraction. ('The Psychological Structure of Fascism' 160n1)

Here, in 1933, Bataille appeals to a conception of experience that is neither the Husserlian *epochē* nor an anticipation of poststructuralism's critique of experience as self-present – yet he explicitly assumes a basis in phenomenology. Bataille aims in this essay at critiquing the homogenizing tendencies of reification under capitalism, suggesting that fascism constitutes a necessary way station between capitalism and utopia. The homogeneity of capitalism, where money and commodification regulate expenditure, resists difference and heterogeneity, and Bataille's essay attempts to resolve this antagonism dialectically by advocating the shock of such heterogeneous elements as the unproductive expenditures and excesses of, variously, conspicuous consumption, warfare, mourning, and fascism. While Bataille stresses that such expenditures are not means to an end but rather ends in themselves – *en-soi* rather than *pour-soi* – he none the less implies that transgressions possess a utopian component corrosive to the homogenizing tendencies of capitalism. Echoing Heidegger, Bataille argues that fascism erupts with the promise of a valued and emancipatory heterogeneity, but in practice it becomes more homogenizing than capitalism.

Bataille will discard this crude dialectical structure – as well as its highly questionable fascination with fascism – and his naïve formulation of experience will undergo a thorough transformation in his first full-length philosophical text, *Inner Experience*, where this tenuous and barely articulated link to phenomenology will be radicalized. In *Inner Experience*, unlike 'The Psychological Structure of Fascism,' there will be a remainder of negativity that escapes the economy of the dialectic. Phenomenology and psychoanalysis become remainders in Bataille, in the same sense in which the philosophical context in which his writing takes place – that is, in an area bounded by Freud, Sartre, and Hegel, among others – cannot be made to resolve itself into a seamless and unified whole: their crossings and conflicts themselves generate remainders within the general economy of their combined thought, leaving us with a potentially productive way to reconsider the sprawling body of Bataille's work. At the intersection of psychoanalysis and phenomenology in Bataille, beyond his anthropological and social investigations, he is a thinker of subjectivity who attempts to surpass phenomenology in both its transcendental and existential forms: Bataille's inner experience equals psychoanalysis minus the unconscious, with a phenomenological remainder.

Inner Experience seems an unpromising point of departure for such an investigation: stylistically it shows Bataille at his most uncompromisingly oracular. More challenging, however, is the concept of inner experience itself: there is little – if anything – about it that depends on interiority, but neither is it an experience as such. It is in his refusal to sublate dialectically the opposition of inner and outer that Bataille begins to distance himself from Hegel, but it is in his detailing of the relationship between inner experience and action that Bataille critiques contemporary phenomenology:

> ... [I]nner experience is the opposite of action. Nothing more. 'Action' is utterly dependent on project. And what is serious, is that discursive thought is itself engaged in the mode of existence of project. Discursive thought is evinced by an individual engaged in action: it takes place within him beginning with his projects, on the level of reflexion upon projects. Project is not the only mode of existence implied by action, necessary to action – it is a way of being in paradoxical time: *it is the putting off of existence to a later point.* (*Inner Experience* 46)

'The opposite of action': this will be no Sartrean project then. The temporality of the limit experience opposes a conception of experience as mediated by discursive thought which admits a deferral, a 'putting off of existence to a later point.'[3] Such an opposition, however, should not be related to the transcendence of self-reflection: Bataille, extending his ideas from his earlier work, sees inner experience as immanent, opposed to any discursive thought or project that would externalize it. Sartre, responding to this, Bataille's first full-length philosophical text, could not help but see himself as the target of this critique, where the project – what, for Sartre, gives the subject self-consistency, what is directly responsible for the subject's coming into being – becomes for Bataille only a ruse that defers authentic being.[4] Derrida, more helpfully than Sartre, sees inner experience as challenging the precepts of phenomenology:

> That which *indicates itself* as interior experience is not an experience, because it is related to no presence, to no plenitude, but only to the 'impossible' it 'undergoes' in torture. This experience above all is not interior: and if it seems to be such because it is related to nothing else, to no exterior (except in the modes of nonrelation, secrecy, and rupture), it is also completely *exposed* – to torture – naked, open to the exterior, with no inner reserve or feelings, profoundly superficial. ('From Restricted to General Economy' 272)

Although he never mentions it by name here, Derrida parallels the tradition of existential phenomenology, examining extreme or borderline states of consciousness that have also fascinated such diverse thinkers as

Julia Kristeva, Rollo May, and R.D. Laing. Martin Jay stresses that Derrida's description of inner experience here emphasizes only its negative qualities, and argues that 'inner experience at its most negative is indistinguishable from limit-experience itself' (71). While Jay is at some pains to distinguish between the negative and positive characterizations of inner experience – even and especially when it seems ambiguous for Bataille himself – ultimately inner experience remains fundamentally negative.[5] Here inner experience demonstrates the transformation of experience for Bataille since 'The Psychological Structure of Fascism' – indeed, this limit experience is associated with *Erfahrung* rather than *Erlebnis,* and to this extent takes part in and even anticipates poststructuralism's critique of experience as essential and foundational under phenomenology.[6] *Erlebnis,* with its qualities of immediacy and self-presence, cannot be invoked as an adequate characterization of the phenomenological act of perception: Husserl, for instance, argues that perception implies a past and a future in the 'protentions' and 'retentions' that accompany the moment. But it is in particular this very lack of commensurability of perception with itself that Derrida will use to deconstruct Husserl's phenomenology.[7]

In a parallel sense, Bataille's inner experience contests the restricted economies of philosophy in general and phenomenology in particular: thus inner experience as such is never really defined in his text, but rather represented as an elemental power explicitly opposed to language and philosophy:

> It is through an 'intimate cessation of all intellectual operations' that the mind is laid bare. If not, *discourse* maintains it in its little complacency. Discourse, if it wishes to, can blow like a gale wind – whatever effort I make, the wind cannot chill by the fireside. The difference between inner experience and philosophy resides principally in this: that in experience, what is stated is nothing if not means and even, as much as a means, an obstacle; what counts is no longer the statement of wind, but the wind.
> (*Inner Experience* 13)

Just as discursive thought is on the side of action, of the project, and thus not commensurate with inner experience, so discourse too gets cast as an epiphenomenon, not to be mistaken for the limit experience itself. Despite his rejection of discourse and discursive thought, though, inner experience for Bataille occurs within an economy of the formation and grounding of the subject – therefore we will need to consider

Bataille's articulation of subjectivity in terms of the then-dominant philosophical discourse of phenomenology.

Bataille's assessment of phenomenology is explicitly antagonistic: in his reply to Sartre's review of *Inner Experience*, Bataille goes so far (perhaps unsurprisingly) as to dismiss *tout court* what he refers to as modern phenomenology: 'A *phenomenology of the developed mind* assumes a coincidence of subjective and objective aspects and at the same time a fusion of subject and object ... Clearly, instead of responding to it [Hegel's phenomenology], modern phenomenology, while replying to changing human thought, is only one moment among others: a sandcastle, a mirage of sorts' ('Appendix IV: Reply to Jean-Paul Sartre,' *On Nietzsche* 186).

In levelling this charge, Bataille rejects the negativity – and a perceived lack of attention to the history of philosophy – of an existential phenomenology that unlike its Hegelian counterpart separates subject and object, and he enacts a phenomenological reduction of a sort in distinguishing existential phenomenology from its object: it loses itself, is incapable of distinguishing itself, and becomes just another mode of thought with no particularly strong truth claim to make.[8] Bataille must respond to Hegel even as he attempts to surpass the dialectical method, and it is this debt to transcendental phenomenology – the notion that subject and object can be united – that distinguishes Bataille's philosophy from Sartre's. For Bataille, such transcendence must be possible both for the subject and for any philosophy that desires to be more than a sandcastle or mirage: '[I]n order to become the whole universe, humankind has to let go and abandon its principle, accepting as the sole criterion of what it is the tendency to go beyond what it is' ('Appendix IV: Reply to Jean-Paul Sartre' *On Nietzsche* 186–7). Far from eschewing transcendence, Bataille sees the transcendental impulse as immanent in the individual and constitutive of inner experience's relation to philosophy, though it is this transcendence itself that furnishes Bataille with a remainder of negativity that escapes synthesis. This negativity, however, is the result of the transgressive impulse of thought and not, as in Sartre, tied to the structure of the subject: but in so far as this negativity remains, Bataille is closer to existential phenomenology – and Sartre – than he would care to admit.

Bataille will trace an identical arc when in 1947 he reasserts his ties to surrealism against the oncoming tide of Sartrean existentialism: just as this transcendence cannot be brought about by an act of will on the part of the subject, so freedom cannot be achieved by the will:

The profound difference between surrealism and the existentialism of Jean-Paul Sartre hangs on this character of the existence of liberty. If I do not seek to dominate it, liberty will exist: it is poetry; words, no longer striving to serve some useful purpose, set themselves free and so unleash the image of free existence, which is never bestowed except in the instant. ... If we were genuinely to break the servitude by which the existence of the instant is submitted to useful activity, the essence would suddenly be revealed in us with an unbearable clarity. ... For surrealism is not only poetry but overpowering affirmation and, in this way, negation of the meaning of poetry. (*The Absence of Myth* 66–7)

'Surrealism' here later becomes life itself, for 'Life is essentially extravagant, drawing on its forces and its reserves unchecked; unchecked it annihilates what it has created' (*Erotism* 86). Phenomenologically speaking, Bataille wants to preserve the possibility of integrating the for-itself of the social subject and the in-itself of 'inner experience'; it is at precisely this point, however, that the negativity that is synthetically transmuted and transcended in a social paradigm (as in 'The Psychological Structure of Fascism') leaves its own excremental excess in the realm of inner experience – which is to say that there exists a negativity that Bataille's Hegelianism cannot assimilate.[9]

To suggest what and why such a non-recuperable negativity must be, I wish to return to Bataille's response to Sartre: sand seems to be a favourite trope of Bataille's for representing the contingency of systems, whether of thought or of language. Language is like sand:

The sand into which we bury ourselves in order not to see, is formed of words ... and it is true that words, their labyrinths, the exhausting immensity of their 'possibles,' in short their treachery, have something of quicksand about them. ... If we live under the law of language without contesting it, these states are within us as if they didn't exist. (*Inner Experience* 14)

It is not just that inner experience cannot be represented in language, but also that it cannot be said to exist 'under the law of language.' Were Bataille's text to attempt to represent inner experience in a language that did not seek to transgress itself, its very object would sink and disappear beneath its representation. Given Foucault's acknowledged debt to both Bataille and Nietzsche,[10] it becomes difficult to ignore the echoes of Bataille's 'sandcastle' of modern phenomenology and quicksand of language in Foucault's famous conclusion to *The Order of Things*:

If those arrangements [of knowledge] were to disappear as they appeared, if some event of which we can at the moment do no more than sense the possibility – without knowing either what its form will be or what it promises – were to cause them to crumble, as the ground of Classical thought did, at the end of the eighteenth century, then one can certainly wager that man would be erased, like a face drawn in the sand at the edge of the sea. (387)

Surely this is the anti-enlightenment discourse Habermas has in mind when associating Bataille and Foucault. Bataille's image of the contingency of modern philosophy and language is trumped by Foucault's evocation of the contingency of the very notion of 'man.' As if to underscore this allegiance, Foucault again deploys the same figure in one of his most direct assessments of Bataille, 'Preface to Transgression':

We have not in the least liberated sexuality, though we have, to be more exact, carried it to its limits: the limits of consciousness, because it ultimately dictates the only possible reading of our unconscious; the limit of the law, since it seems the sole substance of universal taboos; the limit of language, since it traces that line of foam showing just how fast speech may advance upon the sands of silence. (30)

Foucault points to the crucial crossing of sexuality and consciousness that goes some ways towards explaining Bataille's description of the nihilating powers of surrealism and life, as well as his frequent deployment of psychoanalytic terms to describe social and aesthetic phenomena. For Foucault, as for Bataille, the subject and the social cannot be thought of in terms of the simple opposition of inner and outer. If, as Foucault suggests, the limits of sexuality parallel the limits of consciousness, then in so far as sexuality is utterly constitutive of the *un*conscious, a psychoanalytic methodology becomes necessary for the investigation of the subject in any mode of her being in the world, especially at the contingent, culturally defined limits of such being.

Bataille's most extended study of sexuality, *Erotism: Death and Sensuality*,[11] typically oscillates between theorizing sexuality as integral to inner experience and cultural/historical depictions and constructions of sexuality. At precisely this point where one would expect the unconscious to come to the fore in Bataille's writings, it is conspicuous by its absence: Freud is cited only twice, and then only in his most anthropological mode. Relying on *Totem and Taboo*, Bataille alludes to Freud only in

examining the taboos associated with sexuality – a significant lack, given
the extent to which Bataille's notion of sexuality depends on subjectivity: 'The animal itself does not have a subjective life but this life seems to
be conferred on it like an inert object, once and for all. Human eroticism differs from animal sexuality precisely in this, that it calls inner life
into play' (*Erotism* 29). Bataille's 'inner life' – inner experience – is thus
apparently not to be mistaken for the Freudian unconscious. However,
Bataille's conception of taboo is informed by both social *and* unconscious aspects – but this formulation of the unconscious is little more
than a perpetual crossing and recrossing of an internal reserve of socio-
cultural taboos and the transgressive impulse to overcome those limits.
Even though transgression informs the unconscious for Bataille, it
nonetheless is not identical with it: rather, the unconscious for Bataille
is this perpetual antagonism between the fundamental social dynamic of
taboo and transgression within the individual.[12] How then is such a formulation to be reconciled with the negativity of an inner experience
that is nonetheless capable of disrupting and destabilizing the social?
On one hand, erotic transgression is for Bataille a privileged example of
transgression as such, in so far as the limits it transgresses are imposed
on the subject from without; but within the general economy of
Bataille's theories, this negativity, this transgressive impulse, is non-
recuperable by the restricted economy of the social, and, as such, must
properly be discussed in the context of *la parte maudite*.

The status of phenomenology in Bataille's texts also engages our
attention most particularly at this point where it is necessary to define
what the nature of this excremental remainder is, and how it can escape
the synthetic paradigm of the general economy. What is the status of a
mode of thought that seeks to celebrate waste, excess and negativity, the
accursed share that cannot be accommodated within a restricted economy, and yet conversely valorizes a sub-version of the Hegelian synthesis? In his broad concern with the states of consciousness associated with
social formations, Bataille would seem to be closer to existential phenomenology than he may at first appear. Not only his critical vocabulary
but his attention to marginal states associates him with the psychoanalytic concerns of the manner of the subject's insertion into the world – a
mode of thought that shares more with existential than transcendental
phenomenology. Yet it would be reductive to suggest that Bataille's
interest in the irrecuperable and marginal is enough on its own to align
him with a more existentially nuanced phenomenological paradigm, as
we have seen in his relation to Sartre – it remains to be seen if these

marginal states really do resist recuperation within a synthetic, general economy – rather, the status of negativity in Bataille's thought is inextricable from the status of value itself.

Surrealism, the site of the quarrel between Bataille and Breton, gets entangled in this charged matrix: most significantly, surrealism cathects the unconscious and the transcendent, achieving a seemingly contradictory status, in effect positing the unconscious as transcendental structure, noumenal, beyond experience and history. Foucault's reading of Bataille argues that it is rather the movement of sexuality to its limits that permits us to examine the unconscious at all. How can such a structure be reconciled with the particularities of Bataille's project? These contradictions must be considered as productive, in much the same fashion as Bataille sees the excremental as liberating and productive – which of course begs the question of its negativity.

Such a valorization of the limit experience is contingent on the marginal or abject status of the negative and transgressive. In addressing this dilemma in Bataille, Foucault writes

> Transgression contains nothing negative, but affirms limited being – affirms the limitlessness into which it leaps as it opens this to existence for the first time. But correspondingly, this affirmation contains nothing positive: no content can bind it, since, by definition, no limit can possibly restrict it. Perhaps it is simply an affirmation of division; but only insofar as division is not understood to mean a cutting gesture, or the establishment of a separation or the measuring of a distance, only retaining that in which it may designate the existence of difference. ('Preface to Transgression' 35–6)

Articulate and cautious as Foucault's framing is, nonetheless it raises difficulties to the extent that it conflates negativity with difference. For his own purposes of deploying phenomenology against structuralism, Foucault utilizes these – and, elsewhere, other – limit metaphors to raise ontological questions concerning fundamental structures of experience and existence.[13] In Bataille's case, the question then becomes: does transgression function in the manner that Foucault describes? For Bataille, the critique of structuralism is not an issue; yet there remains a place for ontology in Bataille's writings:

> For some time now, the only philosophy which lives – that of the German school – tended to make the highest knowledge an extension of inner

experience. But this *phenomenology* lends to knowledge the value of a goal which one attains through experience. This is an ill-assorted match: the measure given to experience is at once too much and not great enough. Those who provide this place for it must feel that it overflows, by an immense 'possible,' the use to which they limit themselves. What appears to preserve philosophy is the little acuity of the experience from which the phenomenologists set out. This lack of balance does not weather the putting into play of experience proceeding to the end of the possible, when going to the end means at least this: that the limit, which is knowledge as a goal, be crossed. (*Inner Experience* 8)

Starting from a valorization of Heidegger – the association of experience with living as a kind of shorthand for being-in-the-world or *Dasein* – Bataille goes on to distance himself from phenomenology, arguing that knowledge of Being is never equivalent with Being itself. He implies a critique of the transcendental, too, in that knowledge of inner experience entails essentializing it. Bataille argues that phenomenology and, by extension, philosophy itself are not fully conscious of the extent to which 'knowledge as a goal' is radically surpassed by the experience that informs philosophical and phenomenological investigations at their outset: the limit experience will always exceed any attempt to ascertain its essential structure. This radical surpassing underwrites Bataille's conception of transgression.

Phenomenology is, then, rejected: 'it is a matter of putting to rest the analytic division of operations, of escaping by this from the feeling of the emptiness of intelligent questions' (*Inner Experience* 8), which is to say that phenomenology for Bataille cannot succeed in attaining the fundamental structures of phenomena as they appear to consciousness as long as it pledges its allegiance to 'knowledge as a goal,' as the attempt to determine the essential structures of the limit experience will always founder because of the division between the experience of knowledge and inner experience. Thus any attempt to understand the limit experience must remain within the limit experience. Already inherent in such a critique is a characteristic devaluation of the rational and its accompanying use value; yet at this point it is important to consider in a more precise fashion exactly why the limit experience holds such a privileged position. Consonant with his critique of Sartre, Bataille writes that

Experience attains in the end the fusion of subject and object, being as

> subject non-knowledge, as object the unknown. ... This attained as an extremity of the possible, it stands to reason that philosophy properly speaking is absorbed – that being already separated from the simple attempt at the cohesion of knowledge that is the philosophy of sciences, it is dissolved. And being dissolved in this new way of thinking, it finds itself to be no longer anything but the heir to a fabulous mystical theology, but missing a God and wiping the slate clean. (*Inner Experience* 9)

Experience, then, will not be bracketed or transcended: the fusion of subject and object sought by transcendental phenomenology becomes virtually unrecognizable. One can see what Foucault found so appealing in reading Bataille: what is 'being as subject non-knowledge, as object the unknown' if not an attempt to think the unthought of phenomenology? Moreover, how is that unthought to be described without falling into the same trap as the philosophy of sciences or religion[14] for that matter with their troubling mystical foundations?

Such issues return us to the problem of value. Where Foucault is able to contextualize his exploration of the unthought within a framework of discursive regimes, Bataille's attitude towards history is, at best, eclectic: he constructs this particular and peculiar fusion of subject and object that pushes past the limits of knowledge and the known such that it threatens to escape even the metaphors that describe it. Such a methodology has a distinct appeal for Foucault, who borrows heavily from Bataille's critique of phenomenology in the 'Preface to Transgression': as Rajan argues, 'Foucault's essay performs rather than defines Bataille's *expérience intérieure*, as a transgression that transgresses nothing, an inside that is not an inside because there is no outside against which to define it' (459). The fusion of subject of non-knowledge and the object as unknown exceeds the distinction between inner and outer. This is the negative aspect of Foucault's description of Bataille's project, of how transgression can by definition be neither negative nor positive without succumbing to the very logic of value it seeks to undermine or overcome. Yet such a conception of limits is inscribed within Bataille's reworking of the Hegelian dialectic whereby the metaphor of limit itself serves to illustrate the limits of metaphor: rather than being part of the logic or restricted economy that alternates both positivity and negativity as positive qualities, the transgression of limits becomes a negation of a negation. Even given that Bataille's thought relies heavily on images of value and economy, waste and surplus, it does so in order to bring about a dissolution of the evaluative impulse itself, in order to suggest how transgression may avoid its own reincorporation as resistance or positivity. Put another way, Bataille's general economy subsumes a restricted economy and maintains its transgressive potential to the extent that it refuses simply to negate tradition but rather incorporates it in such a fashion as to *resist* synthesis. How, then, does Bataille's work successfully negotiate the paradox most succinctly articulated by Steven Connor?

> [F]or a body of work which promotes loss, waste, excess, refuse and excrement, along with everything which stands against the principles of bourgeois utility, to have become such a rich resource for knowledge is a strange kind of failure. How is it possible to maintain a serious commitment to the values of pure and non-productive expenditure, the value of non-value, when Bataille's own work increases so steadily in positive value? (71)

It is difficult – if not impossible – to finally clarify what 'inner experience' is for Bataille. It is certainly not the will, but neither is it the unconscious; it is informed by the social, but transgresses the social; and thus it is an in-itself that cannot remain an in-itself since it depends on the for-itself, in contradistinction to Sartre; and in seeking transcendence, it must also have limits in order to surpass them. It is not a positivity but rather a negativity that becomes a positivity through transgression, and finally it is a positivity that is itself transgressed and undone by its own transgression. Borges' story 'The Book of Sand' recounts an unnamed scholar who comes into possession of a book of infinite pages which, for the sake of his sanity, he must ultimately abandon: 'I thought of keeping the Book of Sand in the space left on the shelf by the Wiclif, but in the end I decided to hide it behind the volumes of a broken set of *The Thousand and One Nights.*' To my mind this monstrous volume parallels the status of philosophy in particular and other restricted economies in general in Bataille's work: the sand that demarcates the limits to be transgressed by the radical thinker are ever shifting and expanding in response to the surge of the transgressive impulse. And though such thought cannot in the end take the place of philosophy or religion – the Book of Sand, infinite though it is, cannot fill the space of the absent Wiclif Bible on the narrator's shelf – or supplant culture, filling in for the missing volumes of *The Thousand and One Nights*, it does not have to: *it already includes them*, it exists only in so far as it surpasses the limits of philosophy, language, faith, or literature. Behind the 'broken set' of Bataille's narratives drifts, as Habermas intimates, an infinite capacity to reinscribe his philosophy, not just outside 'the language of triumphant subjectivity' but outside whatever mode of thought mistakes the sandcastle it has built for a more enduring structure.

NOTES

1 My thanks to Tilottama Rajan for this and other important suggestions about Bataille's relationship to poststructuralist thought.
2 There is an important parallel between the dispersal of Bataille's thought and Deleuze and Guattari's figuration of subjectivity: both try to resist oppressive totalization, preferring intensity. Such an avoidance has consequences not just for the structure of their thought but also for their style: the occasionally opaque texts of these theorists enact the resistance to totalization.
3 Bataille will go on to articulate this 'Principle of inner experience: to emerge through project from the realm of project' (*Inner Experience* 46). The project seems to be both an essential component of inner experience and also a component that must be, again, transgressed and left behind.
4 See Sartre, 'Un nouveau mystique.' *Situations.*
5 Bataille's *Inner Experience* has not always been so sensitively read: Fred Botting, for instance, characterizes it as a mystically charged text, in which writing becomes ecstasy. Bataille does not go so far himself: 'What characterizes such an experience which does not proceed from revelation – where nothing is revealed either, if not the unknown – is that it never announces anything reassuring' (*Inner Experience* xxxii). See Botting's 'Literature as Heterological Practice: Georges Bataille, Writing and Inner Experience.' Jean-Luc Nancy's *The Inoperative Community* offers a more socially nuanced reading of this difficult text.
6 See Rebecca Comay, 'Gifts without Presents: Economies of "Experience" in Bataille and Heidegger.' Comay, citing Adorno and Benjamin, argues that '*Erlebnis* would be that clammy sensation of proximity which marks our radical alienation from the depths of history' (84). She continues, suggesting the proximity of Heidegger's contrast of 'the vitalist "stream of experience" [*Erlebnis-strom*] to the homogenous flux of accumulative now-points – to a modality, that is to say, of the inauthentic' (85). Ultimately, for Comay, Bataille's inner experience is profoundly negative and never present, but always referring back to an originary plenitude: '*Erfahrung* – the experience lost – is nothing other than the experience of loss' (85).

7 See Derrida's *Speech and Phenomena, and Other Essays on Husserl's 'Theory of Signs.'*

8 Bataille uses similar strategies to further differentiate himself from André Breton in the essay 'Surrealism and How It Differs from Existentialism' (*The Absence of Myth* 57–67), where Bataille's philosophical investments put him at odds with both Sartre and Breton, despite the essay's professed admiration for the latter. For an overview of the often turbulent relationship Bataille and Breton shared, see also Allan Stoekl's introduction to *Visions of Excess*, ix–xxv.

9 This is one of Derrida's points in his reflections on Bataille and Hegel: 'how, after having exhausted the discourse of philosophy, can one inscribe in the lexicon and syntax of a language, our language, that which nevertheless exceeds the oppositions of concepts governed by this communal logic?' ('Restricted' 253). Bataille's debt to Hegel is most evident where he is most critical of Hegel. Leslie Anne Boldt-Irons is surely correct to write that 'In Bataille's view, the movement of Hegel's system towards closure of the circle denies the movement of negativity to which the entire circle could be subjected. ... The systematic thought which Bataille's thought denies is only possible under these conditions: either a ground or a closure [is] needed to satisfy the demands of the project to sustain a philosophical "system"' (Introduction 5) – but, as I hope to show, Bataille is not immune to system building himself, as the negativity of his critique is inevitably recouped – sublated, even – at another level within his corpus of thought.

10 See, for instance, *The Order of Things* 328.

11 Again, the title itself compels one to wonder how well Bataille has been served by his English translators and publishers. While 'erotism' would seem to be a literal translation of the book's French title, *L'Érotisme* (Paris: Minuit, 1957), it is also conspicuously absent from the dictionary.

12 It would be useful to read *Erotism* against Lacan's description of how the Law of the Father – the *nom-du-père/ non-du-père* – creates the desire for its own transgression. Žižek's critique of Bataille follows a different path: 'Bataille's "subject" is not yet the pure void (the transcendent point of self-relating negativity), but remains an inner-worldly, positive force. Within these co-ordinates, the negativity which characterizes the modern subject can express itself only in the guise of a violent destruction which throws the entire circuit of nature off the rails. It is as if, in a kind of unique short-circuit, Bataille projects the negativity of the modern subject backwards, into the "closed," pre-modern Aristotelian universe of balanced circular movement, within which this negativity can materialize itself only as an "irrational," excessive, non-economical expenditure' (125; italics in original). While Žižek's cri-

tique may be apt in its characterization of Bataille's theory of the subject as, in a sense, anachronistic, such a description is perhaps truer to Lacan's notion of being 'between two deaths' than it is to Bataille. In Foucault, for instance – who can hardly be accused of projecting Bataille's notion of the subject into a 'pre-modern Aristotelian universe' – the transgressive impulse of the subject serves precisely both to challenge and to reinscribe the limits of subjectivity of such a 'closed' world.

13 For a detailed account of Foucault's relationship to phenomenology see Tilottama Rajan, 'The Phenomenological Allegory: From *Death and the Labyrinth* to *The Order of Things.*'

14 Were this paper to be more comprehensive, it would be necessary to include a consideration of Bataille's extensive comments on religion. Even though his *Theory of Religion* is, again, a largely anthropological and even dialectical work, it would be valuable to trace the intersection of inner experience with ecstatic religious experience.

WORKS CITED

Bataille, Georges. *The Absence of Myth: Writings on Surrealism.* Ed., trans., and intro. Michael Richardson. London: Verso, 1994.
– *The Accursed Share: An Essay on General Economy.* Trans. Robert Hurley. Vol. 1. New York: Zone, 1988.
– *Erotism: Death and Sensuality.* Trans. Mary Dalwood. San Francisco: City Lights, 1986.
– *Inner Experience.* Trans. and intro. Leslie Anne Boldt. Albany: SUNY P, 1988.
– *On Nietzsche.* Trans. Bruce Boone. Intro. Sylvère Lotringer. New York: Paragon, 1992.
– 'The Psychological Structure of Fascism.' *Visions of Excess: Selected Writings, 1927–1939.* Ed. and intro. Allan Stoekl. Trans. Allan Stoekl, Carl R. Lovitt, and Donald M. Leslie, Jr. Minneapolis: U of Minnesota P, 1985.
– *The Tears of Eros.* Trans. Peter Connor. San Francisco: City Lights, 1989.
– *Theory of Religion.* Trans. Robert Hurley. New York: Zone Books, 1989.
Baudrillard, Jean. *Symbolic Exchange and Death.* Trans. Iain Hamilton Grant. Intro. Mike Gane. London: Sage, 1993.
– 'When Bataille Attacked the Metaphysical Principle of Economy.' *Ideology and Power in the Age of Lenin in Ruins.* Ed. and intro. Arthur and Marilouise Kroker. Trans. David James Miller. Montreal: New World Perspectives, 1991. 135–8.
Beckett, Samuel. *Worstward Ho.* New York: Grove, 1983.
Boldt-Irons, Leslie Anne. Introduction. *On Bataille: Critical Essays.* Ed. Leslie Anne Boldt-Irons. Albany: SUNY P, 1995. 1–38.

Borges, Jorge Luis. 'The Book of Sand.' *The Book of Sand.* Trans. Norman Thomas Di Giovanni. New York: Dutton, 1978.

Botting, Fred, and Scott Wilson. 'Literature as Heterological Practice: Georges Bataille, Writing and Inner Experience.' *Textual Practice* 7.2 (1993): 195–207.

Comay, Rebecca. 'Gifts without Presents: Economies of "Experience" in Bataille and Heidegger.' *Yale French Studies* 78 (1990): 66–89.

Connor, Steven. *Theory and Cultural Value.* Oxford: Blackwell, 1992.

Derrida, Jacques. 'Différance.' *Margins of Philosophy.* Trans. Alan Bass. Chicago: U of Chicago P, 1982. 1–28.

– 'From Restricted to General Economy: A Hegelianism without Reserve.' *Writing and Difference.* Trans. and intro. Alan Bass. Chicago: U of Chicago P, 1978. 251–77.

– *Speech and Phenomena, and Other Essays on Husserl's 'Theory of Signs.'* Trans. David B. Allison. Evanston: Northwestern UP, 1973.

Foucault, Michel. *The Order of Things: An Archaeology of the Human Sciences.* Trans. Alan Sheridan. New York: Vintage, 1973.

– 'Preface to Transgression.' *Language, Counter-Memory, Practice: Selected Essays and Interviews.* Ed. Donald F. Bouchard. Trans. Donald F. Bouchard and Sherry Simon. Ithaca: Cornell UP, 1977. 29–52.

Habermas, Jürgen. 'Between Eroticism and General Economics: George Bataille.' *The Philosophical Discourse of Modernity: Twelve Lectures.* Trans. Frederick Lawrence. Cambridge: MIT P, 1987. 211–37.

Jay, Martin. 'The Limits of Limit Experience: Bataille and Foucault.' *Cultural Semantics: Keywords of Our Time.* Amherst: U of Massachusetts P, 1998. 62–78.

Nancy, Jean-Luc. *The Inoperative Community.* Trans. Peter Connor, Lisa Garbus, Michael Holland, and Simona Sawhney. Minneapolis: U of Minnesota P, 1991.

Rajan, Tilottama. 'The Phenomenological Allegory: From *Death and the Labyrinth* to *The Order of Things.*' *Poetics Today* 19.3 (1998): 439–66.

Richardson, Michael. *George Bataille.* London: Routledge, 1994.

Richman, Michele H. *Reading Georges Bataille: Beyond the Gift.* Baltimore: Johns Hopkins UP, 1982.

Sartre, Jean-Paul. 'Un nouveau mystique.' *Situations.* Paris: Gallimard, 1947.

Žižek, Slavoj. *The Indivisible Remainder: An Essay on Schelling and Related Matters.* London: Verso, 1996.

TECHNOLOGIES

Theory *avant la Lettre*: An Excavation in Early Modern England

LINDA BRADLEY SALAMON

Those who read and deploy critical theory are accustomed to thinking (to borrow a dashing phrase from that most dashing of modernists, Virginia Woolf) that 'human character changed on or about December, 1637,' when Descartes published the *Discourse on Method* that attempted to evacuate from the thinking subject all acculturated content, including naturalized culture and, via the body, nature itself. Given the origin of the modern *sciences humaines* in France, it is understandable that Descartes's move in the *cogito*, positing reason alone as the essence of the human condition, should be taken as the conventional baseline for the seventeenth-century *epistemē*. Descartes fathers the binary distinction, multiplying across the centuries but always signifying related referents, between mind and body, between Kantian *Theorie* and *Technik*, between Foucauldian ideology and procedure, between – the dichotomy I wish to foreground in this essay – theory and practice. For early modern England, however, the archaeological exploration into the prehistory of twentieth-century theory that I undertake can derive that fundamental distinction equally well from the more empirical, less sceptical, quintessentially English discourse of Sir Francis Bacon, particularly from his *Advancement of Learning* (1605). It is Bacon who sets a fatal stamp, for England, on the permanent division between 'knowledges which respect the Body' and 'knowledges that respect the Mind'; Bacon who establishes the ambitious project of surveying, systematically categorizing, and setting a research agenda for those knowledges; Bacon who – in this early work, before his ultimate project of 'the scientific method' was clear – organizes all of them under the general rubric of 'arts' (206–7, 217–19).

Use of the term 'art' to signify a discipline that lays claim to a defined body of knowledge is as old as the *trivium* and *quadrivium* of the medieval seven liberal arts – grammar, rhetoric, logic, arithmetic, geometry, astronomy, music – and as contemporary as the nominal labelling of faculties and courses of study in American colleges and universities. Within Bacon's immediate discursive space, however, was a chorus of native voices that privileged a certain kind of 'art.' Beginning with printing itself, the earliest books published in England from the fifteenth through the seventeenth centuries include more than seventy texts, many in multiple editions, on particular arts: the art of angling (or fishing), the art of falconry, the art of fortification, of gardening, of hunting, of logic, of navigation, of plucking chickens, of riding, of war, of woodworking, and a dozen other themes. These texts, and the work they describe, are about performance, about material production, about ways of being and doing, about manoeuvring in the world of affairs. They present (not yet 'represent') human skill when it is conducted with efficacy, economy, and – in the more sophisticated of them – with grace, or 'ease,' or other qualities that we recognize as aesthetic effect.

These little books – literally little, for many are the *octavo* or even *duodecimo* size that may be held in one hand or carried in a pocket – were patently successful, a publishing phenomenon as popular in the sixteenth and early seventeenth centuries as sonnet cycles and as consistent, over two hundred years, as the drama. Their successors sit today on crowded bookstore shelves and best-seller lists with titles like *On Golf: Lessons from America's Master Teacher, The Nine Steps to Financial Freedom*, and the perennial seller, *How to Do Just About Everything*. Manuals of practical advice available to any literate person who can afford a paperback book, they are the ultimate 'self-consuming artifacts.' Like modern 'how-to' books, early modern art-texts (as I shall call them) do not eschew knowledge; rather, they appropriate the authority of inscribed history and philosophy as mere confirmation for the wisdom that comes from practical experience, not from the experience of reading. Though each skill is transcribed and presented – sometimes proudly so – as the work of one author, in fact each text is the product of accumulated practice by many people over decades or longer. They represent, in short, the 'discourse on non-discursive practices' described by Michel de Certeau in *The Practice of Everyday Life* as the 'remainder' that is excluded from (Baconian) scientific discourse by the very process of its constitution (61). These texts, as de Certeau might recognize, present specific incarnations or 'hypotheses' – brought to consciousness – of what Pierre Bourdieu has unforgettably named the *habitus* (*Logic* 53 and passim);[1] for the early modern period, they offer important interventions in the emerging dialectic between *habitus* and cultural field.

In the twentieth century, aside from studies in the history of the verbal science of rhetoric, art-texts were approached largely in an antiquarian mode, explored archivally as sources on particular cultural practices or mildly patronized in exhibits of herbals or cookbooks that focus on the specific, usually domestic techniques they purvey. In such a gaze they are made quaint, feminized, set apart from the orbits of power.[2] In this essay, however, I wish to explore the *artes* as constituting an independent, powerful quasi-genre of their own, running much deeper than mere pedagogical treatises with immediate practical use. I find these texts firmly embedded in the pre-history of theory; they offer readers what Bourdieu pointedly calls 'the truth of what science is constructed *against*' (*Logic* 36). My warrant for such a claim is drawn in part from Bourdieu's *The Logic of Practice*, but still more directly from de Certeau. For the texts are precisely the transcription of cultural practices that lack an 'interrogating apparatus,' of 'strategies which do not know what it is they know.' De Certeau himself cites the 'art' as a pre-articulated practice, rather than a text that presents it; the mode by which the Enlightenment appropriates the inchoate knowledge of the *always-already* he calls 'ethnologization' and even 'colonization' by science. 'Science will make princesses of these Cinderellas' (63, 65, 64, 67), he says, whether the weaving of twentieth-century Berber women or the sundial-making of Elizabethan Englishmen. In everyday life in the sixteenth century, to be sure, such an appropriation could not yet be envisioned. To grasp the cultural work that the art-texts do, as Bourdieu says, 'one has to situate oneself *within* "real activity as such," ... in ... the active presence in the world through which the world imposes its presence, with its urgencies, its things to be done and said ... which directly govern words and deeds without ever unfolding as a spectacle' (*Logic* 40, 52).

To locate the art-text in the archaeology of theory, I shall examine both its generative principles (recognizing with Bourdieu that in *praxis* 'genesis implies amnesia of genesis') and the cultural work that its writers desire to accomplish, again warned by Bourdieu that 'there is every reason to think that, as soon as he reflects on his practice, adopting a quasi-theoretical posture, the agent loses any chance of expressing the truth of his practice' (*Logic* 91). In that spirit, I conclude by considering some ways in which this genre, by expressing early modern practices unmediated, intersects with contemporary cultural studies. Focusing on the earliest examples, I shall illustrate primarily from *The Treatyse on*

Fysshing with an Angle (1496), probably by Juliana Barnes; *The Art and Science of Preserving Bodie and Soul* (1579), by John Jones; *The Arte of Limning* (1600), by Nicholas Hilliard; and particularly *The Arte of Brachygraphie* (1597), by Peter Bales.[3]

A minor difficulty in reconceiving these texts for today's academy needs preliminary address. As constituted in the modern university, the 'arts' – as in 'bachelor of arts,' not including the fine or *beaux* arts which have a very different genealogy and a different relation between theory and practice – are those disciplines that study texts, artifacts, institutions, and systems like religion: the products of human culture over time, and the meanings that have been (or can be) invested in them. In the academy more familiarly called 'the humanities,' these are the hermeneutic disciplines, each at work upon a reasonably well defined body of material. The modern 'sciences' (biological, physical, or social), on the other hand, are viewed by their practitioners as procedures of inquiry, increasingly technical, increasingly dependent on complex instrumentation, increasingly intent on 'methodology' as the criterion for accurate outcome. Natural scientists say 'her science' to signify the unique processes a colleague uses in her lab, more than her results; they describe their work as '*doing* science.'

This binary in the objects of discourse – between cultural products and patterns of investigation, between knowing and doing, between the complete and the emergent – has equal valence for the intellectual realm of the early modern world. But, through what de Certeau calls 'the ruptures separating separate configurations of knowledge' (70), the terms that denote the two domains are exactly the opposite. For the fifteenth to seventeenth centuries, a 'science' is a settled body of doctrine – not necessarily, indeed not often, about nature – while an 'art' is a practice, a set of skills for doing or making that *is* most frequently concerned with the physical realm. (Then as now, ironically, it is science that is valorized, whatever the term signifies.)[4] The lineage for the early modern usage comes directly from the medieval academy: *scientia* is knowledge, even truth, while *artes* – in the plural in part because they are multiple, contingent, indeterminate in outcome – are technical accomplishments. The original liberal arts, we readily forget, were higher-order skills, mental exercises to be practised by well-born schoolboys.[5] In the classroom, arithmetic and logic of course, but also rhetoric and music; in everyday life, more practical forms of arithmetic and music, but also 'tricks of the trade.' As Ben Jonson shows in *Volpone*, even parasites and mountebanks on the criminal fringes have their mysterious 'art' that yearns to be a 'science.'[6] This 'know-how,' 'composed of multiple but untamed operativities,' as de Certeau says, 'claims to conquer and annex not contemptible practices but "ingenious," "complex," and "effective" forms of knowledge' (65). This '*reserve* of knowledge one can inventory in shops or in the countryside' (67) is the object of early modern English art-texts.

The texts of Tudor England may, of course, be situated in the history of discourse. A relatively distant ancestor is the Socratic *technē* of Plato as mediated by Aristotle. Often translated as 'art,' *technē* is Plato's general term for skills of the body, informed by the mind and brought to a high level of mastery. From the *Ion* through the *Protagoras* and quintessentially in the *Gorgias*, Socrates unites medicine, military strategy, the production of musical instruments, the composition of poetry, hunting, statesmanship, navigating, and the work of the personal trainer, all as forms of special expertise. *Technē* connotes deftness not so much in making an object as in using it well. Focused not on science/knowledge but on conduct, it contains an ethical or aesthetic dimension, but it is not merely a capacity for pleasing: cosmetics, cookery, and – for Socrates' ironic purposes – rhetoric do not rise to *technē*. The body's crafty mastery, hard-won in measured practice; tough dexterity of hand and eye ... *fly-fishing*, as Juliana Barnes knew. I call Socrates only a godfather, however, because the first hundred years' worth of writers of art-texts had neither read Plato nor (most of them) even heard his name. And of course they need not have; as Bourdieu says, 'the *habitus* – embodied history, internalized as a second nature and so forgotten as history – is the active presence of the whole past of which it is the product' (*Logic* 56). Rhetoric changes regularly, fishing – in its essentials – very little.

The more immediate genealogy of the art-texts, however, is drawn from two almost opposite streams. The organization of medieval artisanal groups, craft industries, and craft merchants into guilds had as one strong purpose the protection of their 'trade secrets,' closely held among the initiated; hence vocations are, in early modern England, also called 'mysteries.' Several of the early art-texts show signs – within a culture that was in various ways secretive, surreptitious, and given to obliquity – of literally 'telling tales out of school': committing to writing, and the costly new medium of print, precious private information. Nicholas Hilliard's *Arte of Limning* publishes the technique of painting miniature portraits, an offshoot of the ancient skill of manuscript illumination: painting in watercolours on vellum on a minute scale. Half of his treatise figures the Italian Renaissance come at last to England, but the other half is a medieval recipe book for making paints out of ground stone or vegetable matter and fixative, for preparing the surface, and similar matters of craft. Why would a member in good standing of the Goldsmiths' Company reveal their secrets? He kept some tricks of the trade under wraps, to be sure – one could not paint a miniature following only his directions – but I want to maintain that he also affirmed, and formally laid claim to, what he had come to recognize as his own unique contributions to the craft, a craft that had until that time been – in Bourdieu's term – an 'intentionless invention of regulated improvisation' (*Logic* 57).

The other parental strain for the Tudor/Stuart art-text is the Greek and Roman learning of the classical revival, hybridized onto the native stock. Many of the Elizabethan art-texts simply naturalize the *trivium*; Ralph Lever's 1554 *Art of Reason*, for instance, is a logic primer, with the Latinate nomenclature carpentered into clumsy Anglo-Saxonisms. And *Art[s] of Logic, Art[s] of Rhetoric* abound in the years when humanist education was expanding. As the 'new learning' of the Renaissance spread in England, the literate grew acquainted with Horace's *Art of Poetry* – as perhaps the best known of these texts (at least to literary scholars), George Puttenham's *Arte of English Poesie* (1579), shows – and with Ovid's *Art of Love*, as Christopher Marlowe amply reveals.[7] The learned even knew that the Greek title for Aristotle's *Poetics* is based on *poiein*, 'to make,' and posits 'production' in general, not literary terms. The poet is a 'maker,' who practises an art.

Many of the writers, however, simply borrow the *arte* title with its inherent implications of authority in order to add stature, lustre, and shelf-appeal to their texts. *The Art and Science of preserving the Bodie and Soule in Health, Wisdom, and the Catholic Religion* sounds very impressive, but what John Jones actually proffers is the Dr Spock's *Common Sense Book of Baby and Child Care* (1946) of its day, full of detailed advice for choosing a wet nurse and her diet, mixing a newborn's bathwater, rocking a cradle very gently after meals, spinning as an art suitable for women of every rank, and so on – with a segue to the cost to the commonwealth of poor relief, as he turns from his real interest (the quotidian culture surrounding the child under seven) to the parade of learning from Galen, Aristotle, Avicenna, and the like that he expects will convince the learned reader of his credentials. Although practice and theory are ingenuously quilted together in Jones's text, he clearly privileges the 'common phrase' and 'daily experience' over 'lawful authority' (2).

The hybrid art-text, that is to say, frames within the formal concepts of medieval schooling a wide range of actual practices that constitute the texture of everyday Tudor/Stuart life, in all its particularity. By inscribing aspects of the *habitus*, these texts perform cultural work that gives a common matrix to Tudor society; they are Bourdieu's 'conductorless orchestra' (*Logic* 59) whose music we hear across early modern England. Through description and through presentation of method, de Certeau says, this discourse about tasks of daily experience adumbrates what will become – in Durkheim, in Freud – a theory of practices (64–5). Albeit inscribed, in Bourdieu's terms, in 'regularities' rather than 'rules,' theory can arise from the *habitus*.[8] After all, the hero of the age, Sir Philip Sidney, begins his ultimately theoretical *Apology for Poetry* (1595) by analogizing writing to horsemanship – as it is presented by an equerry who loves his art. Conversely, Juliana Barnes describes a dozen flies that still hold a high place among the thousands in the modern fishing repertoire, but she also teaches us to 'break no man's hedges in going about your sport'; courtesy and discretion are part of her art.

To my knowledge the art-text is the earliest example in England of a polysemous 'writing culture,' in part in the sense that interpretive anthropologist Clifford Geertz presents in *Local Knowledge* and elsewhere. The genre's writers are precisely writing down – describing the boundaries, announcing the purposes, providing the categories, listing the tools and ingredients – traditional practices that have heretofore gone unvoiced; the writers have fixed each practice in their, and their culture's, gaze for the first time, and thus begun to unveil its mysteries. Bourdieu has located the logic that 'generates an infinity of practices adapted to situations that are always different, on the basis of schemes so generally and automatically applied that they are only exceptionally converted into explicit principles' (*Logic* 101), and the art-texts present such exceptions. They appropriate what has been natural and give it cultural shape, expressing an entire world. While the writers are codifying traditional practices in which they have taken part, moreover, they are very rarely the originators of the practices they transcribe; only in special cases (usually later in the history of the genre) do they claim the personal authority of the subjective 'I.' The skills they present have been perfected collaboratively over time, each individual building upon the work of hundreds of predecessors; thus the text itself, even though signed, often seems impersonal and objective. Given the nature of the work that is presented, many of those practitioners – those silent collaborators – will have been women whose voices are lost in the history, or rather the ethnology, of the discourse.

The art-texts represent 'writing culture' in a material, even technological meaning, as well.[9] They occupy the social space of literacy, with all its early prestige, at just the moment when writing gains the added glamour – and the overwhelming power – of the printed page. Although the texts naïvely present themselves as unmediated, of course that is impossible; inevitably, their appropriation does violence to the textured richness of the *habitus*. These writers have learned that falconry can be tied down, navigation anchored in the harbour, by the constraints of print; thus they help us see that pushing customs into dead letters – circumscribing the free play of activity – has its costs. For the most part, though, they rejoice in the culture of writing. A pointed example is Peter Bales's *Arte of Brachygraphie*, a text so succinct that, to be more marketable, its second edition has been packaged together with others of Bales's compositions, *The Order of Orthographie* and *The Key of Kalygraphie*, into a handy seventy-five-page trilogy on writing as a physical activity. Calligraphy is penmanship, a serious challenge to the newly literate, and orthography is spelling, especially demanding in the sixteenth century when no dictionaries had achieved any agreement on what was 'correct.' The mysterious 'brachygraphy,' we learn from the title-page, is the skill 'to write as fast as a man speaketh, treatably, writing but one letter for a word': shorthand. A handwritten product, Bales repeatedly tells his readers, should be made 'swift,' 'true' (accurate), and 'faire,' or attractive; his treatise is aimed at achieving those goals, though the aesthetic value gets short shrift in his strenuous depiction. Repeatedly he remarks that shorthand can also make a document so secret that 'the curious Decipherer may sooner breake his braine, than reach to your meaning.' Sir Francis Walsingham, Elizabeth I's secretary of state and the father of all intelligence services, might take note.

The format of *The Arte of Brachygraphie* is exemplary for many of the briefer art-texts. Following the usual Elizabethan liminal matter of epistle to patron and commendatory poems from famous associates, it opens with a preface that flourishes some classical learning as a further warrant of the writer's credentials. In this case, the reader is told that Bales has not tasted of the herb Iris to gain eloquence, as Trojan orators did, and that he aims to persuade not with Aristotle's axioms but with Mercury's figs. The lesson, that is, will be short and sweet, not dry and long-winded. In the middle of the preface comes an exotic scholarly touch, appropriate to this topic: his art is similar to 'Aegiptian Hieroglyphickes,' though easier because it uses alphabetic characters rather than pictures. Metaphorical language of a certain charm characterizes the preface, as well: 'insatiable contempt from the Panther, foolish scoffing from the ... Asse, and unskillful deceit from the Camel' imagine new beast-fables. Of his opponents Bales says, with pantherian contempt, 'Their breath is like the Northwinde, bitter and tempestuous; their judgments rash, and no lesse perillous than the headlong Races of the Mauritanian Asses, that breake their neckes before they end their journeyes' ([Aiii(v)]–Biv). Blowhards, and their speech like their punishment is a phenomenon of nature, not mind.

Statements of purpose for an art are also usual, and Bales follows his preface with a handy list (at once 'defence' of the art and sales-pitch for the book) of the benefits inherent in the practice it will present. Abbreviated note-taking is, on the one hand, very valuable for students 'in all Arts and Sciences' both as a means to spare the memory by recording lectures and as a fast way to copy for themselves both books and manuscripts 'never yet imprinted' (this, at a time when books were expensive and copyright non-existent); on the other, more lofty hand, note-taking can preserve the sermons, lectures, and orations of learned men which are 'worthie the writing,' for the benefit of all 'posterities.' It is particularly useful for ambassadors and travellers into distant countries, who need to make quick notes of the manners and customs, policy and government they find in each nation. Purposes noble and pragmatic, learned and grubby – something for everyone. Brachygraphy, moreover, is like riding a bicycle: once you learn it, you retain it forever with very little practice, 'to your singular delight.' And a child of twelve can master it (Bales Bi[r]–Bii[r]).

Reached at last, the instructions *per se* – again, in generic fashion – are technical and explicit, utilizing terse rules and graphic tables, providing exercises for practice, and summarizing how to progress from the basic steps to full perfection. In good humanist fashion, the text rails against learning 'tittles and places by roate'; varied practice, not mere memorization, is the key to Bales's highly active skill. The probable reason why this early form of shorthand never caught on, however, is that memorization is virtually the only way to master it. The symbol for each word is its initial letter accompanied by an additional mark (a 'prick' or 'tittle,' which is to say a period or comma) placed in one of twelve specific places around the letter; since the placement of the mark is relatively arbitrary, it must be memorized. A and the first prick means 'abound,' A and the second 'about,' A and the third 'accept.' Even in an era when illiteracy demanded prodigious feats of memory, the challenge of learning much English diction in this way is Herculean; Bales advises the use of synonyms for words not so memorized. (He insouciantly acknowledges some of the wide range of problems: 'All wordes of like sounds, though of contrary sense, are to be written alike with the same letter and tittle, as, Sound and Swound; Here and Heare; Rod and Rode; and suchlike' – the mysteries multiply [Bvii(r)].) Once the student has memorized the tables of words, he is admonished to practise taking dictation, using sentences like 'Bishops begin to bestow both benefices and bookes, before they bargaine for birds that byte and break your bones' (Cvi[v]).[10] Yet again, making marks that act as signs is all that matters; sense will be no help whatsoever in transcribing such a sentence. Brachygraphy is writing entirely for its own sake.

Liminal matter, often in the form of quasi-appendices, is common at the conclusion of the art-texts, as well as the beginning. Bales, however, has elevated his afterthoughts with new titles. Truly filler, the ten-page essay on spelling gives – within a framework of praising Queen Elizabeth – the only advice possible for the uncertain orthography of the early modern era, still more than today: memorize lists of 'spelling words.' Half of the text has modest value as a reference for social historians, for it provides lists, by letter of the alphabet, of 'Christian or proper names' in current use; interestingly, masculine and feminine names are interleaved. For 'P,' the collection is Parnell, Paule, Penelope, Percivall, Persida, Peter, Petronilla, Philip, Philodelpha, Prudence, Prisilla (Bii[v]). From the perspective of discourse on knowledge, however, the chief value of this tiny treatise is to underline the passion for orderly categories.

The art concerned with handwriting, though it confirms Bales's practice of categorization as a compulsion, has its own quirks. Most pertinent is the emphasis on writing as a bodily activity that engages technical tools. The quill (to be chosen from the second or third feather on any wing, distinguished by its narrowing towards the end), once honed by a (specifically) Sheffield knife and smoothed on the dry upper leather of a shoe, becomes virtually a prosthesis of the body. The would-be penman must sit at a desk, leaning forward just the right amount to prevent pain and weariness, protect his sight by every possible means (such as covering the desk in green), hold the pen gently between two fingers and thumb, and ... proceed. In this description of practice, the words to be written are thoroughly erased; it is their formation from letters as physical signs that matters. Thus dry tracing to attain the correct feeling in the fingers – going through the motions in a gesture – is the only follow-up instruction that is proffered. 'Whosoever will write well,' Bales says, 'must let his minde, his eye, and his hande, goe all together in the making of every letter'; the role of the mind in this mysterious equation is, however, invisible. This treatise too is ingenuously extended; it is divided into eight hardly necessary chapters, each with its own flourished title, and as a handy mnemonic the content of each is summarized in a little doggerel that manages, more or less, to scan and to rhyme on alternate lines.

> Than exercise of everie
> Art the ground;
> Without the which
> no cunning comes to man;
> No rule can helpe but this,
> doe what we can.
> Wheretoo belongs
> both labour and delight,
> With diligent heede of minde,
> hand, and sight.   Evi[r], Fiii[r–v]

Writing serves poetry, of a sort; the 'delight' is not so easily to be found.

In this miniature trilogy, Bales – writing a text that explains how to write – has put serious effort into making that new-fangled object (and foremost technology of its day), a printed book. The emphasis on physically transcribing dictated words serves to underline the importance of spoken knowledge and its preservation, to suggest the rarity in 1597 (and therefore the value) of printed books, and to indicate that a culture of writing was, while in its earliest stages, still triumphantly recognized as a skill useful far beyond the aristocracy. By coming under the gaze of Peter Bales, by having certain boundaries drawn, by being constituted as both practical and potentially beautiful, by showing itself subject to order and regularities, writing enters the field of discourse. A theory of the practice will not be far to seek.

The art-texts, clearly, operate at a distance from the academic and intellectual worlds of Tudor/Stuart England. In a variety of ways – some readily visible but others needing to be teased out – many of them subvert the dominant culture in, and on, which they work. I have noted that some of them strip veils from the trade secrets of the mercantile guilds that dominated much commerce in early capitalism. More to the point of implicit subversion are the subject-positions of the writers: most are of course practitioners – artisans, craftsmen, in the case of falconers and huntsmen upper servants. The very fact of their writing is an assertion of significance, and status, that has gone unacknowledged by literary history. By the end of the sixteenth century, when a glover fathered Shakespeare, such audacity was no longer wholly unusual. But the notion that fishing might be anatomized by a woman was nonetheless regarded as shocking by early twentieth-century scholars – more so, no doubt, than in the fifteenth century, when the work of preparing food, and using the tools and practices related to it, was probably less gendered. It is true that we have no extrinsic evidence about Juliana Barnes, but her 'legendary' authorship speaks for an entire culture of working women.[11]

A clearer case of social subversion is Nicholas Hilliard, a lapidary and jeweller who became Queen Elizabeth I's sole licensed portrait-painter, a position that (since she wished to be represented as forever young) was inherently vulnerable. Hilliard's era was one of great social fluidity, hence social anxiety; with Leicester and Ralegh and Essex as his subjects, Hilliard felt his own status painfully and, in his *Arte of Limning*, played the game of striving to contest it. He claims that painting is an art most suitable for gentlemen, with their 'tender sences, quiet, and apt'; its materials have 'sweet odors [that] comforteth the braine and openeth the understanding' (113). I cannot help reading here the converse of his premise: not that gentlemen should be painters, but that painters should be made gentlemen. Hilliard's only cultural capital is his taste and his talent, embodied in his eye and his hand; he has a great stake in claiming both the originality of his work and his desire for the broader horizons that his agency ought to provide. Self-creation, self-authorization through control of the works of the body as informed – and expressed – by the mind is the implicit goal for many writers of art-texts; *praxis*, not birth or education, should define social place.

To the discourse of systematic science on the rise, wrapped in grand theory, these small texts apparently formed a modest threat. In *The Advancement of Learning*, Bacon at least nods to multidisciplinary seamlessness and the value of experience. In a form of proleptic footnote to his survey of human philosophy – 'knowledge of ourselves' – he remarks,

> All partitions of knowledges [should] be accepted, rather for lines and veins, than for sections and separations; and ... the continuance and entireness of knowledge be preserved. For ... particular sciences [have] become barren, shallow, and erroneous ... while they have not been nourished from the common fountain. (205)

But Bacon cannot sustain that breadth of vision for the future constitution of discourse. To be sure, in his defence of the learning to be found in books, he offers substantial sidebars on the uses of empirical experience, on the challenge of the world of (political) affairs, on the importance of applying knowledge to 'the benefit and use of men ... and the relief of man's estate,' even on the desirability of uniting contemplation (the mind's work) with action (the body's work) (147).[12] But these are merely the concessions required of a practising lawyer and statesman. The overwhelming assertion of *The Advancement* is 'the dignity and excellency of knowledge and learning in that whereunto man's nature doth most aspire' (167). And by 'knowledge' there is no doubt that he means canonical *scientia*.

In the realm of the academy, in fact, Bacon tried to erase the *artes*. A major intellectual error, he holds, is 'the over-early and peremptory reduction of knowledge into arts and methods; from which ... commonly sciences receive small or no augmentation.' Arts are not 'matter[s] of fact' but – spoken with disdain – a 'matter of opinion.' Bacon is coolly dismissive of 'some barren relations touching the invention of arts or usages,' for in 'arts mechanical ... artillery, sailing, printing, and the like ... the first deviser comes shortest ... and [they] were grossly managed at the first' (142–5).[13] In his bold claims for the authority of the individual investigator, Bacon cannot imagine that the 'first deviser' merely inaugurates the practice upon which the cultural *habitus*, thickly described, is built. In the stately march of systematic reason, intellectual effort is superior to material production, the sciences to practice, abstraction to quotidian life. By *The Great Instauration* (1620), Bacon easily proves himself the distant impetus for the contesting egos engaged in the Human Genome Project.

Whether conceptualized by Bacon or by Descartes, the new, rationalist science of the seventeenth century eclipsed the texts that 'do not know what it is they know'; science is, as Bourdieu says, constructed against them. As a genre, the English *arte* fades into a mannerist, indeed self-parodic phase in the politics of the Restoration and the drolleries of eighteenth-century London. Thus my initial analogy with 'how-to' advice books, offered for easy identification, is far from representing linear genealogy. The modern non-books – thin, repetitive, graphically designed to be skimmed, focused on fetishist topics like diets and the stock market – clearly have no other goal but success as commodities in the marketplace responding to social desires or anxieties; any attempt at enlightenment or serious instruction is derisory. And (despite the frequent presence of a more- or less-visible collaborator) they normally proclaim the unique authorship of a single, privileged expert whose advice is, or should be, sought after: Martha Stewart, Warren Buffett, and so on.

By what warrant, then, can I name the art-texts pre-theory, or even pre-history of theory? First, the longer and more elaborated of them display a capacity for analysis and for generalization, thinking practices that seem to me to initiate the construction of theory. Leaving aside the Oxbridge-educated Philip Sidney, Hilliard's *Arte of Limning*, for instance, exhibits a habit (like Peter Bales's) of 'distinction,' drawn from scholastic disputation, which we would call categorization and see as a prime attribute of intellect at work. Hilliard also deploys – not to make, but simply to buttress, claims – self-conscious citation of 'authority' from published texts as well as experience, and from the contemporary art-theorists Lomazzo and Dürer as well as standards like Cicero; again like Bales, he makes structural uses of analogy, as well as ornamenting his prose with homely metaphors. To be sure, these learned gestures are a façade over the core of personal narrative, definitions, recipes for paints, and shy parades of terms-of-art that form the genuine charm of his text; their presence helps Hilliard – like many other *arte*-writers – to claim personal authority in a literate world that privileges such forms. They take the first steps towards what Bourdieu has called 'a critical objectification of the epistemological and social conditions that make possible both a reflexive return to the subjective experience of the world and also the objectification of the objective conditions of the experience' (*Logic* 25). And the formal theorizing gestures point in the direction the genre takes: by 1609, John Blagrave can valorize his text as the 'theorick of the arte' of dialling, or clockmaking.[14] These early modern texts may not show us 'theory as practice,' but they adumbrate a technology of writing 'practice as theory' for their *habitus*.

The more potent positioning of the art-texts, however, is as a form of early modern cultural studies that de Certeau might relish. The great majority of them are thoroughly embedded in the material world in its spatial order – whether clocks or cradles, guns or compasses – and in the radical agency of bodies in interaction with material objects; what they describe, though in some cases pursuits of leisure, is work. The performances that the art-texts prescribe occur in what de Certeau calls a 'nowhen,' a synchronic 'place' that incorporates the remembered past of the writer/teacher and the imagined future of the reader/user. Each writer circumscribes and names, in an unsystematic fashion that creates his own system, the 'local habitation' that his *technē* maps, and he walks his readers along the pathway through it. (I might have said he composes his own grammar and gives us the phrasebook to manage, as tourists, in his language.) 'The art of turning phrases,' says de Certeau, 'finds an equivalent in an art of composing a path' – and vice versa (94, 100).[15]

The technologies available to sixteenth-century operators are not complex, but their products, whether objects or ideologies, can be both sophisticated and revealing. And the texts that describe these productive practices are themselves products: contributions to an information economy that not only make available that knowledge that has been buried in the *habitus* but shape new vocations, new (or reconstituted) social identities, hence new subjectivities. In telling their writers' crafty secrets, in revealing the secret code of such techniques as shorthand, they enter the cultural field. Bourdieu's trenchant remark in *Distinction*, 'Most products only derive their social value from the social use that is made of them' (21), is applicable equally to the art-texts and to the products of their eponymous practices. Those practices are, moreover, subversively democratic: anyone who can read – through the course of the sixteenth century, an increasingly large proportion of the populace – and get access to a craftsman's materials may perform these practices. (Nicholas Hilliard hoped that the unwashed would not try their hands at limning – he did not publish his manuscript – but, in a clear operation of *habitus*, others pirated and printed it; his hope was utterly vain.) Everyone can do it, and (just as important, in the long run) almost anyone can write about it.

As I have said, the writers of these texts, with rare exceptions, were drawn from the middling sort, and the lower middle, at that. Standing outside the academic or 'public intellectual' world of Bacon, Newton, and that ilk, these writers deterritorialize the social space both of the university's structure for the liberal arts and of the imminent university scientific machine. With the audacity of a fishing woman, they claim specific knowledges as their own and thus, although with little visible intent, insouciantly subvert the hegemonic pretensions of an increasingly powerful academy. What begins in expression of control over one's own bodily skill and a carefully defined domain of *praxis* can evolve into a (largely inchoate) desire for a larger world attained by one's own agency. Their implicit recasting of the social field for information technology did not formally succeed, but it could not be repressed forever. The early modern theorists are perhaps best imagined, among modern figures, by Gramsci:

There is no human activity from which every form of intellectual participation can be excluded: *homo faber* cannot be separated from *homo sapiens*. Each man, finally, outside his professional activity, carries on some form of intellectual activity, that is, he is a 'philosopher,' an artist, ... he participates in a particular conception of the world, ... and therefore contributes to sustain a conception of the world or to modify it, that is, to bring into being new modes of thought. (9)

There is, in short, a ready dialogic relation between the polysemous writing culture of Elizabethan craftsmen and emerging intellectuals and the late twentieth-century turn towards the discourse of material culture and its multiple meanings. Contemporary cultural studies, contesting the distinction between (high) dignified knowledge and (low) 'barren usages' made by Bacon and enormously elaborated in the seventeenth and eighteenth centuries, can relish the confidence with which *arte*-writers set about their task. In the first flush of claiming status for newly printed (though rarely new-minted) knowledge, they exhibit no defensiveness. To them, *all* knowledge is worth having, all practices located within their historical and social conditions are valuable to situate, to analyse, to weave into a texture of meaning. And with rare exceptions, no cult of personality surrounds the transcriber of a practice, who is absorbed, and sometimes effaced, in a rich cultural pattern that is decades, often centuries old. Boundaries between 'high' and 'low,' intellectual and practical, are erased in this writing; the body in space is as central to experience as the mind in discourse, and procedures have equal status with ideologies as 'structuring structures.' These writers are the first in English to explore cultural, rather than literary, philosophical, or historical, texts; they begin in tentative ways to theorize, but more important, they undertake the cultural work – provide the instantiations – that makes possible the theorizing work of a Bourdieu, a LeFebvre, a de Certeau. They precede the sharp boundaries, and the hierarchies, among disciplines of formal academic knowledge that would be rigidified in the Enlightenment – and they foreshadow the troubling of those boundaries by many contemporary theorists. As the study of material culture moves away from the discourses of high theory, the art-texts may be a welcome reminder that cultural studies, as well as theory, has a history. De Certeau, to be sure, sees another outcome; he says that, when 'scientific' knowledge is objectified and removed from the realm of practice, 'what remains on the margins or in the interstices of scientific or cultural orthopraxis' – the 'everyday virtuosities that science doesn't know what to do with' and that are inherently subjective – takes a different form. 'The poetic or tragic murmurings of the everyday ... enter massively into the novel or the short story'; 'everyone's micro-stories' turn into literature (70).

NOTES

1 De Certeau, who believes that the concept of *habitus* (61) has been fetishized, would presumably not make this connection – in part because, on his reading, analysis of particular, empirical practices as such is gradually erased in Bourdieu's theory-building (50ff). I find *habitus* unusually illuminating for study of the cultural space of early modern England. Not casting his gaze behind Bacon, de Certeau imagines *artes* (65) as '"know-how" without a discourse, essentially without writing'; my project is situated in that absence.

2 Rudolph Bell's 1999 study *How to Do It* explores some of their counterparts, the sixteenth-century Italian manuals of advice on family life from conception to widowhood. Valuable as a compendium delimiting these texts as a subgenre of knowledge and instruction, Bell's study only minimally theorizes the manuals as cultural products; he misses an opportunity to look beyond printing history and reading practices. Other scholars (Rebecca Bushnell on gardening manuals, Gail Paster on medical texts), are inquiring into sixteenth-century manuals 'vertically,' on specific individual topics, from multiple optics; they do not treat the *artes* as a genre.

3 First editions of the Bales and Jones texts, published in London (Bales facsimile also available as STC #1311, Amsterdam, 1972, not paginated by modern convention), are available at the Folger Shakespeare Library, Washington, DC.

4 De Certeau locates the reversal to the modern opposition in Diderot and the *encyclopédistes* (66).

5 In the Renaissance, the *artes* gave way in educational practice, at the hands of the *humanista*, to the *auctores* – or 'great books' of a canon – precisely because humanist scholar/teachers wished to claim the authority of discursive doctrine.

6 See Ben Jonson, *Volpone*, Mosca's 'soliloquy' at 3.1.7–32.

7 An English translation of Ovid was published by the early printer Wynkyn de Worde in London in 1513.

8 See Bourdieu, *The Logic of Practice* 53: 'Objectively "regulated" and "regular" without being in any way the product of obedience to rules' does not cite Foucault but is strongly reminiscent of his thought.

9 This analysis is brilliantly presented in Jonathan Goldberg's *Writing Matter*, in which he illustrates his argument not only with Richard Mulcaster's *Elementarie* (1582), a text on the early institutionalized training of young boys, but also with a Spanish handbook called *Arte Subtilissima* (1550), which focuses on *escrevir* as elegant handwriting itself. De Certeau, extending the problematic of relations to the act of writing and the written text (98), adds further illumination.

10 The text concludes with a passage for 'dictation,' fortunately not alliterative, to be used for practice.

11 Antiquarians and scholars at the turn of the twentieth century spare little scorn on the mere 'attribution,' 'assumption,' or 'legend' that the text could have been written by a woman who is otherwise unknown to history, though usually credited with the title 'Dame'; G.E. Bentley (*The Art of Angling* 1–2) reviews the controversy, including the suggestion of Wagstaff that 'Julian the Berner' was a keeper of hunting dogs on a medieval estate. Lyla Foggia rhetorically inquires, 'Are we to believe that 500 years ago a woman would be credited with authoring a document she did not write – when it's extraordinary enough that a woman would be credited at all?'

12 The greatest error in the pursuit of knowledge, he says, is using it to distract from boredom, to achieve reputation for learnedness, to win in debate – illustrations of pride.

13 The context is credulousness: the public succumbing to ideas without the 'observation and rule' of true science.

14 See John Blagrave, *The Art of Dyalling* (London, 1609) – one of the exceptional cases where the writer claims 'the greater part wrought by diverse new conceits of the Author, never yet extant, now published' – on the title-page.

15 See also Bourdieu, *The Logic of Practice* 53–5.

WORKS CITED

Bacon, Francis. *The Advancement of Learning. Francis Bacon.* Ed. Brian Vickers. Oxford: Oxford UP, 1996.

Bales, Peter. *The Arte of Brachygraphie.* 1597.

Barnes, Juliana. *The Treatyse on Fysshing with an Angle.* Ed. W.L. Braekman. Brussels: Scripta, 1980.

Bell, Rudolph. *How to Do It.* Chicago: U of Chicago P, 1999.

Bentley, G.E. *The Art of Angling.* Princeton: Princeton UP, 1958.

Blagrave, John. *The Art of Dyalling,* London 1609. Amsterdam: Theatrum Orbis Terrarum; New York: Da Capo, 1968.

Bourdieu, Pierre. *Distinction.* Trans. Richard Nice. Cambridge: Harvard UP, 1984.

– *The Logic of Practice.* Trans. Richard Nice. Stanford: Stanford UP, 1990.

de Certeau, Michel. *The Practice of Everyday Life.* Trans. Steven Rendall. Berkeley: U of California P, 1984.

Foggia, Lyla. *Reel Women.* Hillsboro, Oregon: Beyond Words, 1995.

Geertz, Clifford. *The Interpretation of Cultures.* New York: Basic Books, 1973.

– *Local Knowledge.* New York: Basic Books, 1983.

Goldberg, Jonathan. *Writing Matter.* Stanford: Stanford UP, 1990.

Gramsci, Antonio. *Selections from the Prison Notebooks.* Trans. Quintin Hoare and Geoffrey Smith. New York: International Publishers, 1971.

Hilliard, Nicholas. *Nicholas Hilliard's Art of Limning.* Ed. Arthur F. Kinney and Linda B. Salamon. Boston: Northeastern UP, 1983.

Derrida, Foucault, and the Archiviolithics of History

MICHAEL J. O'DRISCOLL

I shall hold myself, once again, to the instance of the archive.

Derrida, Archive Fever

I. Materiality and S/Citation

From the tangled underroot of ideas that is Ezra Pound's 'paideuma' to the textual 'assemblages' of Deleuze and Guattari; from the labyrinth of Joyce's *Finnegans Wake* to Derrida's inferno in the house of Freud; from the fantastical imaginings of Borges to the very rule of Foucauldian discourse; the archive may well be the central figure of twentieth-century literary and theoretical engagements with questions of knowledge.[1] As, in Borges' words, a technology 'whose hazardous volumes run the constant risk of being changed into others and in which everything is affirmed, denied, and confused as by a divinity in delirium' (86), the archive has served as a consistent but conflicted figure of otherwise disparate constructions. Each of these authors – not to mention many, many others – takes up a subject-position within the archive in a manner that suggests that this cultural space of the imagination, while ever shifting and resistant to the limitations of its own definite article, nonetheless bears directly on a variety of literary and theoretical practices dispersed across a single epistemic field. With that in mind, I would like to argue that in our attempts to engage the histories of theory, the archive must be regarded as other than purely figural – as other than organic growth, fiery destruction, or deranged god. Indeed, I would like to argue further that such metaphoric reconstructions of the twentieth-century condition of knowledge effectively sublimate what might otherwise be regarded as crucial to the conceptualization of the archive as a site of theoretical and cultural exchange: that is, the socio-history of what I will call 'textual management,' or that range of material practices that bear the trace of the archive's emergence into discourse, and that simultaneously constitute the possible conditions of an archival discourse.

This paper will suggest, through a rehistoricizing of poststructuralism's fascination with the archive as figure, that contemporary theories of knowledge – too often understood in absolute, ahistorical, universal terms – are, in fact, the by-product of a lengthy and dramatic shift in the way in which we manage material texts and the manner in which that materiality is brought into being by discursive practices. That is to say, the archive is not only *constructed by* theoretical discourse, but also *constructs* theoretical discourse. Indeed, the archive serves as the very *technology of theory*, in the sense that discursive technologies are assemblages that perform further intellectual work in the same manner that any technology (as we may conceive of that notion in more materialist terms) is caught up in a cycle of (re)production without origin or end. Contemporary theories of intertextuality, challenges to the status of the book as a bound embodiment of meaning, could only be realized amidst a proliferation of printed material and corresponding anxieties over the burgeoning archive that is the cumbersome inheritance of twentieth-century thought. At the same time, however, it must be recognized that the material archive itself neither exists prior to its discursive representations nor is entirely constructed by that discourse; rather the archive as the site, or situation, of theory is an effect of power, and specifically the effect of what Judith Butler has called the 'reiterative citational practice by which power produces the effects that it names' (2).

Butler's work, while directed towards the field of gender theory and the politics of sexuality, intervenes productively in more general philosophical debates over materialism, and in a manner that will inform the following argument. 'Sex,' Butler tells us, 'is part of a regulatory practice that produces the bodies it governs' and 'is an ideal construct which is forcibly materialized through time' (1). In this sense, Butler sets sex in relation to bodies in the same manner as Foucault sets the archive in relation to discourse; indeed, one might surmise that the body functions as an archive of sorts, constituted by the discourse in and around sex, at the same time that it provides the repertoire of statements that constitute the discourse of sex. However, unlike Foucault, Butler refuses to posit 'sex' – which she insistently, and correctly, places between destabilizing quotation marks – as somehow existing prior to its materialization or as a 'static condition of the body.' Indeed, sex is not some pre-given material condition upon which the cultural constructs of gender are imposed, but, rather, sex as a regulatory norm is indissociable from the bodily materializations that it governs through the process of re-iterative, performative citation. To eradicate this process of materiali-zation – from either the standpoint of a crude materialism or a radical constructivism – is to deny critical access to those effects that are the workings of power:

> The production of material effects is the formative or constitutive workings of power, a production that cannot be construed as a unilateral movement from cause to effect. 'Materiality' appears only when its status as con-tingently constituted through discourse is erased, concealed, covered over. Materiality is the dissimulated effect of power. (251)

In considering the material archive as a 'dissimulated effect of power,' my attempt here is to avoid broaching the subject of the archive in a manner equatable with those thinkers of sex challenged by Butler, for whom, she tells us, '"sex" becomes something like a fiction, perhaps a fantasy, retroactively installed at a prelinguistic site to which there is no direct access' (5). One might well contend that Foucault's archive enjoys such a privileged site, but that contention extends equally to post-structural thought in general, or at least to its most exemplary moments. This results, in part, from the insistent dissociation of the archive as *site* from the archive as *citation*, from the binary opposition between materiality and ideality, from an uncontested logic of causality, that would see the archive as either constructive of discourse, or con-structed by discourse, but never at one and the same time both that which names and that which is the effect of naming.

Indeed, in naming the archive, this paper gathers around the homo-phonic coincidence of the infinitives 'to site' and 'to cite.'[2] In their most archaic forms, the two terms are variant spellings of each other, but oth-erwise the relationship is one of pure, however fortuitous, contingency. The former derives from back-formation of the Latin noun *situs*, mean-ing 'local position'; the latter from the Latin term *citare*, meaning to move, excite, or summon. It is this very tension, however, between the material conditions of one's socio-historic position and the dynamics of writing practices that are at once both transgressive in their movement or ex-citation and regulatory in their summoning or legal citation that is in question. What is the relationship, we might ask, between the archive as a poststructural *site* and the archive as the scene of poststructural *cita-tion*? What does it mean, in the many senses of the word, to *s/cite* the archive? My reference to ex-citation, which we might well consider the pleasure principle of the incessant *fort/da* of poststructural theory,[3] should bring to mind the countervailing, destructive impulse of the Freudian death-drive, the 'archive fever,' that Derrida locates in psycho-analytic practice, and at the same time should invite us to consider the outside of citation, to ask what is excluded by the theorization of cita-tional practices; my reference to citation as a legal summoning, mean-while, should bring to mind the Foucauldian archive that functions as the regulatory system that, Foucault tells us, determines the emergence of certain statements into discourse and the relationship between the elements of that discourse. In other words, the summons of the archive serves us with the reminder that we are regarding here both, and at once, a site of power and a citation of law.

What is curious about the seemingly common focus on the archive in contemporary theory is the tendency of poststructuralism, particularly at its, again, most exemplary moments, to situate the writing subject squarely within the archive, as a central figure of that theory's own histo-ricity, even while effacing the machinations of theory's own archival technologies of power: the operations of s/citation. This paradox emerges in chiasmatic fashion in Derrida's critique of the archaeologi-cal as origin in *Archive Fever* and Foucault's analysis of the archival as law in *The Archaeology of Knowledge*. Both writings share in an intellectual genealogy that draws from cultural anthropologies and practices of tex-tual management mediated by the poetics of modernism. In this sense, whether understood in Derrida's terms as the space of living memory in its 'insistent impression through the unstable feeling of a shifting figure' (*Archive Fever* 29), or in Foucault's terms as a network of discursive regu-larities that constitutes 'the general system of the formation and trans-formation of statements' (*Archaeology of Knowledge* 130), the archive shifts from its literal status as the space in which we might situate (or site) Derrida's and Foucault's writing practices of citation, to its figural status as the realm of a metaphoric construct that ideally might remain always outside those practices. In both cases, what we are witness to is poststructuralism's continuing effort to extricate itself from the s/cite of the archive. My hope is to demonstrate in what sense the deconstructive and the archaeological – or the future anterior of various technologies of writing and the anticipatory sedimentations of discursive power – sublimate the archive as poststructural *site* in favour of regarding the practices of textual management as pure *citation* without consideration for its emergence into the material practices of our everyday lives.

The re-cursive (one might say re-iterative or citational or performative) effect of the Derridean and Foucaultian reduction of the archive to its purely figural status is to reenact, rather than cancel, the dissimulation of power that constitutes materiality. If the coming into being of matter conceals the very power effects of the citational performance that delimits and demarcates its existence, the sublimation of that materiality also precludes the resistances, gaps, disidentifications that gather around the reiteration of the law of the archive, the archive as either regulation (Foucault) or commandment (Derrida). One cannot, in contesting the inscribed space of a purely figural archive, cite that which is excluded by – and therefore defines the boundaries of – the materialization of the archive as site. In other words, to reduce the material status of the archive to a pure figurality not only conceals the very concealment of power (a mode of representation we might consider analogous to the third order of Baudrillard's simulacrum),[4] but also effectively disavows any possible resistance to that power. Furthermore, to fail to account for the citation of the archive as site – to argue for an archive that is either prior to or outside of discourse – is to fail to recognize, as it were, the archive of the archive, or the archive as its own regulatory ideal.

II. Epistemic and Textual Management

To distinguish between *citing* the archive and *siting* the archive is to distinguish also between the management of ideal knowledge and the management of material texts. This heuristic opposition is, however, as critical as it is illusory – the by-product of a centuries-long shift in the status of encyclopedic projects as well as cataloguing and indexing practices, in which the emergence of a burgeoning material archive serves, following Butler, actually to dissimulate the machinations of power of which it is an effect. Nonetheless, to foreground the management of texts is to bring into relief those processes by which the archive emerges as an effect of s/citation. On the one hand, epistemic management is charged with the organization of knowledge and seemingly elides or evaporates what are actually overwhelming quantities of material inscriptions. Of course, while epistemic management is figured as the transcendence of the archive, it can do no more than displace temporarily the material documents on which it is dependent. On the other

hand, textual management recognizes and privileges the sheer materiality of the text and, through the manipulation and juxtaposition of documentary materials, seeks to situate itself advantageously within the space
of the archive. Historically, this difference first comes to the fore in the
shifting metaphorics that undergird encyclopedic projects of various
kinds, but most specifically in the split between Diderot's and d'Alembert's understanding of the *Encyclopédie* and their commentaries on that
most important of Enlightenment projects. In practising an overt brand
of materialist textuality, Diderot demonstrates that such polymathic literary forms cannot be understood as transparent containers of their
contents. Rather Diderot's encyclopedia accounts for the materialization of the archive as a process of reiterative citation.

In the wake of Bacon's revision of the encyclopedic project as an
organic tree of knowledge – laid out in *The Great Instauration* and *The
New Organon* – and his recognition of the disorder of the world, and
given that 'an encyclopedic tree which attempted to portray it would be
disfigured, indeed utterly destroyed' (d'Alembert 46), Enlightenment
encyclopedists attempted to supplement the metaphor of the tree with
that of the map – a restriction or localization of knowledge that still per-
mitted a mastery of the world through the privileged viewpoint of
figures like d'Alembert's colossal cartographer, for whom the encyclopedic project consists of

> ... collecting knowledge into the smallest area possible and of placing the
> philosopher at a vantage point, so to speak, high above this vast labyrinth,
> whence he can perceive the principal sciences and the arts simultaneously.
> From there he can see at a glance the objects of their speculations and the
> operations which can be made on these objects; he can discern the general
> branches of human knowledge, the points that separate or unite them; and
> sometimes he can even glimpse the secrets that relate them to one another.
> It is a kind of world map which is to show the principal countries, their
> position and their mutual dependence, the road that leads directly from
> one to the other. This road is often cut by a thousand obstacles, which are
> known in each country only to the inhabitants or to travelers, and which
> cannot be represented except in individual, highly detailed maps. These
> individual maps will be the different articles of the *Encyclopedia* and the
> Tree or Systematic Chart will be its world map. (49)

This towering encyclopedist is, in d'Alembert's conception, an emblem
of epistemic mastery that looms over the landscape of knowledge direct-

ing readers across its winding roadways and through its labyrinthine passages. This is the central conception of the encyclopedic writer – the persona who oversees intellectual history from a privileged viewpoint. Given that such figures as the labyrinth and the winding path are capable of 'disfiguring' the metaphor of the tree, d'Alembert invokes the metaphor of the map in a telling bid to arrest the flux of knowledge.

The successive and supplementary metaphors (circle, tree, mirror, map, and storehouse) that govern encyclopedism amid the proliferation of texts that characterizes typographic culture suggest an emerging crisis in the field of epistemic management: the gradual recognition of the unwieldiness of the encyclopedic project in the face of a burgeoning textual archive. Indeed, in a passage towards the end of his entry 'Encyclopédie' in the fifth volume of the *Encyclopédie*, Diderot describes a world crushed beneath the weight of accumulated texts and calls for the dis-accumulation of knowledge in a gesture that recognizes physical textuality as a threat to epistemic mastery.[5] Diderot's rather bold solution is an encyclopedia grounded in a materialist discourse.[6] Diderot privileges radial reading – the term is Jerome McGann's – that works against a static or linear *Encyclopédie* in favour of a text that functions as a dynamic set of cross-references or intertexts.[7] Such a reader – in contradistinction to the passive d'Alembertian reader – makes intuitive poetic leaps between the subject matter of the *Encyclopédie*, creating revolutionary advances in thought and generating further texts. Diderot articulates a materialist theory of poetics that recognizes the *Encyclopédie* as a series of interanimated conversations in the form of material documents. However, Diderot's poetics is not quite the inverse of d'Alembert's in that the encyclopedia is not a map of knowledge created by a masterful cartographer, but is rather generated by and generative of discourse (in that it provokes speculation and, thus, further knowledge) as a site that marks the accumulation of reiterative citations of power. Not surprisingly, Diderot's conception of the encyclopedic project is not at all typical of the genre; indeed, his reconstruction of the problem of epistemic management as a problem of textual management drew severe critical attacks: Diderot was berated by his contemporaries for creating a system of cross-references and interdependent texts that forged gaps that could only be filled – as Diderot himself maintained – by an advanced, intuitive poetic reader, thus making self-evident the materialization of discourse as an effect of power. It could be argued that the materialist poetics envisioned by Diderot in the production of the *Encyclopédie* has been suppressed in a tradition of intellectual discourse that could not tolerate the instability of such radical poetic materialism and textual dynamism even while maintaining the illusion of an epistemic mastery founded, ironically, on the act of supplementation (either encyclopedic or metaphoric). In either case, the delimitation of textual and epistemic management, of the material and metaphoric archive, of the archive as site and the archive as citation, is reiterated in the anxious investment of modern poetics and contemporary theory in siting or citing, but never s/citing, the archive.

This burgeoning material archive to which I've referred, coextensive with pressing issues of location reference or the situation of texts, is manifest in the technologies of textual management formulated with an intensity that is specific to the last century and a half: that is, document retrieval (such as the codification of cataloguing systems, the redescription of shelving methods), institutional structures (including the formation of indexing societies, the professionalization of librarianship), architectural movements (for example, the adoption of expansive reading rooms such as the former BML), and discursive representations (including histories and pedagogical programs). Such practices mark the archive as a process, rather than a product, of materialization that adopts its own boundaries and fixities over time, and invites us to consider the practice of textual management as an effect of power, as the materialization of those regulatory ideals or reiterative citations that constitute the archive. The archive is always, first and foremost, historical – that is, it is neither event nor object. Furthermore, such a focus on the practice of textual management recognizes, considers axiomatic, the notion that the law of the archive, the summons of the archive, is dependent on the very citations it apparently commands or authorizes. To refuse the materiality of the archive, and thereby the materiality of those writing practices that take place within the archive, is to fail to take into account, in Foucault's own terms, the archive (like the prison) as 'an instrument and vector of power' (*Discipline and Punish* 30).

The reconceptualization of the archive in the late nineteenth and twentieth centuries – that is, at the apex of typographic technology and at the dawn of what we now recognize as the age of information – marks a significant rupture in our relationship to the materiality of that institution. This rupture, which I would regard as the emerging emphasis on textual management rather than epistemic management, can also be traced in modern literature, however, an equally reliable register of this shift. The reconfiguration of the imaginative space of the library is contemporary with the composition of *Bouvard and Pécuchet*, serves as the background to the futile bibliographic endeavours of Flaubert's clerks, and, as Foucault has suggested in his discussion of *The Temptation* in his essay 'The Fantasia of the Library,' marks the inaugural moment of modernism in which the imagination 'grows among signs, from book to book, in the interstice of repetitions and commentaries; it is born and takes shape in the interval between books. It is a phenomenon of the library' (90–1). Flaubert's *encyclopédie en farce*, as Ezra Pound describes it, ushers modernism, in its growing awareness of the materiality of discourse, into the archive.

Pound himself, in elaborate documentary assemblages such as the *Cantos* and *Guide to Kulchur*, attempts to engage the problematics of the archive: in employing systems of reference rather than meaning, Pound navigates and exploits the intertextual in an overtly graphic, particular, and concrete manner. It is important to recognize, however, the agonistic, decidedly traumatic, nature of Pound's project. Consider, for example, a moment recorded by Pound in 1938, more than thirty years after the fact. In his *Guide to Kulchur*, the author recalls what might be best characterized as the primal scene of his introduction to the tangled complex of the European archive and a startling encounter with the sheer materiality of discourse:

> About thirty years ago, seated on one of the very hard, very slippery, thoroughly uncomfortable chairs of the British Museum main reading room, with a pile of large books at my right hand and a pile of somewhat smaller ones at my left hand, I lifted my eyes to the tiers of volumes and false doors covered with imitation bookbacks which surround that focus of learning. Calculating the eye-strain and the number of pages per day that a man could read, with deduction for say at least 5% of one man's time for reflection, I decided against it. There must be some other way for a human being to make use of that vast cultural heritage. (53)

Pound's decided unease with his seat in the BML – which may well be synecdochic for the larger unease he feels between and beneath the daunting, circular stacks of the reading room – is met with a rage to order manifest in the tidy stacking of books into large and small piles and the calculating mind that reckons days, minutes, and percentages into his prospective plan of study. Pound also seems to recognize an insidious risk that his conjecture presents. He takes note of 'the false doors' and 'imitation bookbacks' – the threatening errancy of hidden passages and deceptive texts – that promise either to mislead the reader or to derail any strategic approach to the volumes surrounding the reading room. This moment in the BML functions in *Guide to Kulchur* as the *raison d'être* of the ideogrammic method of the *Cantos*, Pound's attempt to create a textual utopia out of what he calls 'the mass of undigested heteroclite materials' of twentieth-century Euro-American culture. However, despite its reliance on, and even foregrounding of, its own documentary processes, the *Cantos* is ultimately intended to be a self-effacing text that dissolves in the plenitude of its own meaning. The heterotopia that is Pound's *Cantos* – that compendium of archival documents and textual fragments, that sum of countless gestures towards fictive and factive images – is intended to give way to a linguistic utopia in which its real-world textual referents might somehow coexist in the non-space of language and citation, or within the walled city of Dioce, the archetypal *polis* of human order that is itself a purely textual referent.

III. Archiviolithics

It is, I would argue, this agonistic dimension of Enlightenment encyclopedism and such high modernist projects as Pound's *Cantos* that is the unwitting inheritance of poststructuralist theory that seeks, among other things, to achieve the belated modernist dream of the self-effacing archive, a dream conceived in response to the very conditions of the history of textual management that I've merely intimated here. Indeed, we might well regard poststructural theory as the Freudian *Nachträglichkeit* of Pound's encounter with the archive, the return from the future that demarcates the import of such traumatic moments.[8] While I will shortly consider the history of the Derridean archive itself as a series of returns and loops, this more local question of traumatic return can be recognized in a number of forms: not only in such wonderful textual constructions as *Glas*, which derives its strategies of collage and montage from high modernism, but also in his pronouncement that the modern literary text is more likely to destabilize the self-presence of logocentric thought: 'This,' Derrida writes,

> is the meaning of the work of Fenollosa whose influence upon Ezra Pound and his poetics is well-known: this irreducibly graphic poetics was, with that of Mallarmé, the first break in the most entrenched Western tradition. The fascination that the Chinese ideogram exercised on Pound's writing may thus be given all its historical significance. (*Of Grammatology* 92)

Despite his awareness of this 'first break' – which comes dangerously close to the promise of an origin, of the commencement of the *archē* – at no point, unfortunately, does Derrida really describe this 'historical' significance. On the contrary, he gestures quite generally towards a causal relationship through which some mysterious agency of intellectual history works towards the 'death of the civilization of the book, of which so much is said and which manifests itself particularly through a convulsive proliferation of libraries' (*Of Grammatology* 8). This agency, however, is in no way mysterious and the book and the archive are in no way at odds with each other. In fact, the proliferation of libraries – and this historical actuality is crucial to the emergence of textual management – reinforces the status of the book in all its materiality. Such a notion demands a reconsideration of Derrida's claim that

> The idea of the book, which always refers to a natural totality, is profoundly alien to the sense of writing. It is the encyclopedic protection of theology and of logocentrism against the disruption of writing, against its aphoristic energy, and, as I shall specify later, against difference in general. If I distinguish the text from the book, I shall say that the destruction of the book as it is now under way in all domains, denudes the surface of the text. (*Of Grammatology* 18)

To associate the book with the encyclopedia, as Derrida does here, is to claim the precise opposite of what I am contending: the encyclopedic project (as a form of epistemic management) is about the very effacement of books, not about their actualization; the encyclopedic is about the warding off of the threat of material textuality in order to ensure the mastery of knowledge and the dissimulation of power of which the materialization of knowledge is an effect. With his pronouncement of 'the end of the book and the beginning of writing,' it is to the daunting presence of this burgeoning archive of material culture that Derrida responds in a manner commensurate with his modernist predecessors.

The excision of material books in favour of ideal texts in these early stages of the grammatological program is a clear gesture of epistemic mastery. In the later stages of Derrida's project, however, he tends to exploit the graphic qualities of archival documents in a manner that, ironically enough, reinforces the materiality of discourse. The early Derrida effects a sublimation of the archive – a treatment of the archive as pure citation – in a manner that follows the modernist bid for mastery; the later Derrida desublimates the archive, reverting to a form of determinism in which the archive is understood as pure site, prior to the discourse to which it gives shape. One might contend that Derrida's theorization of the archive serves as a legitimating, retrospective account of his earlier bricolated, citational archive in which thinkers such as Husserl, Saussure, Lévi-Strauss, and Rousseau figure prominently. Regardless, in both the early and later work, Derrida effectively passes over the relationship between sites of power and reiterative citation, refusing to recognize the s/cite of the archive.

The claim that it is the s/citation of the archive that functions as the repressed of the Derridean project finds its most salient evidence in Derrida's recent publication *Archive Fever: A Freudian Impression*. The claim is, I recognize, counter-intuitive in more than one sense. On the one hand, Derrida recognizes the archive as a 'topo-nomological' structure, invoking simultaneously in that neologism both the sense of archive as place or site and the archive as naming or citation. The archive, Derrida tells us, can be located 'at the intersection of the topological and the nomological, of the place and the law, of the substrate and the authority' (3). The claim is important, potentially productive, and moves towards an understanding of the archive as neither object nor event, but as an operation of s/citation. Yet, as this geometrical metaphor of 'intersection' itself suggests, Derrida's text as a whole will privilege the notion of sitation over citation, rendering the topo-nomological in a manner that will always posit *topos* as somehow prior to *nomos*. On the other hand, such a claim to a repression of archival s/citation is counter-intuitive in that *Archive Fever* is ostensibly dedicated to 'the *impression* left ... by the *Freudian signature* on its own archive, and of archivization, that is to say also, inversely and as an indirect consequence, on historiography' (5), and as such constitutes an examination of the archive – not to mention various and related technologies of inscription – as the techno-prosthesis of memory. Yet, in this particular case, Derrida elides the socio-history of the archive as a technology of textual management and s/citation in at least four conflicting ways, despite his focus on electronic technologies and their phantasmatic effect on the history of psychoanalysis as 'archival machines of which one could hardly have dreamed in the first quarter of this century' (14).[9]

First, Derrida subordinates the archive as the s/cite of textual management to the operations of memory. Derrida's Freudian *impression* is, admittedly, at once 'scriptural and typographic' (26), only a 'notion ... of a schema, or of an in-finite or indefinite process' (29), and a mark on the institutional body of psychoanalysis itself. Yet these impressions in the first sense he offers, these techno-prosthetic forms of memory, are substrates within an 'archiviology' or general science of the archive that makes primary the 'economy of memory' (34). In constructing such a general science one must, Derrida tells us, either include psychoanalysis within such an archiviology or subject that general science to the critical authority of psychoanalysis from outside such an archiviology, in that the Freudian impression will have always already made its mark. As substrata, then, such technologies of archivization are, indeed, secondary; yet they also, as Derrida maintains, are 'hypomnesic' (11) or underlie the operations of memory, and, hence, are also foundational. In challenging Yerushalmi's claim in *Freud's Moses* that, contra Freud, had Moses actually been murdered by the Jewish people the act would not have been repressed, Derrida writes:

> This, in my opinion, is the sinews of the argument in this book. Now to affirm this, Yerushalmi must again suppose that the contradiction between the act of memory or of archivization on the one hand and repression on the other remains irreducible. As if one could not, precisely, recall and archive the very thing one represses, archive it while repressing it. (64)

Of course, Freudian psychoanalysis would tell us that, indeed, one might 'recall and archive the very thing one represses,' and so Derrida's point is well taken; significantly, however, he here conflates memory and the archive in a manner that would suggest not only that the archive and repression are synonymous, but also that it is the archive itself that is repressed, is displaced by an archiviology that is, first and foremost,   a counter-mnemonics, a forgetting of the archive in the memory of memory.

Second, and perhaps in contradiction to the first, Derrida, in asking 'in what way has the whole of [psychoanalysis] been determined by a state of the technology of communication and archivization?' (16) posits the archive as a site anterior to or outside its own citational reiterations – '*There is no archive ... without a certain exteriority*' (11), Derrida tells us – in his insistence on the archive as an origin or site of commencement that exists prior to its reiterative citations in what is, surprisingly perhaps, the most blatant form of techno-determinism:

> the archive, as printing, writing, prosthesis, or hypomnesic technique in general is not only the place for stocking and conserving an archivable

content *of the past* which would exist in any case ... the technical structure of the *archiving* archive also determines the structure of an *archivable* content even in its very coming into existence and in its relationship to the future. The archivization produces as much as it records the event. (16–17)

Derrida makes this point by way of challenging the very possibility of a Freudian 'living memory' that might be prior to its own archival inscriptions. Living memory cannot speak without the archive, without the techno-prosthesis that Derrida tells us is prior to the iteration that it, indeed, conditions. Yet, such a challenge fails to account for the manner in which living memory, or the citational practices of everyday life, are constitutive of, without being prior to, the archive. Nonetheless, Derrida unwittingly provides us with an example of that very process in an act of reiterative citation that makes of *Archive Fever* an act of critical repetition – following, indeed invoking, the argument of 'Freud and the Scene of Writing' – the effect of which is the materialization of a Derridean archive, an archive by, and of, Derrida. At the same time, his critique of a Freudian psychoanalysis that insists 'the *arkhe* appears in the nude, without archive' (92) returns us, revealingly, to Derrida's suggestion in *Of Grammatology* that 'the destruction of the book as it is now under way in all domains, denudes the surface of the text' (18). The destruction of the book, the destruction of the archive, are one in the same. In either case, what we have is an archival discourse predicated on the forgetting of its own socio-history, its own materialization as the s/cite of the archive. What we also have is a demonstration of the inability of the materializations of discursive power to be fully adequate to the reiterative citations of which they are the effect.

Third, and briefly, as a result of these conflicting positions, Derrida treats the dynamics of archival citation without serious consideration of the archive as a s/cite of socio-political power. While Derrida clearly acknowledges the 'unlimited upheaval under way in archival technology' today (*Archive Fever* 18), he also offers merely conciliatory gestures in the direction of the material archive as a site of ideological conflict: an initial, single footnote that recognizes that 'there is no political power without control of the archive' (4) serves to frame the text alongside the concluding comment, some ninety-one pages later, that 'in his theoretical theses as in the compulsion of his institutionalizing strategy, Freud repeated the patriarchal logic' (95). That the archive operates as a s/cite of power does not – indeed, cannot, given Derrida's rendering of sitation and citation – constitute an even incidental focus in Derrida's deconstruction of the archive.

Fourth, and most important then, in a strategic writing practice that is most pronounced both here and in his *Spectres of Marx*, Derrida practises the strategy of a pervasive auto-citation that situates (sites) Derrida himself among the *archons*, those superior magistrates who are 'accorded the hermeneutic right and competence' and who 'have the power to interpret the archives' (2), in a reiterative citational performance that materializes the Derridean archive as the dissimulating site of its own commencement. This is, quite possibly, inevitable, and of course the Derridean archive remains open to the future, but it seems imperative to me (as an ethical responsibility) that we recognize this instance of the archive – the moment, or better yet moments, of its materialization. A fleeting instance this may be, however, in that the archontic function of Derrida's text depends on its own anarchontic, archiviolithic force, a force difficult to trace in that it works by 'silent vocation' and 'leaves nothing of its own behind.' Nonetheless, we are witness to the fact that time and time again, Derrida will invoke the constituents of his own writings in a manner that seems expressly tied to questions of ethical and political import – a gathering up, of sorts, of the less explicitly engaged fragments in a manner that promises to reshelve them within the archival space of the, as of late, more overtly politicized Derrida. In the case of *Archive Fever*, the most evident example of this is Derrida's already noted citation of his 1966 essay, 'Freud and the Scene of Writing,' which should remind us that *Archive Fever* is part of a much more concerted return to Freud marked by Derrida's recent publication of three key essays in his 1998 *Resistances of Psychoanalysis*, and part of a much larger pattern of returns in Derrida's reformulation of his critical project.

More to the point, however, the half dozen or so Derridean texts to which the author makes explicit reference are matched by an at least equal number of implicit, but nonetheless very evident, references to his other major analyses: readers of Derrida will recognize the significance of the 'truth in painting' (12), 'postal technology' (17), 'circumcision' (20ff), 'some proper name or ... some body proper' (45), the 'domination of the constative over the performative' (51), and 'self confirmation in a *yes, yes*' (79), as the central motifs, respectively, of the following texts: *The Truth in Painting, The Post Card, Glas, Signsponge, Limited Inc*, and 'Two Words for Joyce.' The frequency and thoroughness with which Derrida invokes many of the key texts in his own archive – and my examples are not at all exhaustive – invite some kind of commentary, for certainly the cumulative effect of this reiterative citational performance cannot, as a rhetorical strategy, go without notice.[10] What is the import of such a strategy? Simply put, if materiality is the effect of reiterative citation, if materialization is the dissimulation of the power of which it is an effect, then Derrida himself writes, to cite his own words, an 'archive that would confuse itself with the *arkhē*' (98) in that it both archives and represses its archival origins by materializing the Derridean corpus and, thus, dissimulating the ideological dimensions of Derrida's own reiterative citations. If the archiviolithic is an archive-destroying force that, like the Freudian death-drive, like *le mal d'archive* or archive fever, violates all principles, then Derrida's project is itself 'archiviolithic,' it engenders the destruction of the very archive in which it takes shape – that is, the archive of Derrida's own archive, historicity itself. As such, this 'force leaves nothing of its own behind' and 'not only incites forgetfulness, amnesia, the annihilation of memory, as *mneme* or *anamnesis*, but also commands the radical effacement, in truth the eradication, of that which can never be reduced to *mneme* or to *anamnesis*, that is, the archive' (11). That Derrida's project enacts two contradictory movements, both the repression and the archivization, sublimation and desublimation, of the archive, might come as no surprise to Derrida himself, for he explicitly imparts the same contradiction to Freud, importantly recognizing his analysis as descriptive, rather than evaluative:

> This contradiction is not negative, it modulates and conditions the very formation of the concept of the archive and of the concept in general – right where they bear the contradiction. (90)

What is at stake here, in my own analysis, is not so much the description of the seemingly inevitable archivization of the archive, but the relationship of that operation to poststructural theory, or more appropriately to what I would like to call the 'technologies of theory' in general.

IV. The Technologies of Theory

From within the house of Freud, the archive of the father of psychoanalysis, Derrida directs our attention to 'an incessant tension ... between the archive and archaeology' (*Archive Fever* 92). The methods of archaeology, Freud's own passionate diversion, Derrida tells us, insist on the effacement of the archive so that the origin may speak by itself. Such a methodology is *en mal d'archive* as a technology of desire:

> It is to burn with a passion. It is never to rest, interminably, from searching for the archive right where it slips away. It is to run after the archive, even if there's too much of it, right where something in it anarchives itself. It is to have a compulsive, repetitive, and nostalgic desire for the archive, an irrepressible desire to return to the origin, a homesickness, a nostalgia for the return to the most archaic place of absolute commencement. (91)

Freud's recourse to archaeological parables, such as that of the archaeologist who discovers that *Saxa loquuntur* or 'stones talk' in 'The Aetiology of Hysteria,'[11] is testimony to the archive fever of psychoanalysis. Such a fever is characterized by repetition and compulsion disorders (again the *fort/da* of little Ernst), but also by the movement of the return gathered around the notion of the site, and specifically the site of archaeology:

> The archaeologist has succeeded in making the archive no longer serve any function. It *comes to efface itself*, it becomes transparent or unessential so as to let the *origin* present itself in person. (93)

The excavation, materialization, of such a site, seemingly without citation, those markers of power and the historicity of the archive, effectively mask what is the 'archontic' principle of the archive, the nomological function of the archive as regulatory ideal and the commandment of law.

Derrida is speaking here more generally of Freud's *Moses* and his *Studies on Hysteria*, but the radical incompatibility of the archaeological and the archival, which stems from the forgetting of s/citation, returns to haunt Derrida's own project. Ideally, as I've tried to suggest, the Derridean archive either dissolves in the plenitude of its own meaning, or effaces its own process of archivization in the materialization effected by reiterative citation. If, indeed, we recognize the practice of textual management, of s/citation, as what Foucault would call a 'technology of power,' Derridean deconstruction – in its repression of the material archive – implicates itself in the bid for textual mastery that is the totalizing project of modernism, that is complicit with the technologies of theory.

Technology is, of course, integral to Derrida's conception of the archive, which, in the opening pages of *Archive Fever*, he carefully sets in relation to the historical, as part of a larger schema that remarks upon the schism within the archive itself as both commencement and commandment, as both origin and law:

> This name apparently coordinates two principles in one: the principle according to nature or history, *there* where things *commence* – physical, historical, or ontological principle – but also the principle according to the law, *there* where men and gods *command*, *there* where authority, social order are exercised, *in this place* from which *order* is given – nomological principle. (1)

In turn, the natural and historical introduce a further schism, in 'a chain of belated and problematic oppositions between *physis* and its others, *thesis*, *tekhne*, *nomos*, etc., which are found to be at work in the other principle, the nomological principle of the *arkhe*, the principle of the commandment' (1). Derrida thus makes complicit the idea of history with the notions of place, technology, and name. To that I would like to add, however, the important observation that the technological, as the middle term here, assumes the role of the trait, stroke, or line that both separates and joins together sitation and citation. The archive, then, as a technology of theory is a marker of historicity and power; but the rendering of the archive as either pure site, or pure citation, is the effacement of the operations of s/citation.

As the phrase 'technology of theory' might suggest, my earlier enumeration of Derrida's reiterative citations is certainly incomplete, for his juxtaposition of the archive and archaeology returns us again, inevitably, to the Derridian archive, and to the exchange that gathers around historiography and the publication of Foucault's *Madness and Civilization*.[12] Of course, the archive and the archaeological 'will always be close the one to the other, resembling each other, hardly discernible in their co-implication, and yet radically incompatible' (*Archive Fever* 92). What Derrida offers us, among many other insights, in *Archive Fever* is an implicit critique of the early Foucault, whose own archaeological methodologies intersect with an archive, understood in an entirely different sense, but nonetheless relegated to the purely figural status of a mysterious agent of history. Foucault's reluctantly named 'archive' is the self-determining rule of discursive formations that is expressly divorced from its institutional manifestations, from the matrix of discourse/practice that Foucault will recognize in the work that follows *The Archaeology of Knowledge*. Here, the possibility that the material archive might well serve as a locus of social struggle, as a discipline rooted in power relations, goes without serious consideration. Even in the later Foucault, however, it is curious that the institutional critiques of *Discipline and Punish* and *The History of Sexuality*, and so on, are not extended to the materialization of the archive itself. Foucault's suggestion that 'it is not possible for us to describe our own archive, since it is from within these rules that we speak' (*Archaeology of Knowledge* 130) may well hold true here, for it is the institution of the archive itself, the discourse/practice of textual management, that constitutes the archive in Foucault's own sense of a network of discursive regularities. If we have moved beyond this archival moment – in, say, the shift to the digital management of texts – then we may well now be in a position to recognize the materialization of the archive itself as poststructuralism's *very condition of possibility*. The practice of textual management, the twentieth century's unprecedented and concerted regard for the interrelation between physical books, may well constitute the 'historical a priori' of both Derrida's and Foucault's programs – the condition of emergence of those statements, along with such literary texts as are caught up in the fantasia of the library, that constitute an archival discourse. Together, it is these statements that bring the archive-as-object into existence at the same time that archival practices enable such a discourse.

But what, then, of the archive if, indeed, the archival discourse of Derrida and Foucault effects a return to such modernist moments in their failure to locate their own writing practices in the materialization of the archive? What is the consequence of recognizing the archive as a technology of theory? That the archive-as-object can now be brought into view suggests a possible response to the all too common rejection of Foucault on the grounds that his convincing genealogical critique deprives the subject of agency in the face of shifting and excessive technologies of power. It's worth contending that such agency as can be formulated might well take the shape of a poetics of archival resistance that emerges – so Foucault reminds us – coextensive with the formulations of power.[13] Such a poetics demands both an awareness of the archive itself as a technology of theory, a technology that works silently behind even such thoroughgoing critiques as Derrida's and Foucault's own, and a method of textual practice that takes this into account. If the early, archaeological, Foucault proves problematic in this case, then it could well be that the later, genealogical, Foucault, as well as those who extend the work of this politically and ethically engaged philosopher, might prove instrumental in formulating a practice of s/citation in the writing of intellectual historiography. If it is Butler's contention that materialization is never fully adequate to the citational practices of which it is an effect, then what we require is an exemplary model that in its s/citation of the archive, in its formulations of the archive as a technology of theory, foregrounds that which is inadequate to the reiterative s/citations of theory.

Such an exemplary model might well be located in the critical practices of a number of German scholars now working in the wake of poststructuralist theory inflected by the central precepts of a cultural materialist methodology. Indeed, such a nuanced shift in poststructuralist critique provides further insight into the manner in which theories of intellectual historiography and the intellectual history of theory succeed each other in dialectical fashion. This corrective gesture, in effect, returns to itself by way of the very writings under consideration reinvigorated by the recognition of the boundedness of all discourse, including those theories of technology that serve as self-effacing technologies of theory. In particular, the work of Friedrich Kittler in his *Gramophone, Film, Typewriter* and Bernhard Siegert in *Relays: Literature as an Epoch of the Postal System* provides a strong instance of what I would like to call, in all its wonderful irony, *material theory.* Kittler's advances in media studies, broadly understood, and Siegert's engagement with the history of central European postal systems make possible the historicization of the central metaphors informing Derrida's investigation of a primordial writing embodied in the technologies of the gramme, the graph, and the post. Primarily regarded as antithetical critical schools, the idealism of French theory and the materialism of cultural studies rather find themselves here in a productive relationship that more than anything else demonstrates their ongoing interdependence. Moreover, such a convergence in the history of ideas retains the subtleties of poststructuralist thought while addressing the concerns raised at the outset of this article regarding the dissimulation of power in the sublimation of the archive as its material effect. That is to say, Kittler and Siegert s/cite the archive.

To be sure, Kittler, to focus on just one of my examples, is as much a technological determinist as Derrida might, particularly in his more recent work, prove himself to be. 'Media,' Kittler writes in the opening moment of his *Gramophone, Film, Typewriter,* 'determine our situation' (xxxix). The volume as a whole is dedicated to establishing, and following up on, Kittler's earlier contention in *Discourse Networks* that writing technologies lose their monopoly on the word with the invention of the gramophone and film. This dramatic shift in media history coincides, roughly, with the demise of humanism in Foucault's *The Order of Things* – and the influence of Foucault permeates Kittler's historical methodology. Kittler writes from the position, as Nietzsche tells us in commenting on his own typewriter, that 'our writing materials help write our thoughts' (Kittler, 'Technologies of Writing' 731). However, Kittler's unabashed determinism in this regard is mitigated by a number of factors: his deployment of multiple and diverse socio-historic factors into his analysis; his construction of historical schema analogous to dialectical materialism; and his privileging of the material in a manner that does not fail to account for the discursive production of the technological.

Kittler, furthermore, foregrounds his recognition of the mediality of all discourse – i.e. the notion that traditional historiography is dependent on the ideal of linear narrative because of its reliance solely on the written word, that the way we understand history is itself an effect of the material technology of writing. 'History was the homogenized field that, as an academic subject, only took account of literate cultures. Mouths and graphisms were relegated to prehistory. Otherwise, stories and histories (both deriving from *historia*) could not have been linked. All the orders and judgements, announcements and prescriptions (military and legal, religious and medical) that produced mountains of corpses were communicated along the very same channel that monopolized the descriptions of those mountains of corpses. Which is why anything that ever happened ended up in libraries' (*Gramophone* 4–5). This brutalizing tautology of history is what makes Foucault's archaeological pronouncements both insightful and limited:

> For the libraries in which the archeologist found so much rich material collected and catalogued papers that had been extremely diverse in terms of addressee, distribution technique, degree of secrecy, and writing technique – Foucault's archive as the entropy of a post office. Even writing itself, before it ends up libraries, is a communication medium, the technology of which the archeologist simply forgot. It is for this reason that all his analyses end immediately before that point in time at which other media penetrated the library's stacks. Discourse analysis cannot be applied to sound archives or towers of film rolls. (Kittler, *Gramophone* 5)

What is remaindered in Foucault's work, then, is the technology of the archive itself, the key perhaps to understanding even Foucault's most (ostensibly) revealing analyses as a pure exteriority. Writing stores no more than writing itself; writing records its own authorization. To overlook the s/citation of the archive is to champion the false promise of a causal-expressive history, to fail to recognize that manner in which 'bodies themselves fell under the regime of the symbolic' (Kittler, *Gramophone* 8).

What Kittler reminds us of here is that all media, and our experience of them, are constituted by language even as they constitute the representation of the Lacanian Real. He refuses the presumption, in articulating his determinist histories, that while there is nothing outside the media, the media is itself interior, expressive, and subject to totalizing analysis – demonstrating that the very precepts of exteriority, mediality, and corporeality that inform his argument are themselves rendered in the written language that serves as the crucible through which all media studies – indeed, all cultural studies – must pass. Kittler, it might be argued, succeeds in inverting the poststructuralist privilege of the ideal over the material without committing an analogous fault – failing, that is, to s/cite the archive, to move to a third term that does not, in some manner or another, reinforce the very binary opposition that is at stake here.

With Kittler's project in mind, I return to, reiterate now, the citation that began this analysis, the wonderfully epigraphic 'I shall hold myself, once again, to the instance of the archive' that Derrida articulates only in passing, with seeming innocence, but which actually may be the key to unlocking the archive of the archive that is the very movement of s/citation. The statement is clearly a performative, self-reflexive, promise articulated by a multiplied subject capable of speaking of, and holding, himself. That the speaker can hold himself suggests both potential security and cessation – a wonderful instance of indeterminacy, but an instance that is confounded by the 'once again' of repetition and reiterative citation. The indeterminacy of such a citational performance is even more radical, however, in that the *instance* to which we will return again and again, to which we will hold ourselves, can be understood only in its most radical multiplicity: as a moment, an urgency, a legal precedent, a presence, and an example. In its most irreducible historicity, the *instance of the archive* is at once any and all of these, as a technology that hovers along the trait of sitation and citation, object and event, the literal and the figural, materiality and ideality – and it is to that multiple instance that historiography must inevitably return.

NOTES

1 While a number of these authors deal explicitly with the archive – Derrida in *Archive Fever*, Borges in the stories of *Ficciones*, and Foucault in the chapter devoted to that key term in *The Archaeology of Knowledge* – for others the concept is more implicit. Pound's 'paideuma' in *Guide to Kulchur* is the 'tangled underroot of ideas' that informs particular moments in intellectual history in a manner not unlike Foucault's own archive; Joyce's *Finnegans Wake* is a concerted effort to construct an archive of cultural intertexts and linguistic semes; Deleuze and Guattari's *A Thousand Plateaus* offers the figures of the assemblage and the rhizome in a retrospective account of Deleuze's earlier constructions of a philosophical archive. In either case, the term assumes a certain correspondence between the various bricolated projects of high modernism and poststructural theory.

2 In effect then, this homophonic coincidence plays a similar role to that of Lee Edelman's 'homographesis,' as a writing that troubles the space of sameness and difference, that, in effect, queers the archive and the presuppositions that gather around it. See *Homographesis* 3–23.

3 By this I refer to the playful masteries of both Derridean deconstruction and Freud's grandchild Ernst. See Freud's 'Beyond the Pleasure Principle' and Derrida's reading of the movement of *fort/da* in his *The Post Card: From Socrates to Freud and Beyond*.

4 See Jean Baudrillard's *Simulations*.

5 Diderot's entry has not yet been translated fully into English. The original can be found in volume 7 of his *Oeuvres Complètes*, 174–262. An important, but brief, translated fragment can be found in Diderot, 'Necessity for an Encyclopedia and Method for Compiling One.'

6 For more on this notion, see Wilda Anderson's 'Encyclopedic Topologies,' to which this portion of my argument is partly indebted.

7 McGann first discusses the idea in an article in the *London Review of Books* titled 'Theory of Texts' and later returns to it in *The Textual Condition*, in which he notes that radial reading is the movement that directs the reader outside of the principal text to a series of juxtaposed texts or, more generally, 'radial reading involves decoding one or more of the contexts that interpenetrate the scripted and physical text. It necessitates some kind of abstraction from what appears most immediately. The person who temporarily stops "reading" to look up the meaning of a word is properly an *emblem* of radial reading' (119).

8 Freud most carefully explicates the notion of *Nachträglichkeit*, or deferred action, in the wolf-man case history; see 'From the History of an Infantile

Neurosis.' For an important reading of *Nachträglichkeit* in twentieth-century avant-garde and theoretical discourse, see Hal Foster's *The Return of the Real*, 1–34.

9 Derrida will ask, in relation to his own text written three decades earlier: is 'the psychic apparatus *better represented* or is it *affected differently* by all the technical mechanisms for archivization and for reproduction, for prostheses of so-called live memory, for simulacrums of living things which already are, and will increasingly be, more refined, complicated, powerful than the "mystic pad" (microcomputing, electronization, computerization, etc.)?' (*Archive Fever* 15). In keeping with Derrida's move towards technological determinism here, the answer is 'yes.' For Derrida's engagement with the mystic writing pad, see 'Freud and the Scene of Writing.'

10 It is worth noting, furthermore, Derrida's own strategy in his analysis of Yerushalmi's 'Monologue with Freud' of repeatedly citing the same passage. That Derrida returns to, or reiterates, Yerushalmi's interrogation of psychoanalysis as a 'Jewish science' no less than five times – in order, it would seem, to put into play the internal schisms or differences of that particular passage – invites us to question whether such reiterative citation enjoys a different status in this case. Indeed, s/citation, as one might expect, follows Foucault's argument that power and resistance are co-emergent.

11 See the *Standard Edition*, 3:192.

12 This brief but important exchange between Derrida and Foucault begins with Derrida's critique, in 'Cogito and the History of Madness,' of Foucault's reading of the Cartesian *cogito* in the second chapter of *Madness and Civilization*, and concludes with Foucault's response in 'My Body, This Paper, This Fire.' Following Foucault's death, Derrida reengages the work of Foucault, in a manner tangentially related to this debate, in his 1991 address '"To Do Justice to Freud": The History of Madness in the Age of Psychoanalysis.'

13 See, for example, Foucault's contention in *The History of Sexuality* that where 'there is power, there is resistance, and yet, or rather consequently, this resistance is never in a position of exteriority in relation to power' (95).

WORKS CITED

Anderson, Wilda. 'Encyclopedic Topologies.' *Modern Language Notes* 101.4 (1986): 912–29.

Baudrillard, Jean. *Simulations*. Trans. Paul Foss et al. New York: Semiotext(e), 1983.

Borges, Jorge Luis. *Ficciones*. New York: Grove P, 1962.

Butler, Judith. *Bodies That Matter: On the Discursive Limits of 'Sex.'* New York: Routledge, 1993.

D'Alembert, Jean Le Rond. *Preliminary Discourse to the Encyclopedia of Diderot.* Indianapolis: Bobbs-Merrill, 1963.

Deleuze, Gilles, and Félix Guattari. *A Thousand Plateaus: Capitalism and Schizophrenia.* Trans. Brian Massumi. Minneapolis: U of Minnesota P, 1987.

Derrida, Jacques. *Archive Fever: A Freudian Impression.* Trans. Eric Prenowitz. Chicago: U of Chicago P, 1995.

– 'Cogito and the History of Madness.' *Writing and Difference.* Trans. Alan Bass. Chicago: U of Chicago P, 1978. 31–63.

– 'Freud and the Scene of Writing.' *Writing and Difference.* Trans. Alan Bass. Chicago: U of Chicago P, 1978. 196–231.

– *Glas.* Trans. John P. Leavey, Jr, and Richard Rand. Lincoln: U of Nebraska P, 1986.

– *Limited Inc.* Evanston: Northwestern UP, 1988.

– *Of Grammatology.* Trans. Gayatri Chakravorty Spivak. Baltimore: Johns Hopkins UP, 1974.

– *The Post Card: From Socrates to Freud and Beyond.* Trans. Alan Bass. Chicago: U of Chicago P, 1987.

– *Resistances of Psychoanalysis.* Trans. Peggy Kamuf et al. Stanford: Stanford UP, 1998.

– *Signéponge/Signsponge.* Trans. Richard Rand. New York: Columbia UP, 1984.

– *The Truth in Painting.* Trans. Geoff Bennington and Ian McLeod. Chicago: U of Chicago P, 1987.

– 'To Do Justice to Freud': The History of Madness in the Age of Psychoanalysis.' Trans. Pascale-Anne Brault and Michael Naas. *Foucault and His Interlocutors.* Ed. Arnold I. Davidson. Chicago: U of Chicago P, 1997. 57–96.

– 'Two Words for Joyce.' *Post-Structuralist Joyce: Essays from the French.* Ed. Derek Attridge and Daniel Ferrer. London: Cambridge UP, 1984. 145–59.

Diderot, Denis. 'Encyclopédie.' *Encyclopédie III (Lettres D–L). Oeuvres Complètes.* Vol 7. Ed. John Lough and Jacques Proust. Paris: Hermann, 1976. 174–262.

– 'Necessity for an Encyclopaedia and Method of Compiling One.' *French Thought in the Eighteenth Century.* Ed. Romain Rolland et al. New York: Books for Libraries P, 1971. 304–13.

Edelman, Lee. *Homographesis: Essays in Gay Literary and Cultural Theory.* New York: Routledge, 1994.

Foster, Hal. *The Return of the Real.* Cambridge: MIT P, 1996.

Foucault, Michel. *The Archaeology of Knowledge.* Trans. A.M. Sheridan Smith. London: Routledge, 1992.

– *Discipline and Punish: The Birth of the Prison.* Trans. Alan Sheridan. New York: Vintage, 1979.
– 'Fantasia of the Library.' *Language, Counter-Memory, Practice: Selected Essays and Interviews.* Ed. Donald F. Bouchard. Trans. Donald F. Bouchard and Sherry Simon. Ithaca: Cornell UP, 1977. 87–109.
– *The History of Sexuality Volume I: An Introduction.* New York: Vintage, 1980.
– *Madness and Civilization: A History of Insanity in the Age of Reason.* Trans. Richard Howard. New York: Vintage, 1988.
– 'My Body, This Paper, This Fire.' Trans. Geoff Bennington. *Oxford Literary Review* 4–1 (1979): 9–28.
Freud, Sigmund. 'The Aetiology of Hysteria.' *The Standard Edition of the Complete Psychological Works of Sigmund Freud.* Vol. 3 (1893–9). Trans. James Strachey. London: Hogarth P, 1962. 191–221.
– 'Beyond the Pleasure Principle.' *The Standard Edition of the Complete Psychological Works of Sigmund Freud.* Vol. 18 (1920–2). Trans. James Strachey. London: Hogarth P, 1963. 7–64.
– 'From the History of an Infantile Neurosis.' *The Standard Edition of the Complete Psychological Works of Sigmund Freud.* Vol. 17 (1918–19). Trans. James Strachey. London: Hogarth P, 1963. 3–122.
Joyce, James. *Finnegans Wake.* London: Paladin, 1992.
Kittler, Friedrich. *Discourse Networks 1800/1900.* Trans. M. Metteer with Chris Cullens. Stanford: Stanford UP, 1990.
– *Gramophone, Film, Typewriter.* Trans. G. Winthrop-Young and Michael Wutz. Stanford: Stanford UP, 1999.
– 'Technologies of Writing.' Interview with Friedrich Kittler, M. Griffin, and S. Herrmann. *New Literary History* 27.4 (1996): 231–742.
McGann, Jerome. *The Textual Condition.* Princeton: Princeton UP, 1991.
– 'Theory of Texts.' *London Review of Books* 10.4 (1988): 20–1.
Pound, Ezra. *Guide to Kulchur.* New York: New Directions, 1970.
Siegert, Bernhard. *Relays: Literature as an Epoch of the Postal System.* Trans. K. Repp. Stanford: Stanford UP, 1999.

De Man, Marx, Rousseau, and the Machine

ORRIN N.C. WANG

In his one sustained commentary on his former colleague, Fredric Jameson states that Paul de Man

> was an eighteenth-century mechanical materialist, and much that strikes the postcontemporary reader as peculiar and idiosyncratic about his work will be clarified by juxtaposition with the cultural politics of the great Enlightenment philosophes: their horror of religion, their campaign against superstition and error (or 'metaphysics'). In that sense, deconstruction ... can be seen to be an essentially eighteenth-century philosophical strategy. (*Postmodernism* 246)[1]

What does it mean for both deconstruction and Marxism to consider de Man as a postcontemporary version of eighteenth-century mechanical materialism? Jameson provocatively situates deconstruction within his larger argument for the immanent and nominalist nature of postmodern theory. But in doing so he unleashes analytic energies that extend beyond his own strategies for absorbing deconstruction within the overarching conceptual frameworks of a Marxist analysis of capital (*Postmodernism* 181–259). Dialectically, Marxism's own valence changes from one emphasizing the hermeneutic coordinates implicit in Jameson's investment in narrative and representation (*Darstellung*) to a more uncertain topos, configured not in terms of an interpretive solution but instead as a tropological problematic, here in this essay signalled by the conceptual irresolution of abstract labour and value in Marx's *Capital*.

Jameson argues for the continuity between de Man and eighteenth-century intellectual thought by recovering from *Allegories of Reading* a Kantian-inflected dilemma regarding generalizing from particulars and a noumenon of 'what language cannot assimilate, absorb, or process' (*Postmodernism* 246). *Allegories* is actually as tough on the integrity of the particular as it is on the process of general, conceptual abstraction. Similarly, Jameson's argument for the noumenon as the repressed *non-dit* of de Man's book is complicated by the later, explicit use of the Kantian noumenon in de Man's *The Aesthetic Ideology*, in which the term specifically expresses the 'inward experience of consciousness' (74) and functions as a counterpart to the phenomenal world.[2] Most compelling, however, is the way in which Jameson's analysis notes but does not dwell on the most overt evidence for de Man's eighteenth-century mechanist materialism, the figure of the machine that runs through the *Allegories* essays on Rousseau.

Contrary to Jameson's implied subsumption of de Man's mechanical materialism under the larger exigencies of a dialectical materialism, the machine demonstrates how both de Manian deconstruction and Marxism share a 'technological unconscious' knotted around the mental scandals of instrumentality, *technē*, and simulacra.[3] These issues intertextually connect de Man and Marx through Rousseau's *Confessions* and Marx's *Capital*. In Rousseau's work the machine marks a historical literalization of self, contingency, and value that opens up the question of the literal and the figural congealed in deconstruction's own economy of equivalence. In *Capital* the machine allegorizes the robotic catachresis underwriting abstract labour and value, making Marxism more than a transparent historicism even as deconstruction becomes something else besides an attack upon history's literal nature.

First, a qualification: my point is not that the machine in de Man provides better proof of his affiliation with eighteenth-century mechanist philosophy. Rather, by responding to Jameson's proposition we reorient analysis around the machine in de Man, a topos that both overlaps and diverges from a more traditional concept of mechanist materialism. It is worth remembering, for example, that philosophic mechanism is not simply tied to non-philosophic, prosaic ideas of what a 'machine' is. But it soon becomes clear that the machine in de Man is also much more than such a definition.

In the essay in *Allegories* on the *Social Contract* the image of the machine operates in two ways. First, citing Rousseau's description of the *Social Contract* as a 'machine ready to go to work,' de Man argues that Rousseau's political creation is less a 'piece of property or a State' than a text, a grammar which operates 'like a logical code or a machine' (268). Such a 'quasi-mechanical pattern' has less to do with any recognizable, intelligible structure on the part of the text than with the way the functioning of grammar is independent of referential meaning, much as an abstract law does not depend on any one of its particular applications for its existence (268). This gap between grammar and referential meaning also occasions the essay's second usage of mechanical rhetoric, how Rousseau's analogy between the 'wheels of the State' and the 'principle of inertia of machines' is best understood as a 'debilitating entropy [that] illustrates the practical consequences of a linguistic structure in which grammar and figure, statement and speech act do not converge' (272). This predicament appears to be for de Man a second-order repetition of the initial divergence between grammar and referential meaning, in so far as de Man earlier defines figure as precisely that gap: for him, rhetoric, or figure, cannot unite with grammar to overcome that division (try as it might, as in the case of metaphor); consequently, the complicated, asymmetric, and mutually disabling relations among all of de Man's linguistic categories – grammar, reference, figure, statement, and speech act – function in a 'quasi-mechanical pattern,' a logic that constantly blunts or displaces its own constative or performative force. The final example of this mechanical logic would be the promise of the *Contract.* Equally empty and inevitable because a promise always rejects the particular present for a future moment when grammar and reference might converge, this linguistic act dramatizes the functioning of the text as a machine, in the service of neither itself nor any external referent.

The implications of the machine in this essay are several. The machine underscores a certain linguistic dynamism that sublates the mechanical 'entropy' illustrating the gap between grammar and figure. This dynamism, or set of forces, vehemently effects the mixed sense of aimless repetition and random patterning that de Man reads in Rousseau's mechanical references, and asserts the inevitability of language's self-evacuations (as in a promise), distinguishing self-constitutive error from avoidable mistake. This dynamism also coincides with one characteristic of traditional mechanism, in so far as both eschew Aristotelian final causes, or teleological thinking, as explanations for their functioning. In de Man this rejection takes the further radical step of eschewing organic meaning altogether. As such, the machine also describes how language and the phenomenal world constantly diverge, and how language through reference and figure constantly tries to erase that bifurcation.

In de Man's essay on the *Confessions* this final key issue carries a particular resonance, in so far as the importance of the machine lies not simply in the machine's ubiquity but in what it explicitly suppresses: the figure of the text as a body, and, by extension, the human body itself. That for de Man the metaphor of the text as body in Rousseau refers not simply to a general, phenomenal organicism but to the specifically human form is made clear by de Man's stress on the moments of bodily mutilation – nearly broken heads and crushed fingers – that punctuate Rousseau's writings. The machine of grammar threatens the body, ultimately replacing the latter and all its possible desires and emotive meanings with language's own implacable, unmotivated logic. This displacement reaches the violence of a metalepsis. For 'as soon as the metaphorical integrity of the text is put in question, as soon as the text is said not to be a figural body but a machine,' this predicament occurs:

> Far from seeing language as an instrument in the service of a psychic energy, the possibility now arises that the entire construction of drives, substitutions, repressions, and representations is the aberrant metaphorical correlative of the absolute randomness of language, prior to any figuration or meaning. It is no longer certain that language, as excuse, exists because of a prior guilt but just as possible that since language, as a machine, performs anyway, we have to produce guilt (and all its train of psychic consequences) in order to make the excuse meaningful. (*Allegories* 299)[4]

These sentences climax a discernible narrative in de Man's chapter on the *Confessions*, and, in a sense, his book's entire section on Rousseau. For if the human self stands for an exemplary moment when language and phenomenology, text and body, coincide, de Man's machine of language tears at this synthesis, first refusing to obey the vagaries of human intention, then turning upon the human form, and finally demonstrating how human subjectivity is itself a mere symptom of language's mechanical action. This radically perverse instrumentality, in which language first disassociates itself from and then endangers human purpose, and then displaces that purpose altogether, is described elsewhere in a famous quote by de Man: 'Literature as well as criticism – the difference between them being delusive – is condemned (or privileged) to be forever the most rigorous and, consequently, the most unreliable language in terms of which man names and transforms himself' (*Allegories* 19).

Given that non-literary or non-critical language, like the phenomenal world, is acknowledged but never encountered by de Man, his definition of literature can stand for what especially defines language: its existence as that 'most rigorous and ... unreliable' tool for human real-ization; one that not only rebuffs its own role in naming and transform-ing human existence but that also exacts a chiasmatic exchange, in which the result is one with Kleist's inhuman marionette, a reoccurring image in de Man, the machine as the 'anamorphosis of a form detached from meaning and capable of taking on any structure whatever, yet entirely ruthless in its inability to modify its own structural design for nonstructural [i.e., aesthetic or formalistic] reasons' (*Allegories* 294). As a human extension, or prosthetic, language actually dramatizes the absence of any human animation or purpose behind the prosthetic. It is in that sense that language is a radically perverse instrumentality, an instrument divorced from the human aim that defines it as a tool, a *technē* that displaces any higher, non-contingent aim, any human truth or meaning, which are in fact products of its machinery. De Man's mechanism is first and foremost an obsession with this problematic, a topos of robotic simulacrum and mutilating instrumentality that decon-structs the intelligibility of language as a tool, a sign or extension, of human intent.

We are thus faced with a predicament equally impossible and aborigi-nal: that which defines us, our ability to extend ourselves, to make our-selves and our world, what can equally go by the name of either tool-making or language, is that which is radically disjoined from us, from human motivation and being. Within this 'anthropological' context, one which paradoxically but also emphatically disarticulates its own object of analysis, de Man's well-known references to the 'inhuman' nature of language gain their full force (*Resistance* 86, 94–7, 99–102). Language is not simply a tool, a thing, that we use to know ourselves and our world. It is that breach into the stable oppositions between making and knowing, means and ends, instrument and intention, machinery and human identity, that underscores the degree to which human nature is realized by its prosthetic character, by its dependence on the machine of language. As a repetitive patterning, simultaneously tra-versed by the aberrant and arbitrary, the machine of language is the logic of the inhuman. As an effect of language, the human is a non-human, inhuman, thing.

The mechanist materialism in de Man's deconstructive writings is something else besides Jameson's interpretation of eclectic philosophi-cal nominalism, just as deconstruction in general is something else besides a radically linguistic scepticism, in so far as that scepticism also reorganizes the distinction between the human and the non-human (that is, language) as the problem, or condition, of instrumentality. Such a view not only defamiliarizes de Manian deconstruction by giving it an anthropological cast; it also cannily hails Marxism as a body of discourse largely imbricated by these newly highlighted de Manian concerns.

Such an interpellation not only reiterates how Marx's dictum about freeing humanity from the necessity of Nature resonates with a desired liberation from instrumentality. It also more specifically stresses and clarifies the degree to which Marxism's persuasive cognitive force, what Jameson in another context calls a 'kind of shock to the mind,' rests on the chiasmic scandal that dramatizes how in bourgeois life humans are things and things are living beings (*Ideologies* 121). The apotheosis of this reversal is the commodity fetish in *Capital*, a non-human thing putatively in the service of human life, but that in truth reorients human means in the service of its ends (163–77). As a supernatural being, an idol of our mind, the commodity fetish displaces human intention much in the same way that Rousseau's inhuman grammar replaces the sovereignty of human desire. And, as in de Man, human existence is not merely shunted aside by this displacement; it is transformed, unveiled as part of the machinery of instrumentality. The status of the commodity fetish is inversely reflected in the plight of the worker, now made a machine to serve the production of the living fetish. The machine defines the human, as in Marx's case of the child labourer, outfitted with machinery specifically tailored to its size, so as to increase the efficiency of its production: 'The machine accommodates itself to the *weakness* of the human being in order to make the *weak* human being [the child] into a machine' (*Manuscripts* 95).[5] 'Human being' becomes a simulacrum of itself as human labour becomes an extension of the machine. Radically separated from human identity, the child labourer's actions take on the linguistic dynamism, the formal patterning, of Kleist's marionette, the 'anamorphosis of a form detached from meaning,' locked within 'its own structural design,' the non-human design of capital.

To understand Marx's argument as the assertion of capitalism as non-human, as fundamentally *without* meaning, is to approach the conceptual force behind Marxism's and deconstruction's shared investment in instrumentality, what, poaching from both Jameson and de Man, we might call the asymptotic point of their metonymic contiguity. From another level of Marxist analysis, of course, capitalism is fraught with the meaning of dialectical materialism. The prosthetic objectification of Marxism's child labourer is not simply the sign of a condition of a radically perverse instrumentality that goes by the name of language; it is the symptom of a set of social and economic relations, whose intelligibility depends upon the historical analysis that Marxism both presupposes and interrogates.

Marx also distinguishes between good and bad machines, tools and machines, and single machines and systems of machinery. But these and other crucial differences of contrasting affect and political prescription should not stop us from considering the implications that a shared focus on the machine and instrumentality have for the two discourses. De Manian deconstruction, for example, is today chiefly identified by a certain proscription of the literal, an active exposure of how language constantly confuses itself with the phenomenal world.[6] The images of machines in Rousseau actually complicate this injunction in two ways: by their literal status as machines and, paradoxically, by their simultaneous existence as figures for language.

'Literalizing' the images of machinery in Rousseau means his encounters with machines are just that: encounters with instruments that thwart his plans, threaten his body, and challenge his subjectivity as the origin of his own agency and value. Such a challenge resonates, of course, with the many scenes of psychic self-conflict in Rousseau, such as the famous episode of Marion and the stolen ribbon in the *Confessions*, the very episode that de Man transforms into an allegory of how human intention and subjectivity depend on the contingency – the machinery – of language. The point is, however, that such psychic self-division also reflects Rousseau's interaction with a world of deadly man-made objects, instead of simply the other way around.

Conceivably, the ribbon in the Marion episode is itself a tool or machine that in the unpredictability of its purpose and effect splits Rousseau from his intentions, his subjectivity from the fiction of an originary desire. But a later anecdote in the *Confessions* also vividly confuses the vagaries of machinery with the mercurial nature of Rousseau's desires, his account of the toy heron-fountain. This episode is less immediately structured in an ethical mode than the guilt-saturated theft of the ribbon and framing of Marion. The absence of such an ethical context is actually an advantage, in so far as it allows us to recover from the *Confessions* another series of coordinates. Rousseau relates how this toy figured in his designs with his friend Bâcle, when they planned to leave the home of Rousseau's benefactor, Mme de Warens, for a journey across the Alps:

We constantly played with this fountain as we talked of our journey and so conceived the idea that the one might contribute to the other, and the toy be instrumental in adding days to our travels. For nothing was more curious than a heron-fountain. That fact was the foundation on which we built the edifice of our fortune. All we had to do in each village was to gather the peasants around our fountain, and victuals and good cheer would be showered on us in abundance ... our fountain would pay our way through Piedmont, Savoy, and France, and the whole world.

This extravagant journey proved almost as pleasant as I had expected, but not quite in the same way. For although our fountain amused the landladies and their female servants for a minute or two, we still had to pay when we left. But that hardly worried us, and we did not think seriously of using this resource till our money failed. An accident spared us the trouble. The fountain broke somewhere near Bramant, and indeed it was time. For, though neither of us cared to say so, we were both getting rather bored with it. (102)[7]

Trivial and useless, the heron-fountain is also the 'foundation' upon which Rousseau builds the 'edifice' of his fantasized fortune. The changing meanings of the fountain become an accurate index for the impractical and peripatetic nature of Rousseau's journey, as well as for his own inconstant attitude towards the trip: from being bored with the toy, and thus the grandiose plans associated with it, to laughing at his and Bâcle's foolishness as their clothes and shoes wear out, and to brooding over the outcome of his return to Mme de Warens. Within such a confusion of affect, of means and ends, the fountain could be said not only to reflect but also to generate Rousseau's journey and desires. 'Instrumental' in adding days to the planning of the travel, the 'foundation' of Rousseau's excited imaginings, the fountain is at once what refers to the trip and what the trip refers to, the 'it' that gradually bores Rousseau; literally and figuratively, the toy and its abrupt destruction structure the contingency of his journey, organizing his desires as well as serving them. The fountain is radically instrumental in the perverse sense that we have applied to de Man. At once at the centre and the periphery of Rousseau's narrative, the fountain foregrounds the conflation of aim and pointlessness, of desire and apathy, that underwrites his wanderings. By laughing gaily as their plans for the fountain disintegrate, Rousseau ostensibly asserts a discontinuity between the toy and his emotions; yet the *meaning* of that laughter depends on that very discontinuity, on the very ineffectiveness of the fountain. Rousseau's narrative is as much a reaction to the fountain as what the toy reflects.

The indeterminacy of the fountain as either instrument or motive also tellingly takes place within two explicit systems of exchange: Rousseau's imagined exchange of the toy's performance for food and lodgings, and the actual money economy that rejects the toy as part of its system of substitution. Rousseau's journey is thus a continuous encounter with objects – toy and money – that stress not only the threatening unpredictability of their effects but also the degree to which those effects are questions of value and exchange. That Rousseau also specifies these systems of exchange in terms of class and gender – the imagined economy with peasants and the real one with landladies and their servants – is no coincidence. For the question of the toy's performance, of its value and what it does, could just as well be applied to Rousseau and his relation to Mme de Warens. Entertaining but impractical, of what value or use is Rousseau to his patron? As de Man argues, Rousseau is not simply threatened by the actions of objects; his subjectivity is itself objectified, made a thing. But to equate Rousseau with the heron-fountain is also necessarily to detail the relation between Warens and Rousseau in terms of class and gender difference, terms that in their specificity are, for want of a better term, 'historical.' If Rousseau is a toy whose value and purpose are unclear, that volatility is also at once the historical uncertainty of Rousseau's situation, of a petit-bourgeois man in the ambivalent service, and keep, of his 'Maman,' the wealthy Mme de Warens.

Both Rousseau's and Warens's positions could be particularized in even more complex fashion, but that is exactly the point: seeing Rousseau as the heron-fountain of Mme de Warens occasions this historical specification. Conversely, the question driving this specification – what function Rousseau and the fountain serve – has a paradigmatic power that structures the entire book. Indeed, the *Confessions* can be understood as an extended response to the question of what value, what use, is 'Rousseau,' a name that is almost always associated with the assertion of the interiority of Romantic imagination, the fantastic expression of a heron-fountain. As de Man argues, however, that interiority is paradoxically the consequence of a perversely instrumental world, what he describes as the machine of grammar and what we have depicted as the literal world of machines. In that sense the heron-fountain is not an authentic mode of Romantic expression but an eighteenth-century mechanist work. But, more important, Rousseau's interiority is *itself* a machine in that, like the heron-fountain, it is marked by the question of its use and of the system of relations, the economy, that gives it 'genuine' value. Understanding that economy means understanding that system historically, which means seeing how the question of Rousseau's objectification is simultaneously the question of Rousseau's vocation in life, the question of a career, any career, that cannot by itself be understood without understanding what makes such a question possible: in Rousseau's century the spread of market forces in Europe and the advent of other levelling events, one of which after his death Rousseau will retroactively become the emblem of, the French Revolution. Born the son of a watch-maker, Rousseau might become something else, a fact that is grounded in this historical moment, as well as one that is the occasion for his book: the possibility, the opportunity and crisis, that his vocation, the writing of his life and desires, might be something else beside the making of a watch. The perverse instrumentality recovered from de Man's reading of the machine in Rousseau can thus be linked to the historical instrumentality that resonates with the move from *Gemeinschaft* to *Gesellschaft*, the increasing dissolution of 'organic' society under capitalism.[8]

The apparent hyperbole of such an analysis seems less an issue when juxtaposed with an episode from the *Reveries of the Solitary Walker*, one made famous by de Man's reading of it in *Allegories*. The scene is Rousseau's encounter with a machine that crushes the ends of two of his fingers. De Man does not mention what the machine specifically does. Instead his quote from Rousseau emphasizes the machine's formal properties, as seductive to Rousseau as they are empty to the reader of any apparent purpose or meaning: 'I looked at the metal rolls, my eyes were attracted by their polish. I was tempted to touch them with my fingers and I moved them with pleasure over the polished surface of the cylinder' (*Oeuvres complètes* 1:1036).[9] De Man goes on to stress how the machine's power of suggestion

> reaches far beyond its illustrative purpose, especially if one bears in mind the previous characterization [in Rousseau] of unmotivated, fictional language as 'machinal.' The underlying structural patterns of addition and suppression as well as the figural system of the text all converge towards it. Barely concealed by its peripheral function, the text here stages the textual machine of its own constitution *and* performance, its own textual allegory. (*Allegories* 298)

But what is the 'illustrative purpose' of the 'textual machine'? Rousseau's anecdote actually refers to a calender owned by an uncle who operates a calico works business. The 'textual machine' is, literally, a textile machine. The intelligibility of both machines comes from the common Latin root of what they both produce, *textus*, a 'woven thing.' The status of this 'thing' is, of course, precisely the issue. But the two machines' commonality in this thing, *textus*, also suspends any clear resolution to this issue. By resolving this predicament in favour of his deadly machine of grammar, de Man cannot avoid a clarity of meaning that at once denotes a suppression of history. Indeed, that clarity defines what such a suppression is.

The contours of this suppressed history become clearer when we remember not only the famous role of linens and coats in *Capital*, but also how its discussion of machinery and large-scale industry begins with a number of references to the spinning machines and looms of Europe's eighteenth- and nineteenth-century textile industry (*Capital* 131–50, 493–6). Marx notes how the spinning machines of the industrial revolution create an odd dislocation in scale between the embodied human subject and the productive capacities of the machine, which leaves 'the worker, in addition to his new labor of watching the machine with his eyes and correcting its mistakes with his hands, the merely mechanical role of acting as the motive power' (496). The spinning machine is at once human size and something much larger, a predicament that speaks to the inevitably hyperbolic nature of any narrativization of one individual's experience of capitalist history, as well the odd combination of triviality and menace that Rousseau's encounter with machines thematizes. Indeed, if the machine in de Man comes from both the eighteenth and nineteenth centuries, from the random patterning of vertiginous clockwork and the dynamism and entropy of steam locomotion, that spectrum is embedded in a historical set of social relations that the 'literalization' of Rousseau's machinery reveals. The uselessness of the heron-fountain and the mutilating power of the calico calender – these are the linked symptoms of a historical horizon that coincides with the structure of Rousseau's texts.

It might appear that this 'literalization' of the machine completely diverges from de Man's focus on language in *Allegories*, as well as from contemporary deconstructive proscriptions of the literal. But this is not the case. Separating the literal from the figural becomes a much more complicated proposition when, paradoxically, Rousseau's machines are seen as de Manian figures for language. Far from simply inscribing language within the definitive closure of the figural, such an articulation occasions the question of language's literal meaning: its purpose and

value, which, like the machine's, inhere in the deconstruction of its subordinate role to the presumed originary force of human intention. A
combination of the arbitrary and the formal, machine-like and like a
machine, language *is* a machine. The mechanical and the linguistic are
thus caught in a metonymic relation of mutual displacement, an oscillation of referential properties that subtends how Rousseau's mechanical
references are at once figures for machinery and figures for a language
which is literally a machine. Signs of machinery can refer to both
machine and language, which refer to each other; the machine is language, while language is a machine. That both could be figures for each
other, that both could *be* each other, signals the tension of a metonymic
displacement rather than simply a metaphoric subsumption which
would allow the figural and literal to exist in naïve opposition. Rather,
the mutual displacement between machine and language asserts a condition that repudiates the *a priori*, separate existence of the figural and
literal. This predicament prevents, or resists, the existence of de Man's
allegories as the literality of pure figure.

Contrary to such a pure existence, the literal is the foreign semiotic
that deconstruction's own constative performance cannot quite sub-
sume.[10] As such, the literal is still held out as a possibility within a discourse that seems vehemently organized around the constant exposure
of the literal as a false or blind figure. This possibility, rather than any
pure realization of the literal, structures the aporia between the figural
and literal that makes the 'literalization' of machinery in Rousseau,
along with the attendant historical specification, something else beside
a pure, complete break from de Man's readings. The question then
becomes whether this aporia has any other consequence for the intelligibility of historical thought: whether the machine conversely affects
Marxist discourse in a way that is more complex than simply conceiving
of Marxist historicity as the literalization of deconstruction's instrumental concerns. If the presence of the machine in Marx clarifies the social
character of the dilemma of Rousseau's value and use in the *Confessions*,
how might the machine also interrogate the conception of those very
terms in Marx?

One could respond by considering Marx's many explicit statements
about machinery and automatons in *Capital*, the *Grundrisse*, and elsewhere. A surprisingly more pertinent approach plays off one reading of
Marx's theory of value in the first volume of *Capital*, what Gayatri Spivak
might call a 'continuist' version of the Marxist relation between use
value and exchange value.[11] Within this reading, use value is not blind

radical instrumentality. Rather, it is the self-evident usefulness of a product or object, fundamentally separate from the value of something that occurs within a system of substitution, or exchange. With the advent of capitalism and the ubiquity of the commodity form, use value is shunted aside by the increasingly corrosive powers of exchange value. In dissolving the organic integrity of use value, exchange value, with its mystifying social relations among commodities rather than people, subverts the stability of means and ends that use value underwrites; the result is the general loss of organic meaning that is the invidious signature of capitalist, bourgeois exchange.

Such a reading associates Marx with a nostalgic longing for foundational use value. In his well-known critique of *Capital*, Jean Baudrillard attacks this nostalgia, deconstructing use value by way of a supplementary exchange value that he claims always contaminates use value's pure originary force. For Baudrillard capitalism, rather than mystifying genuine social relations, most perfectly emphasizes a constitutive ontological fissure that always places 'authentic' value and identity within a system of exchange, unmoored from any ultimate referent, adrift within an economy of signs. Use value and production are hollowed out, made phantasms of the equally surface phenomenon of commodities, consumption, and, in Baudrillard's later works, simulacra.[12] Like Kleist's marionette, Baudrillard's simulacrum, a copy with no origin, evinces the radical non-human instrumentality of the machine: an object that not only is unable to account for itself within any system of human reference or design but has also replaced that system, made it a simulacrum effect. Marx's commodity fetish is normalized, with the intelligibility of human affect and subjectivity becoming one more non-human thing.

This familiar argument depends, of course, on the truth of Marx's nostalgia, his investment in a metaphysical essentialism. Gayatri Spivak's meditation on Marxist value comes up with a very different *Capital*, one composed of a much more radical textuality, a vehemently 'discontinuist' performance that foregrounds the 'invagination' of use value's spatial relation to exchange value, and the moments of parataxis that interrupt the dialectical bindings of the transformation of value into capital (159–66). Such blockages turn *Capital* into a very different text from the one that Baudrillard deconstructs. Another tactic is possible, however, one that stays within the boundaries of a text developing a continuous, architectonic argument about value: more specifically, an argument about the relation between value and labour. But rather than supporting Baudrillard, this move demonstrates the degree to which

Capital anticipates the question of the simulacrum, a predicament that says much about the roles of machine and *figure* in Marxist thought.

As Marx explains, exchange value does not occur simply through a set of relational differences, unmoored from the ultimate referent of use value. Exchange value occurs because of Marx's theory of equivalence, his belief that different commodities still share a fundamental commonality that allows them to form relations of value that are both quantitatively *and* qualitatively equivalent. That commonality is 'human labor in the abstract,' homogeneous objectified labour, as opposed to heterogeneous concrete labour which produces use value (*Capital* 128). Indeed, a 'use-value, or useful article ... has value only because abstract human labour is objectified (*vergegenständlicht*) or materialized in it' – a commodity might have a certain utility, but its value lies in the amount of abstract labour, the labour time, that was expended in making it (129). This identity, value as abstract labour, comes to structure the equivalence among commodities that allows them to circulate within the realm of capitalist exchange.

While subtending Marx's entire theory of value, abstract labour has been the source of a continuing controversy, since it begs two thorny, interpenetrating questions. How do we define abstract labour, and when does it occur? *Capital* does conceive of abstract labour in a physiological sense, the 'productive expenditure of human brains, nerves, and muscles' (128) that allows for the temporal measurement of 'identical labor power' (134). Of course, to *measure* one homogeneous identity is to insert questions of relation and difference within the very objective nature of that identity. More troublesome is what this definition also implies, that abstract labour as embodied labour need not be restricted to the human production of a capitalist society. Paradoxically, Marx is also quite emphatic as to how the uniformity of abstract labour occurs only through the exchange of commodities; exchange value might not make sense without the equivalence of abstract labour, but abstract labour cannot happen completely without a society within which exchange value dominates. At the very least, then, abstract labour becomes a constitutive quality of human production that only gains hegemony during the capitalist era. Some readers of Marx have gone further, however, arguing that abstract labour is completely a symptom of capitalist exchange, an abstraction of quality that is in fact alienated labour, the reification of human subjectivity under capitalism. Thus, Marx's text, even its continuist version, occasions two competing conceptions of abstract labour that clash over the metalepsis between abstract labour and historical periodization, and abstract labour itself as either embodied being, constitutive property, or historical effect.[13]

Several passages from *Capital* forcefully convey these tensions. They occur towards the end of Marx's discussion of 'The Equivalent Form of Value,' where he unpacks the consequences of achieving an equivalence between coats and linens by turning the specific concrete labour of tailoring into a measure for weaving through the concept of undifferentiated, abstract labour:

> But because this concrete labor, tailoring, counts exclusively as the expression of undifferentiated human labor, it possesses the characteristics of being identical with other kinds of labor, such as the labor embodied in the linen. Consequently, although, like all other commodity-producing labor, it is the labor of private individuals, it is nevertheless labor in its directly social form. It is precisely for this reason that it presents itself in the shape of a product which is directly exchangeable with other commodities. Thus the equivalent form has a third peculiarity: private labor takes the form of its opposite, namely labor in its directly social form. (150–1)

The organization of this paragraph implies a certain uni-direction, with the transformation of private, concrete labour into social, abstract labour being the 'third peculiarity,' the final consequence of the equivalent form of value. Such a teleological movement would intimate the logic of perceiving the exchange of commodities as being a prerequisite for this transformation. Yet, at the same time, the commensurability between coat and linen through abstract, or social, labour results 'in the shape of a product which is directly exchangeable with other commodities'; far from simply being the effect of exchange, such commensurability seems to present *itself* as the prerequisite for the exchange of commodities.

This chiasmus is exacerbated by the language earlier used to describe the first two peculiarities of the equivalence form, how 'use-value becomes the form of appearance of its opposite, value' (*Capital* 148); and how 'concrete labor becomes the form of manifestation of its opposite, abstract human labor' (150). In contrast to the third peculiarity, terms associated with private labour ('use value' and 'concrete labor') are described as vehicles for core identities associated with social labour ('value' and 'abstract human labor'). To complicate matters more, the 'mysteriousness' of the equivalent form and its first peculiarity, the manifestation of value through use value, is solved by the second peculiarity, the manifestation of abstract labour through concrete labour (149–50). The equivalent form of value thus produces several conflicting, asymmetric relations between abstract labour and its converse. The third peculiarity of equivalent form seems to narrate the transformation of private labour into social labour. At another level, however, the very 'riddle' of value in the equivalent form seems to be explained by the already existing presence of abstract labour in the form's second peculiarity (150). Finally, in the first and second peculiarities value and abstract labour are embodied in their opposites; they are not simply what their opposites teleologically become. Indeed, the 'expression' of abstract labour through concrete labour appears to initiate the transformation of private labour into social labour. At the very least these different scenarios stress the huge complexity in *Capital* of abstract labour's theoretical and historical conception. More radically this complexity stages a scandal of, rather than a challenge to, thought. The meaning of private labour not manifesting but 'tak[ing] the form' of social labour, the question of what refers to what, is simultaneously foregrounded and stalled at the very moment that that transformation's relation to commodity exchange is asserted in the text.

Trying to order these varying levels of conflicting cause and effect, of primary and secondary identity, is exactly what the controversy over abstract labour has tried to adjudicate. Marx himself appears to offer his own solution, with his discussion of Aristotle that immediately follows the description of this third peculiarity of the equivalent form. The question of abstract labour's relation to exchange is once again engaged, this time in terms of the difference between pre-capitalist and capitalist societies. Marx relates how Aristotle's *Nichomachean Ethics* at first seems to understand how an equivalence between unlike things is possible, how five beds equalling one house is indistinguishable from five beds equalling so much money, but then denies their fundamental commensurability. Marx argues that Aristotle's denial was the result of the 'lack [in his analysis] of a concept of value':

What is the homogeneous element, i.e. the common substance, which the house represents from the point of view of the bed, in the value expression for the bed? Such a thing, in truth, cannot exist, says Aristotle. But why not? Towards the bed, the house represents something equal, in so far as it represents what is really equal, both in the bed and the house. And that is – human labor.

However, Aristotle was unable to extract this fact, that in the form of commodity-values, all labor is expressed as equal human labor and therefore labor of equal quality, by inspection from the form of value, because Greek society was founded upon the labor of slaves, hence had as its natural basis the inequality of men and of their labor-powers. The equality and equivalence of all kinds of labor because and in so far as they are human labor in general, could not be deciphered until the concept of human equality had already acquired the permanence of a fixed popular opinion. This however becomes possible only in a society where the commodity-form is the universal form of the product of labor, hence the dominant social relation is the relation between men as possessors of commodities. Aristotle's genius is displayed precisely by his discovery of a relation of equality in the value-expression of commodities. Only the historical limitation inherent in the society in which he lived, prevented him from finding out what, 'in truth,' this relation of equality consisted of. (*Capital* 151–2)[14]

In this difficult passage the 'common substance' of abstract labour seems to inhabit both the identity of a constitutive embodied property and a historical effect. By stressing Aristotle's historical inability to understand this idea, Marx seems to reiterate the degree to which abstract labour is fundamentally tied to capitalist society. But in stressing this inability as a question of historical *understanding*, Marx also seems to imply that the objective nature of abstract labour was something that Aristotle *could* have perceived except for the social inequalities of the Greek world. Indeed, only the advent of the 'fixed popular opinion' of human equality allows abstract labour to be 'deciphered' by modern understanding. This tension is further complicated by the cause of this opinion: the moment in capitalist history when the dominant human relation inheres in those that occur among commodity owners. Commodity production and exchange do seem to enable abstract labour, but only as a second-order effect, by creating the popular opinion that paradoxically allows us to see, through the heterogeneity of concrete labour, what itself had been codified by such pre-capitalist modes of social inequality as slavery. The mediating terms that determine abstract labour's presence are thus themselves of differing ontological weight. This situation destabilizes any simple narrativization of Marx's historical comparison: what is the status of an abstract labour unavailable to Greek antiquity because of the historical fact of slavery, as opposed to that of an abstract labour available to modernity because of the fixed popular opinion of equality? What is the status of the historical difference that inheres in Aristotle's 'historical limitation'? Furthermore, abstract labour is itself *exteriorized* from commodity exchange as a second-order effect of that phenomenon, exactly what abstract labour, within those societies in which the capitalist mode of production prevails, should subtend. Yet abstract labour is also unable to secure simply the identity of a universal property: if such labour was '"in truth"' at the bottom of the equality that Aristotle theorized, its constative effect is inscribed within a phrase whose scare quotes stress rather than elide the figural disjunctions of the passage, the degree to which abstract labour seems at once to occupy and displace itself from both historical moments of Marx's story.[15]

Given the complexity of such passages, solving the controversy of abstract labour seems less pertinent than considering why Marx's text describes this idea in such emphatically ambiguous terms – why his writing creates this controversy in the first place. *Capital* installs within its analysis the concept of abstract labour as a problem of the relation between abstract labour and *something else*: between an entity and its abstraction, homogenization, or objectification, an entity that has been diversely interpreted as the heterogeneity of a concrete labour subtended by the pure physiology of undifferentiated labour and as the prolepsis of an unalienated labour negatively defined by the present expropriation of reified labour. The ambiguity of abstract labour is simply a sign of the ambiguity of its referent, what it abstracts, what we might try to circumscribe by the term 'labour' except for the fact that that idea has no analytic force in Marx's theory of value without the initial divisions between abstract and concrete labour, and labour and labour power. Indeed, depending on what moment of analysis is occurring in Marx's theory, it is unclear whether that entity is abstract labour's referent or abstract labour is *its* referent. One could chalk this up to the mobility of dialectical positioning that characterizes Marx's thought. But one could also see this referential indeterminacy inserting a bar between abstract labour and what it abstracts, an absolute separation that would disrupt their putative mimetic grounding in one another. An abstraction of something else, abstract labour does not need anything else to be itself, to organize and generate Marx's theory of value. This sense of tautology is exactly what Gayatri Spivak criticizes in the continuist version of 'Marx's scheme of value': 'Yet even in this ... version value seems to escape the onto-phenomenological question: what is it (*ti esti*). The usual answer – value is the representation of objectified labor – begs the question of use-value' (155).

To operate within a historically continuous argument of Marxist value, abstract labour does not need what it historically abstracts. What *Capital* marks by such terms as 'concrete labour' and 'use value' *does not need to exist.* An abstraction without a referent, abstract labour functions like a copy with no origin. Baudrillard's deconstruction of Marx is beside the point, in so far as Marx's theory of value is already underwritten by the simulation, the simulacrum of abstract labour. It is no coincidence that Marx so often explicitly or implicitly describes one trait of abstract labour, its homogenization, in mechanical terms. In doing so Marx also signals abstract labour's robotic independence from what it abstracts, an independence that coincides with the metaphysical unmooring of the simulacrum.

When Marx places abstract labour within the realm of a 'phantom-like objectivity,' he could just as well be describing that concept's rhetorical effect on his text (*Capital* 128). Accounting for Marx's theory of value, abstract labour as a simulation cannot account for itself. It is a catachresis at the core of Marx's theory, a figure that cannot account for its figurality in literal terms; it cannot simply be absorbed by the exigencies of concrete labour or use value. If the machine in deconstruction produces the possibility of the literal in a discourse that constantly exposes the literal as a moment of figure, abstract labour is the machine of figure that enables the analysis of the literal in Marx. As a catachresis, abstract labour is also the preeminent figure of the machine, an example of language's robotic quality, the component within a pattern that cannot be accounted for even as it generates a network of constative and performative effects. Far from simply literalizing deconstruction's figural application of the machine, from simply conflating machinery and literality, Marx's theory demonstrates its textual awareness of a radically perverse instrumentality based on the simultaneous articulation of figure as machine, and machine as figure. Such simultaneity demonstrates that any vision of history is at once a rendering of its non-identity, or form. The form in history that is not history: that is the machine, as much as the literal in deconstruction that is not pure figure, history in Rousseau.

NOTES

1 I am indebted to David Kaufmann and Marshall Grossman for their challenging responses to this essay.

2 De Man's immediate point refers to how the Kantian sublime is, paradoxically, 'a noumenal entity [that] has to be phenomenally represented
(*dargestellt*)' (*Aesthetic Ideology* 74).

3 There are, of course, a number of thinkers, such as Heidegger, Adorno, and
Derrida, whose writings explore these issues, and who could just as well have
provided access to the topos considered here. The goal of this essay, then, is
as much to clarify the specific rhetorical and conceptual operations of the
specific writings examined as to suggest a more general overlapping of
deconstructive and Marxist discourse. A possible comparison with particularly timely suggestiveness might contrast the role of the machine in this
piece with the references to 'the external, nonsensical, "machine" – automatism of the signifier' of Pascal and the concept of 'ideological fantasy' in
Slavoj Žižek's *The Sublime Object of Ideology* (30–3, 36–7). Consider also the
New Historicist reading of the machine in US literature, as in Mark Seltzer's
Bodies and Machines. See also notes 4 and 15. I am indebted to Tilottama
Rajan for the phrase 'technological unconscious.'

4 Perhaps unavoidably, this passage seems today pretty much joined to the his-
torico-biographical coordinates of the young Paul de Man's writings for the
collaborationist paper *Le Soir* during the Second World War. For two helpful
– that is, complicated – leftist responses to this situation, see Jameson, *Postmodernism* 256–8; and Ernesto Laclau, 'Totalitarianism and Moral Indignation.' See also my *Fantastic Modernity: Dialectical Readings in Romanticism and
Theory* 35–68. Moving in another direction, we might also consider the American translation of Jacques Lacan's use of the Freudian *Wiederholungzwang* as
'repetition automatism' in his famous 'Seminar on "The Purloined Letter"'
39, as well as that concept's relationship to Lacanian intersubjectivity and his
assertion that the 'displacement of the signifier determines the subjects in
their acts, in their destiny, in their refusals, in their blindnesses, in their end
and in their fate, their innate gifts and social acquisitions notwithstanding,
without regard for character or sex, and that, willingly or not, everything
that might be considered the stuff of psychology, kit and caboodle, will follow the path of the signifier' (60).

5 By citing both *Economic and Philosophic Manuscripts of 1844* and *Capital* I am,
of course, qualifying Althusser's argument for an epistemic break between
Marx's earlier and later works. See Louis Althusser, *For Marx*, and *Reading
Capital.*

6 See, for example, Paul de Man, *The Resistance to Theory* 10–11; Cathy Caruth,
'The Claims of Reference'; and Geraldine Friedman, *The Insistence of History:
Revolution in Burke, Wordsworth, Keats, and Baudelaire.*

7 Cohen notes that the toy is rightly termed the 'Hiero-fountain, after its

inventor, Hiero of Alexander; a toy that depended on air-pressure' (*Confessions* 102). Linguistically, then, a metonymic confusion displays itself as figurative resemblance. My argument is that while this mechanical contingency certainly resonates with the indeterminate actions of Rousseau, the mechanical condition in this passage is more emphatically structured by a contingency that can be 'literalized' by Rousseau's historical moment.

8 The use of such terms does not necessarily imply a fundamental belief in the organic essentialness of pre-industrial, capitalist society. Rather, they allude to the new questions of value, destiny, and worth associated with the vocational choices of a capitalist subject increasingly unmoored from the traditional roles and strictures of that earlier society. For an application of these issues to a twentieth-century moment of modernity, one still generated by the European history of Rousseau's eighteenth century, see Fredric Jameson, *The Political Unconscious: Narrative as a Socially Symbolic Act* 249–50. But see also this essay's discussion of the interpretation of Marx's exchange value as a corrosion of traditional, organic society.

9 Cited in *Allegories* 298.

10 While this reformulation of de Man's terms might sound similar to the way in which the Lacanian Real cannot be subsumed by the symbolic, the propositions are not the same. The Real's resistance to signification more properly recalls Jameson's neo-Kantian noumenon, or de Man's notion of the 'materiality' of language, while the literal is the result of figure confusing itself with the phenomenal world. (In his own reading of Kant, de Man does not locate this materiality simply in the noumenon; rather, he identifies it with the more complex event of the sublime [*Aesthetic Ideology* 119–28].) My reading tries to reinterrogate the certitude of that error *as* error, or as the literality of pure figure. Deconstruction's internal resistance to such literality, or purity, would be, paradoxically, the foreign, unsubsumable element of the literal *in* deconstruction, the possibility of historical narrative.

11 See Gayatri Spivak, 'Scattered Speculations on the Question of Value' 155–8.

12 See Jean Baudrillard, *For a Critique of the Political Economy of the Sign* 130–63; and *Simulations*.

13 For further readings about this debate, see Piero Straffa, *Productions of Commodities by Means of Commodities*; Lucio Colletti, *From Rousseau to Lenin* 87; Diane Elson, ed., *Value: The Representation of Labor in Capitalism*; Ian Steedman, *Marx after Straffa*; and Ian Steedman et al., *The Value Controversy*.

14 For a discussion of this passage as a reflexive allegory of the commodification of social and economic theory after 1848, see Friedman 169–70.

15 Another, more radically Hegelian reading of this passage would consider the objective knowledge of commodities and abstract labour a retroactive effect of the reconstructed historical memory of the subject under capital. In that

sense Aristotle could not have had access to this knowledge, in so far as it is the outcome of an analysis that can only come from the position of a subject secured within the historical nexus of capital and commodity exchange. Within this scenario 'popular opinion' is not a second-order effect, but the index of this nexus, the 'ideological fantasy' that Slavoj Žižek argues actually undergirds social reality (30–3). As such, 'popular opinion' has as much ontological weight as the slavery of Aristotle's Greek society. Indeed, the relations of domination and servitude that inhere in Greek slavery, unequal labour, become under capitalism the fetishized relations among commodities, and, consequently, their owners (26). The fetishized social relations of commodities can only be calculated, however, if there exists their 'common substance,' the 'popular opinion' or 'ideological fantasy' of equal labour – what '"in truth"' human equality actually is.

While securely embedding abstract labour within the historical *epistemē* of capitalism's subject, this retroactive construction of the difference between that subject and Aristotle is structured by the impossibility of answering when that difference – when capitalism, in effect – occurs. (Similarly, Žižek asserts the impossibility of asking when capitalism attains the self-realization that would dialectically lead to its end: 'When can we speak of an accordance between productive forces and relations of production in the capitalist mode of production? Strict analysis leads to only one possible answer: *never*' [52].) Abstract labour is the index of a historical difference that history cannot account for; in so far as capitalism's retroactive memory structures the very parameters of that memory, the moment before that memory objectively begins becomes an impossible point in time. Abstract labour signifies capitalist (and Marxist) history as a simulation that needs no other prior history for either its existence or its historicizing force. Abstract labour is the historical insight into capital's procedures that is Žižek's social 'dream' or 'ideological fantasy,' more real than the waking origins of pre-capitalist history and heterogenous social labour (44–6). Rather than dialectically solving the rhetorical tensions in Marx's passage on Aristotle, an interpretation based on the retroactive remembering of unequal labour, or slavery, ends up reemphasizing the robotic, catachrestic nature of the remembering subject of capitalism in relation to its own history. See also note 3.

WORKS CITED

Althusser, Louis. *For Marx.* Trans. Ben Brewster. London: NLB, 1977.
– *Reading Capital.* Trans. Ben Brewster. London: NLB, 1970.
Baudrillard, Jean. *For a Critique of the Political Economy of the Sign.* Trans. Charles Levin. St Louis: Telos, 1981.

– *Simulations.* Trans. Paul Foss, Paul Patton, and Philip Beitchman. New York: Semiotext(e), 1983.

Caruth, Cathy. 'The Claims of Reference.' *Yale Journal of Literary Criticism* 4 (1990): 193–205.

Colletti, Lucio. *From Rousseau to Lenin.* New York: Monthly Review, 1973.

de Man, Paul. *The Aesthetic Ideology.* Minneapolis: U of Minnesota P, 1996.

– *Allegories of Reading: Figural Language in Rousseau, Nietzsche, Rilke, and Proust.* New Haven: Yale UP, 1979.

– *The Resistance to Theory.* Minneapolis: U of Minnesota P, 1986.

Elson, Diane, ed. *Value: The Representation of Labor in Capitalism.* Atlantic Highlands: Humanities P, 1979.

Friedman, Geraldine. *The Insistence of History: Revolution in Burke, Wordsworth, Keats, and Baudelaire.* Stanford: Stanford UP, 1996.

Jameson, Fredric. *The Ideologies of Theory: Essays 1971–1986, Volume 1: Situations of Theory.* Minneapolis: U of Minnesota P, 1988.

– *The Political Unconscious: Narrative as a Socially Symbolic Act.* Ithaca: Cornell UP, 1981.

– *Postmodernism, or, the Cultural Logic of Late Capitalism.* Durham: Duke UP, 1991.

Lacan, Jacques. 'Seminar on "The Purloined Letter."' *Yale French Studies* 48 (1973): 39–72.

Laclau, Ernesto. 'Totalitarianism and Moral Indignation.' *Diacritics* 20 (1990): 88–95.

Marx, Karl. *Capital: Volume 1.* Trans. Ben Fowkes. London: Penguin, 1990.

– *Economic and Philosophic Manuscripts of 1844.* Trans. Martin Milligan. *The Marx-Engels Reader.* Ed. Robert C. Tucker. 2nd ed. New York: Norton, 1978.

Rousseau, Jean-Jacques. *The Confessions.* Trans. J. M. Cohen. New York: Penguin, 1982.

– *Oeuvres complètes, Les confessions, autres textes autobiographieques.* Ed. Bernard Gagnebin and Marcel Raymond. Paris: Gallimard [Bibliothèque de la Pléaide], 1959.

Seltzer, Mark. *Bodies and Machines.* New York: Routledge, 1992.

Spivak, Gayatri. 'Scattered Speculations on the Question of Value.' *In Other Worlds: Essays in Cultural Politics.* New York: Routledge, 1988. 155–8.

Steedman, Ian. *Marx after Straffa.* London: Verso, 1981.

Steedman, Ian, et al. *The Value Controversy.* London: Verso, 1981.

Straffa, Piero. *Productions of Commodities by Means of Commodities.* Cambridge: Cambridge UP, 1960.

Wang, Orrin N.S. *Fantastic Modernity: Dialectical Readings in Romanticism and Theory.* Baltimore: John Hopkins UP, 1996.

Žižek, Slavoj. *The Sublime Object of Ideology.* London: Verso, 1989.

Contributors

Ian Balfour is Director of the Graduate Programme in English and Associate Professor of English at York University, where he also teaches in the Graduate Programme in Social and Political Thought. He is the author of *Northrop Frye* (Twayne, 1988) and essays on the Romantics, Paul de Man, Walter Benjamin, and topics in popular culture. He is co-translator of Walter Benjamin's dissertation, *The Concept of Criticism in German Romanticism*, in vol. 1 of *The Collected Writings* (Harvard UP, 1997), and a founding editor of *Alphabet City*. His recently completed book *The Rhetoric of Romantic Prophecy* is forthcoming from Stanford University Press, and he is currently at work on a book on the sublime.

Stanley Corngold is Professor of German and Comparative Literature at Princeton University. His publications on the intersections of literature and theory include *Complex Pleasure: Forms of Feeling in German Literature* (Stanford UP, 1997) and *The Fate of the Self*, 2nd edition (Duke UP, 1994); those on Franz Kafka include *The Commentators' Despair* (Kennikat, 1973), *Franz Kafka: The Necessity of Form* (Cornell UP, 1988), and two translations and editions of Kafka's *The Metamorphosis* (Bantam, 1972, and Norton, 1996). He has also coedited two anthologies of essays – one on the literature of the Goethezeit and one on Thomas Mann – and co-written a novel, *Borrowed Lives* (SUNY P, 1991). He is now at work on a book on doubling in European Romanticism.

Peter Dews is Professor of Philosophy at the University of Essex. He is the author of *Logics of Disintegration: Post-Structuralist Thought and the Claims of Critical Theory* (Verso, 1987) and *The Limits of Disenchantment: Essays on Contemporary European Philosophy* (Verso, 1995). He has edited

Jürgen Habermas: Autonomy and Solidarity: Interviews (Verso, 1986/92) and *Habermas: A Critical Reader* (Blackwell, 1998), and is the coeditor of *Deconstructive Subjectivities* (SUNY P, 1997). He has published numerous articles, most recently on Habermas, Lacan, and Žižek.

Rodolphe Gasché is Eugenio Donato Professor of Comparative Literature at State University of New York (SUNY) at Buffalo; he has previously taught at the Freie Universität Berlin and at Johns Hopkins University. Besides translating major works by Derrida and Lacan into German and publishing numerous articles in a variety of scholarly journals, he has published a number of books: *Die hybride Wissenschaft* (Metzler, 1973), *System und Metaphorik in der Philosophie von Georges Bataille* (Lang, 1978), *The Tain of the Mirror: Derrida and the Philosophy of Reflection* (Harvard, 1986), and *Inventions of Difference: On Jacques Derrida* (Harvard UP, 1994). His most recent books are *The Wild Card of Reading: On Paul de Man* (Harvard UP, 1998), and *Of Minimal Things: Studies on the Notion of Relation* (Stanford UP, 1999).

Mani Haghighi lives in Tehran and Toronto. He is the Persian translator of Michel Foucault's *Ceci n'est pas une pipe* and the editor of *The Aporia of Signs: A Postmodern Reader*, published in Tehran in 1995. His recent articles include ones on Deleuze and Guattari in a collection published by the University of Minnesota Press and in a special issue of the *Canadian Review of Comparative Literature*. He is currently writing a book on the 'Rushdie Affair.'

Victor Li is Associate Professor of English at Dalhousie University. His recent publications include 'Policing the City: Modernism, Autonomy and Authority,' *Criticism* 34 (1992); 'Selling Modernism: Resisting Commodification, Commodifying Resistance,' *English Studies in Canada* 19 (1993); 'Habermas and the Ethnocentric Discourse of Modernity' in *Constructive Criticism: The Human Sciences in the Age of Theory* (U of Toronto P, 1995); 'Towards Articulation: Postcolonial Theory and Demotic Resistance,' *Ariel* 26 (1995); 'What's in a Name? Questioning Globalization,' *Cultural Critique* 45 (2000); and 'Marshall Sahlins and Apotheosis of Culture,' *CR: The New Centennial Review* 1:3 (forthcoming).

Michael J. O'Driscoll is Assistant Professor of English at the University of Alberta. His recent publications include 'Whitman in the Archive: *Leaves of Grass* and the Culture of the Book,' *English Studies in Canada*

25 (1999); 'Ezra Pound's Cantos: "A Memorial to Archivists and Librarians,"' *Studies in the Literary Imagination* 32 (1999); and 'Silent Texts and Empty Words: Structure and Intention in the Writings of John Cage,' *Contemporary Literature* 38 (1997). He is currently at work on a book-length project titled *Mosaic Textualities: Literature, Technology, and Culture*, a study that traces a series of ruptures in our understanding of the material text through philosophical, literary, and technological discourse.

Arkady Plotnitsky is Professor of English and University Faculty Scholar at Purdue University, where he is also Director of the Theory and Cultural Studies Program. He is the author of *In the Shadow of Hegel: Complementarity, History, and the Unconscious* (Florida UP, 1993); *Reconfigurations: Critical Theory and General Economy* (Florida UP, 1993); *Complementarity: Anti-Epistemology after Bohr and Derrida* (Duke UP, 1994); and *The Knowable and the Unknowable: Modern Science, Nonclassical Thought, and the 'Two Cultures' via Bohr, Heisenberg, Lacan and Derrida* (U of Michigan P, 2001). He has coedited *Mathematics, Science, and Postclassical Theory* (Duke UP, 1997), and has published papers on Barthes, Bataille, Derrida, Hegel, Kant, and Nietzsche. He is currently working on two books tentatively entitled *Physis, Nous, Eros: Shelley and Scientific Modernity* and *The Invisible and the Unknowable: Modernist Literature and Twentieth-Century French Philosophy*.

Tilottama Rajan is former director of the Centre for Theory and Criticism and now Canada Research Chair in English and Theory at the University of Western Ontario. She is the author of *Dark Interpreter: The Discourse of Romanticism* (Cornell UP, 1980), *The Supplement of Reading: Figures of Understanding in Romantic Theory and Practice* (Cornell UP, 1990), and *Deconstruction and the Remainders of Phenomenology: Sartre, Derrida, Foucault, Baudrillard* (forthcoming, Stanford UP). She has edited Mary Shelley's *Valperga* (Broadview P, 1998) and has coedited *Intersections: Nineteenth-Century Philosophy and Contemporary Theory* (SUNY P, 1995) and *Romanticism, History and the Possibilities of Genre: Reforming Literature 1789–1832* (Cambridge UP, 1998). In addition to articles on Blake, Coleridge, Godwin, Hays, Keats, Mary Shelley, Percy Shelley, Wollstonecraft, and Wordsworth, she has also published on de Man, Foucault, Hegel, Kierkegaard, Kristeva, Nietzsche, and Schopenhauer.

Linda Bradley Salamon is Professor of English at George Washington University. Her publications deal with the prose and cultural history of early modern England, Shakespeare, early novels and narratology, and theorizing the 'Renaissance.'

Anthony Wall is Department Head and Professor of French, Italian, and Spanish at the University of Calgary. He is the translator of Renate Lachmann's *Memory and Literature: Intertexuality in Russian Modernism* (U of Minnesota P, 1997), and the author of *Superposer: Essais sur les métalangages littéraires* (XYZ, 1996). He has published articles on Bakhtin in the *Bakhtin Newsletter, Dialogism and Cultural Criticism* (Mestengo, 1995), and in *Recherches sur Diderot et sur l'Encyclopédie* (1994), and prepared *Bakhtin and the Future of Signs* for *Recherches Sémiotiques/Semiotic Inquiry* (1998).

Brian Wall teaches in the Department of English at the University of Western Ontario, where he is currently involved in research on the relationships among modernity, technology, and cultural production in Beckett's media plays. He has published on Beckett, Adorno, and Lacan.

Orrin N.C. Wang teaches English and Comparative Literature at the University of Maryland. He is the author of *Fantastic Modernity: Dialectical Readings in Romanticism and Theory* (Johns Hopkins UP, 1996), and the editor of *Romantic Circles Praxis*. He is currently working on a study of High Romanticism in an era of local knowledge.

Index

Dunn, Allen, 102
Duvakin, Viktor. *See* Bakhtin, Mikhail,
  and Viktor Duvakin

Edelman, Lee, 306n2
Einstein, Albert, 158
Emerson, Caryl, 218

Fenn, Richard, 211
Fenves, Peter, 219n11
Fichte, J.G., 181
Flaubert, Gustave, 292
Foggia, Lyla, 282n11
Foucault, Michel, 4–5, 6, 8, 13–14, 66,
  83–4n38, 156, 172, 212, 227–41,
  245–6, 260n12, 281n8, 285–6, 305;
  The Archaeology of Knowledge, 18–19,
  74, 287, 301–2, 306n1; *The Birth of
  the Clinic: An Archaeology of Medical
  Perception,* 75, 77; *Discipline and Pun-
  ish: The Birth of the Prison,* 291, 302;
  Dream, Imagination, Existence, 75;
  'The Fantasia of the Library,' 292;
  *The History of Sexuality: An Introduc-
  tion,* 302; *Madness and Civilization: A
  History of Insanity in the Age of Reason,* 301; 'Maurice Blanchot: The
  Thought from Outside,' 80; *Mental
  Illness and Personality,* 75, 83–4n38;
  'Nietzsche, Genealogy, History,' 15,
  229–34, 237, 242n6; *The Order of
  Things: An Archaeology of the Human
  Sciences,* 54, 64, 71, 73, 75–8, 79,
  232, 251–2, 304; 'Preface to Trans-
  gression,' 16, 252, 254, 256; 'The-
  atrum Philosophicum,' 130; *This Is
  Not a Pipe,* 232–3
Freud, Sigmund, 169–70, 172, 174,
  179–81, 252–3, 284, 297; 'The Aetiology of Hysteria,' 300; *Moses and*

Monotheism, 300; *Studies on Hysteria,*
  300
Frie, Roger, 83n36, 84n40

Gadamer, Hans-Georg, 132, 140,
  150n8
Gane, Mike, 89
Gasché, Rodolphe, 7, 10–11, 81n16,
  105
Gauss, Karl Friedrich, 158
Geertz, Clifford, 104, 271
Genosko, Gary, 91
Geuss, Raymond, 25, 38n5, 40n14
Gil, José, 237–8
Godelier, Maurice, 91, 107n6
Godwin, William, 169
Godzich, Wlad, 149n6
Goethe, Johann Wolfgang, 120
Goldberg, Jonathan, 282n9
Gramsci, Antonio, 279–80
Greco, El, 168
Grosz, Elizabeth, 14, 198; *Space, Time,
  and Perversion,* 209, 210–13, 221–
  2n22; *Volatile Bodies: Toward a Corpo-
  real Feminism,* 209–13
Grosz, Elizabeth, and Elspeth Probyn:
  *Sexy Bodies: The Strange Carnalities of
  Feminism,* 209–13, 221n22
Guattari, Félix. *See* Deleuze, Gilles,
  and Félix Guattari

Habermas, Jurgen, 107n6, 245–6,
  252, 257–8
Haghighi, Mani, 13, 14–15
Haverkamp, Anselm, 222n23
Hebrew Bible, 118–19
Hefner, Robert, 92, 94
Hegel, G.W.F., 11–12, 43, 54–5, 57–8,
  65–7, 73, 77, 113–24, 152–4, 156–7,
  161, 164–71, 173–5, 177n14, 245,